No Swinging on Sundays

To Maggie

No Swinging on Sundays

The Story of Bath's Lost Pleasure Gardens

Kirsten Elliott signature

Kirsten Elliott

AKEMAN PRESS

Published by AKEMAN PRESS
www.akemanpress.com

© Kirsten Elliott 2019

ISBN 978-0-9933988-2-7

All rights reserved. No part of this publication may be reproduced, stored in a retrieval system, or transmitted, in any form or by any means, electrical, mechanical, photocopying, recording or otherwise, without the prior permission of Akeman Press.

Front cover: The riverside swings at Grosvenor Gardens c1800 by John Nixon

Back cover: The canal through Sydney Gardens c1800

Printed in the UK by the Pureprint Group

CONTENTS

Foreword by Professor Elaine Chalus	vii
Introduction	ix

PRELUDE

From Pilgrimage to Promenade	
Why Parks and Gardens became part of Spa Culture	1

I
GRAVEL WALKS AND GROVES
THE RISE OF PLEASURE GARDENS IN BATH 1700-1750

1	The Company Goes Walking	
	Bath's Earliest Pleasure Grounds	13
2	Riverside Pleasures	
	The Early Years of Harrison's Walks and Spring Gardens	27
3	Out of Town	
	Gardens on the Edge of the City	39

II
CHANGING FASHIONS AND FLUCTUATING FORTUNES
THE DEVELOPMENT OF THE GARDENS 1750-1800

1	A Most Delightful Spot	
	The Transformation of Spring Gardens	57
2	Winners and Losers	
	How Competition changed Pleasure Gardens in Bath	75
3	Fireworks and Birdsong	
	The Battle for Supremacy between Spring Gardens and Villa Gardens	99

4   Bold Ideas and Broken Dreams
    How Sydney Gardens triumphed over Grosvenor, Spring Gardens
    faded away, Botanic Gardens came and went, and a Glaciere Garden
    came to Lansdown   117

III
THE PROUDEST BOAST OF THIS EMPORIUM OF FASHION
THE STORY OF SYDNEY GARDENS

1 First Impressions
   The Happy Accidents of the Swing   147

2 Fixtures and Fittings
   Open for Business   155

3 That Celebrated and Fashionable Resort of Pleasure,
   1796-1839   171

4 The Autumn of a Form Once Fine,
   1839-1891   217

5 From Private Parties to Public Park,
   1892 onwards   259

POSTLUDE

1 Lost Pleasures
   The Fate of Bath's Georgian Pleasure Gardens   315

2 In Conclusion: Welcome to the House of Fun
   How Pleasure Gardens became Fun Parks   335

   Notes   345
   Bibliography   358
   Picture Credits   363
   Index   364

FOREWORD

Bath in the eighteenth and nineteenth centuries provided its residents and the visiting Company with a plenitude of venues and opportunities for fashionable sociability. While the town's emergence as the 'queen' of England's spas in the early eighteenth century rested upon the perceived healing qualities of its spring waters, it quickly attracted investors, speculators and entrepreneurs keen to cater to the needs and desires of its elite visitors. Soon, Bath could boast of the tasteful elegance of its Pump Rooms, Assembly Rooms, and subscription walks, and of its wide and carefully paved parades — all places where promeneurs and flâneurs alike could see and be seen.

And then there were the pleasure gardens. These private commercial ventures repeatedly chanced England's uncertain weather conditions. Their owners and leaseholders invested extensively, sometimes disastrously, as they competed for attendance. While their offerings varied and the events they hosted extended from local cat, dog and flower shows to musical and firework extravaganzas, they uniformly offered their guests carefully constructed 'natural' settings. Gravelled paths wound through stylishly planted landscapes; buildings, grottoes or temples offered shelter from the elements; music was provided; and palates were tempted with a range of foods and refreshments. Hot buttered buns and Sally Lunns were especially popular, particularly in the eighteenth century.

In this volume, Kirsten Elliott goes a long way to present us with a much more complete and comprehensive picture of the pleasure gardens of Bath. Not only does she recover the history of various shadowy and short-lived pleasure gardens, such as the Hand and Flower, King James's Palace and the Bagatelle, but her detailed research also provides us with real insights into Bath's two most influential and long-lasting gardens: Spring Gardens, which marked Bath's aspirations to polite society in the early eighteenth century; and Sydney Gardens, Bath's last great pleasure garden, whose failure in the early nineteenth century is often linked to the intrusion of modernity. Most importantly, for students of Bath's history, Elliott breaks the link between the failure of Sydney Gardens and the coming of the railroad in the 1830s; instead, she explores Sydney Garden's survival through the nineteenth century. What she uncovers is a richer, more complex and more extended history than has often been assumed. The story of Bath's pleasure gardens is one of changing tastes, developing notions of class and respectability, and the ever-shifting balance between private commercial ventures and a perceived public good. There is much here for future historians to explore.

Professor Elaine Chalus
University of Liverpool, 2019

INTRODUCTION

This book is the result of nearly 35 years of sporadic study, sometimes carried out as part of a project, sometimes serendipitously as information fell into my lap while I was looking for something else. The topic of Bath's Georgian pleasure gardens is, however, dear to my heart, as it was the very first piece of historic research that I ever carried out. It was suggested to me as a project by my tutor, John Ede, when I was training to be one of the Mayor's Corps of Honorary Guides in Bath. I do not think either of us had any idea where this would take me, but after my very first afternoon in the Bath Reference Library, I knew that historic research was what I wanted to do.

At first, I was making notes for my own interest, but I soon discovered that the story of the gardens, and how they developed, captured the public's interest. The tales of public breakfasts, with their abundance of buns and quantities of coffee, of concerts and circus acts, balloon ascents and terrifyingly dangerous scientific experiments, and, above all, the firework displays – sometimes splendid and sometimes disastrous – held people enthralled. They listened attentively, on walks and during talks, as I explained how, popular though these gardens were, they were a risky enterprise which all too often ended in bankruptcy.

As I continued to delve into the hidden histories of Bath's long-lost pleasure gardens, it was not long before I had amassed far too much material to pack into a short walk or talk. But I felt that the story of the gardens, with all the magic, mystery and tragedy it involved, was one that deserved to be told. The only answer was to write a book.

Acknowledgements are due to the many people who have helped and collaborated with me over the years. Staff at Bath Record Office and Bristol Archives were most helpful in seeking out documents and offering helpful suggestions of where to look. At an early stage I met Peter Atkinson, who was then writing his dissertation called *Sydney Gardens and the Development of Eighteenth Century Pleasure Gardens in Bath*, (published in 1989) and we spent a happy afternoon throwing ideas and theories at each other. Thanks are also due to members of Bath Parks Department. In the past year, Susan Palmer, Sydney

Gardens Community Ranger, and Hannah Myall, intern at Bath and North East Somerset Council, who worked on the historic features of Sydney Gardens for the Heritage Lottery Fund application, gave their time to me freely. In addition, Sydney Gardens Project Manager, Keith Rowe, ensured that I have my facts straight on the projected restoration, not least the rather complicated financial arrangements with the Heritage Lottery Fund and other sources. Above all I would like to acknowledge the help and friendly co-operation from Glenn Humphreys, for many years Heritage Parks Manager for Bath.

Several members of the Facebook page Born & Bred or Live in the City of Bath gave me helpful clues and leads. In particular I would like to thank Jayne Williams, who recalled her aunt and uncle running up Bathwick Street to the shelter in Sydney Gardens during the Bath Blitz of April 1942. I am also most grateful to Mary Britton and her twin brother Tom Harper for allowing me to use photographs of the model railways and model village at the Larkhall Inn, and to Patricia Humphrys, who lived at the Folly as a child, for kindly providing the unique photograph of the Folly from her family collection

Thanks also go to Toussaint Clarke, who confirmed that the Barbadian Steel Band which played in Sydney Gardens in 1956 was the forerunner of the present day Rainbow Steel Band.

At the Paragon School, various documents dating from when the building was Lyncombe Spa had been safely stored away when it became the junior school for Prior Park College – so safely that no one remembered where they were. Emily Hughes, the marketing manager, eventually tracked them down, and I am most appreciative of her efforts. They cast a fascinating light on life at the spa.

I would also like to thank the various museums and galleries who make their picture collections freely available, in particular the Wellcome Collection and the Yale Centre for British Art. Special thanks go to Kate Igoe of the Smithsonian National Air and Space Museum in Washington, who, in the middle of the US Government shut down at the end of 2018, still found time to deal courteously and efficiently with a request to use a picture by what must have seemed a very obscure publisher across the Atlantic.

Last and not least I would like to thank my husband, Dr Andrew Swift. Wearing his academic hat, he has rigorously edited the book, and as co-partner in Akeman Press he has created its design. Above all, he has always supported and encouraged my work.

PRELUDE

FROM PILGRIMAGE TO PROMENADE

Why Parks and Gardens became part of Spa Culture

During its Georgian heyday, Bath's pleasure gardens were among the glories of the city. With their groves and grottoes, fêtes and fireworks, they mingled artifice and nature to create a world of fantasy and illusion. Along their tree-lined, lamp-lit avenues, well-heeled visitors sought refuge from the dusty streets. Assignations and intrigues, revels and reveries, all played their part in these green retreats, where tortuous labyrinths vied for distraction and delight with artificial cascades and ruined castles. Perhaps the most astonishing aspect, though, was the sheer number and diversity of these hedonistic havens.

Even at their most extravagant, however, they all had their roots in a Europe-wide tradition that went back centuries. Visit almost any European spa town and you will immediately notice that most have parks and gardens, often set off by wide boulevards. From small spas like Bagnoles de l'Orne and Bad Pyrmont to the resorts of Montecatini, Aix en Provence, Baden-Baden and, above all, Spa itself, gardens play an important role in spa culture. Bath itself is well supplied with parks and open spaces great and small. Yet most spas began as places of worship. How did a stroll in the park develop into a crucial part of taking the waters?

In all early civilisations, worship was centred around nature. Although we think of the four classical elements – earth, air, fire and water – as a Greek concept, similar notions were found right across the ancient world, from Egypt to Tibet, India and Japan. One of the first places where water worship was combined with a pleasurable place to walk was Persia, with its formal, geometric gardens created by Zoroastrians, in particular Cyrus the Great. Indeed, the word paradise comes from an old Iranian word meaning 'exceptional gardens'. These gardens influenced Islamic and Indian gardens. Water was used to divide the gardens into four, the rills representing the four rivers which flow from paradise. Four is a highly symbolic number in Islam, with many meanings, including a reference to the four elements.

There is symbolism in oriental gardens, but the emphasis is different. The Chinese style of gardening

The Moghul Emperor Babur laying out the Garden of Fidelity

reflected the natural world, often including views of distant mountains, but with water as an essential component. In these gardens it was the plants and even the rocks which were imbued with historical significance. The yin energy of water was seen to balance the yang energy of the rocks. In Japan, where this style was copied, Shinto still adheres to these ideas, and gardens are a crucial part of its religious practices.

So we can see that, throughout history, gardens have held a mystical and symbolical significance in which, of the four classical elements, water is the most magical. As a result, all sorts of legends and beliefs attach themselves to water in cultures all over the world. Life itself depends on its presence but too much of it can cause death and destruction. The Greek god Poseidon, ruler of the sea, and brother of Zeus, represented this savage aspect. He was unforgiving and quick to be roused, much like the sea itself. The Naiads, however, the nymphs of springs, represented its gentle face. We can surely understand the fascination of water. Even today, we like to have a 'water feature' in our gardens, even if it is only a shallow pool of moulded fibreglass. Water was linked with death: one crossed the River Styx to enter the underworld. King Arthur, on nearing death, returned his sword to the Lady of the Lake, before sailing off to the Isle of Avalon. Other folk legends link water with ghosts and spirits. Even a gentle flow of water can be destructive, by wearing away solid rock over centuries. The appreciation of such qualities resolved itself into water worship, with votive offerings being offered to the gods and goddesses of springs. So strong is this instinct that we still readily toss coins into fountains, pools and wishing wells.

If water on its own can exert this compelling attraction, we can hardly begin to guess how extraordinary hot springs must have seemed to early humans, especially when, as in Britain, they are a rarity. It is thought possible that the area which is now central Bath was so holy to the Celtic people that it was left in its natural state as a shrine to the goddess Sulis. The only interference with the site may have been the tending of a sacred grove and the construction of a causeway to approach the springs. Gazing down from one of their settlements to the wooded valley below, so often shrouded in mist and steam, the local people must have regarded it as a mysterious and perhaps frightening place.

The Romans, however, who arrived sometime between 44 and 47 CE, were more pragmatic in their approach. If the gods had provided water, especially ready heated, it was meant to be used. Wherever springs occur in the Roman world, the Romans could be guaranteed to use them, no matter how obscure they might seem. The salt springs near Vézelay in Burgundy, for example, are not easy

Looking down through layers of history – Georgian and Roman – to see the hot spring bubbling up through the earth

to find even now, but the Romans heard about them and laid out suites of baths along with temples. Such a combination of practicality and worship is also found at Bath, or Aquae Sulis, as it was known. While the Romans were determined to use the waters, it was obviously necessary to placate any deities guarding them, either by replacing local gods with Roman ones, or, if the resident spirit was sufficiently awesome, by combining it with one of their own, thus presumably propitiating all the gods. The Celtic Sulis was such a goddess: the Romans linked her with Minerva. Even to such an intensely practical people, the traditions of water worship ran too deeply to be ignored. Thus along with their relaxation in the baths went devotions at the temple, and votive offerings in great numbers were cast into the steaming waters. From time to time the goddess was even asked to wreak terrible vengeance on enemies.

The story was much the same at the warm springs of Buxton, which were dedicated to the Goddess of the Grove. Nor was it necessary for the water to be warm. At Chedworth Roman Villa, for example, there was a Nymphaeum, or shrine to the goddesses of the spring which fed the reservoir for the villa's water supply. Nothing was taken for granted.

At the mouth of the Roman drain from the Sacred Spring, the iron-rich waters leave a bright orange deposit. Here is where many Roman offerings were found, and today people are still casting coins into the water.

The Roman goddess Minerva and the Celtic goddess Sulis combined to create a guardian deity of the spring, called Sul Minerva

With the coming of Christianity, it might be thought that these pagan sites would be abandoned. On the contrary, many simply became absorbed into the new religion, thanks to the broad-minded Pope Gregory. His policy was to win converts by gently welding new ideas on to the old, rather than by destroying long-held beliefs. Just as Bath became a centre for Christian worship, many wells and springs became holy wells. Water worship had already insinuated itself into the new rituals with baptism, and cures that followed immersion in the old sacred places became miracles. This strange muddling of two cultures probably explains some of the odd customs associated with holy wells, such as well-dressing, where the pre-Christian deities of the spring are placated with floral pictures showing Biblical events. At Madron, in Cornwall, the waters from the spring were channelled into a Christian baptistery, but at the well itself the local girls used to cast straws upon the surface, and the time it took the straws to sink would indicate how long it would be before they met their intended husbands. The well had a reputation for healing, and a cripple called John Trelilie found a complete cure there in 1650. Those who sought a cure dipped a cloth into the well and knotted it into the branches of nearby bushes. Daphne du Maurier, in *Vanishing Cornwall*, suggests that this was a votive offering to the spirits, but it is more likely to have been sympathetic magic. As the cloth rots away, so the illness vanishes. Today, despite modern medicine and science, the old traditions die hard here. The trees and shrubs in

At Madron well there was a Christian baptistery ...

... but the sympathetic magic of the old pagan religion still has a powerful hold on people's imagination

the vicinity of Madron Well have their branches profusely covered with strips of cloth and coloured ribbons. So at a supposedly Christian site there is a fine confusion of magic, divination, and belief in miracles. However, in most cases, the introduction of Christianity seems to have broken the link with nature, and gardens lost their important symbolism.

In Bath, the Christian abbey was built as close as possible to the hot springs, actually on the site of one Roman temple

Bath in 1610, from John Speed's map of Somerset. All the emphasis was on the baths – there were no pleasure gardens.

It was with the advent of the Protestant church in England that holy wells became a matter of concern to the authorities. Being associated with Roman Catholic saints, their use was suppressed, but high-ranking English Catholics used this as an excuse to visit foreign spas, in particular Spa itself. Here they met, and were suspected (probably rightly) of plotting with Catholics from Spain, Spa being under Spanish control. Obviously there had to be a change of policy, and it became acceptable to visit English spas not for religious reasons, but for one's health. However, the waters needed to possess unusual properties caused by minerals. From about this time we see an enthusiasm for water that has an unpleasant taste, looks rusty, or, best of all, causes food or drink to change colour (preferably to black or purple). Miracles were out and minerals were in. Curative properties had to be proved, or the buildings attached to a spring could be destroyed. Courtiers close to the Earl of Leicester, the Queen's favourite, promoted the 'politically correct' spas, and Elizabeth I herself helped to set the fashion for watering-places by visiting Bath. She also allowed Mary, Queen of Scots, to visit Buxton to take the waters. In the meantime a kind of passport was introduced for those wishing to visit Spa, making this potential trouble-spot more inaccessible. The names of those determined to visit were also registered on a list.

Yet, despite all this, spas were to retain an aura of popery until this was swept away in the social whirl of the eighteenth century. This was probably due in part to the Stuart enthusiasm for spas. Ironically, this enthusiasm began with Anne of Denmark, the wife of the staunchly Protestant James I of England and VI of Scotland, who came to Bath in 1613. So satisfied was she with the efficacy of the waters that she made another visit the same year and a third in 1615. It was fortunate that she did not come in 1605, for some of the conspirators in the Gunpowder Plot gathered in Bath, ostensibly for the sake of their health, but actually to provide a cover for their meetings.

Taking the waters had now received the royal seal of approval, yet it was the iron-rich waters of Spa which were still deemed to be the most efficacious. Anglican invalids mixed with Catholic plotters, all equipped with the medical certificate which was necessary to get a passport. Some even took their doctors with them. There was a substantial import trade in Spa waters. If anything, this worried the Privy Council even more, but relief was at hand. Some doctors and other entrepreneurs realised that if similar waters were promoted here in

Spa in 1647 – note the area for walking already well established as part of the town

Vauxhall – the model for all the British pleasure gardens

England there was scope for making a fortune. The hunt for iron-rich waters was afoot, although springs with other chemicals proved equally popular. With the search for health and wealth came a desire to make the experience pleasurable. To create a successful spa, the promoters needed to provide places of entertainment throughout the day, and promenades, where the company could meet and gossip, caught on. From these small beginnings sprang the inspiration for Georgian pleasure gardens. Yet the gardens which were the model for all those that followed had nothing to do with spas or springs, despite their name.

These trend-setting gardens were at Vauxhall, which opened as the New Spring Gardens in 1661. They were named after the original Spring Gardens, a fashionable meeting place near Charing Cross. They also had nothing to do with water – the name derived from an archaic use of word spring meaning 'a plantation of young trees, especially one inclosed and used for rearing and harbouring game'.[1] This is precisely how these gardens started out – as a place to get away from the bustling streets of the city. At Vauxhall, set in open countryside, with avenues for people to stroll alone, one of the popular diversions of an evening was to listen to the nightingales, although the gardens were also open throughout the day. It was only later, in the eighteenth century, that concerts and other entertainments, especially fireworks, became a feature. Vauxhall and other London gardens such as Marylebone were also notorious as gathering places of prostitutes. In Fanny Burney's *Evelina*, the eponymous heroine is pursued by drunken young men down the alleys of Vauxhall, and, in another encounter with drunken fellows, seeks the protection of two young women – who, it soon transpires, are prostitutes – at Marylebone. This is a world Burney's readers would have recognised. In fact, the prostitutes turn out to be very much better guardians of the innocent young woman than the young men in her party, returning her safely to her family and friends, but then insisting on joining the party.

All the aspects of these gardens were incorporated into the pleasure gardens in Bath – including their rather risqué reputation. Bath's first pleasure gardens – whose story is told in Part One – opened as the city reinvented itself in the early eighteenth century. Having long been accustomed to seeing itself as the country's premier spa – thanks to its hot springs – its complacency was shattered when new spas started opening, offering the latest attractions and the newest fashions. Pleasure gardens were only one of a raft of measures – which crucially included the appointment of Richard 'Beau' Nash as Master of Ceremonies – that sought to restore the city's pre-eminence.

The success of this initiative was beyond anything its architects could have predicted, and saw Bath transformed from a fusty watering place living on past glories, to the most fashionable city in the land. Part Two looks at how this led to new gardens opening up, trying to stay one step ahead of fashion and competing with each other in a cut-throat bid for the attention of the *beau monde*.

Part Three moves forward to the end of the eighteenth century when Sydney Gardens – the only one of Bath's pleasure gardens to survive, albeit in a different form – saw off an upstart rival to become the greatest of them all. Even as it was being created, however, Bath was once again sliding out of fashion, as Cheltenham and Brighton set the standards for Regency style and sophistication.

The final nail in the coffin of Bath's spa society (and Sydney Gardens' Georgian elegance) was the coming of the Great Western Railway (GWR). Already competing with public parks, it finally became a public park itself. Part Four provides a gazetteer of lost pleasure gardens, before looking at the final throw of the dice for pleasure gardens, when pub gardens, notably the GWR-owned Folly, took on this role. It ends, however, on a hopeful note. Despite our age of austerity and uncertainty, the news that Bath and North East Somerset Council has been awarded Heritage Lottery Funding for restoring and reviving Sydney Gardens means that it may be looking forward to a new role as a garden of pleasure and delight once more.

I

GRAVEL WALKS AND GROVES

THE RISE OF PLEASURE GARDENS IN BATH
1700-1750

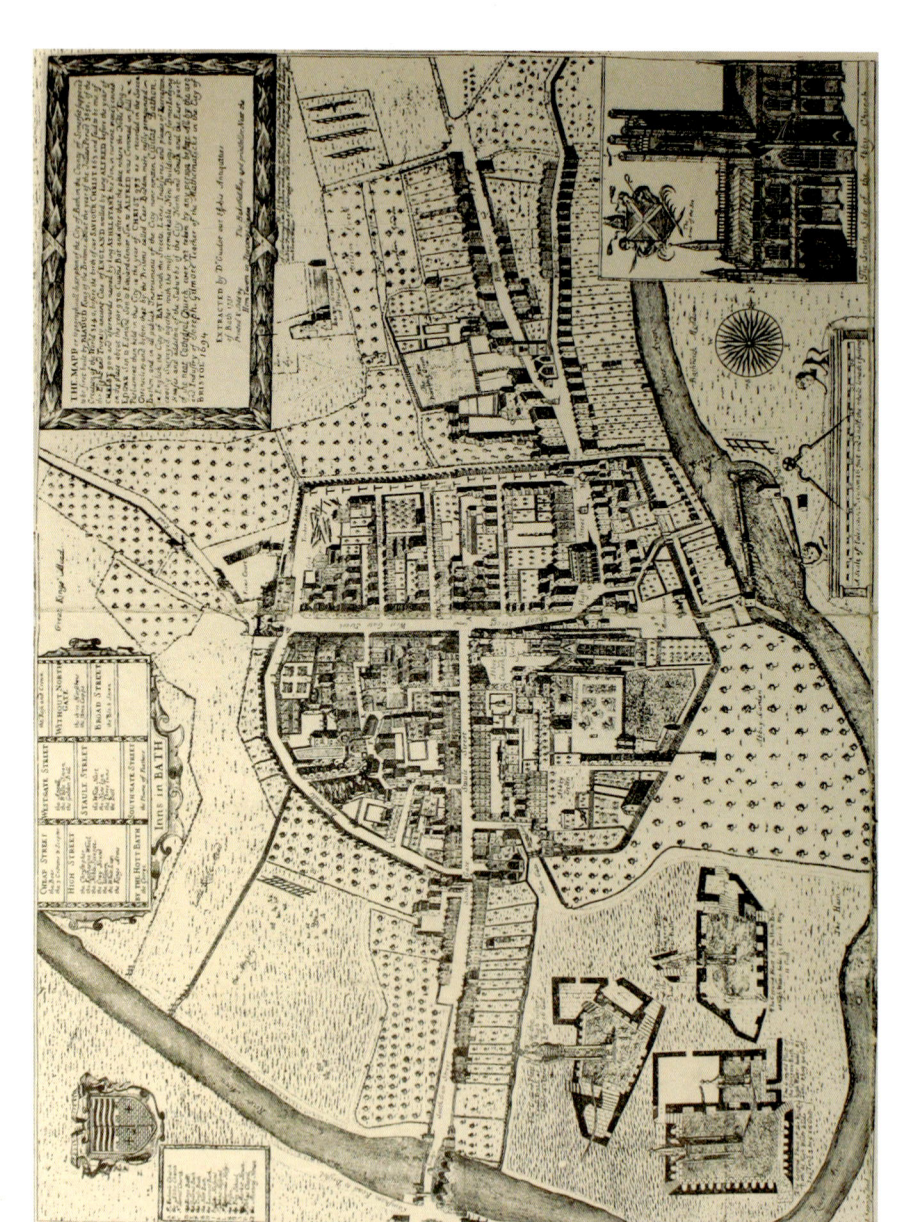

1

THE COMPANY GOES WALKING

Bath's Earliest Pleasure Grounds

As holy wells turned into spas, attracting fashionable society as well as genuine invalids, there was a need to construct places where the company could amuse itself when not taking the waters. The first and most successful of the new spas was Tunbridge Wells, with its chalybeate – or iron-rich – waters. At the peak of its popularity, it challenged Bath itself. Indeed, the history of the two spas became entwined when Richard 'Beau' Nash was appointed Master of Ceremonies in both of them – thanks to Tunbridge having a summer season while Bath's season ran from late autumn to spring.[1]

Tunbridge supposedly owed its discovery to Dudley, 3rd Baron North. Having suffered ill-health and tried spas in England and abroad, he decided to take a rest at the Kentish home of his friend Lord Abergavenny (or Bergavenny). On his way back to London, so the story goes, he came upon some springs, tried them, and immediately felt an improvement. This conjures up an amusing picture of the sickly aristocrat frantically trying every spring he came across, but it is likely that these springs already had a local reputation and Lord Abergavenny suggested he try them. This is borne out by Lord North himself, who says he popularised the springs, rather than discovered them. Since the nearest town of any size was Tunbridge (now spelt Tonbridge) the spa became known as Tunbridge Wells. At first there was very little there. Lord Abergavenny cleared the area around the springs and laid on facilities for drinking the waters, but there was nothing much in the way of entertainment.

Opposite: Gilmore's map of Bath in 1697, showing the city surrounded by meadows, many of which were the venue for healthy exercise

Tunbridge Wells, circa 1700, with the terrible state of the roads clearly evident.
The well is visible at the far end of the street.

It was perhaps for that reason that Queen Henrietta Maria at first shunned Tunbridge and turned to Wellingborough when she decided to try an English spa. Wellingborough, with its iron-rich Red Well already had court patronage and the Queen's visit seemed to set the seal on its success, particularly after she gave birth to her first child in 1629. Alas for Wellingborough, the child did not survive, and the Queen was persuaded to try Tunbridge Wells instead. The court camped out in elaborate tents on the downs, and a merry time seems to have been had by all, except the poor Queen who did not greatly care for the chalybeate waters. Nevertheless, she later gave birth to the required heir, and Tunbridge's success was assured, despite its lack of facilities and the appalling state of Kentish roads.

Another new spring to find favour was at Epsom, which was discovered when a local farmer noticed his cows refusing to drink from a particular water supply. Since the general rule of thumb for deciding if a spring had medicinal qualities was that if it had an unpleasant taste it must be good for you, the wells were tested and proclaimed to have healing qualities. Epsom Salts were put on sale, and despite its rural situation, the spring became famous, until over-exploitation caused it to fail. Like Cheltenham in later years, Epsom's waters had a purging effect, and purging in all its forms was regarded in the eighteenth century as highly desirable.

Yet another Kentish spa was at Sydenham, though this never really flourished to any great extent. Meanwhile, in the north, the hitherto rather neglected Harrogate was attracting attention. With its variety of wells, including the chalybeate Tewit Well, and the aptly named Stinking Well, its fame grew, although at this stage it was still part of Knaresborough, rather than being a town in its own right.

Suddenly, the structure of society was shaken by the cataclysmic events of the Civil Wars. With our modern tendency to categorise political figures as left wing or right wing, it is easy to imagine that the Royalists were right-wing capitalists and the Puritans left-wing socialists. This was not the case. The underlying cause of the war was a power struggle in which religion merely played a part. As a result, many among the peerage were to be found in the ranks of the Puritans while merchants joined the Royalist cause. Aristocratic families were split down the middle as their principles and loyalties clashed. There was also a pragmatic reason for such divisions, however – whichever side won, the estates would remain in family hands. Thus, although there were great rents in the fabric of society, its pattern remained essentially the same. If aristocrats were imprisoned, it was because they espoused the wrong principles, not because they were aristocrats. There was not the urge to sweep away what had gone before which resulted in the bloodbath of the French Revolution. Wherever possible, social life went on as before. If Royalist prisoners could plead a medical reason to visit spas, they could be given temporary leave of absence from their place of confinement to do so. This was very similar to the earlier passport scheme for visiting Spa, although the ailing prisoners also had to pay substantial bonds. For most spas, therefore, it was business as usual, but Bath was not so lucky. It became caught up in the skirmishing, changing hands a couple of times. Not only did the city have to entertain its latest rulers; it also had the expense of finding billets for soldiers. The soldiers may have been Puritans, but in 1644 they wreaked so much damage on an inn, the

Katherine Wheel in the Market Place, that in 1650 Mrs Power, the landlady, was excused from paying rent for five years as compensation.

Once hostilities were over, society was again welcome, even if its members were there by permission of Oliver Cromwell. Rather less welcome were the humble war-wounded sent by parliament. The council refused point-blank to pay for them and so the state decided to fund them instead. This scheme proved to be good for Bath's reputation as a centre of healing, but did little to promote it as a fashionable resort. It is not surprising to learn that, on the restoration of Charles II, Bath was the first city in England to proclaim him as the new King. It must have seemed that happy days were here again, especially as the court's passion for spas was greater than before. There was, however, to be a determined battle for precedence before Bath was able to re-establish itself as the leading watering-place. This marks a shift in the spa culture from health to pleasure, but, as will be seen, the entertainments would include healthy activities such as riding and walking – pastimes the court in exile in France would have enjoyed. Bath does not seem to have grasped the importance of this immediately. There was nowhere where fashionable society could indulge in the pleasure of a stroll. In 1668, when Pepys came to Bath, his first port of call on the first morning was the baths, where he admired the 'very fine ladies', despite thinking to himself that it could not be clean 'to go so many bodies together in the same water'. His exercise consisted mainly of walking, either about the town, admiring the buildings, or around the walls. Finally, on Sunday afternoon, he went 'to the fields a little and walked, and then home'. At this time the city was still encircled by meadows, those most favoured for walking being the Ambrey and the King's Meads, to the southwest.

It was Tunbridge Wells, however, not Bath, which was the first place to make its name as a fashionable resort after the restoration. It had a great deal to commend it. It already had connections with the Royal family, and was close to London. Walks had been laid out where visitors could take the air. It had suffered little under the Commonwealth, and although it was still necessary for the court to set up camp when Charles II went there in 1663, there was considerable improvement in the years which followed. The King considered he was travelling light, claiming he was 'bringing just my night bag' because he had a mere forty to fifty horsemen with him. He also brought the Queen and his favourite mistress of the day, Frances Stewart.

When they left the resort, the Queen was still not pregnant – unlike several of her ladies.

Before long, new walks were laid out in Tunbridge Wells; assembly rooms and lodging houses were built. A chapel dedicated to King Charles the Martyr was added in 1678, and a fire on the walks in 1687 was the excuse for extensive rebuilding. The spa was reported as rising glorious from the ashes. It had a pleasant informality, and that connoisseur of spas, Celia Fiennes, was most enthusiastic. The market was well stocked and cheap, there were shops full of 'toys', silver, china, and 'all sorts of curious wooden ware ... the delicate neate and thin ware of wood both white and Lignum vitae wood'. This is what we now call Tunbridge Ware, and shows it was already on sale.[2] Her account lists coffee houses 'for tea and chocolate', rooms for gambling, different areas for walking in wet or dry weather, as well as bowling greens where the gentlemen bowled while the ladies walked or danced. There were places of interest to visit nearby, such as Penshurst, although the house, Celia said dismissively, was 'but old'. Even the iron-smelting works attracted her attention. Tunbridge Wells had everything. What could go wrong?

The first sign of trouble came when Queen Anne's son, the Duke of Gloucester, tripped and fell on the uneven walks. She gave £100 for the walks to be levelled and paved with pantiles, but the work was not carried out properly.

The Upper Walk or Pantiles in Tunbridge Wells, circa 1780

When she discovered this on a subsequent visit, she rode off and turned her patronage to Bath. She liked Bath. It welcomed her while her sister Mary was Queen, and received a royal reprimand for its pains. It already had some of the entertainments which high society expected, and, in the years since Pepys' visit, had started to catch up with Tunbridge Wells. As early as the 1680s, when Celia Fiennes visited, the gentle exercise in meadows indulged in by Pepys had

Detail from Gilmore's map, showing the gravel walks laid out at the east end of the abbey, with a bowling green to the south

become more sophisticated and the walks were a notable part of her visit. Here is how she described them, in her inimitable, stream-of-consciousness style:

> Y^e places for divertion about ye bath is either ye walkes in that they call ye Kings Mead which is a pleasant green meaddow, where are walkes round and Cross it, no place for Coaches, and indeed there is little use of a Coach only to bring and Carry ye Company from ye bath for ye wayes are not proper for Coaches ... I now proceed to describe the rest of the town. There are green walkes very pleasant and in many places, and out of the Cathedrall you walk into ye priory which has good walkes of rows of trees, which is pleasant – there are ye deans prebends and doctors houses which stand in ye green which is pleasant, by ye Church called the Abby, wch is lofty and spacious and much Company walke there especially in wet weather. Y^e Quire is neat but nothing extraordinary – in that Kings mead there are severall little Cake-houses where you have fruit lulibubs and sumes Liquours to entertaine y^e Company that walke there.[3]

Two early photographs of Bath Abbey, giving a glimpse of its spacious interior before the pews were added in the Victorian restoration

From this we can deduce that the fields where Pepys passed his time now had walks laid out around and across them, and little shops constructed to supply refreshments.[4] By lulibubs, we must assume Fiennes meant syllabubs. Pepys called them sullybubs, so this 'lulibubs' may even be a misreading of Celia Fiennes' hand-writing. Within the walls, the area east of the abbey was planted in 1675 with eighty sycamore trees, protected by a hawthorn hedge and arranged in straight lines, in the French style. Walking had become so much part of the social scene that, as Celia tells us, in wet weather people walked in the abbey.

So here begins in Bath the notion that the company needed somewhere to walk as part of their social daily round. The year before planting the sycamores, the council had set up a fund to provide railings along sections of the city walls, thinking this would create a pleasant promenade. As the city moved into the eighteenth century, exercise became an established part of a visitor's day. Formal walks were laid out near the abbey with various diversions available. In Ned Ward's rather scurrilous description of the city, *A Step to the Bath*, written in 1700, he describes how,

> bathing being over for that Day, we went to walk in the Grove, a very pleasant Place for Diversion; there is the Royal-Oak and several Raffling Shops: In one of the Walks, is several Sets of Nine-Pins,

and Attendance to wait on you: Tipping all Nine for a Guinea, is as common there, as two Farthings for a Porringer of Barley-Broth, at the Hospital-Gate in Smithfield. On several of the Trees was hung a Lampoon on the Marriage of one Mr S— a Drugmonger, and the famous Madam S— an old B— of London.[5]

It was plainly a popular and fashionable place to walk. Ward describes sitting with a friend on a bench in the Grove, as the friend tells him who the various people are. Eventually he tires of this, as

for Fops, Beaus, and Bellfa's, this Place exceeds Greys-Inn-Walks on Sunday Evening; and consists of greater variety of Persons, Remarkable for some Vice or Folly, than there are Ingredients in a Lombard-Pye for a City Feast.[6]

However, walking in the fields was still a popular recreation. The following evening, Ward goes out with the rich widow he has hastily married and her sister. Simple meadows they may have been, but they were crowded with people of all sorts:

In the Evening we took a Walk into the Meadows, much resorted to for pleasant Rivers, and delicate Walks; 'tis a second Hide-Park for Coaches, and a St. James's for Beau's and Belfa's of all sorts; there was Chaucer's Sempstress, my Lord R— Mantua-Makers dandled by Cringing Fops, Antick Beaus, and Blustering Bullies Innumerable, London-Jilts with Tails like Countesses, and case-harden'd Impudence; bantering Young Squires, and Shopkeepers Prentices: Nay my Millenian Landlady, and her Sister, was there Intriguing, and as well match'd as a pair of Nice Coach-Horses; much Admired, the one for an obliging Temper, the other for a Beauty; but ask honest Punch the Pastry-Cook, he'll tell you they Rival each other in their own proper Qualifications. After an Hour or two's Walking, I Treated my Ladies with the best the Place afforded, and then returned Home.[7]

Walking eventually became elevated to the social event known as parading, when fashionable society strolled out, dressed in their best afternoon clothes, to meet each other and exchange the latest gossip. As the idea of formal groves went out of fashion, people started laying out gardens, with water features and rooms for entertainments. However, according to one oft-quoted source by a famous writer, little had changed in Bath since the seventeenth century, despite Queen Anne's visit. That writer was Daniel Defoe, who, in his Journey through Britain, published in 1724, declared that

> the rest of the diversion here, is the walks in the great church, and at the raffling shops, which are kept (like the cloyster at Bartholomew Fair,) in the churchyard, and ground adjoyning.[8]

Defoe does not seem to have looked very hard. Change had certainly happened, and it was largely thanks to the energetic organisational skills of Beau Nash. In 1714, another visitor, John Macky, wrote that

> most of the company go to church in the morning in dishabille, and then go home to dress for the walks before dinner. The walks are behind the church, spacious and well shaded, planted round with shops filled with everything that contributes to pleasure, and at the end a noble room for gaming, from whence there are hanging-stairs to a pretty garden for everybody that pays for the time they stay, to walk in.[9]

This mention of a 'pretty garden' is extremely significant. The 'noble room' he refers to was the first set of Assembly Rooms, which Beau Nash persuaded Thomas Harrison to have built. They were constructed outside the walls but with their first floor rooms level with the ground inside the walls. To enter them, Harrison knocked a way through the walls, to enable people to walk straight in, thereby causing a dispute with the council. He also laid out walks, which soon became known as Harrison's Walks, in the former Abbey Orchard. John Wood, ever critical of the council and always ready to praise Beau Nash, explains why this was done, and how the council reacted:

> In the midst of all this Splendour, the Company were driven to the Necessity of meeting in a Booth to drink their Tea and Chocolate, and to divert themselves at Cards, till Mr Thomas Harrison, at the Instigation of the new King of Bath, erected a handsome Assembly-House for those Purposes. This House was begun in the Spring of the

Year 1708; to which Mr Harrison added Gardens for People of Rank and Fortune to walk in: But his Works were soon looked upon as prejudicial to the Gravel Walks, and as an Invasion of the Liberties of the City in as such the Corporation opposed them with the Power of Men determined by Might to overcome all Manner of Right.[10]

This seems to have been the first attempt to create gardens dedicated to pleasure, and may have come about because the King's Meads were being developed for building, making it necessary to find somewhere else for strolling.

Nevertheless, the King's Meads had one last moment of glory in 1728, when Princess Amelia stayed in the lodgings over the west gate. To celebrate her birthday,

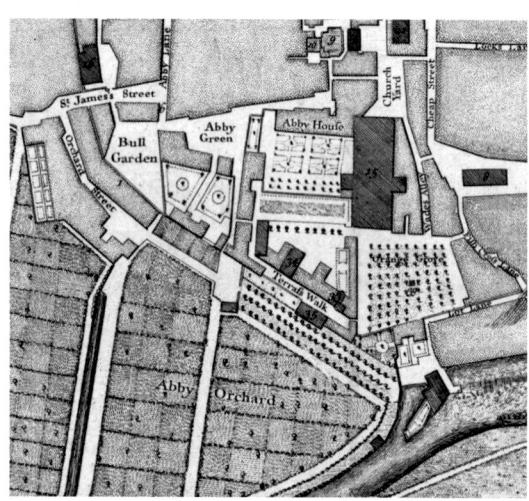

Detail from Wood's 1735 map of Bath, showing the expanded Orange Grove with the added trees, Harrison's Rooms and the original layout of Harrison's Walks

Capt Goulding's Ox, with head and horns on, was spitted, and put to the Fire ... in the Mead, just without the West Gate, and in sight of the Princess's Lodgings. Next the said place, was an Arbour covered with green Boughs, and two of the Captain's Grenadiers in Effigy fronting. The Morning was spent with a handsome and inoffensive Regale, of numerous spectators, from all Parts. And a select Set of Maurice-Dancers serenaded her Royal Highness for near an Hour, before her Window. Soon after that, Captain Goulding, at the Head of his Troop (being rang'd in good Order) saluted her Royal Highness in a very handsome Speech. After that, the Troop made a tripple Discharge of their Arms, and then march'd off. The Smiling Goodness and Condescention of her Auspicious Highness on this Occasion, was so great, that she appear'd publickly at her Sash Window, during all the Procession, being in perfect Health. At night, there were Rockets and Fireworks discharg'd in Little King's Mead, which were brought from the Tower of London, for that Purpose, but they did not all answer Expectation. The Honour of this Day was so successful, that 'tis modestly computed, this City was never so Populous since built before; so that the numerous Concourse and Advantage must accrue from the generous Undertaking of Capt Goulding.[11]

Although the King's Meads disappeared soon afterwards, the gardens laid out by Harrison still survive in part today as a small park, known as Parade Gardens. We will look at Harrison's Walks, as they were known, in greater detail in the next chapter.

One area which was redesigned and extended was the Grove. The garden at the east end of the abbey, described by Celia Fiennes, was expanded northwards into the space formerly known as Mitre Green, which was planted with trees in a similar fashion.[12] The whole area then became known as the Orange Grove. Again, we can turn to John Wood for an explanation:

> ORANGE GROVE has all the Advantage of Situation to render it a fine Place: It is one hundred and ninety eight Feet in Length, from North to South; one hundred and sixty nine Feet in Breadth; and it contains four and twenty Houses. So much of this Open Area as lies behind St. Peter and Paul's Church, and is of the fame Breadth with that Structure, has, for its proper Name, the Appellation of the *Abbey Litten*; and the Remainder of it was called the *Grove*: Litten is a *Wiltshire* Word for a Church Yard; from whence it seems evident, that that Part of the Grove behind the Church was the Church Yard belonging to it; the other Part of this open Place had its Name preserved by the Trees upheld in it; and that Name had its Origin in Pagan Times, as I have already set forth. In the Center of this Grove there is a small Obelisk, set up by the Order of Mr *Nash*, in the Year 1734, with Inscriptions upon the Pedestal under it, to set forth the Benefit the Prince of *Orange* received by Drinking the *Bath* Waters, as well as to give the Grove the proper Name of *Orange*, in Compliment to that Prince; whose Arms adorn the West Side of the Body of the Pedestal ... On the South Side of this Open Area

there is a paved Walk of two hundred Feet in Length, and twenty seven Feet in Breadth, which, not many Years ago, was the only Place of general Resort in the City for Pleasure and Exercise. Here the Company repaired in the Afternoon, when they had drank the Hot Waters, to compleat the Day with walking, while the Musick was playing to them; and this Alley was then large enough for the Purpose to which it was applied: Three Rows of tall Sycamore Trees lined out two other Alleys, Parallel to the former, which were spread with Gravel, for the Use of the common Sort of People; and these three Walks, with the Houses on the South Side, and the Fence on the North Side, took up the whole *Abbey Litten*; but were generally called the *Gravel Walks*, as two of them were covered with that Kind of Sand. In the tall Trees of these Walks, I remember, Rooks were used to build their Nests; but those Birds of Prey proving a great Nuisance to the Company who frequented the Alleys below, were therefore expell'd their lofty Seats: Since which this Open Area hath grown more and more in Repute; and People of Fortune have lately preferred it to any other Place, within the Walls of the City, to take up their Abode in, during their Stay at *Bath*.[13]

The Jardin du Luxembourg in Paris, laid out in 1620, with its straight rows of trees – originally elms – with gravel beneath them

The Orange Grove in 1737 as depicted on a fan by G Speren

Modern archaeological excavations have shown that Wood was correct in supposing there was a sacred grove in the area of the springs – but it was not where he thought it was. What we learn from these accounts by Macky and Wood is that there were now two places where people could walk. The gravel walks laid out in alleys or straight rows in the Orange Grove was very much in the French style. Almost every French town, even today, has similar areas for people to wander or play boules, while in Paris, parks such as the Tuileries Gardens or Les Jardins de Luxembourg exemplify this formal style.

During the seventeenth century, Mitre (or Outer) Green was used as a public area for bowling, though this ceased about 1680. However, a more private bowling green immediately to the south of Orange Grove remained popular with the aristocracy, until that too was built over in the early eighteenth century. Its northern boundary is marked by the row of shops which look northwards over Orange Grove.[14]

At the same time as the Grove expanded, Harrison created his walks on the low-lying area of the former Abbey Orchard. These were the first of Bath's true pleasure gardens, although, as we shall see, there was not a great deal there beyond gravel walks. It was enough, however, to attract comment and even poetry when they first opened. Although formal parading and informal exercise would continue to be very much part of the social day, with Harrison's Walks the age of pleasure gardens was dawning and has never really gone away.

2

RIVERSIDE PLEASURES

The Early Years of Harrison's Walks and Spring Gardens

When Thomas Harrison added walks to what was then just a single room intended for gaming, he had to lease land between the city and the river from the landowner, John Hall of Bradford on Avon. The area was larger than the present day Parade Gardens, including, as it did, the area now known as Terrace Walk – or Bog Island.[1] When the Parades were first built, the whole of North Parade overlooked the gardens, as did the houses in Terrace Walk.

Although his walks could be described as Bath's first true pleasure gardens, it is hard to know exactly what they contained. The evidence is somewhat confusing. Macky describes them as a 'pretty garden', so it is possible that right from the start there were flower beds. John Wood, however, simply calls them gardens where people could walk. Both the panorama of 1734 by Samuel and Nathaniel Buck and Wood's map of 1735 show an avenue of trees parallel with the city wall leading to a riverside walk. This too is lined with trees on the landward side, and what appears at first sight to be a rather odd-looking fence or hedge on the river side. Thanks to a poem by Mary Chandler, published in 1734, we have an authentic, albeit rather gushing, description, which explains what we are looking at:

Opposite: Part of a panorama of Bath in 1735 by Samuel and Nathaniel Buck, with Harrison's Assembly Rooms clinging to the city wall. Between the rooms and the river lie Harrison's Walks, with espalier trees along the riverside walk. Also visible at the southern end of the walks is the grotto – known as Delia's Grotto – where Sheridan and Elizabeth Linley left notes for each other before eloping to France in 1772. At the northern end is the riverside lodge. The trees in Orange Grove can also be glimpsed between the buildings.

> Now leave the Terrace, and th'extended Scene
> Of Hills inclos'd, and Meadows ever-green.
> Descend to Walks, 'twixt Limes in adverse Rows,
> And view the gay Parterre, that ever blows.
> This fair Pavilion view; around its Base
> Observe the sporting of the scaly Race.
> A cool Recess, the Muses chosen Seat,
> From Crouds, and empty Noise, a blest Retreat!
> The lovely Landscape and the silent Stream,
> Inspire the Poet, and present the Theme.
> Round the green Walk the River glides away,
> Where 'midst Espaliers balmy Zephyrs play,
> And fan the Leaves, and cool the scorching Ray.[2]

This poetic description actually contains much useful information. It tells us that there was a flower bed – the 'gay parterre'. It also tells us (and Wood's map and the Bucks' panorama confirm this) that Delia's Grotto – the 'cool recess' – was there, and that the odd looking fence in the Bucks' panorama was in fact a row of espaliers. When we compare the eighteenth century drawing with a

A nineteenth-century copy of Thomas Robins' picture of Harrison's Walks

RIVERSIDE PLEASURES

Espaliered trees in winter at Norton St Philip, showing how accurately they are shown in the panorama

photograph of espaliers in winter, we can see how accurate it is.

There is also the little ornamental lodge near the weir. This is seen clearly in Thomas Robins' View of Bath (c 1745) which shows it with chimneys. The accuracy of this is confirmed in a letter of 1752 from Mr Hutton Perkins to his employer, Lord Hardwick, in which he tells him that Princess Amelia was visiting the city, and that, in addition to playing cards (mainly a game called Commerce) and going horse-riding, she has discovered a new pastime:

> [She] amuses herself almost every day some hours in angling in the river, in a summer house by the river side in the garden, formerly known as Harrison's Walks, which has two fire-places in it, and to secure her against cold, puts on a riding habit, and a black velvet postillion cap, tied under the chin.[3]

However, most illustrations show the central area given over to grass, with no flowerbeds, shrubs or trees. Indeed, John Wood's 1735 map suggests that the central area was still orchard, with a path running across it to the river bank. As Wood developed the Parades, he also put forward a scheme for this orchard. A plan drawn in 1749 indicates that he proposed a

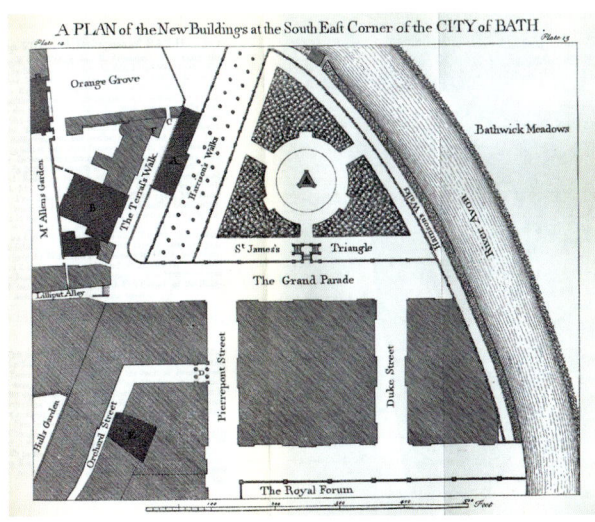

John Wood's never-realised plan for Harrison's Walks

formal design for the major part of the gardens, which he called St. James's Triangle.

Wood's design was geometric, incorporating a circle within a triangle, and within that what appears to be a triangular obelisk or perhaps a small pond. It possibly reflected some of the obscure philosophies that drove Wood's creative genius. Instead of lawns, the plans suggest a planting of Mediterranean plants such as santolina and lavender within box hedges, in the French style, as in the garden at Ham House in Surrey.

Santolina parterres at Ham House in Richmond, Surrey. This appears to be what Wood had in mind for his garden.

This plan never came to fruition. The circle may have been marked out, but only as a bowling green. To discover why the central area was left undeveloped and the opportunity for formal gardens was lost, we need to make a short diversion to examine the history of Bath's earliest Assembly Rooms.

They were a highly speculative venture. Promoted by Beau Nash to attract the aristocracy, Harrison's first room had been intended solely as a casino, not for concerts or balls. Almost certainly, at this stage, Harrison had no thought about developing the gardens – this would have been risking money unnecessarily. His nickname was 'Thrifty', which suggests that he could be penny-pinching, although his entrance charges were regarded as high. The walks would have been considered adequate for the sort of visitors then coming to Bath. However, Harrison extended his building in 1720 by adding a ballroom. This was possibly in response to competition from a ruthless rival. Mary Lindsey – known as Dame Lindsey – was one of Bath's first female entrepreneurs and proved to be a determined and manipulative operator. With the help of what Wood described as her sister Kitty – who was probably her housekeeper Catherine Lovelace – and an elderly servant called Fanny, she set up a gaming house which by 1721 was well established. It also offered entertainment, supper and dancing. Dame Lindsey had been one of England's top opera singers, and although she had retired from the stage, she could still sing beautifully. The Countess of Bristol described her as singing like a nightingale at a private party in her rooms in 1721.

A year later, there was an outbreak of smallpox in the city. Visitor numbers fell drastically and Harrison decided to close his rooms – which turned out to be a somewhat rash decision. By November, the smallpox epidemic had receded, and a visitor to Bath, Mrs Francis Vaughan, reported that

> wee have a good dell of company in town and thay met every night ither at hayis rooms, linsees or cornishis'.[4]

It is clear these were all operating as Assembly Rooms. 'Linsees' is obviously Lindsey's. 'Cornishis' was a double-width building in the middle of the south side of the Grove, owned by a milliner called Thomas Cornish. It still exists but is much altered. But the most interesting is 'Hayis'. About 1720, the apothecary and city councillor, William Collibee, had built a large house up against the north wall of the abbey chancel, which he shortly afterwards leased to Lord Francis Hawley. Even at the time many people did not realise that this impoverished nobleman had, in 1718, after the death of his first wife, remarried to a woman described in the register as Elizabeth Hayes, widow. For many years she seemed to have been content to be considered Hawley's partner – in business as well as pleasure. Even fewer realised she was a widow – John Wood said she always used her maiden name. However, it was known that she was the sister of Dame Lindsey, and the two of them had great plans. These small rooms were but a stepping stone to a larger empire.

Dame Lindsey approached Humphrey Thayer to persuade him to build her a much grander set of rooms. Thayer was a speculator who had acquired several pieces of the former Hall estate, which had come into the Duke of Kingston's family by marriage. In 1728, Wood designed rooms for her, which overlooked Harrison's, and which, although smaller, had a larger ballroom. When they opened in 1730, they were a serious threat to Harrison, who by now was possibly ailing. He passed the lease of his rooms officially to Lord

A drawing of Terrace Walk circa 1750, with Lindsey's – later Wiltshire's – Rooms to the left and Simpson's Rooms to the right

Hawley, but it was Elizabeth who was in charge. The sisters were now in complete control of both sets of rooms. Harrison died in January 1735, and his two daughters inherited the rooms, although the Hawleys continued to run them. The income they paid to Harrison's estate was sufficient to pay a regular annuity to his sister-in-law, while still turning a profit for themselves.[5]

Dame Lindsey and her sister Elizabeth may have persuaded Wood to design formal gardens, but if so the cost probably deterred them. They were set on making as much money as possible. So rapacious were the two that Nash insisted they reduce their prices. However, their scheming came to an abrupt end when Dame Lindsey died in 1737. For a short time the rooms passed to her housekeeper Catherine Lovelace before passing to the Wiltshire family in 1740. Lord and Lady Hawley survived at the former Harrison's Rooms until he died in 1743, followed by Lady Hawley in 1745. The lease of the rooms then passed to Charles Simpson, Lord Hawley's principal servant.

All this competition and greed, as well as the changes of management, meant that an opportunity to carry out a coherent design for the gardens was lost. There was the occasional firework display, and Beau Nash's cannons, which he acquired in 1746 for royal salutes, were kept there, but there were no further additions to the grounds. By the time the dust had settled and the proprietors of the rooms had established a more settled routine, a competitor had sprung up on the other side of the river. It was called Spring Gardens.

These were Bath's first true pleasure gardens. Their name derived from the original name of the famous gardens at Vauxhall in London, and, as with their successors, the word Vauxhall was often added to their name. Styling them Spring Gardens Vauxhall, however, was somewhat presumptuous, as they were very much smaller, especially at the outset.

Their story begins with Bathwick Mill, which stood by the weir on the east side of the river. Savile's Map of about 1600 shows a building close to Bathwick Mill. Since it has tenters – or drying racks – for newly dyed cloth beside it, and faces east and west, to give maximum light, it may have been a weaver's house. A survey of 1727, drawn up a year after William Pulteney, the future Earl of Bath, bought the land from the Earl of Essex, shows the house surrounded by a triangle of land. This may already have been an informal garden. Samuel and Nathaniel

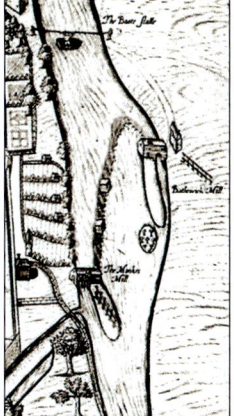
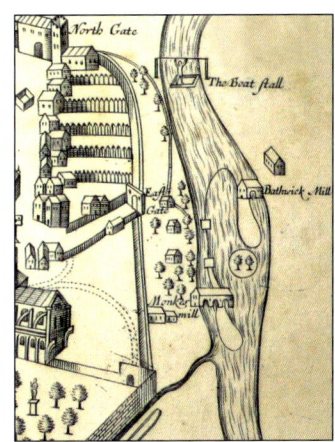

Above left: Henry Savile's map showing Bathwick Mill and Monk's Mill, both with tenters alongside them

Above right: The same location on John Speed's map of 1610

Below: Detail from the Bucks' panorama showing Bathwick Mill on the right., with Monk's Mill and the summer house on the other side of the river

Bucks' panorama of 1734 shows both the mill and the house, with what appear to be shrubs around them. We can also see that a wing has been added on the east side of the house. This is confirmed by Wood's map of 1735. There are what seem to be vegetable gardens to the north, and to the south the first indication of formal gardens.

In 1737, William Pulteney let the land to

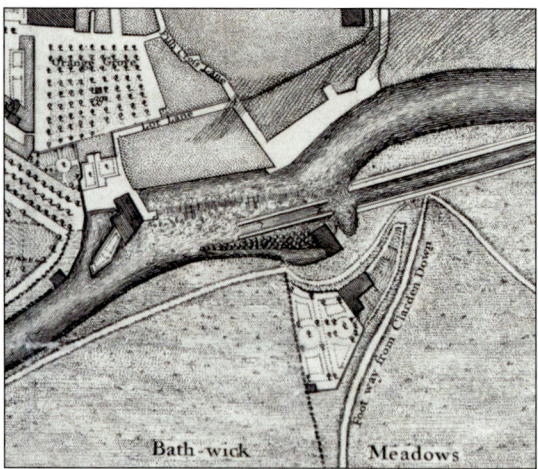

Wood's map of 1735 showing gardens in Bathwick Meadows but no Long Room. It also shows a proposed lock, which would have opened up the river, but was never built.

William Hull, a gardener. Perhaps Hull had been involved in laying it out, but if so his tenure was now on a formal basis. It is clear from an inventory of 1742 that it had been a place of entertainment, and that he had been using the building like a pub. There were five coffee pots, four dozen pewter plates and fourteen chairs in the kitchen, a further fourteen chairs in the room over the kitchen, and more in other rooms. There was a tap room, with two kilderkins of draught ale, two barrels of beer, a cask of cider (almost empty) and two other casks with what was described ominously as sour liquor, although this may simply have meant vinegar.[6] There were also fifteen pint bottles and eight quart bottles of white wine, and twenty-eight pint bottles and seven quart bottles of red wine.

William Pulteney, first Earl of Bath

This all suggests the building was used for entertainment and refreshment. Sadly, the reason the inventory was drawn up is that in 1742 Hull was evicted for non-payment of rent. He did not go quietly, and the row rumbled on for another ten years but, in the meantime, Pulteney and his solicitor Jarrit Smith looked for new tenants. A draft lease was drawn up in September 1742 to let the land to a group of people, but the deal fell through. However, the lease is interesting because it describes the property and lays down conditions as follows:

> All of those gardens and buildings lately leased and let to Wm Hull gardener, commonly called Spring Garden, with the fish pond, fish therein, fruit trees and garden stock therein ... to keep in good repair all the said premises and all buildings now or that shall be erected thereon ... to keep gardens, fruit trees and walks in good order and the fish ponds well stocked with fish.

This suggests that Hull had come up with the name Spring Gardens several years earlier. Thorpe's map, which also dates from 1742, not only features Spring Gardens, but also shows that the site had been extended a considerable way south of the area shown by Wood in 1735. However, we have to wait until 1770 to find a map showing larger and more elaborate gardens filling the whole site, suggesting that originally the southern part of the plot was not fully laid out. All we know for certain is that by 1742 there were ponds and fruit trees. This implies that, besides being pleasurable, the gardens

Thorpe's Map, showing Spring Gardens and the Long Room

were also productive. The draft lease indicates that further buildings had been erected or were planned, and Thorpe's map shows what became known as the Long or Great Room, commissioned by Pulteney and completed in 1743.

We do not know why this lease fell through but it appears that Pulteney was pleased about it. He wrote to Jarrit Smith in May 1743 that the lease would be granted for three years 'to the person I first intended of Spring Gardens, and I will therefore have the new building finished there, according to the plan and agreement'. He added that the building would be 'very good of its kind'.

Pulteney may have fallen out with Jarrit Smith over this and from now on he would use Samuel Purlewent, a London lawyer who had moved to Bath, to handle his Bathwick estate. Smith was told to hand over the plan to Purlewent and the lease was granted to Francis Edmondson for three years. When it expired, the *Bath Journal* of 2 May 1748 carried the following advertisement:

> To be Lett at *Michaelmas* next:
> A Messuage or Tenement, with the Gardens and Fish-ponds thereto belonging, called *Spring-Gardens*, in the Parish of *Bathwick*, near *Bath*, in the County of *Somerset*, now in the Possession of Mr *Edmondson*: And also a Messuage and Garden in the same Parish, late in the Possession of *William Lewis*. – Enquire of Mr *Purlewent*, Attorney in *Bath*.

The advertisement only appeared in one issue, because it seems that Edmondson renewed the lease and stayed there until 1759. The gardens seem to have been little more than a pleasurable retreat. We can guess that music was played, but there are no known accounts of public breakfasts, dancing or fireworks. No advertisements appeared in the local papers, probably because Bath was still small enough for any events to be advertised by word of mouth. Furthermore, to reach the gardens, one either had to take a ferry or walk down to the old bridge and back along the river bank.

However, a more vigorous entrepreneur was waiting in the wings to change the fortunes of the gardens. This was William Purdie, a lodging-house keeper who, in the same year that Edmondson renewed his lease of the gardens, advertised that he sold 'all sorts of Mineral Water, viz: Spaw,

A sketch by Thomas Robins with Bathwick Mill in the foreground. The wall of Spring Gardens can just be seen alongside the river path. On the other side of the river are Simpson's Walks, with the summer house in the foreground.

Pyrmont, Cheltenham, Bristol, Road, Holt, &c, &c'.[7] Purdie was an astute business man who eventually became rent collector for the Earl of Bath and on certain occasions his trustee. His lodging-house and premises in Orange Court overlooked the gardens, and he must have seen their potential. He saw, too, how to overcome the problems of access from the city. When he took over, in 1759, he would make Spring Gardens into one of Bath's most popular places of resort. While retaining features such as the fishponds, fruit trees and parterres, the gardens were completely transformed, and retained their popularity until the development of the Pulteney estate and the coming of Sydney Gardens finally led to their demise.

Map of Bath and surrounding area, showing Kings Mead, Amery, Bath Gardens, Dont Mead, Key Bridge, Rotton way, Beachen Cliff, Mr Allens Wharfe to Bath Wick, Gardens, To Claverton, Wicksteed Machine, Parsonage House, Mr Bennets, Witcombe, Lyncombe, Mr Chapmans, Lyncombe Span, Gibbs Mill, To Comb, Park House, One Mile from Bath, One Mile, Mr Allens House, Mr Allens Free Stone Quarry.

3

OUT OF TOWN

Gardens on the Edge of the City

As we have seen, walking in the countryside was viewed as pleasurable exercise, so we should not be surprised to find that gardens developed outside the city, both to north and south.

The steep slopes of Lansdown made it difficult to create the formal gardens popular in the early eighteenth century. It was only later, when views or 'prospects', as they were known, became fashionable with the development of landscape gardens in the 'picturesque' style, that the hillsides were seen as offering opportunities. However, a public house called the Hand and Flower on the west side of Lansdown Road seems to have had small pleasure gardens attached to it quite early on. In a 1740 survey of Walcot, the landlord of the Hand and Flower pub is listed as Mr Rogers, who also held the lease of a plot of land owned by Widow Bishop. We have little evidence of what went on there, but it may have been a pleasant refreshment spot for people keen to take the air on Lansdown. It would certainly have had a wonderful view, for the houses on the other side of Lansdown Road had not yet been built. We know it was a popular spot for florists to meet, as the *Bath Journal* of 13 July 1747 included the following advertisement:

> All florists are desir'd to meet their brethren at the Sign of the *Hand & Flower* on Lansdown Road, on Wednesday, the 29th of this instant

Opposite: Part of Thorpe's map of 1742, showing the course of Ralph Allen's tramway from his freestone quarry at Combe Down, past his house at Prior Park, to his wharf on the river. It also shows Lyncombe 'Spaw', Wicksteed's Machine and Philip Bennet's house at Widcombe Manor.

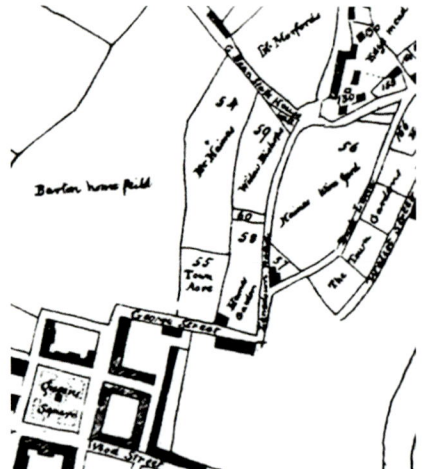 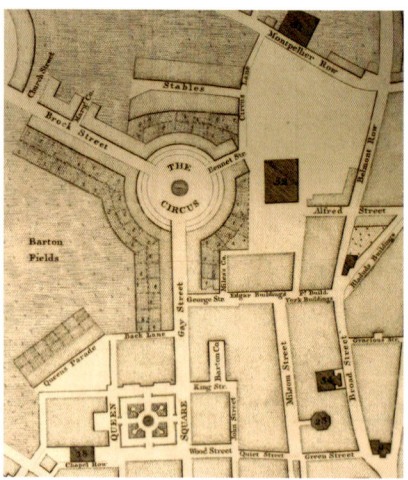

On the map accompanying the 1740 survey of Walcot, seen above left, Widow Bishop's land, on which the Hand and Flower Ground stood, is number 59. On the map from 1775, seen above right, houses on Alfred Street and Belmont Row already cover part of the area.

July, and to bring with them their choicest carnations. He that shows the best will be entitled to a silver cup.

Rogers continued to run the Hand and Flower until the leases were transferred to the ruthless developer Thomas Warr Atwood, who turned him out and subsequently re-leased the plots at great personal profit.[1]

Thus ended the story of the Hand and Flower.

Despite being on the far side of the River Avon, the land south of Bath proved more fertile ground for pleasure gardens. These included the estate surrounding Ralph Allen's house at Prior Park. Although it was private, illustrations show its grounds were visible from the road and were meant to be enjoyed by passers-by. Philip Thicknesse described Prior Park as 'a noble seat which sees all Bath, and which was built, probably for all Bath to see'.

At about the same time that Prior Park was being laid out, John Wicksteed, who ran a 'toy shop' – or gift shop – in Orange Grove, invented a machine for engraving seals. At first his studio was based in Bathampton, but about 1737, he moved

> Stone Seals Engrav'd by
> J. WICKSTEED, at his Machine
> up Mr. ALLEN's Road.

An advertisement from 1741

to Widcombe. Here he built a house where people could go to see his machine, which was driven by water power. It became such an attraction that it is shown as Wicksteed's Machine on Thorpe's map of 1742. At this stage, though, Wicksteed had not developed the area around the house as pleasure gardens. That came later, as we shall see in the next section.

First, we must consider the strangely-named King James's Palace, whose pleasure gardens stood on the north side of Lyncombe Vale. Most authorities agree that they opened about 1777, taking their name from the local legend that, when Mary of Modena, wife of James II, came to take the waters in Bath in 1687, the King stayed at a house in Lyncombe. There appears to be no evidence for this. Thorpe's map certainly shows no building on the site, let alone one grand enough for a King. However, a reference in *The Memoirs of Capt. Peter Drake*, published in Dublin in 1755, provides a more plausible explanation. Drake was an Anglo-Irish Jacobite who fought for the French. Captured and convicted of treason, he received a royal pardon in 1709. By the 1720s he was running various gaming rooms and tables in London and occasionally, on an *ad hoc* basis, in Bath. During a visit to the city about 1724, he met with some potential business partners, and recorded that

> one Sunday they all invited me to dine with them at a thatched Cabbin, within a Mile of the Town, called King James's Palace.

This suggests that there was some kind of drinking establishment on this site, which was perhaps used for discreet meetings. As Captain Drake was a Jacobite, it is likely that his friends and acquaintances were of a similar persuasion. So perhaps this cabin, well away from the prying eyes of the authorities, was a meeting place for Jacobites. A pub in Walcot, on the north side of town, known as the Hat and Feather, may have possibly served a similar purpose. If so, as the Hanoverian grip on the country tightened, it seems likely that the meeting place in Lyncombe fell out of favour, only to be revived later in the century, a story which will be picked up in the next section.

But let us return to Prior Park, Bath's first landscape garden. Many will say this was not a pleasure garden in the sense that Vauxhall and Ranelagh were, but created to give people a pleasing vista to enjoy. Nevertheless, it would have a major influence on the development of later pleasure gardens. Although not a public garden, Allen worked with Philip Bennet of Widcombe Manor to

Ralph Allen's tramway running past Prior Park

create a picturesque rural landscape in the valley, while making elements of the industrial infrastructure connected with this quarrying business, such as his tramway and Padmore's crane, attractions in their own right.[2] The design of the mansion which overlooked the garden was partly to show off Bath Stone, and to demonstrate how it could enhance the area, but was also intended to show off Allen's power. Despite his polite and quiet demeanour, he could be a ruthless operator when he chose, as John Wood found to his cost. Visiting the tramway and enjoying the scenery from outside the wall proved immensely popular. We can see this in an illustration of 1750 entitled *A Perspective View of Prior Park, the seat of Ralph Allen*. Not only do we see details of the garden, with its formal area on one side, and Wilderness on the other, we also see the tramway, lined with

A detail from the Bucks' panorama showing Allen's wharf and stoneyard and the crane designed by John Padmore

visitors, some agog at the new technology, others peering over the wall at the garden. Within the grounds, privileged visitors stroll, admiring the view from near the house. The popularity of Prior Park as a visitor attraction is doubtless why Wicksteed decided to move his seal-cutting device to Widcombe.

The mansion itself, set on high towards the top of the combe, was the star of the show. The garden tumbled away from it, with nothing to block the view from the house. The Palladian Bridge was added later in 1755, and even then was set to one side to avoid interfering with the spectacular vista from the house. The first adviser on landscape gardening to whom Allen turned was Alexander Pope, who took a great interest in the grounds, which were laid out as the house was being built. Later, Lancelot 'Capability' Brown seems to have advised Allen on developing the design to keep up with fashion, as there was a payment of £60 due to him in Allen's accounts after his death, but it is not known if he actually visited. Whatever form his intervention took, it resulted in a softer, more natural appearance. In 1761, the *Bath Chronicle* published a poem entitled 'Prior Park: or Industry and Art's Triumph'. The first few lines run:

> To please the Eye, and entertain the Mind,
> The Powers Of Art and Industry combin'd;
> In Prior-Park their mutual Labours wrought
> Beauties, scarce imag'd by the Strength of Thought:
> Soon as the ravish'd Eye the Scene surveys,
> New, curious Strokes of Art the Mind Amaze;
> While by the Force of Industry around,
> A second Eden, blissful Seat! is found.[3]

It continues in a similar vein, conveying the amazement felt at the combination of the beauty of the garden with industry. This industry included two mills, one on Allen's land and one on the land of Philip Bennet, to whom Allen was related by marriage. The former fishponds, a relic of Bath's monastic past, not only fed the mills but also added to the beauty of the setting.[4]

Bennet's mill was also fed by the Lyn Brook which flowed down Lyncombe Vale. It was fed by springs in the other pleasure gardens on this side of Bath, at Lyncombe Spa. Like Prior Park it was built about 1735, and, as with Prior Park, there are historians who deny that its gardens can be described as pleasure gardens. Although it was a place of recuperation, however, its grounds were laid out attractively and there are strong indications that it was also a place to visit and to enjoy refreshment. Lyncombe Spa and Prior Park were, if you prefer, proto-pleasure gardens.

The land on which it stands came into the Hickes family in 1691, and by the early eighteenth century it was leased to Charles Milsom. Much of the land was taken up with a fishpond, of a similar size to those in Prior Park. John Wood takes up the story:

> Mr Charles Milsom, a Cooper of Bath, commonly called Doctor Milsom, having, in Partnership with four other People, rented an old Fish-Pond at Lyncomb, for twenty Shillings a Year; and there having been Leaks in the Pond, Mr Milsom, about the latter end of June in the Year 1737, searched the Ground under the Head of it, then over-ran with Briars, Willows, &c. in order to discover and stop the Chinks; at which Time he perceived a void Piece of Ground, of about six Feet long, and three Feet broad, which, as he approached it, shook, and looked much like the Spawn of Toads: This, upon Examination, he found to be of a glutinous Substance; to have a strong sulphurous Smell; and to be of the Colour of Oaker [ochre].
>
> This Slime, as it was not above fifteen Inches thick, Mr Milsom soon removed with a Shovel; and then perceiving several little Springs to boil up, and emit a black Sand, like the filings of Steel or Iron, he dug a small Hole to collect all the Springs together: The Soil he threw out was partly a petrified Earth, in Lumps, which at first resembled Cinders; but when those black Lumps of Earth were exposed to the Air, and dried, they turned grey, and grew less, like pieces of Spunge taken out of Water, squeezed and dried. The other part of the Soil was a white Earth, like Chalk, so soft that he could thrust his Cane, horizontally, up to the Head in it; but this Strata of white Earth was not above four or five Inches thick; it was about nine Inches under the Surface of the solid Ground; and the Water that run thro' it was of the Colour of White-wash, made with Lime and Water. These things, and the Taste of the Water, made Mr Milsom conclude it to be a strong Mineral.[5]

OUT OF TOWN 45

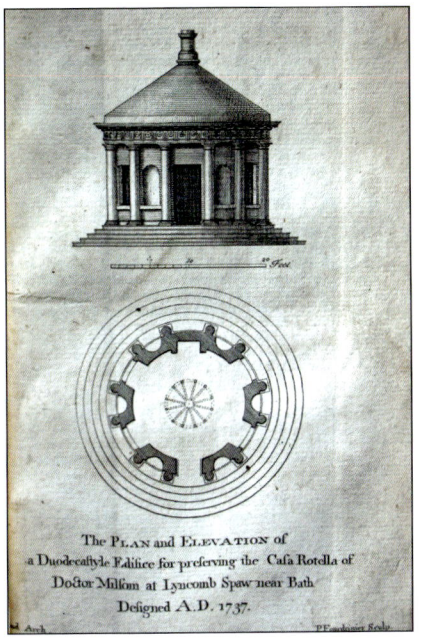

John Wood's design for the spring at Lyncombe Spa

The plan from the deed between Hillary and Hickes. At the bottom is the main buildng, with the court in front and 'the spaw' on the left. Behind it, surrounded by walks, is the fish pond.

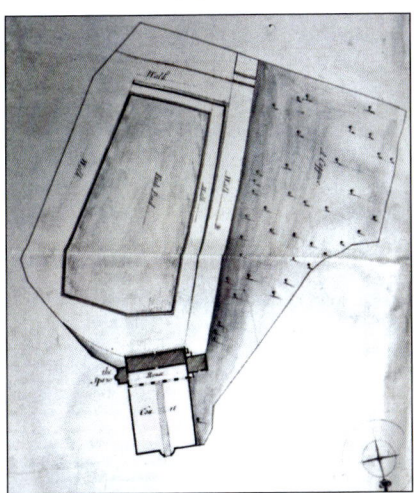

At this point, the story becomes confused, as Wood's account conflicts with that of someone else connected with the spa who, like Wood, had his own agenda. What we do know is that, in 1740, John Hickes, who had an agreement with Milsom, died, and his son, also John, inherited his property. By now, a doctor who had come to live in Bath, William Hillary, had taken an interest in the spring. He is the author of the other account, and John Wood soon fell out with him. Suffice it to say that, when water from one of the springs discovered by Milsom was mixed with brandy, it turned it deep purple. Word of this having reached Dr Hillary's ears, he analysed the water and declared it to be a chalybeate spring. Milsom decided to exploit the spring, and, according to Wood, commissioned him to design him a cover for it. However, Hillary and Hickes had other ideas, and Milsom was apparently persuaded to leave the site. Perhaps he was paid off. If so, he used the money to good effect. It is about this time we see him becoming involved in property development and by the time he died he owned property all over Bath, as well as in Lyncombe and Widcombe, and as far afield as Bathford. In Lyncombe, he leased land from Richard Maltby

The front of Lyncombe Spa about 1910. The small extension on the left was a bath-house, fed by the spring. It was there by 1809, when the property was sold to a Dr Jones. When he let the house a year later, it was described as an excellent cold bath.

on the other side of the road from the spa and built a new house there after demolishing the existing one. It is likely that the one he demolished was the 'thatched Cabbin ... called King James's Palace' visited by Captain Drake, for, although we do not know what Milsom called his new house, by the 1770s it had taken the name King James's Palace.[6]

With Milsom out of the way, Hickes and Hillary set out to build not just a cover over the well, as Wood had suggested, but a spa house, which would also serve as lodgings. They also dispensed with Wood's services and drew up a design of their own. Hence Wood's ire with Hillary, of whom he said scornfully that he should not have 'taken upon him more of the Architect than the Physician in this Work'. Wood declared that the ground was too weak to bear the weight of the building, and the foundations needed to be so deep that the spring was ruined. Why Wood made this manifestly false claim is unknown – the spring still flows vigorously even today.[7] However, giving the lie to his claim about the spring is a comment from an anonymous traveller who wrote in 1743 that Lyncombe Spa was 'famous for a well of water in high repute hearsay'd [sic] to be as good as the German Spaw water'.[8]

By 1742, the spa house was complete and fully equipped, at a cost of £1400. The work included building the house, enclosing the ground, putting the fishpond and grounds in good order, covering over the spring and building a brewhouse with a vault. The gardens were laid out with walks, parterres and a mound like one in Bennet's garden at Widcombe. An illustration by Thomas Robins has been identified by John Harris, who catalogued his drawings, as showing the gardens at Lyncombe, and though some modern researchers have disputed this, a later plan of the spa house gardens shows the identification to be correct. Although intended as a curative resort, Lyncombe Spa also offered accommodation and had several apartments. An inventory of 1746 suggests that it also catered to day visitors. There was a coffee room, amply supplied with crockery, including tea, coffee and chocolate pots. The Great Room had eighteen black leather chairs, with another eighteen chairs in the parlour. The apartments, which each consisted of a dining room and at least one and occasionally two bedchambers, were also capable of accommodating guests for meals. Each apartment had matching colours in the bedchambers and dining rooms, with crimson in the best one, blue damask in the second best, and green, yellow and blue apartments on an upper floor. The kitchen too was well equipped to provide meals, with two dog wheels, suggesting this was a sizeable operation. In 1754, a visitor described it as

> a sweet retirement, where there is a Chalybeat water, and a very good house for lodgings, &c, on the same terms as Bath.[9]

All this points to the house being rather more than a retreat for the poorly. People came to Bath to take the waters and enjoy themselves and this cold water spa was designed to serve a similar purpose. There may even have been occasional concerts there, although only one was advertised. In May 1751, the *Bath Journal* carried a notice about a concert at Lyncombe Spa House by Messrs Charles, the French-Horn makers. There was to be a 'Band of Musick' with a variety of instruments, to accompany a public breakfast. If ladies so wished, there would be Country Dancing afterwards, with 'proper hands ready to attend'. There would be no other expense for people attending 'than what they please to spend', as the concert was for the benefit of John Taber, who kept the house at that time. It has been suggested that this concert was a one-off, but it can equally be argued that the spa seems to have been well-

This sketch of the grounds by Thomas Robins was drawn from the balcony. The mound – or rather the part of a hillside – to the side is still there today, with paths leading up it, but the other paths have gone.

prepared for such an event, and that there are likely to have been similar events on other occasions.

However, there is no doubt that its medicinal facilities were the driving force behind the operation. Hillary made a scientific study of the waters, which he published in 1742. He found there were two springs, one which deposited what he called yellow ochre – lime-scale discoloured by iron in the water – and the other, which ran intermittently, leaving a black deposit. Both had a temperature of 52°F (12°C).[10] He listed some of the cases that the water had cured, one in particular which still resonates with us today:

> A Girl of 13 had violent Pains in her Stomach, Belly, and Hips, accompanied with very frequent Purging, and almost total Loss of Appetite, for near two years; she sometimes complained of a Pain in her Head, and Dizziness, but was never free from the Complaint of her Stomach and Belly, which were always increased after eating, and sometimes were so violent as to force her to vomit, which for the present gave her Ease. The long Continuance of these Disorders had

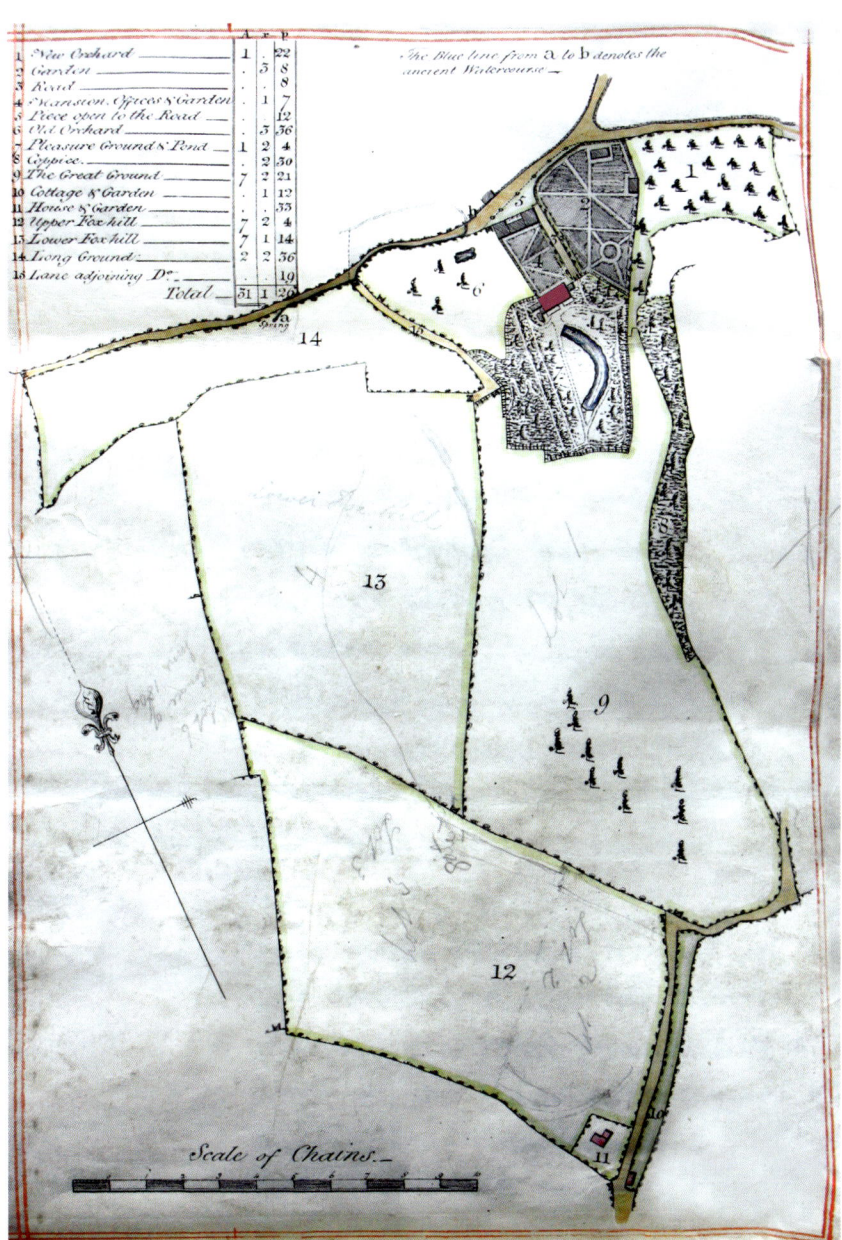

A plan of Lyncombe Spa from a deed of 1809. Comparison with the sketch by Robins shows how the paths still conform to those in his sketch. However, changes have taken place since the spa became a private house: the fish pond has been replaced by a crescent-shaped pool and a bath house has been added on the west side of the house.

reduced her to a very low Condition, though several Methods had been tried to relieve her, but without Success.[11]

Today, we recognise such a combination of symptoms as a textbook case of anorexia nervosa. Interestingly, Hillary did not try to make her eat but persuaded to her to drink the Lyncombe Spa waters, and, according to him:

> In a few Days her Pains abated, the Vomiting and Purging stopp'd, her Appetite returned and in about Six Weeks she got quite well, without the Assistance of any other Medicine.

This may not be as unlikely as it first appears. A recent scientific analysis of the water shows that it contains many of the chemicals regarded as essential nutrients for a healthy human body.

Managing the spa seems to have been up to Hickes. Hillary spent much time abroad, and Hickes simply supplied him with accounts from time to time. Between them, they must have thought they had a winning formula, but medical science was beginning to make inroads into the fashion for taking the waters. In addition, many other little spas sprang up in and around Bath during the Georgian period, though none had the facilities offered by Lyncombe Spa.

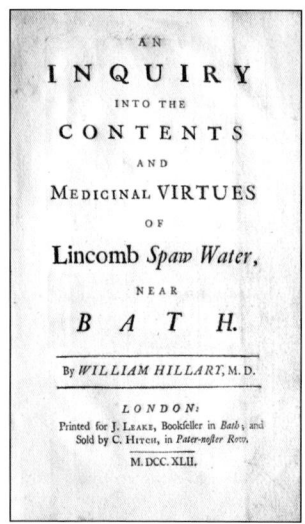

The title page of Hillary's book on 'Lincomb Spaw Water'

As the century wore on, Bath itself was changing. As its popularity grew and the number of lodgings increased, the city needed to offer better facilities to visitors, whose expectations had risen. In particular, they wanted a greater variety of events to amuse themselves during their stay. They wanted music, fireworks, and public breakfasts in delightful settings. As the city moved into the second half of the eighteenth century, new pleasure gardens were created which provided more sophisticated entertainments. In the case of Spring Gardens, they would be transformed by a new proprietor, eclipsing Harrison's Walks, and remaining pre-eminent until almost the end of the century.

Information on the early years of Bath's pleasure gardens is scant in the extreme. Some records have survived from Lyncombe Spa, however. One of them is an inventory drawn up in 1746, listing the contents of the spa in meticulous detail. The first and last pages of this three-page document are reproduced above, while a transcript of the entire inventory appears on the following three pages. Although much of the information relates to the catering and lodging arrangements, its rarity value and the light it sheds on life in early Georgian Bath more than justifies its inclusion here.

Inventory of the Goods at Lyncombe Spaw House &c
Linnen &c

Four pair of fine Holland Sheets. Five pairs of Irish Holland Do.
Eleven pair of Servants Do.
Two Large fine Table Cloths.
Twelve Single fine Table Cloths.
Two Doz fine Napkins
Two Doz fine Diaper Towells
One Doz Huckaback Towells
Nine Rubbers
One Doz & 10 Glass Cloths. Rushy Cloth
Six Long Kitchen Towells.
Twenty Pillow cases.

Aug 5   Sent up 8 New Rubbers

First in the Coffee Room

Two Doz and Half of China Plates
Two Doz and Half of Cups and Saucers
Two Doz Coffee Cups wanting One
Three Pint Slop Basons, and 2 Half Pint Do
Three Sugar Dishes, and 3 Milk Pots
Five Teapotts and 1 Large China Dish.
One Plate Baskett, One Chest of Drawers an Iron Hearth
2 Doz of Large Knives and forks. Two doz and an Half
of Breakfast Knives. Six Large Hand Boards, and four small
Do One Tin Chocolate pot and Mill. One Large Copper Chocolate
Pot and Do a pair of Scales with two Oz-Weights, and 2 Quarters
of an Oz weight. A Coffee Mill and a Gallypot for Sugar, four
Quarts, and four pint Tin Coffee Pots.

In the Great Room

One Doz and Half of Black Leather Bottom Chairs Two Square
Deal Tables, A Brass Fender, fire Shovell poker & Tongs, a large
Glass, & a Hearth Brush

In the Parlour

One Doz and a Half of Black Leather Bottom Chairs , Two Square
Deal Tables, A Brass Fender, and a Hearth Brush.

In the Best Dineing Room

One Mahoganny Table and a Round Do. A Crimson Damask
Settee Six Chairs with Crimson[stuff] Damask bottoms One Pair of Crimson
Harrateen Window Curtains A Chimeny Glass with A Gilt Frame and
2 Brass Arms A Stove Grate A Brass Fender fire Shovell poker &
tongs and pair of Bellows

In the Best Bed Chamber

A Crimson Damask Bed A feather Bed, Bolster and two Pillows
Three Blanketts and a White Quilt. Six Crimson Damask Chairs
And a Crimson Damask Dressing Chair. One pair of Crimson
Harrateen Window Curtains. A Brass fender fire Shovell poker and Tongs.
A Chest of Drawers and dressing table, and One Large Swinging Glass.
A Blue & White Mattrass and a Close Stool Box & pewter pan.

In the Middle Chamber on the dineing Room floor

A White Dimitty Bed A Feather Bed, Bolster 2 pillows, 3
Blanketts, a White Quilt, and a pair of Dimmity Window Curtains
a Small Chest of Drawers and a Swinging Glass.

In the Least Dineing Room

Six Wallnut'ree Chairs with Blue Damask Stuffed Bottoms Two
Pair of White Dimitty Window Curtains. A Wallnutt Oval table A Round
Mahoganny table, A Chimney Glass. A Stove Grate fire Shovell poker and
Tongs, and a Brass Fender

In the Bed Chamber within the Least Dineing Room

A Worked Bed, Feather Bed Bolster 2 pillows, three Blanketts, a White Quilt
2 pair of ^{white} Dimitty Window Curtains A Walnutt Chest of Drawers. A Wallnutt
Dressing Table and Glass. A Brass Fender fire Shovel Poker & tongs. Two
Walnutt Chairs with blue stuffed Damask Bottoms. A Blue and White Mat
=rass, & a Close Stool & pewter pan.

In the Green Dineing Room two pair of Stairs

A White Dimitty Bed & feather Bed, Bolster, 2 pillows, three Blanketts,
& a White Quilt. Six Wallnutt Chairs with Green Damask Bottoms. Two
pair of Green Harrateen Window Curtains. One Sconce with a Gilt frame and
Arms, and a Brass Fender.

In the Green Bed Chamber

A Green Harrateen Bed, Feather Bed, Bolster, and 2 pillows. Three
Blanketts, & a White Quilt. Two pairs of Green Harrateen Window curtains
four Wallnutt tree Chairs with Green damask Bottoms A Wallnutt Chest
of Drawers, Dressing table and Glass, and a Hearth Brush. An Oak Close
Stool Box and pewter pan.

In the Little Bed Chamber, 2 pair of Stairs

A Yellow Harrateen Bed, a Small Chest of Drawers, and Swinging
Glass

In the Blue Dineing Room

A Blue China Settee Bed. Feather Bed, Bolster, one pillow and
3 Blanketts, and a Quilt. Four Wallnutt Chairs with Blue damask
Bottoms, Two pairs of Blue Harateen Window Curtains One Sconce
With a Gilt frame and Arms. A Brass fender.

In the Blue Bed Chamber

A Blue Haratten Bed, Feather Bed, Bolster, two pillows, three
Blanketts, and a White Quilt. Tow pair of Blue Harateen Window
Curtains A Wallnut Tree Chest of Drawers, Dressing table & Glass, and
two Chairs with Blue damask Bottoms. A Close Stool Box and pewter
pan.

In the Great Garrett:

A Worked Bed, Feather Bed, Bolster, three Blanketts, four Old
Cane Chairs and an Oak Table.

In one of the Garretts, on the East End of the House &c.

A Green Half Tester Bed, a Feather Bed, Bolster, three Blnaketts, & a Rugg, and 2 Small common Looking Glasses.

In the next Garrett:

A Green China Bed; A Dressing Table, & 3 Black Cane Chairs

In the Blue Garrett.

A Blue China Bed, and two Old Chairs. A Green Settee Bed, Feather Bed, Bolster, and 3 Blanketts.

~~*In the Boy's Garrett*~~
X

In the Kitchen.

Two Spits A Tin dripping pan and an Iron frame. Three Tossers One Large Saucepan, and Cover and four small Saucepans. A Brass Cullander three Brass pots and Covers. Two pairs of Brass Candlesticks Two [word deleted]^{hand} Brass Candlesticks, & One Iron Do. A Tinder Box and five Pairs of Snuffers. A Box Iron and two Clamps. A flesh fork, A Brass Scummer. A Brass Ladle, an Egg Slice. A Copper frying pan. A Chaffing dish. Two Gridirons, Fire Shovell poker and tongs. Two Iron Racks. Two dogwheel chains. Two Kitchen tables, four Kitchen chairs. A plate Rack. A pair of Bellows. Two tea Kettles, two pails and a Baskett. A Brass flower Box. A tin pepper Box. A Bread grater. A Market Basket. two Glass Salts, One Crewett, A Chopping Knife. A Cle^{a}ver A Copper fish Kettle Cover and tin plate. A Chopping Board and a Chopping Block. A Washing Bench. A Large Ockamy Spoon. A large tin Ladle for Soop. A Copper Soop Kettle and cover. Seven Dozen of pewter plates, twenty pewter dishes an Odd Copper Cover for A Cooler A Mashing Vatt, and Tubb. A Tunddish. Mashing Shovel An Iron Fender A coal Shovel a Hatchett, Two Iron cole Boxes Two Irons for the Stoves. An Iron Crane in the Chimeney. 3 pott Hooks, and a Woodden Horse.

In the Serv^{ts} Hall

A Table and four Chairs

WH
18 June) Sent to Lyncombe a new feather bed, Bolster and 2 pillows
1745)

At Mr Hickes House in Bath not yet Sent up to Lyncombe....

four pairs fine Holland Sheets
Two Large fine Diaper table cloths.
12 fien Diaper Napkins.
13 Russia Towells.
Sixty two yards of coarse Rushia cloth

We allow this to be ^{a} true inventory Witness our Hands this 12th Day of November 1746.

                                                  Wm Hillary
                                                  Jno Hickes

II

CHANGING FASHIONS AND FLUCTUATING FORTUNES

THE DEVELOPMENT OF THE GARDENS
1750-1800

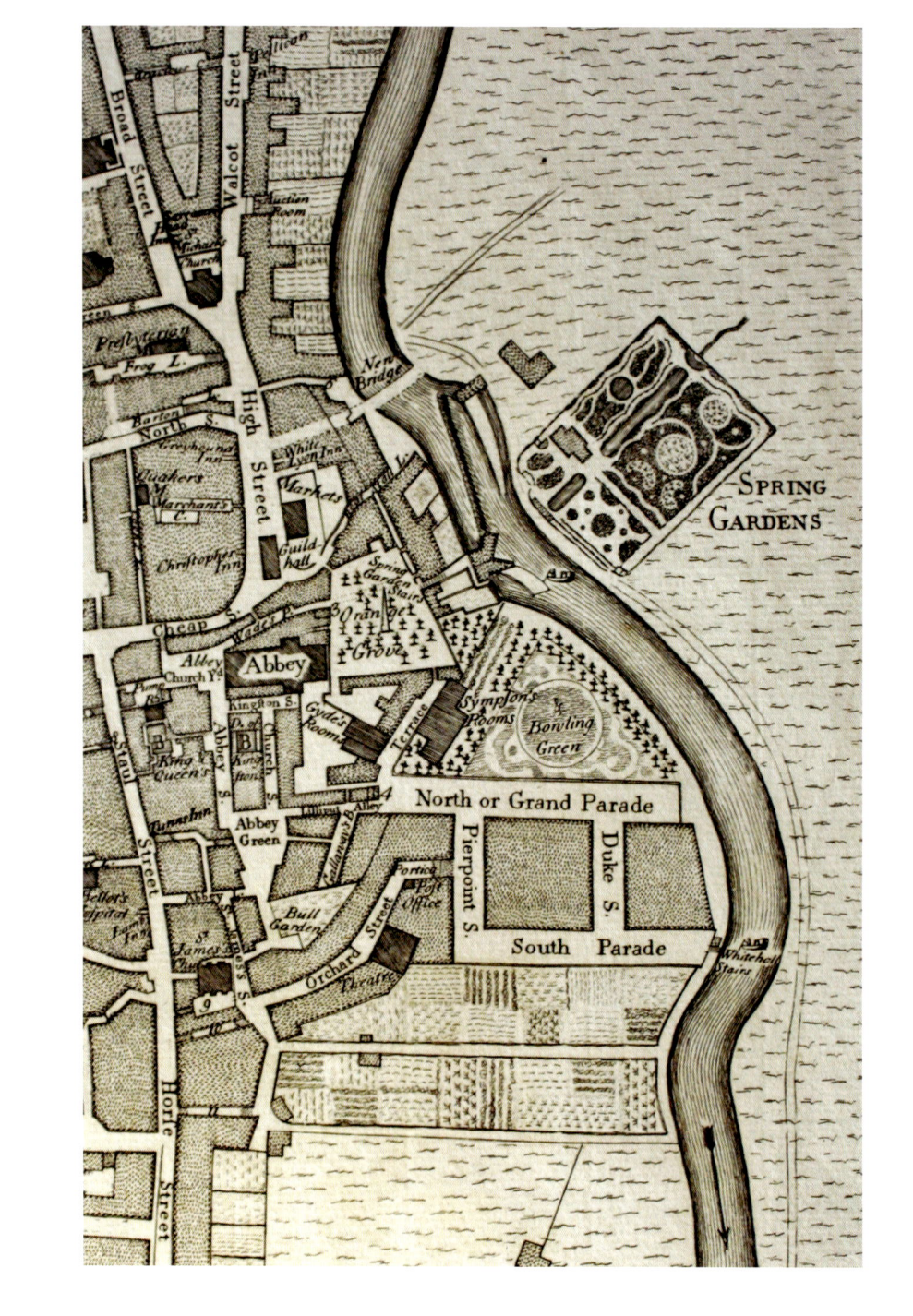

1

A MOST DELIGHTFUL SPOT

The Transformation of Spring Gardens

As we saw in Part One, Francis Edmondson ran Spring Gardens without incident for over ten years, from 1748 to 1759. However, we hear almost nothing of what went on there. A search through copies of the *Bath Journal* for those years reveals no advertisements for events. It seems merely to have been a pleasant place to visit and take refreshment while on an excursion to Bathwick through the fields. We do not know why Edmondson left, but as William Pulteney was notorious for his love of money perhaps he felt that he was not fully exploiting the gardens' potential. In addition, the popular seasons in Bath were autumn and spring. More sophisticated entertainment of the kind offered in London by Vauxhall, and even more so by its new rival Ranelagh, was needed to attract visitors all the year round.

The lease was taken by William Purdie, whose lodging house and wine merchant's in Orange Court overlooked the gardens. His landlord was Bennett Stevenson, the minister of the Unitarian Chapel in Frog Lane, which Purdie attended on a regular basis.[1] The chapel's christening register shows that many of Bath's successful tradesmen, as well as minor landowners, also attended the chapel. They would have provided Purdie with useful social contacts. He was very much a self-made man, having started his career as a servant, but by 1752 was described in a deed as a 'gentleman'.

So it is not surprising that Pulteney turned to the energetic, businesslike and respectable Purdie to take on Spring Gardens. It proved an excellent choice.

Opposite: A map of 1775, showing Spring Gardens Steps and the ferry crossing the river

As new gardens opened, Spring Gardens could have sunk into oblivion, but Purdie rose magnificently to the challenge. Maps show that, from the time he took over, the gardens expanded. In April 1764, an advertisement in the *Bath Chronicle* announced that

> the Proprietor of these Gardens having been, and is still, at a considerable Expence, in making and keeping them in proper Order for the Amusement of the Company; he was advised by many Ladies and Gentlemen, frequenting the Gardens, to open a Subscription for walking therein; which he has accordingly done, to commence this Day, at the trifling Expence of Half-a-Crown for the Season.[2]

The compiler of the 1769 *Bath Guide* was convinced that Purdie's initiative was proving successful:

> The Proprietor has taken much pains, and expended a considerable sum, to bring it to its present flourishing state; however, as much company resort there, 'tis not doubted but it will answer his expectations.

The following year, the *Guide* informed visitors that

> leading from the Grove across the Avon, is a public garden (called Spring-Gardens) very pleasingly and judiciously laid out by Mr William Purdie, for the summer amusement and recreation of the inhabitants of this city, who have a privilege of walking here the whole season on paying a subscription of half-a-crown.

Tobias Smollett featured the gardens in *The Expedition of Humphry Clinker*, written about 1769 and published in 1771. The impressionable Lydia Melford, writing to her dear friend Miss Willis of the delightful entertainments of Bath, tells her that

> there is, moreover, another place of entertainment on the other side of the water, opposite to the Grove: to which the company cross over in a boat – It is called Spring-garden; a sweet retreat, laid out in walks and ponds, and parterres of flowers; and there is a long-room for breakfasting and dancing.[3]

Frustratingly, her uncle, the cantankerous Matthew Bramble, will not let her go because he considers it damp.

A map of the Manor of Bathwick from about 1770 shows how much the gardens had been enlarged since 1755.[4] Formerly, it only reached as far as where the Beazer Maze is today – after Purdie's intervention, it was extended south to where the halfway line on the rugby pitch is now. What had been a stream running beside a hedge supplied water to an ornamental canal and cascade. Purdie appears to have remodelled the grounds based on the Dutch style of garden which

> **SPRING GARDENS**
> Are now open'd, for Breakfasting and Afternoon Tea, as usual.
> A Subscription is begun at the Bar, for Ladies and Gentlemen's walking in the Gardens, at Half-a-Crown the Season. Those who do not chuse to subscribe, may be admitted on their paying Sixpence each at the Gate; for which a Ticket will be deliver'd, entitling the Bearer to its Value at the Bar in Tea, Coffee, Chocolate, Jellies, Wine, &c. &c.
> The Proprietor humbly hopes no Lady or Gentleman will think the above Terms unreasonable, as they are calculated to render the Gardens as agreeable as possible to polite Company; for which Purpose (by particular Desire) no Servant in Livery will be admitted, unless to wait on their Ladies or Masters.
> N.B. The Company may depend on having the best Tea, Coffee, and Chocolate; with hot Rolls, just out of the Oven, from half after Nine 'till half after Ten every Morning, Sundays excepted.—A large Company are desired to give timely Notice.—Music will attend, if requir'd.
> *.* Constant Attendance at the Passage-Boat leading from the Grove to the Cardens.

One of William Purdie's early advertisements from 1760.

Spring Gardens from the Pulteney Map of 1770, showing the extent of the gardens with the 'canals'. The miller's house is now part of the gardens, while the Long Room can clearly be seen, with a smaller building alongside it.

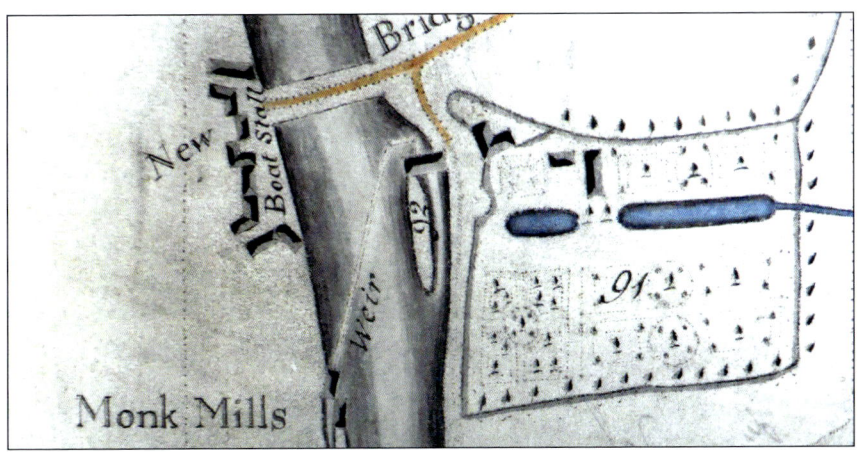

first became popular in the late seventeenth and early eighteenth centuries. Westbury Court Gardens in Gloucestershire are the only surviving example in this country. Originally they were much larger than Spring Gardens, but what survives now must be a close approximation to what visitors to Spring Gardens would have seen.

One of the canals and, below, the parterre at Westbury Court Gardens

Purdie also solved the problem of access. He first improved access to the ferry by utilising a way from the Grove to the riverside. According to Richard Jones, Ralph Allen's Clerk of Works, the stone for building Queen Square had been shipped from the riverside at Widcombe up to Monks Mill, which stood by the weir on the west side of the river. From there, it was 'rolled up in a Road made up into the Grove for that purpose, and then began the building in the Square called Wood Street'. This was the route adopted by Purdie, which meant that visitors could avoid the messy Boatstall Lane, with its slaughterhouses, and walk directly to the riverside and so upstream to the ferry. But soon he had a better idea. He acquired his own passage-boat which became known as the Spring Gardens ferry and could be hired for those coming in a party. Unlike the ordinary ferries, it was covered to protect passengers against the weather.

Purdie was involved in a dramatic river rescue in 1772. Astley's Riding School from London was giving an exhibition in the fields near Bathwick. A certain Mrs Clarke and her friend Mrs Britain decided to watch it from a boat which Mr Clarke kept moored up at the bottom of his garden in Walcot Street. But the boat was not secured properly. The river was already high and the women were swept downstream. The boat went over the weir safely, but the current drove the boat back towards the weir and it overturned. The *Bath Chronicle* takes up the tale:

> Mrs Clarke was instantly left to the mercy of the rapid stream, and with the most amazing heroism kept herself above water for the space of two or three minutes, and swam more than 100 yards, till a boat put off from the mill to her assistance, and took her up safe. Mrs Britain kept her head above water by holding fast to the side of the boat, and was carried by the current 3 or 400 yards at least, till Mr Purdie, in his boat, put off to her assistance.[5]

It was a reminder that visiting the gardens had its hazards. In Christopher Anstey's verse satire *A New Bath Guide,* published in 1766, he relates how unpleasant the trip could be in wet and windy weather, when an aristocratic host takes a group to the gardens. As he makes clear, once out of the boat, visitors still had to walk to and through the gardens before reaching the shelter of the Large Room:

> I'm sure He's a Person of great Resolution,
> Tho' delicate Nerves, and a weak Constitution;
> For he carried us all to a Place cross the River,
> And vow'd that the Rooms were too hot for his Liver:
> He said it would greatly our Pleasure promote,
> If we all for Spring-Gardens set out in a Boat:
> I never as yet could his Reason explain,
> Why we all sallied forth in the Wind and the Rain?
> For sure such Confusion was never yet known;
> Here a Cap and a Hat, and there a Cardinal blown:
> While his Lordship, embroider'd, and powder'd all o'er,
> Was bowing, and handing the Ladies ashore:
> How the Misses did huddle and scuddle, and run;
> One would think to be wet must be very good Fun;
> For by waggling their Tails, they all seemed to take Pains
> To moisten their Pinions like Ducks when it rains;
> And 'twas pretty to see how, like Birds of a Feather,
> The People of Quality flock'd all together;
> All pressing, addressing, caressing, and fond,
> Just the same as those Animals are in a Pond.[6]

Visitors were doubtless pleased to read in the *Bath Guide* of 1770 that

> the company are at present ferry'd over to the above garden in a cover'd passage-boat, which constantly attends for that purpose – But they will soon have the pleasure of walking to it over a new bridge, now erecting at the expence of Wm Pultney, Esq.

It would be another two years, however, before they could do so. In fine weather, of course, the boat trip was an additional pleasure. But what was it that drew people in such numbers to the gardens, even in poor weather? It was not just their beauty – it was the wide range of entertainments devised by William Purdie.

These began in the morning with breakfast. A Cornish visitor, the Rev John Penrose, described taking breakfast at Spring Gardens in a letter to his daughter Peggy in 1766.[7] A friend of his, Dr Stackhouse, had arranged for all

A public breakfast. This drawing, from The Comforts of Bath by Rowlandson is believed to show the interior of the Long Room at Spring Gardens

the Cornish people then in Bath to enjoy such a meal at his expense. Having been ferried across from the Orange Grove, the observant clergyman was able to enjoy a walk in the grounds before breakfast. He gives us perhaps the best description we have of the gardens in their prime:

> The Gardens are a most delightful Spot, laid out in Gravel and Grass Walks, some strait [sic], others serpentine, with a fine Canal in one place, and a fine Pond in another, with the greatest Variety of Shrubs, Trees, and other Vegetables that the most curious could desire. In these Gardens is a large handsome Building, wherein is a Breakfast Room capacious enough to hold many Sets of Company, having six Windows in the side, (so you see it must be long) and proportionately wide.

On this occasion, there were three groups – the seventeen-strong Cornish party, another group of ten and 'a noble Lord' on his own. When the groups entered the room, everything was ready for them:

> When we entered the Room, the Tables were spread with singular Neatness. Upon a Cloth white as Snow were ranged Coffee Cups, Tea

> Dishes of different Sizes, Chocolate Cups, Teapots, and everything belonging to the Equipage of the Tea Table, with French Rolls, Pots of Butter, all in decent order, and interspersed with Sweet Briar, which had a pretty Effect both on the Sight and Smell. At the Word of Command were set on the Table, Chocolate, Coffee, Tea, Hot Rolls buttered, buttered Hot Cakes. What could hinder one from making a good Breakfast? Yet I was so moderate and had so philosophical command of my appetite that, in the midst of all this Plenty I eat but one Roll and one Cake and drunk but one Cup of Chocolate, two of Coffee and two of Tea.

The hot cakes were known as Spring Garden cakes, and the French Rolls may well be what we now call Sally Lunns.[8]

After such a meal, Penrose explained what happened next, His account suggests that Purdie had installed the very latest mod cons in the Large Room:

> From filling we proceed to Emptying ... Everyone's eyes in search of a Fro. As Need required we found Two. Over the Door of one was written: 'for the Ladies only;' over that of the other, 'For the Gentlemen only.' Against the Wall within the Gentlemen's was written with a Pencil: 'Whosoever comes into the Place is desired to be cleanly, to let down the Lid and shut the Door.' Whatever relates to the Ladies Fro, must be kept an inviolable Secret.

This may be the earliest reference to the use of public conveniences for ladies and gentlemen. It seems from Penrose's account that it was quite a novelty.

Penrose does not mention music playing, and, as it was optional in the mornings, it appears it had not been requested. However, during the public breakfasts, which were normally held twice a week, there was music and dancing, which continued until half past two. In July 1767, Purdie placed an advertisement in the *Bath Chronicle* promising that – 'by desire of several Ladies and Gentlemen' – there would be public teas on Wednesday and Saturday evenings with a concert of vocal and instrumental music, beginning at five o'clock and ending at nine. The first concert would include 'a variety of new songs as are sung at Ranelagh, Vauxhall, &c.' In stressing this, Purdie was plainly implying that his gardens were the local equivalent of these great London gardens. This seems to have been regular practice. In June 1770, those attending the Friday evening public tea drinking were promised that

> the Company will be entertained with French Horns, &c, also Violins for those who are disposed to dance, at 1s per person. But in case the company should chuse [sic] to continue Dancing by candlelight, a further reasonable Compensation will be expected.[9]

The dances would have been social country dances, as danced in the ballrooms. These were English country dances, which had been collected by French dancing masters and made more elegant. The word *contredanse* is simply a corruption of the English phrase *country dance*. The dances often returned from France with their English name translated to French. So *Greensleeves* became *Les Manches Vertes* and *Christchurch Bells* became *Le Carillon d'Oxford*. However, a new French dance – the cotillon or cotillion – began to take England by storm. As the London *Gazetteer and New Daily Advertiser* reported in 1768,

Another illustration from The Comforts of Bath shows a country dance in a longways set being danced in the New Assembly Rooms

if the English Country Dances are all the mode at Paris (as mentioned in our last) we are even more with them here, for that the French Country Dances are now equally the 'bon ton' at London; the Cottillons, &c being now taught in all the great boarding-schools, and danced in all the polite assemblies in this metropolis and its environs.

The earliest references to cotillions in London date from 1768, but Bath was ahead of the game – or rather, Spring Gardens were. It was here that the cotillion was first danced in this country, in 1766, and there is more than one reference to this. In Anstey's *New Bath Guide*, after the party have dried themselves off and are safely in the Long Room, they tuck into breakfast and begin to dance as the music strikes up:

> The Company made a most brilliant Appearance,
> And ate Bread and Butter with great Perseverance;
> All the Chocolate too, that my Lord set before 'em,
> The Ladies dispatch'd with the utmost Decorum.

A print from a painting by John Collet of eight people dancing a cotillion. The man in the foreground has contrived to be on the wrong foot. As the poem makes clear, the standard of dancing was not always perfect.

> Soft musical Numbers were heard all around,
> The Horns and the Clarions echoing sound:
> Sweet were the Strains, as od'rous Gales that blow
> O'er fragrant Banks, where Pinks and Roses grow ...
> Miss Clunch and Sir Toby perform'd a Cotillon,
> Much the same as our Susan and Bob the Postilion;
> All the while her Mamma was expressing her Joy,
> That her Daughter the Morning so well could employ.[10]

A year later, a poem appeared in the *Bath Chronicle* entitled 'An Invitation to Spring Gardens, Humbly dedicated to the Dancers of Cotillons'. Despite poking fun at the dancers, it paints an alluring picture of an early morning visit to the gardens:

> Improv'd by soft showers, the shrubs and the flowers,
> New blown, to Spring Gardens invite us;
> Where freely we range, and partake of each change,
> Kind nature can give to delight us.
>
> Then approach ye gay nymphs, and renouncing all care,
> Each party in number increase;
> The boat stands all ready, the rope is quite steady,
> Your passage a penny a-piece.
>
> Without wind or tide, on the opposite side,
> Safe your landed, and hous'd in a trice;
> Coffee, chocolate, tea, spread before you you'll see,
> With provisions, well chosen, and nice.
>
> Of these as you eat, a musical treat,
> All sorrow shall sweetly remove;
> Till breakfasting done, to the garden you run,
> Softer musick invites to the grove.
>
> Then back again haste, no time you must waste,
> When dancing becomes the gay theme;
> The bold hurdy-gurdy, play'd by man stout and sturdy,
> Of pleasure presents you the cream.

> For what can be equal, I pray, to the sequel;
> What compar'd to the gay cotillion?
> Where with step, or without it, quite careless about it,
> You're sure to dance in the *bon ton*.
>
> Here, quite in her prime, miss, for the first time,
> Two very odd things puts together,
> Our own country-dance and another from France,
> So jumbled you cannot tell whither.
>
> Then approach sons of mirth, and with hearts light and gay,
> From the Pump-Room assemble the fair;
> One draught of warm water, then hasten away,
> And quick to Spring Gardens repair.[11]

Occasionally there were evening balls at the gardens. In 1760, Purdie advertised that these would be held every Thursday, but the proprietors of the two sets of rooms, Simpson's and Gyde's, probably objected, as these weekly balls failed to materialise.[12] However, occasional balls were advertised, and in June 1769, regular balls were again advertised on Saturday nights, although only during the summer season.

There were also occasional concerts other than those at the tea drinking. The earliest may have been a demonstration of the glass armonica in 1762. A London maker was advertising sets of musical glasses in the *Bath Chronicle*, and he described them as being like those 'play'd on by Miss Davies at Spring Garden, London, Bath and Bristol'. All three cities had pleasure gardens called Spring Gardens, so it appears Miss Davies chose to play at all of them.[13] In 1777, there was a charity concert at a public breakfast, in aid of a family in difficulty. In April the following year, there was a similar event, for the benefit of two children born blind. The performers

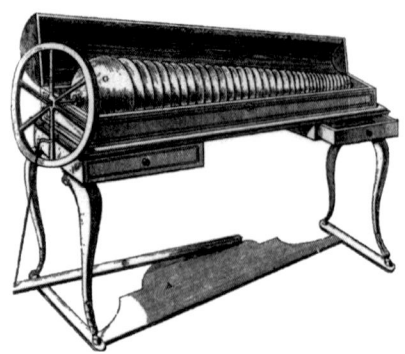

A glass armonica of the kind played by Miss Davies

included Miss Cantelo, who sang glees with Mr Brett and Mr Edwin. In June that year, a Mr Evans performed several pieces on the triple harp during breakfast.

The Cantelo family were well-known Bath musicians, playing at many events. They formed part of the regular band at Spring Gardens, and had a benefit breakfast concert in May 1779, when the members of the band of horns and clarinets were Messrs Cantelo, Loder, Stevens, Whitehead and W Cantelo, while Miss Cantelo and Messrs Brett, Stevens, and Edwin sang glees and Mr Brooks played the first violin. Next year, however, this annual concert was moved from Spring Gardens to Mr Gyde's Garden Walks and Rooms. Cam Gyde was, by this time, running the former Simpson's Rooms, and was a man determined to succeed, so he had evidently lured the musicians to his garden. Although some of the musicians later appeared at Spring Gardens, the Cantelos did not, preferring to play at the Theatre Royal in nearby Orchard Street and the Assembly Rooms. However, when the New Rooms opened in 1771, Gyde could not keep them either, as they moved up to the new venue. It gives an insight into how competitive the business of entertaining visitors could be. It was to get even worse, as we shall see.

There was more competition over fireworks. These were among the eighteenth century's most popular entertainments, and William Purdie introduced them to Spring Gardens almost as soon as he had signed the lease. In July 1761, Bath residents were promised a 'magnificent and curious piece of fireworks' in Spring Gardens. Before it took place, news was received of the surrender of Pondicherry and St Domingo to the British and there was great rejoicing in the city, with ringing of bells and firing of cannons. The cannon were the 21 guns that Nash had given to the city in 1746 to provide royal salutes, which were still held by Simpson in his gardens, although they would later go to Spring Gardens.[14] The *Bath Chronicle* reported that, to celebrate these 'important Acquisitions', there would be additions to the 'Firework' [sic]. When we look at the programme for the order of fire, it is hard to see what additions related to these victories, but nevertheless, it makes interesting reading.

They were divided into what the director, Mr Gill, called three dispositions. The description of the first, which began with a 'salute of cannon', gives us a glimpse of this popular eighteenth-century entertainment. There were rockets of 'various explosions', two pots d'argret, vertical wheels, changing

There are no known illustrations of Georgian firework displays in Bath, but this picture of a display in Green Park in London in 1749 shows a number of popular devices, including, in the foreground, the framework for a yew tree

Opposite: A selection of fireworks engraved by Andrew Bell, from the 3rd edition of the Encyclopaedia Britannica, published in 1797

into brilliant suns, tourbillions, a flight of 'Chinese and Caducher' rockets, two wheels, called the horizontal glory, and brilliant wheatsheafs, two air balloons, with serpents and star, double line rockets, a spiral wheel and yew-tree illuminated.[15] The two following dispositions were ever more ambitious, and among the rockets, wheels (horizontal and vertical) there were set pieces forming stars and cascades, a windmill, a Chinese building, pumps of white fire with blue balls, culminating in a 'brilliant Sun, casting its Rays 50 Feet Diameter'. Doors opened at five o'clock, and the display started at nine and lasted an hour. The warning that, 'if the Weather should prove bad, it will be deferred till the next Night' proved unnecessary. The following week the *Bath Chronicle* reported that

> the Fire-Works exhibited at Spring Gardens on Thursday last ... gave universal Satisfaction, and were acknowledged by good Judges to exceed everything of the Kind ever seen here. A great Concourse of People were present, among whom were many of Distinction.[16]

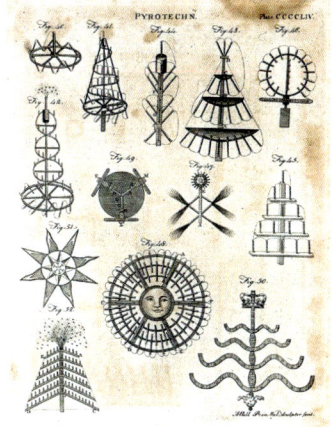

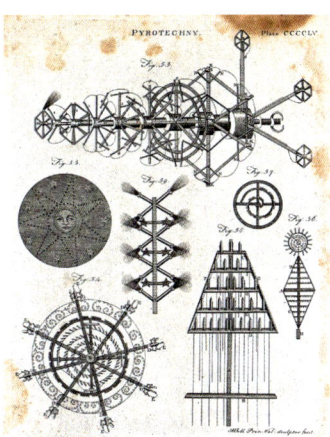

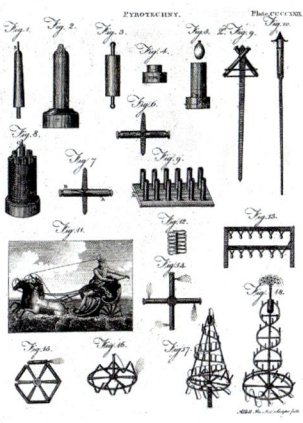

A similar display was held in 1762, when subscribers could book reserved seats and the passage from the Grove to the Gardens was 'properly lighted'. Perhaps there had been complaints – Purdie was always quick to react to feedback from his clientele.

Charles Simpson, of Simpson's Rooms, struck back in November 1765 with a display right on Spring Gardens' doorstep. Simpson was the lessee of the field to the south of the gardens, and here he arranged for 'a large Firework representing an Egyptian Pyramid ... and other pieces' to be displayed. He listed in the advertisement places where 'gentlemen and ladies may have a very good prospect of the fireworks'.[17] Spring Gardens was conspicuous by its absence.

In 1776, Cam Gyde of the Lower Rooms must have been dismayed when Spring Gardens opened in the winter season, offering tea and coffee in the tea room, with Spring Garden Rolls fresh from the oven. 'There will be constant fires kept in the tea-room during the winter', added the advertisement, a trifle smugly.[18] This move must have irritated Gyde considerably, for he was already under pressure after the opening of the New Rooms. It was he who had converted the grass lawn of Simpson's Walks (the former Harrison's Walks) to a bowling green, but Purdie and Spring Gardens had undoubtedly captured the summer audience. Moreover, unlike Gyde, Purdie had other businesses to keep him going. He still ran his lodging house and wine merchant's,

A print of 1773, with Pulteney Bridge nearing completion. To the right, the trees of Spring Gardens are now so well established that they obscure the view of the Long Room. To the left of the picture, Cam Gyde's newly-established bowling green is being rolled.

while one of his daughters ran a successful perfume shop on the Walks. A curious incident in 1777 suggests there were those who looked with envious eyes on his success and were ready to cast aspersions. On Friday 15 August, a young man was bathing in the river by Dolemeads, downstream from Spring Gardens, when he found himself out of his depth. A clergyman, the Rev Mr Eccles, threw off his coat and leapt in to save him, but the terrified man clung to him so desperately, that they both drowned. Various doctors tried for several hours to restore them to life, but in vain. Chief among these was Mr Cruttwell, surgeon to the Humane Society.[19] The following Monday, the *Bath Journal* reported that Purdie had refused to admit the bodies when they were brought to Spring Gardens, and that he was devoid of humanity. Three days later, an anonymous writer, who called himself Phrygian, had a letter published in the London *Public Advertiser,* described by Purdie as a 'most illiberal and false paragraph, reflecting in a more gross manner upon the character of William Purdie'. The letter appears to have been an attempt to blacken the name of Purdie with people likely to visit Bath. Purdie said that, while he had been prepared to ignore the invectives of an anonymous writer, his friends had pointed out that silence might be regarded as guilt. He therefore wrote to the *Bath Chronicle* in early September, stating the facts, which he was sure Mr Cruttwell, the surgeon, would confirm.[20] Cruttwell had been called to the drowning, though at that time he did not know precisely where the bodies were. On the way, he called in to Spring Gardens to see if the bodies (when found) could go there. It was a Friday night, and Purdie began to explain to Cruttwell that not only were the gardens full of people but most of them were ladies. He was going to add that the sudden introduction of two dead bodies might lead to what he called dangerous circumstances – in other words, people leaving in a panic close to the river. But Cruttwell had already agreed with him and left. In the end, the bodies were taken to the White Hart Inn at Widcombe, downstream of where they were found. This was some considerable time after Cruttwell had called at Spring Gardens. Gyde's summerhouse was even closer than Spring Gardens, but it was easier to take the boat with the bodies downstream than upstream.

Given Purdie's public spirited action five years earlier, when he had pulled someone from the river, to call him 'void of humanity' was manifestly unfair. Purdie knew the river and its dangers. His story has the ring of truth. But it is clear that he had managed to upset some people.

By this time, competitors were already making their presence felt, and Purdie and his successors at Spring Gardens would find that they had constantly to keep abreast of the latest fashions to maintain their pre-eminence.

Even more far-reaching changes, that would ultimately lead to the demise of Spring Gardens, were already afoot. In 1764, William Pulteney had died. The Earldom of Bath died with him, but his estates were inherited by his brother, General Henry Pulteney. When he died three years later, the estates passed to William Pulteney's cousin, Frances. Her husband, William Johnstone, changed his name to William Johnstone Pulteney and started drawing up plans to transform Bathwick from a semi-rural domain to an architectural showpiece called Bath New Town. Pulteney Bridge – his first project – opened in 1773, and, although work thereafter proceeded in fits and starts, due to financial constraints caused by wars with America and France, the development would not only change the face of Bath but also lead to the creation of new pleasure gardens on a grander scale than anyone could have imagined.

2

WINNERS AND LOSERS

How Competition changed Pleasure Gardens in Bath

While Gyde and Purdie fought to have the most popular gardens in the city, competitors were setting up new gardens to the south. Lyncombe Spa, with its principal aim of being a health resort, had never quite fulfilled the role of a pleasure garden – indeed, some would argue that it never qualified as one. In 1766, the Rev John Penrose visited his friends, Colonel and Mrs Sewell there. Although they were both there for their health, the dinner given to the Penrose family was sumptuous, and included a pudding, to Penrose's delight.[1] They also drank wine. But this would all come to an end in 1767, when John Hickes sold out to William Street, who, with his business partner, David Kinneir, ran an apothecary's and chemist's at the sign of the Phoenix in Northgate Street.

William Hillary – who must have been Dr Hillary's nephew and heir, for the doctor had died in 1763 – was furious with Hickes, who was very secretive and refused to say who wanted to buy it. Hillary wrote to an attorney in Bath called Jefferys, telling him that the estate was being undervalued, and demanding that John Hickes give a full report so that he could have his fair share. When the accounts were drawn up, one of the items on the list was the cost of wine licences for 1765 and 1766, proving that the Spa was a licensed house. Providing alcoholic refreshment was clearly part of the operation.

Opposite: A blue auricula (Auricula Fille Amoreuse) by Georg Dionysus Ehret, 1757, the kind of bloom which would have featured in the Florists' Feasts at King James's Palace

The north side of Lyncombe Spa. Where there were once gardens there is now a children's playground. The balcony was extended forward in the 1980s to create a school hall, but the original building had such a balcony. The spa was at the side where there is now a bay window, so it can be seen that, despite being used for smallpox inoculation, it was easy to access the waters.

Within a month of purchasing the spa, Street and Kinneir had converted it to a sanatorium where people could be inoculated against smallpox.[2] In June 1767 they placed an advertisement in the *Bath Chronicle*:

> Time and Experience having fully evinced to the greater Part of the People of this Kingdom that the lives of many Thousands of his Majesty's Subjects have been happily preserved thro' the Means of INOCULATION; it has been often lamented by many judicious People, that there was not a House appropriated for that purpose (at a convenient Distance) from every City or great Town in the Kingdom. To conform in some Measure to the Wishes of the People, the house commonly known by the name of Lyncomb Spaw-House, in the parish of Lyncomb and Widcomb, about one Mile from Bath, being a very commodious one for the Purpose, and in a proper situation, is opened this Day for the Reception of those desirous of being inoculated, where they may be assured of finding every Requisite for their well-being.

Not wishing to lose the income provided by those coming to drink the waters, they added that,

> as Applications have been made by Persons who have been accustomed to, and have received Benefit by drinking the Lyncomb Spaw-Water (which is thought to be more strongly impregnated than any other Chalybeate Water in England) and as the Well is so situated, that it is not necessary to go through any Part of the House to it; at their Request we inform the Public that it will still be kept open, and a Servant will be constantly in Waiting to deliver it.[3]

But with nothing else on offer apart from the water, and the house given over to people inoculated with a mild dose of smallpox, it is not surprising that few visitors took them up on the offer. And so Lyncombe Spa's career as a pleasure garden came to an end. Its career as an inoculation hospital was even shorter. The last advertisement for it appeared in the *Bath Chronicle* less than two years later, on 9 March 1769, and by 1773 Street had converted it to his private residence. Kinneir died that same year, and, although Street gave up the shop in Northgate Street, he continued to live at Lyncombe Spa until his death in 1785, when it was put up for sale as a private house.

The stables at Lyncombe Spa, now converted to classrooms. They were built to accommodate several carriages.

When it closed, somewhat abruptly, in 1767, Lyncombe Spa had operated successfully for 25 years, demonstrating the market for a facility of this kind south of the river. This was the cue for the Wicksteed family, who still owned the house at Widcombe where seals were cut by a water-driven engine, to cash in. By now, John Wicksteed was dead, and it was his son James who held the lease of the house and grounds around Wicksteed's Machine, while his mother ran the shop in Orange Grove. Although James had leased the house on the

The Bagatelle from Ralph Allen Drive.
It is now much altered and known as Welton Lodge.

site, he had previously taken leases on adjoining fields and closes, indicating that he may already have had plans to expand the enterprise. After Ralph Allen's death in 1764, the tramway had been lifted, removing one of the attractions that had drawn people to the area, yet this does not seem to have spurred James Wicksteed into action. However, with Lyncombe Spa becoming a sanatorium, he finally acted. In July 1769, he placed an advertisement in the *Bath Chronicle:*

> Mr Wicksteed, of the Machine, presents his most respectful Compliments to the Gentlemen of the Faculty at Bath; and as he has great Reason to believe he has found a good cold CHALYBEATE in his Garden at Widcombe, (which may be, if approved of by them, of Service to Bath in general, and to many Individuals in particular,) he takes the Liberty to request their Opinion of the Water. And he likewise begs their Advice how he may best construct and secure the Spring in the most convenient Manner, for the Accommodation of such Patients as they shall think proper to recommend it to. He will always acknowledge himself highly obliged to those Gentlemen who shall have the Goodness to comply with this Request.[4]

There was no Advertising Standards Authority in the eighteenth century, so we cannot gauge the reliability of his claim to have discovered a spring, and a chalybeate spring at that. The whole area was full of springs and watercourses, and it seems surprising that, the Wicksteed family having been there for over thirty years, he had only just discovered it. Nevertheless, the doctors must have given him the necessary approval. By March the following year, the waters were available and he had plans to build baths, for, by washing only the distemper'd Parts, great relief has been given in the most inveterate Scurvy. As bathing in a cold Chalybeate will be a new Mode of treating that Disorder, its Success cannot be doubted.[5]

The new spring appears to have been popular, although some of the wealthier subscribers did not see why they should pay for a second glass of the water. On 13 September, the *Bath Chronicle* reported that the proprietors had to let the world know that only paupers or their particular friends could have the second glass free, and that payment would be requested before the second glass was dispensed. In the same issue, the garden was called the Bagatelle for the first time, with public breakfasts and dinners available. By this time, the people running the garden were Mr and Mrs Bowers, who were friends of the Linley and Sheridan families. Their connections with the theatrical world led to some interesting innovations.

An extract from the survey of Ralph Allen's estates, made after his death around 1768, showing the three houses which made up the Bagatelle in the top right-hand corner

The west side of part of the Bagatelle, showing the rounded end which may have given rise to its name

In May 1771, public breakfasts were held on Wednesdays and Saturdays, with music, cotillions and country dances. In June, the proprietors promised something new which turned out to be a 'Luminary Cascade' – an illuminated waterfall – which operated to the sound of music. The price of admission on these nights was one shilling and sixpence.[6]

While the Bowers were running the Bagatelle, and introducing new attractions such as cold chalybeate baths 'that will soon brace the Seminal Vessels by Bathing', Wicksteed put the property up for sale as he was moving to London. He received an offer and took it off the market, but when the offer fell through in November 1773, he advertised it for sale once again. According to an advertisement in the *Bath Chronicle*, it was put up for auction because several gentlemen were 'desirous of purchasing the Bagatelle'. This must have been an anxious time for the Bowers. Despite this, they continued to put on all sorts of entertainments. In September that year, during Bath Races, for example, they

> exhibited each morning gratis, the Rise and Fall of the Chalybeate Water at the Bagatelle, with prœpilogical Songs on the occasion, sung by poor William the gardener.[7]

Unfortunately, poor William was taken ill, so the songs did not take place.

The property was still for sale in January 1774, when it was put up for auction as two lots. One lot comprised the gardens, with the canal and the summerhouse housing the machine, while the other included the orchard. However, it failed to sell and was still being advertised to let in May, by which time it had acquired the name Cupid's Garden.

By 1775, control of the Bagatelle had passed to James Guillet.[8] About this time another canal, intended as a men's bathing pool, was created, with convenient changing rooms. Guillet even went to the trouble of repairing the coach road to the Bagatelle, over which he held the rights.[9] Despite all this,

Poor William ...

... and poor Mr Guillet, from the pages of the *Bath Chronicle*

the gossip-mongers soon got to work, and in June 1776 Guillet had to place a pained appeal in the *Bath Chronicle*:

> *To the* LADIES *and* GENTLEMEN *of* BATH
>
> Tis an unspeakable anguish to a feeling mind which industriously tries and assiduously endeavours to merit the Favour of a generous Public, that calumny and detraction should so far prevail, as to operate to the prejudice of a numerous, tho' innocent family – but such there are – enemies to the Bagatelle Gardens – when every Lady or Gentleman may be assured not only the strictest regard is and will be paid to the company admitted, but that every proper accommodation suitable to such respectable personages as shall please to honour this place with the favours, shall be most punctually and duly regarded, by their most obedient and most oblig'd Servant JAMES GUILLET,
>
> NB The Chalybeate Waters, now in perfection, need no encomium to urge their utility. There is a canal detached from the pleasure garden, for the conveniency of bathing.[10]

We do not know what lay behind this outburst. Guillet was clearly genuinely distressed but, despite his efforts, the story of the Bagatelle was nearing its end. In October 1777, when it was put up for sale again, it was described as

> all those two New-Built Messuages, with their Appurtenances, and that small delightful Tenement or Summer-House, lying contiguous thereto, situate in a fine laid-out garden, containing about an acre of land, in which is a canal, and extraordinary fine shrubbery, and one of the most strong and efficacious Chalybeate Waters in this kingdom.

The orchard with its bathing canal was included in the sale, although there were only seven years left on its lease. Prospective purchasers were also apprised of the suitability of the garden for alternative uses:

> In the compass of an advertisement, there is not room to express the encomiums justly due to this delightful elevated situation, not too much exposed to the winds or sun, which many complain of in some of the much-admired situations in this city. It is not only exceedingly well calculated for the business it is now used in (to which a porter

Brewery may be very conveniently annexed) but it is likewise an eligible situation for the temporary residence of a genteel person, who wishes to be retired from the family, as there is a separate dwelling for the children and domesticks, and is an easy distance from the Rooms, Pumps, etc.[11]

It was still being advertised for sale in February 1778, by which time an air of desperation had become apparent. Described as being about half a mile from the city (it is actually a mile from the Guildhall), the contract was available to be 'entered upon immediately', and even more alternative uses had been dreamed up. The bathing pool had also disappeared from the advertisement – perhaps it was considered a deterrent to purchasers:

> That delightfully situated Tavern and Public Garden, for Tea Company, &c called the Bagatelle; consisting of two good dwelling-houses, and a spacious summer apartment, in a garden beautifully laid out, in which is a fine shrubbery, canal, walks, and a very noted efficacious Chalybeate Spring. Also, a large body of water may be had through the premises, sufficient to drive a mill, supply a brewery, &c. Adjoining the above is a kitchen-garden and orchard, well planted, containing near four acres of land.
>
> It is universally allowed by every impartial person, that an active man, acquainted with the business, could not fail making a fortune in it, as it requires but a small capital, and not subject to bad debts, the bane of the present times.

The advertisement then added, rather cryptically,

> it is a place of great resort, and much wanted near Bath, but has never yet been conducted with a degree of propriety.[12]

This may indicate why the gossipmongers had targeted Guillet. The first Cupid's Garden in London – originally called Cuper's Garden – lost its licence due to the loose morals of its clientele, and it is possible that, like its forerunner, the Lyncombe garden attracted ladies of dubious reputation. Nevertheless, in 1778, Mr T Harrison from London took over the gardens and opened them for the reception of company, promising 'a great variety of amusements, and every other convenience to render the place truly agreeable'. He offered lodgings to let, dinners dressed at the shortest notice, and teas, with horn and clarinet accompaniment, on Tuesdays and Thursdays. However, after two advertisements appeared in the newspapers in 1778, no more is heard of the Bagatelle until the end of 1779, when it was offered for sale as

> a Genteel and Commodious RESIDENCE within a quarter of a mile of the city of Bath, which may answer the purpose both of a town-house and country seat, known by the name of the *Bagatelle,* in the parish of Widcomb and Lyncomb, The premises consist of two good dwelling-houses, one of them covered with copper; a summer-house, and garden well planted with curious shrubs; a fine chalybeate spring &c.[13]

Appealing to the public with the novel concept of a house covered in copper fell on deaf ears. The house and gardens went to rack and ruin. In 1786, when Betsy Sheridan, Richard's younger sister, was visiting Widcombe, she walked past the Bagatelle and found it 'quite forsaken and overrun with weeds'. It was a sad ending, and must have been doubly poignant for Betsy Sheridan, whose brother knew the Bowers who had run it successfully despite the constant threat of sale by James Wicksteed. Eventually, the buildings were converted to the houses we see today.

One reason for the downfall of the Bagatelle was the rise of new pleasure gardens opposite Lyncombe Spa. Known as King James's Palace, they were much more in the style of Spring Gardens. Betsy Sheridan was on her way to them when she passed the abandoned Bagatelle. As we have seen in Part One, there seems to have been a clandestine meeting place called King James's Palace in Lyncombe in the 1720s, but it would have been fairly primitive.

In 1774, Charles Waters leased the house which Charles Milsom had built opposite Lyncombe Spa from his son, Charles Milsom Jr. Waters was a master tailor, a churchwarden of the abbey and a member of the Masonic Lodge of Perfect Friendship, which met at the White Hart Inn in Stall Street. Richard Maltby, who owned the freehold of the land on which the house stood, was a member of the same lodge. For all these reasons, he was unlikely to tolerate the lack of propriety which brought the Bagatelle into disrepute in any enterprise with which he was involved. Although he masterminded the development of the gardens, his other commitments led to him leaving the day-to-day running of them in the hands of his son, Harry.

On 24 April 1777, the *Bath Chronicle* published an advertisement announcing that King James's Palace 'is neatly fitted and opened for the reception of Ladies and Gentlemen'. The usual drinks, alcoholic and otherwise, were available, and dinners, as always, could be dressed at the shortest notice. After adding that 'a great variety of flowers, flower-roots, shrubs, plants etc' were also for sale, the advertisement ended with a somewhat curious remark:

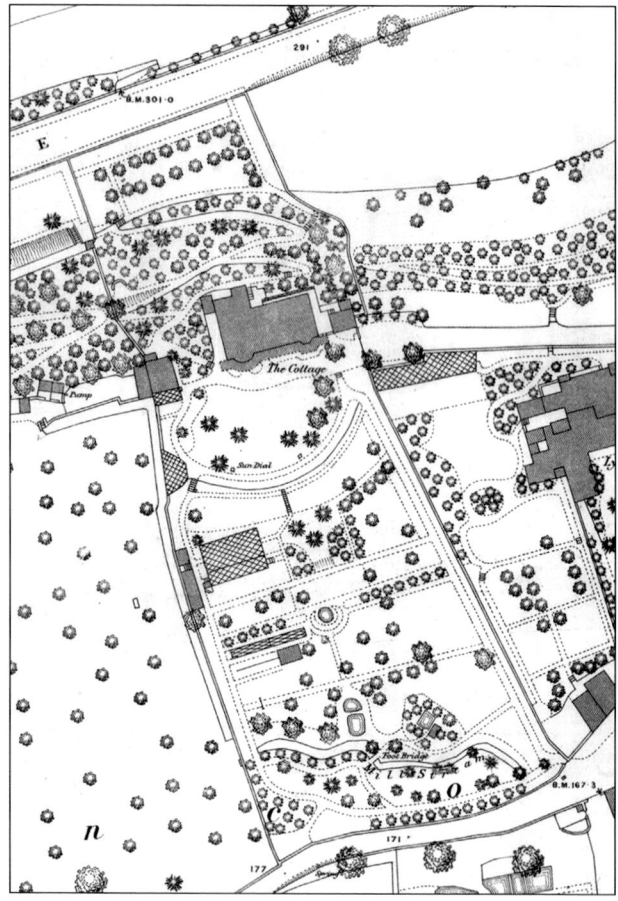

The site of King James's Palace from the 1886 Ordnance Survey map, when it still retained a semblance of what the gardens would have looked like. Since then, houses have been built on the lower part of the site.

> There will be no illuminations, or fireworks, on 1st May as usual; nor will the gates be opened until 5 o'clock in the morning.

This suggests that May Day celebrations had been held here before Charles Waters took over. It also seems probable that, as he had plants ready for sale, there had already been some horticultural activity on the site. The man most likely to have carried this out was Richard Lancashire, who had been hosting carnation and auricula florist feasts at Lyncombe since 1767. On 9 April 1767, he placed an advertisement in the *Bath Chronicle* for 'an auricula florist feast … at Richard Lancashire's, at Lyncomb'. Not only did he lay a dinner on at the feast; anyone who wanted to enter the competition for 'the best blown Auricula' was obliged to dine 'with the company'. There was also 'a great collection to be seen at the above Place in Bloom; which Plants, with Variety of other Sorts of Flower-Roots, are to be sold'.

Frustratingly, the advertisement does not give the exact location of Richard Lancashire's garden. Seven years later, however, on 13 October 1774, when he advertised a large selection of bulbs, shrubs and evergreens for sale, he gave his address as 'Lyncomb Spaw'. As the former spa had by now become William Street's private residence, it would have been impossible for Richard Lancashire to have been operating his business from there. The explanation has to be that, as the spa was still a well-known landmark, despite having closed several years earlier, Lancashire used the proximity of his garden to the spa to indicate its location. Five years later, on 8 July 1779, when King James's Palace was up and running, Charles Waters advertised a 'public tea-drinking' there, advising potential visitors that they would find it 'opposite Lyncombe Spa'. Furthermore, not only was Lancashire selling virtually the same range as plants later sold at King James's Palace; at Lancashire's last carnation feast, one of the stewards was Charles Waters.[14]

The house at the top of the former King James's Palace Gardens, formerly known as the Cottage

All this points to the gardens having been open for at least ten years before Charles Waters took them over and renamed them. Why he chose the name King James's Palace is not known, but he may well have been reviving the name of the establishment visited by Captain Peter Drake over 50 years earlier.

The members of the Masonic lodge to which Charles Waters belonged were invited to visit the garden on 24 June 1777, just a month after it opened.[15] The ostensible reason for the invitation was to celebrate the festival of St John the Baptist. The real reason was that Samuel Woodhouse, the landlord of their former meeting place, the White Hart Inn, had gone bankrupt.

By April 1778, Charles Waters' son Harry had given up running the gardens and a new manager – possibly his son William – was appointed. Plant sales continued to be prominently advertised:

> Great variety of hot and greenhouse plants to be sold, with all sorts of flower-roots, polyanthus, narcissus, at 10s 6d per hundred; the best tulips, many of the new from Holland, at £5 5s per hundred, their offsets at one guinea. The curious in tulips are desired not to miss the opportunity of seeing the bloom; they are very forward, some in bloom.[16]

Lyncombe Vale Road – the 'very good carriage road' – seen here in the early twentieth century. It was built shortly after the visit of the Rev John Penrose to Lyncombe Spa, alongside the Lyn Brook, which here formed a leat supplying the mills in Widcombe.

Opposite: Two more eighteenth-century paintings of the type of flowers which would have been sold at King James's Palace: .six cut Ranunculus flowers, double flowered varieties, by Mrs Montgomery; and tulips by an unknown artist.

Advertisements also continued to emphasise the lack of revelry on 1 May. There were also requests not to bring dogs into the garden 'as much mischief has been done by them'. Public evenings were on Mondays and Fridays, with tea, refreshments and a band of horns and clarinets. Charles Waters assured visitors that there was 'a very good carriage road' to the garden 'and the distance only one mile'. One advertisement advised visitors that 'the best and pleasantest road is by the Bagatelle', even though by the time it appeared, in 1779, the gardens there had closed, their demise possibly hastened by competition from a more salubrious rival. Plants were still for sale, although not on public days, and the polite request not to bring dogs into the garden was soon changed to an order. In February, Edmund Rack, founder of the Bath and West of England Society, visited and wrote approvingly in his journal:

> A fine morning. Walked to King James Palace – the gardens coming forward apace – the snowdrop & the crocus are

ushering in the spring. The green houses are in full beauty and glow in all the radiance of exotic colouring.[17]

The sense that Lyncombe and its gardens were regarded as a peaceful retreat is admirably expressed in a poem which appeared in the *Bath Journal* after the destruction of the Roman Catholic Chapel in Bath. Inspired by the Gordon riots in London, a mob had descended on the chapel, chased the priest through the streets and burnt the chapel to the ground. John Butler, a footman, was hanged in Bath for his part in the disturbances on 28 August 1780. The poem, 'written on the day of the late execution, at a very beautiful spot, laid out for the entertainment of the public, near Bath', was published three weeks later. The spot in question was King James's Palace:

> Far from the curious mob that crowd the streets,
> I seek the shelter of this cool retreat;
> This tranquil scene, for sacred quiet made,
> Where the fresh zephyr breathes around the shade;
> And while the world to yonder city go,
> To gaze upon a spectacle of woe,
> With anxious heart to this recess I fly,
> And feel a generous sorrow bathe my eye,
> E'en as the florid landscapes round me glow
> I drop a tear upon the vale below,
> I bless that hill which screens me from the wind,
> I hail that wood that shuts me from mankind:
> And innocence, with nature, seems to roam;
> Here rave no tumults, riot strays not here,
> But peace smiles softly, tho' the city's near:
> Smooth glides the waters as you pass along,
> And pleasure warbles in the linnet's song;
> Fair, within reach, the ruddy fruits are seen,
> And Autumn decks with various flowers the green:
> The artist here from labour may repose,
> And see health cultivate the blushing rose,
> Here nature for the sick shall court the air,
> And every gale a heavenly balm prepare;

To these calm seats serenity retires,
And every passion, but the best, expires;
And they who sigh for self-improving hours,
Will seek these winding walks, these fragrant bowers.[18]

Although very much of its time, even to our ears this conveys a sense of tranquillity far from the dust and bustle of the city. And that is precisely what the Lyncombe pleasure gardens sought to convey.

In November 1780, Charles Waters advertised King James's Place to let due to 'the present occupier's leaving England'.[19] Although there is no indication of the 'present occupier's' identity, it may have been Charles Waters' son William, who a few weeks earlier had married a Miss Johnson in Kingston, Jamaica.[20] Whether Charles Waters found a tenant or installed another relation is not known, but he continued to be involved in the running of the establishment, and plant sales did so well that in 1784 he started selling surplus stock in his tailor's shop in the High Street. This included 'a great variety

A late nineteenth-century view looking east along Lyncombe Vale and a modern view looking west from Widcombe Terrace – both demonstrating how rural this part of Bath still appears, despite being less than a mile from the city centre

of the curious sorts of ranunculuses' from J Holder of Seend who had given up 'that part of his amusement and study'. Although they cost him from 10s 6d to 21s, he was selling them off at £5 5s per hundred. Having paid for the advertisement, Charles got his money's worth by adding that two rooms were to let at the Palace, and that his fine collection of fossils and a small collection of fine shells were for sale.[21]

Before long, however, Charles Waters seems to have been ailing, resigning from his Masonic Lodge in 1787. Two years later, Robert Lansdown took over the management of King James's Palace, coming up with a new name for it – Lyncombe Pleasure Garden – and declaring it to be 'remarkable for its warmth and healthy situation'. Lansdown described himself as 'many years waiter at the Bear Inn'. He may well have been chosen for the job by Waters, who would have known him through his Masonic connections. Lansdown would have waited at the Masonic dinners held at the Bear, before eventually becoming a Mason himself. He kept the gardens ticking over for a year, with regular advertisements in the papers for breakfasts and teas, but may always have been a stopgap, helping a fellow Mason out until a permanent tenant could be found.

In November 1790 an ambitious perfumer called Robert Tanner gave up his perfumery business, selling all his stock, including snuff and tobacco, to Ann Osman, who ran a rum and brandy warehouse in the High Street, and stepped forward to take the lease of King James's Palace. There is no doubt he had a flair for business. His shop had been in a prominent position opposite the Pump Room, where he doubtless made many contacts with well-heeled visitors and residents. Given that he had 'laid in a stock of excellent old wines, spirituous and malt liquors', he probably did a deal with Mrs Osman. But he should have taken lessons from the Purdie family, and kept another business going. Sadly, it was not going to end well for Mr Tanner.

Things started badly when Charles Waters died in March 1791, just as Tanner advertised that he had opened a subscription book for people wishing to walk in the garden. This left his lease in a slightly precarious position. Nothing daunted, Tanner decided his tenancy should literally start off with a bang. For the first time, in the summer of 1791, there were illuminations and fireworks as well as music at King James's Palace. In September, however, it was announced that King James's Palace would be coming up for auction.

The following March, after the shells, fossils and other items from Waters' collection went under the hammer, the house and gardens were put up for sale. They were advertised as

> a convenient Dwelling-House, with necessary attached and detached offices, large pleasure gardens, hot-houses, green-houses, temples, alcoves, shrubbery, stables, &c.[22]

The advertisement acknowledged that it was being used as a tea garden, but Mr Tanner must have been a trifle alarmed to see that it was also deemed 'particularly eligible for the retreat of a private family'. To his relief, it was not sold, but offered to let, viewers being requested to apply to Tanner for details. There had been a further setback for Tanner the previous November, when his gardener, John Biggs died tragically by bursting a blood vessel while lifting a heavy basket. There was a collection for his widow and her six children, who were living in part of the old Bagatelle House.[23]

The gardens were still open in April 1792, with group bookings for dinner being taken at Tanner's former shop, which was now run by a Mr Cadman. Tanner not only managed to keep going until the end of the season, but opened the gardens the following year. He last advertised their delights in June 1793, but by October the gardens hosted an auction of Tanner's property – he had gone bankrupt, like many other Bath business people in those troubled times. The lease was advertised in December 1793, along with the stock of roots and plants.

A year later, Tanner had bounced back, taking on the former Jennings Stables near Queen Square and converting them to the Elephant and Castle Inn. But King James's Palace – home to Lyncombe's shady groves, as Christopher Anstey had described them – was no more. It had succumbed partly to the financial crisis, but also to the continued popularity of Spring Gardens, which for nearly a decade had been locked in battle with another competitor – Bathwick Villa.

The story of Bathwick Villa begins with James Ferry's retirement from business. He and his brother Peter were silk merchants, who had arrived in Bath in the mid 1740s, to cash in on the lucrative trade generated by wealthy visitors. Their shop stood at the corner of Gallaway's Buildings. By 1769, after over twenty years of successful trading, they decided to call it a day, and held

A sketch of Bathwick Villa in its declining years, but still bearing the words 'Bathwick Villa' and beneath that 'Neat Wines'

a massive sale of all their stock. In March 1770, they had retired, with Peter going to Widcombe and James finally moving to Bathwick in 1777. Here he had a villa built in the Strawberry Hill Gothick-style then becoming popular. Selina, Countess of Huntingdon, had had a chapel in the Vineyards built in this style in 1765.

The architect is unknown, but Bathwick Villa, as the house was called, bore a striking resemblance to it. One possible claimant may be Thomas Jelly. He built Cottle's House, now Stonar School, at Atworth, in 1775 and a villa in Upper East Hayes about the same

The Countess of Huntingdon's Chapel, architect unknown

36 Upper East Hayes designed by Thomas Jelly

time. Both of these were castellated, and Cottle's House, like the chapel and Bathwick Villa, had ogee-headed windows.

In February 1779, after the acquittal of the popular Admiral Keppel on charges of misconduct and neglect of duty, the city went wild, with illuminations at many locations. According to the *Bath Chronicle*, James Ferry, by now chamberlain of the city, had a particularly notable display at Bathwick Villa:

> On the right and left wings, under four superb columns on each side, was a gothic arch embellished with lamps of every colour, and well disposed. In the centre of the house, in every window, were large pyramids of candles, which had a most pleasing effect.
> On the circular plot of grass before the house was placed a ship, compleatly rigged with sails, and colours flying, illuminated, and mounted with brass cannon, which were almost incessantly fired; and over it an ellliptic arch, with lamps in variety of colours. On a pedestal of 12 feet high was the figure of Hercules, and above his head the Great Union Flag of England, Hercules as herald, in transparent letters, proclaiming BRAVE, HONEST, KEPPEL – on the right Montague, on the left Harland.[24]

It is unclear whether Ferry intended to open the Villa as an attraction. It was certainly full of curiosities, as Fanny Burney found out when she visited with Mr and Mrs Thrale, their daughter Queenie and the Bishop of Peterborough. 'Mr Ferry is a Bath alderman,' she wrote,

> his house and garden exhibit the house and garden of Mr Tattersall, enlarged. Just the same taste prevails, the same paltry ornaments, the

same crowd of buildings, the same unmeaning decorations, and the same unsuccessful attempts at making something of nothing.

They kept us half an hour in the garden, while they were preparing for our reception in the house, where after parading through four or five little vulgarly showy closets, not rooms, we were conducted into a very gaudy little apartment, where the master of the house sat reclining on his arm, as if in contemplation, though everything conspired to show that the house and its inhabitants were carefully arranged for our reception. The bishop had sent in his name by way of gaining admission.

The bishop, with a gravity of demeanour difficult to himself to sustain, apologised for our intrusion, and returned thanks for seeing the house and garden. Mr Ferry started from his pensive attitude, and begged us to be seated, and then a curtain was drawn, and we perceived through a glass a perspective view of ships, boats, and water. This raree-show over, the maid who officiated as showwoman had a hint given her and presently a trap-door opened, and up jumped a covered table, ornamented with various devices. When we had expressed our delight at this long enough to satisfy Mr Ferry, another hint was given, and presently down dropped an eagle from the ceiling whose talons were put into a certain hook in the top of the covering of the table, and when the admiration at this was over, up again flew the eagle, conveying in his talons the cover, and leaving under it a repast of cakes, sweetmeats, oranges, and jellies.

Fanny Burney

When our raptures upon this feat subsided, the maid received another signal, and then seated herself in an armchair, which presently sank down underground, and up in its room came a barber's block, with a vast quantity of black wool on it, and a high head-dress.

> This, you may be sure, was more applauded than all the rest; we were *en extase*, and having properly expressed our gratitude, were soon after suffered to decamp.[25]

They laughed about it all the way back to their lodgings in South Parade.

There was, perhaps, a reason for the alderman looking so pensive. He was in deep financial trouble, and owed the council money from his post as chamberlain. Two fellow councillors had to arrange security for his debts, and in March 1782 Bathwick Villa was put up for sale. The advertisement in the *Bath Chronicle* described the Villa as being 'in a most pleasing and healthy situation, on a dry gravelly soil, commanding many beautiful views of Bath, and the countryside circumjacent'. The rooms were spacious and included, on the upper floor, a drawing room 'highly finished with ornamental ceiling, an elegant marble chimney-piece, &c, three spacious windows from the front and illuminated by a well-proportioned dome'. Contemporary accounts also mention that the staircases were magnificent and wide. The gardens, meanwhile consisted

> of about an acre and a quarter of land laid out in the modern taste, with serpentine gravel walks, valuable shrubbery, evergreens, fish-ponds, bridges, fruit-trees, in the highest perfection. The whole premises in compleat repair, with plenty of most excellent water both in the house and garden.[26]

Despite this enticing advertisement, it did not sell, and the property, along with its contents, was put up for auction on 8 May 1783.[27] It was bought by Joseph Marrett, a wine dealer at 45 Milsom Street, who planned to turn it into a pleasure garden.[28]

There may have been a number of reasons for his decision. He had been in partnership with a Mr Guille, who like him was from Guernsey. However, the partnership was dissolved in December 1782.[29] In that same month William Purdie died, and in January 1783 the lease of Spring Gardens was offered for sale. Marrett may well have seen an opportunity to steal custom from Bath's premier pleasure gardens. However, if Marrett thought that the Purdies were no longer going to be involved in Spring Gardens, he was sadly mistaken, because Purdie's widow took over in March.

Nevertheless, in July 1783, Marrett announced that the gardens would open on 10 July for tea and coffee. Newspapers would be available in the coffee room, dinners and suppers would be served, and the choicest wines could be depended on. Given his profession, this comes as no surprise. Ingenuously, he added that, 'as the undertaking has been attended with very great expence, the proprietor humbly requests the favour and encouragement of the public in general, and his friends in particular'. To encourage visitors to venture further than they may have been accustomed to, he pointed out that there was a coach road up to the front of the house, and a ferry which crossed the river from Walcot. As an added attraction, he kept the automata and the perspective view. These featured in an advertisement in the *Bath Journal* of 1786, which stated that 'the curious chair, table and perspective view, &c are in proper repair for the amusement of subscribers'.[30]

The Purdie family at Spring Gardens had seen competitors come and go. But Marrett would soon prove that he meant business. With Bath growing rapidly, the mention of the ferry from Walcot was timely, since it suggested a convenient access for visitors from the developments along the London Road. Mrs Purdie must have been dismayed when a letter appeared in the *Bath Chronicle* in August 1784 from a resident of the Crescent, giving a favourable report of both establishments but singling out Bathwick Villa for particular praise:

> I am at present an inhabitant of Bath, and have long lamented the want of amusements at this season of the year, as the cause why so many people seek for them elsewhere. I cannot therefore too much commend the spirited endeavours of the Proprietors of Spring-Gardens, and the Villa. I must own I have been rather prejudiced against the latter, till last night, when I went in company and at the particular request of some friends; and was really astonished at the beauty and elegance of the place. The House is a perfect Palace in Miniature, and the Garden laid out with the greatest taste imaginable; the situation likewise is greatly in its favour, being at a good distance from the river, on an eminence, and quite free from those damps which, if nearer, it would be subject to. The evening was rather unfavourable, yet, not withstanding, there was a numerous, genteel

company; amongst whom were many persons of distinction. The music, which was well selected, was heard to great advantage from the orchestra here, being opposite the house; the illuminations were on a new plan, extremely elegant, which were heightened by the beautiful emblematic transparency; and the fire-works, some of the best I have seen in a long time, particularly the naval engagement, which was quite a new thought, well designed, and happily executed; and had a very good effect. In short, I never would desire to spend an evening more agreeably than last night, and sincerely wish that the Proprietor, whom I find is Mr Marret, wine merchant in Milsom-Street, may meet with that encouragement he so richly deserves.[31]

While this must have been music to Joseph Marrett's ears, the Purdie family would have been furious. From now on, the two gardens were locked in a bitter struggle, each trying to outdo the other, and sometimes employing dubious tactics. The winners were the visitors who were offered increasingly diverse entertainments. There were concerts, balls, bird impressions, and, most spectacular of all, fireworks – and the best man for fireworks was the ingenious Signor Invetto from Italy.

3

FIREWORKS AND BIRDSONG

The Battle for Supremacy between Spring Gardens and Villa Gardens

At Spring Gardens, the Purdie family must have wondered how they would compete with Villa Gardens. In 1784, the same year that the anonymous resident of the Royal Crescent was so delighted with the Villa, they signed up two people popular with London audiences to perform at their gardens. The first was William Crotch, a child prodigy on the violin and piano.[1] By this time he was nearly ten years old, and his concert on 27 May 1784 was advertised as his last public performance. This may well have been true – in 1786 he went to Cambridge to study and take up an assistant organist's post. In June, at the request of Mrs Thrale, there was a breakfast concert starring James Harris, described as 'a Person equally extraordinary and unfortunate'. His 'misfortune' was that he was only three feet tall, although possessed of a 'peculiar symmetry of form'.[2] He turned this to his advantage and was able to provide for his 'suffering parent, whose only dependence for present support is the singularity of her unhappy boy'. Tickets for the event, at which he would 'show himself in the gardens' after the concert, were quite expensive at 3s 6d each.[3]

By the start of the 1785 season, Spring Gardens, now boldly calling itself Spring Gardens Vauxhall, had clearly upped its game. In May, the management proudly announced the commencement of the usual entertainments in 'this

Opposite: A drawing by Samuel Hieronymous Grimm, showing Pulteney Bridge in 1788, with Bathwick Mill and the miller's house across the river. To the right of them, behind a wall and half hidden by trees, is the Long Room at Spring Gardens. The impact of building work is also apparent, with the causeway on which Argyle Street would be built, and the beginnings of houses in Laura Place and Great Pulteney Street.

much-improved and admired spot'. The opening night's fête consisted of a concert of vocal and instrumental music, with illuminations 'after the manner of Vauxhall'. Mrs Purdie assured 'the nobility and her friends at large, that every effort will be exerted on this and the following evenings to render Vauxhall worthy their patronage and attention'.[4]

However, Marrett had already started his season in April, with a concert at a public breakfast, during which Masters Shell and Cook sang favourite songs and duets between the orchestral pieces. This pair had appeared at Spring Gardens the year before, and Marrett seems to have poached them. To rub it in, he promised that, 'by particular desire of the nobility and gentry', they would appear at a future breakfast concert. In June, despite a postponement due to bad weather, he was promising a brilliant display of fireworks, including a large illuminated yew tree and an enormous vertical wheel. In addition, between the acts, there was to be the launch of a 'very large and beautiful balloon'.[5] Balloons at this time were all the rage. The Montgolfier brothers had made

Huge crowds were attracted to Moorfields in September 1784 when Vicenzo Lunardi made the first balloon flight in this country. It would set a new fashion in hats, clothes, coaches and fireworks.

FIREWORKS AND BIRDSONG 101

A year later, in June 1785 Vincenzo Lunardi arranged for another flight with his assistant, George Biggin, and one of the first female balloonists, Mrs Letitia Anne Sage

their successful flight in 1783, prompting designers to create balloon hats, balloon coaches – intended to make passengers feel as though they were flying – and even balloon curls. In England, the star balloonist was Vincenzo Lunardi, who made his famous maiden flight in 1784. True to his word, on 16 June, Marrett promised that, four days later, a 'large balloon, variegated with purple, yellow, green and white will be launched'. He could not have timed it better, for shortly afterwards Lunardi took off in a balloon from St George's Fields in London.

To coincide with the balloon launch, Marrett also booked 'a gentleman just arrived from Italy' who could imitate birds and play on the viol d'amour. This may have been an imitator of Signor Rossignol, of whom we will hear more later. If it was Signor Rossignol himself, 'newly arrived' would hardly have been an accurate description, as he had first performed in this country in 1774.

By now, it must have been obvious to many in Bath that there was a desperate struggle going on for supremacy, and it was about to turn very unpleasant indeed. In 1786, Spring Gardens pre-empted the opening of Villa Gardens for the season by staging a concert in February, by the 'very extraordinary young musician', Maria Poole, who was invariably referred to as Miss Poole. She had arrived in Bath a few months earlier with her parents, having come to study with the famous castrato Venanzio Rauzzini, who had retired to the city. Although only sixteen, she had already sung at Vauxhall Gardens, and would go on to sing at Covent Garden and star as a delightful Polly Peachum in *The Beggar's Opera*. In this concert she promised to perform airs 'in various styles, serious and comic, ancient and modern'. Following the concert, there was to be a ball.[6]

Throughout that summer, it must have been hard to choose which of the gardens to visit. Spring Gardens were still doing well – in June, on the occasion of the King's birthday, there were over a thousand people in the garden by eight o'clock, and by the time the fireworks started there were over 1500.

Miss Poole married in 1800 and retired from the stage, but her husband, Mr Dickons, contrived to lose their money, and she returned, first of all to Drury Lane, later going on to Covent Garden. This sketch was made in 1812.

In July, visitors could have gone to two firework displays on consecutive nights, with those at Villa Gardens being slightly cheaper. At the Villa, they displayed a flag at the top of the house on public days, so that strangers were able to find it.[7] Spring Gardens had no such difficulty as it was in full view of the Parades. By August, the two gardens were promising ever more stupendous events. For the Prince of Wales' birthday, Spring Gardens promised 'fireworks on a grand scale, such as have never been exhibited in Bath', while the gardens would be 'decorated in an elegant and superb style, for which grand preparations are now making. The paintings for the boxes &c in the manner of Vauxhall, London.'[8]

On this auspicious occasion, for the first time the two gardens were planning to go head to head. The advertisements in the *Bath Chronicle* on 10 August 1786 were actually side by side, which made for some interesting

FIREWORKS AND BIRDSONG   103

The scenes in the boxes at Vauxhall were painted by the artist Francis Hayman. Originally a scene painter (and occasional actor) at Drury Lane, he made his name as an artist with these delightful paintings for Vauxhall. This one is called The Milkmaids' Garland.

reading, especially as it seems that someone at the *Bath Chronicle* tipped off the Purdies about the wording of Marrett's advertisement. Her promise of 'fireworks on an enlarged scale, such as have never been exhibited in Bath before' was countered by Marrett's boast that his fireworks would be on 'so magnificent and enlarged a scale, the proprietor challenges all competition'. To which the Purdies responded that, although 'an opponent has challenged all competition, the publick may be assured that an equality, if not a decisive superiority, will be produced at these Gardens'. She also promised a display of paintings, including a realistic view of Otaheite, as Tahiti was then known.

Another bone of contention was the musicians. Among those scheduled to play at the Villa was Miss Poole – although she was not mentioned by name but simply referred to as 'a young lady of extraordinary talent' – along with Masters Shell and Cook, the other two young singers Marrett had poached from Spring Gardens. Marrett's advertisement stressed that

> the Report so industriously propagated, that Mr Marrett could not procure Musicians for this Night is groundless; he begs leave to assure the Public, that his Band will consist of TWENTY THREE Vocal and Instrumental PERFORMERS, selected by Mr Milgrove.[9]

Marrett was undoubtedly implying that the Purdies were behind the rumours. They retorted that,

> as to the Band, though the proprietor cannot promise twenty-three performers, yet he has three equal to three and twenty, though not selected by Mr Milgrove.[10]

All this proved to be irrelevant, however. There is a Chinese proverb, 'When we speak of tomorrow, the gods laugh.' They were certainly laughing on the night of 12 August because the heavens opened, and both displays had to be postponed. Spring Gardens were first off the mark afterwards, staging a performance on the following Monday. This was so well attended, despite the weather being disappointing, that they promised a repeat on 22 August for those who could not attend or had decided the weather was too bad.[11]

Most artists struggled to convey the excitement of Georgian firework displays. This painting, from 1749, of a firework display on the River Thames at Richmond, gives some idea of how spectacular they could be, as well as illustrating some of the more popular types of fireworks.

By this time, Marrett was seething, and not only because the Purdie family been given the chance to respond to his advertisement. Although, in its report, the *Bath Chronicle* reminded the public that Villa Gardens would be putting on a splendid display as soon as the weather was good, it also raved over the Spring Gardens display, which they claimed that more than 1500 people had attended. To add insult to injury, Spring Gardens had chosen Monday – Villa Gardens' regular day – to stage the fireworks. The advertisement Marrett eventually placed in the *Bath Chronicle* is worth quoting in full as it shimmers with suppressed rage:

> Marrett respectfully informs the Publick, that, conscious of the undeniable preferences of these Gardens after wet weather, it was his full intention to have exhibited on Monday last (being his usual evening) the various performances prepared in honour of the Prince of Wales' Birth-day; but by the advice, and at the particular request, of numerous and respectable friends, they were further postponed.
>
> Anxious to experience as early as possible the defer'd favours of his friends and a generous public, the proprietor proposes to celebrate the said Grand FESTIVAL tomorrow (THURSDAY) on which evening he pledges himself (notwithstanding the *mean aspersions* of some, and the *secret arts* of *others to depreciate and injure him*) to produce a series of Entertainments as shall be an appeal to the impartial judgment of the Company, whether he or any of the performers he has engaged are deserving of the *illiberal attack* which appeared in the papers.
>
> The great musical abilities of the Female Singer, who will make her first appearance at these Gardens, the admired vocal talents of Master Gray and others, a Capital Band of Instrumental Performers, with ILLUMINATIONS and SUPERB FIRE-WORKS; (at the close of the 2nd Act) will, he trusts, give general satisfaction.[12]

While his rage was understandable, this was not perhaps the best way to go about things. Losing one's temper in public is a double-edged sword. Not only had the Purdies been in Bath a long time, they were closely associated with the powerful William Johnstone Pulteney. Marrett's friends seem to have advised him to stop fighting the Purdies by arranging clashing dates.

But then Marrett came up with an idea. A week after this tirade, he thanked the 'Nobility and Gentry' for their support on Thursday, 'surpassing his most sanguine expectations', and offered a repeat performance of the fireworks on Monday 28 August when the 'Young Lady, who gave universal satisfaction' would appear again. His master stroke was to light the way from Villa Gardens to Pulteney Bridge at the close of the evening's entertainment with 'attendants ... stationed at proper distances with flambeaus'. This was taking the battle literally to the very doorstep of Spring Gardens.[13]

However, Spring Gardens had what they thought would be the last word. On the last day of August, the proprietors advertised that they had been 'induced to open the Gardens ONE NIGHT more' on September 5, which would be 'POSITIVELY THE LAST'. Not only that, but during the evening they expected one of the principal vocalists from London's Vauxhall to perform.

Joseph Marrett did not take this lying down. He hastily arranged a concert for 7 September. The advertisement did not appear in the *Bath Chronicle* until the day of the concert, so it was done at very short notice. For the first time, Miss Poole was named as the principal vocal performer. The fireworks were promised to be new and superb, and the illuminations peculiarly brilliant.

Thus the pleasure gardens' 1786 season came to a close, but when a new season began the following year, rivalry soon flared up again. This time, Spring Gardens was completely outgunned, even though they started off well by opening in March, three weeks earlier than Villa Gardens. This, though, was to be the year of Villa Gardens' greatest success. Late in April, Marrett announced that the celebrated Signor John Invetto from Milan would be displaying 'a most superb and brilliant set of fireworks, far grander that ever seen in these parts'.[14]

Invetto arrived in England by 1771, and soon started to make a name for himself. At first, his displays consisted of the usual rockets, pyramids, trees, wheels, and so on. But by 1780 his displays included the set battle pieces for which he became famous. In Derby, for instance, in 1780, he presented an engagement between two English and French ships. By 1786, when he was in Winchester, not far from the great naval base of Portsmouth, the ships had become the *Rodney* and the *Comte de Grasse*. The scene 'astonished every beholder', according to the report in the *Hampshire Chronicle*.[15]

By 10 May 1787, Invetto had settled in Bath with his family, and became a fixture at Villa Gardens. Throughout that season, Villa Gardens outshone Spring Gardens whose advertisements even seem to have shrunk in size compared with those of their rival. The royal celebrations, in which Spring Gardens had led the way, were now dominated by ever more dramatic offerings from Invetto. On the Prince of Wales' birthday in August, the display in Spring Gardens, though splendid, was overshadowed by that in Villa Gardens, which included a representation of the siege of Gibraltar. This was so popular that it was repeated two weeks later.[16] This time, Spring Gardens ended their season in August but Villa Gardens went happily on into September. To celebrate the anniversary of the King's coronation, Invetto presented a display including 'Chinese fire', palm trees and the sun, a crown with the letters GR and a representation of the siege of Portobello. Invetto was, by this time, using Villa Gardens' advertisements to publicise sales of fireworks from his lodgings at the Seven Stars on Upper Borough Walls.

Marrett of Villa Gardens was undoubtedly the winner in 1787, but 1788 brought with it a development that put Spring Gardens back in the lead. As ever, they opened slightly earlier than Villa Gardens, and by early April were taking front page advertisements. This was unusual – most notices for coming events normally appeared on page 3 of the *Bath Chronicle*.

In April came an event that would ultimately lead to the downfall of both gardens. Since its completion in 1773, Pulteney Bridge had led only to Spring Gardens, Bathwick Mill and a track across fields leading to Villa Gardens. This is why Marrett decided he needed to light the way back after evening events at the Villa. Due to war with America, all work on Pulteney's 'New Town' had been put on hold. However, once the political dust from the American War of Independence had settled, work resumed on the estate. Peace was declared in 1783, and work on houses in Argyle Buildings (later Argyle Street) started late in 1787. On the last day of March, the foundation stone of Laura Place was laid, with great celebration. As with other auspicious events, bells were rung, cannon were fired from Spring Gardens, and the crowds were 'treated with plenty of strong beer delivered from the foundation in pails'. However, the construction work meant that visitors to both sets of gardens were now walking through a building site after crossing Pulteney Bridge. Spring Gardens assured its clientele that the bridge and road would be watered if necessary, to keep down the dust, while Villa Gardens strongly recommended that visitors use the ferry from Walcot Parade.

By now, Spring Gardens had found their own pyrotechnic expert. Keeping his name secret at first, they revealed only that he was a 'celebrated artist in London'. What is more, he devised different displays every week, unlike Invetto, who was beginning to recycle displays. Cryptically, they announced in May added that their expert would be assisted by a gentleman of acknowledged abilities in this city. It is not impossible that this was Invetto – as will be seen, he was getting ready to jump ship.

Bit by bit, in a tempting manner, more information about this mysterious expert trickled out. By June, it was revealed that he was not just the first artist in London, but the engineer to Ranelagh Gardens. Later that month, the proprietors informed the public that he was also engineer to Marylebone Gardens, and had had 'the honour of exhibiting several pieces of Fire-Works before his present Majesty and the rest of the Royal Family at Kew, likewise at Gunnersbury and Ranelagh Gardens, for the entertainment of his Danish Majesty'.

Eventually, in August, just in time for the Prince of Wales' birthday, he was revealed as Benjamin Clitherow, a London firework maker used by celebrities such as David Garrick for their galas and fêtes, as well as by the Royal family. The fireworks promised for the Prince of Wales' birthday celebrations included 'water fountains to discharge sky rockets (an entirely new invention)'. Spring Gardens had also upgraded their orchestra for the celebrations, and recruited William Herschel's brother Alexander as a cellist. New vocal performers included a former Villa Gardens regular, Master Gray, while parts of the gardens were to be lit by new illuminations.[17] All Villa Gardens could muster was Invetto's recycled Siege of Gibraltar, and this failure to produce something new increases the suspicion that he had been too busy working with Clitherow at Spring Gardens – an association which would have opened doors for him.

Even more catastrophic for the Villa was that, although once again the weather was poor for the Prince of Wales' birthday, Spring Gardens staged a magnificent display witnessed by over a thousand spectators.[18] There is no mention of Villa Gardens in the *Bath Chronicle's* report of the event. However, as in previous years, Villa Gardens' season was longer, running until early October, when there was a display of Invetto's fireworks, including a 'water fountain that will discharge an air balloon with stars', which sounds suspiciously like one of Clitherow's set pieces.[19]

In April 1789, Invetto moved his lodgings and workshop to the Grove Tavern in Orange Court. This was Purdie territory. It was where William Purdie had had his wine shop, and where Mrs Purdie still ran a lodging house. Although Invetto continued to stage firework displays at the Villa in May and June, it was an ominous development.

June was a busy month for the Purdie family. Mrs Purdie's daughter, Eliza, married the architect John Eveleigh, who, for a time, used the lodge at Spring Gardens as his office. On 4 June, they laid on a grand gala in honour of the King's birthday and his 'happy recovery', and reminded visitors that, to avoid the building works, they could take a ferry from South Parade for 'a pleasant walk thro' the Meadow' to a new gate at the south end of the gardens.

Marrett, meanwhile, was pleased to announce that 'a large and commodious ferry' had recently been introduced on the crossing from Walcot Parade. Although this was not enough to prevent a fall off in visitor numbers, he still

The jetty for the ferry still exists, though much altered, on the Walcot side and is now used by the Bath Canoe Club for launching its craft. Some old stonework still survives to each side. The landing stage on the Bathwick side, however, has vanished.

managed to book some popular acts. In June, for example, appeared three celebrated musical prodigies, the children of Mr Bryson:

> The youngest, but three years, performed before his Majesty and the Royal Family before he was two yours old. Likewise his Brother, who is but 6 years old, has had the honour to perform before the Royal Family of France, and most Courts in Europe. – The Elder Brother will also perform and accompany them on the Guitar.[20]

Then in August came the news that Marrett must have guessed was inevitable. For the Prince of Wales' birthday at Spring Gardens, the fireworks were to be by Invetto, while the entertainment would be bird and animal impressions by Mr Campbell, the 'British Rossignole' or 'Scotch Shepherd'. He had already gone down a storm at Spring Gardens in June, when his repertoire had included hounds going out in the morning and crows feeding their young.

By August, Invetto was briefly back at the Villa Gardens, promising a most magnificent display of fireworks to celebrate the Duke of Clarence's birthday. Not only was there to be a 'curious sea engagement' but also a firework which represented two pigeons going from an alcove to the top of the gardens and back. But Mr Marrett's luck was out. Once again the weather was bad and the show could not go ahead, but this was not just a postponement – Invetto demanded the fireworks back and they were set off at Spring Gardens to

The Grove Tavern in Orange Court, to which Invetto moved in April 1789, and where his wife and son were killed by an explosion in his workshop four months later

celebrate the anniversary of the King's coronation on 22 September.[21]

By this time, Invetto was in mourning. At the end of August, while he was out, there was an explosion at his workshop, and his wife and son were killed. The tavern suffered little damage as his rooms were at the top of the building, but he had lost everything. A collection was held for him throughout the city in October. Although fireworks were so popular, it was a dangerous trade. A year later, Benjamin Clitherow's wife would die in an almost identical accident.

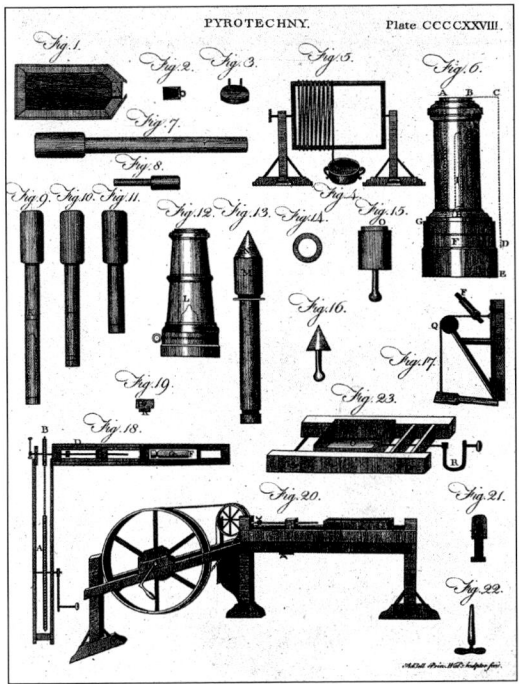

Making fireworks was a perilous business. This selection of firework-making tools was engraved by Andrew Bell for the Encyclopaedia Britannica.

It must have been clear to everyone that Villa Gardens was struggling, but Marrett decided that going slightly downmarket might solve his problems. In late autumn he booked a team from Philip Astley's Riding School to demonstrate their skills.[22] They had appeared in Bath before – it was during one of their performances that the women whom Purdie rescued had fallen into the river. The troupe was led by Benjamin Handy, one of Astley's assistants who eventually started his own circus, and Mr Wilkinson, who not only performed with Astley's group but at Sadler's Wells. The acts included performers on the slack wire and musicians from Sadler's Wells, some of whom played on a double set of musical glasses. The musical Bryson children, who had appeared in June, also travelled with the troupe. There was also 'the learned English dog' and the 'Amazingly Learned Military Horse'. This animal, whose name was Billy, could take a kettle off a blazing fire, set the table for tea, and prepare for company. One account said he was

Astley's amphitheatre in London, which set the standard for the size of a circus ring

so good-tempered that everyone was fond of him, and he would play like a kitten with those he knew.

Among the riders was one referred to as 'Mr Jackson the Black' who could ride on his head. He may well have been the man later known as 'the Famous African, (who is not to be equalled)', who could 'go through the Tilts and Tournaments, and Military Exercises, as performed on Horseback, in the Field and Manage'. Other riders included the 'wonderful Child of Promise' – who was Handy's five-year-old daughter – and the 'Little Devil'.

Doubtless this drew the crowds, but the following year only one advertisement appeared for Villa Gardens, on 19 August. It announced a 'grand entertainment' that evening, with a concert and fireworks, but warned prospective visitors that, as building work in Great Pulteney Street had effectively blocked off access to the gardens from Pulteney Bridge, 'the best Coach Road at present is over the Old Bridge round Claverton-street' – a long diversion. The advertisement ended with the ominous announcement that this would be 'the only Publick Night at the Gardens this Season'. And so it proved. After that, there was silence. In December, goods from the Villa were sold off, and in 1795, the house was put up for sale. As a pleasure garden, the days of Bathwick Villa were over.

It may have been the demise of Villa Gardens which inspired Robert Tanner to take on King James's Palace, but, as we have seen, that too failed eventually. To all intents and purposes, Spring Gardens now had the field to itself. Mrs. Purdie's son-in-law, Meshach Pritchard, took over managing the gardens in March, and he must have experienced a quiet feeling of satisfaction as the Villa closed. Invetto was now working for him, and perhaps feeling more settled. In February, he married again, to Mary Nichols. Although this may seem very soon after the death of his first wife, he had a ten-year-old daughter, Lucy Ann, so this may have been a marriage of convenience, as he needed someone who would look after her.

In this print from 1790, it is just possible to make out, on the extreme right, people wandering in Spring Gardens. Others walk up from the ferry landing, while the ferryman conveys a party back across the river. On the far bank is another ferry at the bottom of the steps leading down from South Parade. The boat moored nearby may have been the covered ferry acquired by William Purdie to protect passengers from the vagaries of the weather. By the time of this print, Spring Gardens had no competitors, but with work on the Pulteney estate well advanced, the advent of Sydney Gardens and the demise of Spring Gardens was just five years away.

Despite the lack of rivals, it was not all plain sailing for Spring Gardens. The fireworks scheduled for the King's birthday were 'by an unlucky accident' delayed due to the theft of musical instruments and music. The *Bath Chronicle* reported that this caused scenes of laughable confusion, relieved only by a display of fireworks.[23] Was this a last desperate attempt by someone associated with Villa Gardens to destroy the reputation of their rival? We shall never know, for the perpetrators were never caught and the instruments never recovered.

Nevertheless, as the *Bath Chronicle* remarked in 1791, now that Spring Gardens was 'now almost the only place of amusement open for the company and inhabitants of this city to resort to', the 'numerous attendance there every publick night' was hardly to be wondered at, especially as it was 'conducted in so liberal a manner'.[24] This did not mean that the quality of performances slipped – on the contrary, Invetto continued to come up with new displays, and the music remained of a high standard. The gardens also attracted the genuine Signor Rossignol (rather than his Scottish imitator) who gave imitations of a multitude of birds, including chaffinches, linnets, goldfinches and – of course – nightingales. On occasion he even used real birds in his act. The appropriate bird would come at its call, and during the finale all the birds would fly around the stage. This refinement was not mentioned, however, in advertisements for his performances at Spring Gardens – if the amusements were outside he may have been frightened they would all fly off. However, he did promise that he would perform a concerto on a violin without strings. He did this by making a noise in his throat, which was not always greeted with approbation.

Even Spring Gardens could not avoid brushes with Bath's darker side. In July, the body of a new-born baby boy, stabbed to death, was found beneath one of the hedges which separated the gardens from the meadows. Another death, in January 1791, just outside Spring Gardens, was due to the encroaching building work. A young man ventured down Johnstone Street in the dark, after seeing two young ladies home.[25] There was no barrier where the building work stopped, and he fell off the edge onto the stones beneath. It was an uncomfortable reminder that Spring Gardens stood in the way of Pulteney's development – and Pulteney was their landlord. What is more he had his plans for another, much larger pleasure garden as the centrepiece of his estate.

In June 1791, the *Bath Chronicle* reported that

> a plan is drawn for a New Vauxhall upon a very extensive plan; it is to be in the centre of Sidney-Place (the area of which measures 19 acres) adjoining the East End of Great Pulteney Street.[26]

However, the architect John Eveleigh, who was married to Eliza Purdie, had beaten Pulteney to it. Two weeks earlier, the newspaper had carried this notice:

> **GROUND TO LETT FOR EVER, ON BUILDING LEASES.**
>
> ALL those Healthy and Desireable MEADOWS, situate on the east side of the London-Road, between the Turnpike and Lambridge, commanding a most beautiful prospect of the serpentine Avon and surrounding hills; the center of the Meadows to be laid out in Pleasure Gardens, which every house will command; and a gravel walk in front, sixty feet wide. In this eligible situation, several Gentlemen and Builders took, the day the plan was finished, ground for *thirty-five* houses.
>
> The plan and elevation will be exhibited on Wednesday next, at York-House, precisely at two o'clock, where all persons desirous of taking ground are requested to attend.—Dinner on table at three.
>
> N.B. Any Lady or Gentleman may have a house built on a large or small scale, by applying to J. EVELEIGH, architect.
>
> Dated June 1st, 1791.

Just as one battle for supremacy had ended, another was to begin, between Sydney Gardens and Grosvenor Gardens.[27]

4

BOLD IDEAS AND BROKEN DREAMS

*How Sydney Gardens triumphed over Grosvenor,
Spring Gardens faded away, Botanic Gardens came and went,
and a Glaciere Garden came to Lansdown*

We cannot know what possessed John Eveleigh to take on the might of William Johnstone Pulteney. It was a high risk strategy. Eveleigh himself not only worked on the Pulteney estate – he also lived and had his workshops there. He was closely involved with the building of Laura Place and had just moved his office from Laura Place to spacious workshops in what we now call Grove Street but was then known as Cheapside.

There may have been a split in the Purdie family – as will be seen, Pritchard and his wife Charlotte had decided to co-operate with Pulteney's plans, though they really had no choice. Perhaps Eliza Purdie, now Mrs Eveleigh, thought she and her husband could do better, or felt they should fight back. If they could have seen into the future, they might have reconsidered. No one realised then that early in 1793, France would declare war on Great Britain, triggering a banking crisis. In 1791, war with France, then in the throes of the revolution, seemed unlikely. George III had recovered from his latest unfortunate bout of 'madness'. The aristocracy and the wealthy were flocking to Bath in ever increasing numbers. In the summer of 1791, even the sun was shining. Bath must have seemed set for a period of unprecedented prosperity. It was surely time for a new style of pleasure garden, not to mention new lodgings for all these extra visitors. Clearly, such a venture demanded something bright and new both in architecture and in entertainment. And if Pulteney planned a

Opposite: William Johnstone Pulteney painted by Thomas Gainsborough. Though always dressed unassumingly, as he is here, Gainsborough has captured the stern gaze of a man who would be a formidable opponent.

pleasure garden on the south side of the river, why should not John Eveleigh have one on the north? One that, moreover, would be more extensive and magnificent than anything seen before – called Grosvenor Gardens.

Questions, and indeed a certain amount of astonishment, must have greeted Eveleigh's announcement of this stupendous project, for three weeks later, he placed a notice in the *Bath Chronicle*:

GROSVENOR GARDENS, VAUXHALL

It having been insinuated, that these Gardens are to be declined, it is thought necessary to inform the publick, that on Friday next will be laid the first stone of

GROSVENOR-HOUSE, VAUXHALL

In a most delectable as well as convenient situation, about half a mile from the Pump-room, bounded by the London road and river Avon. This house will be built by subscription, with every convenience as an HOTEL; containing not only a spacious ASSEMBLY or MASQUERADE ROOM, for Amusements in the Winter; but also commodious GARDENS, laid out with the utmost taste, for the reception of Company in the Summer Season.

Contiguous to the same, will be a pleasure Bath, Bowling-Green, and Accommodations for Angling; with a Grand Entrance from the River, where pleasure and Ferry Boats will ply from the different Stairs to the said Gardens,

The House and Gardens will be finished with all possible dispatch – planted next autumn – and supported in a style of unrivalled magnificence, against any opposition whatever.

For particulars, apply to EVELEIGH, architect.[1]

A week later, the foundation stone was laid, with 'the firing of cannon and a liberal treat of beer'. Beneath the stone was a sheet of lead with the inscription:

This first stone of GROSVENOR-HOUSE, VAUXHALL, was laid the 24th June 1791 by *John Eveleigh*, architect, being the Centre of 143 intended Houses, and at the entrance of Vauxhall Gardens, which will be built by Subscription, laid out with taste and elegance for the reception of Nobility, Gentry, and the publick in general.²

The report in the *Bath Chronicle* (which sounds suspiciously as though it was written by Eveleigh himself) went on to sing the praises of 'this delectable undertaking', reiterating that was was about half a mile from the Pump Room (it is actually more like a mile and a quarter) and adding that it was set 'in a vale so richly surrounded by a variety of well-clothed hills, as to form a scene of rural elegance scarcely to be equalled'. The assembly room would, the report continued, 'entertain upwards of 2000 people', and the pleasure gardens would 'be planted next Autumn, (regardless of expence or opposition) with the utmost exertions of taste and fancy'.

This was foolhardy. Not only did Eveleigh not have the money to carry out the project, and had to advertise for subscribers – what today would be called crowd-funding – but he was apparently throwing down the gauntlet. If the figure of 143 houses quoted in the report is correct, he was always going to be hopelessly overstretched. The Pulteneys maintained a dignified silence, but their architect, Thomas Baldwin, for whom Eveleigh worked as a builder,

Ranelagh Gardens in London, which stood beside the Chelsea Hospital, may have been one of Eveleigh's inspirations for Grosvenor. Its masquerades were famous – or perhaps notorious would be a better word.

must have been embarrassed. The report also boasted that 'full one third of the ground for the houses is already taken'. However, the plans included side streets. These were never built, and it would take years for the terrace to be completed. What is most interesting is that it seems to have been Eveleigh's desire to design a pleasure garden that drove this scheme.

Eveleigh and Pulteney had watched the success of Spring Gardens but realised that it was much smaller than Vauxhall Gardens in London. Both of the schemes they proposed – Sydney Gardens and Grosvenor – were closer in size to the twelve acres of Vauxhall.[3] Unlike Ranelagh Gardens, which, although much smaller than Vauxhall, had been designed as pleasure gardens, Spring Gardens had metamorphosed from a small quiet garden into a popular resort with large scale events. The obvious next step was to design a purpose-built, extensive pleasure garden – but there would never be room in Bath for two. However, Eveleigh had always been a risk-taker. He broke the rules of Palladian architecture, and he built where the ground was unstable – but somehow he always got away with it. It was the developers who were left to pick up the pieces. This time, however, through no fault of his own, his luck was going to run out.

Pritchard, now managing Spring Gardens, soon laid his cards on the table. In 1792, while Eveleigh was trying to sell houses he had built in Laura Place and Cheapside, as well as promote his project at Grosvenor, Pritchard allowed subscribers to the Sydney Gardens scheme to use Spring Gardens as their meeting place and office. When the subscribers agreed to have a wall built round the gardens, it was to Thomas Baldwin at Spring Gardens that applications were to be made. One of these subscribers was none other than Joseph Marrett, the old rival. He had lost the battle of the gardens, but this decision to put money into the Sydney Gardens project would put him back on the winning trail.

In May 1792, Eveleigh published an enticing account of the proposed facilities at Grosvenor Gardens:

> A large and commodious Hotel, Saloon, with Organ, Mechanism, and Orchestras; Hot, Green, Succession, Fruiting, and Ice Houses; Conservatories, Pinery, Fruit, Flower, and Kitchen Gardens, with Framing; Aviary, Temple with Chimes, Swimming Bath, two Bowling

Greens, Labyrinth, Merlin's Swings and Cave, Grotto, Fireworks, Cannons, Accommodation for Angling, Fish-Ponds and Bason, Ferry and Pleasure Boats, Meadow for Alderney Cows, Alcoves, Boxes, Retreats, Pleasant and Rural Walks, with lamps, &c. &c. both for Summer and Winter Amusements.[4]

Ambitious it certainly was, and it was also far-sighted. Much of it was quite new to Bath's pleasure gardens, in particular the notion of providing facilities for exercise other than walking. In addition to the Merlin, or chair, swing, there were ordinary A-frame swings. Unfortunately, while Sydney Gardens was depicted by several artists in its early years, virtually no contemporary

Above: Although this sketch by John Nixon is captioned Sydney Gardens, these are the two swings at Grosvenor, with a boat sailing past on the river in the background. They are simple A-frame swings, but clearly gave rise to a great deal of enjoyment. Bathampton Down is just visible in the background.

Left: This is roughly the site of the swings today – very overgrown

illustrations of Grosvenor Gardens survive. There are just three cartoons by John Nixon, two of which show nothing more than people sitting in the arches of the saloon.[5] The third has caused endless confusion because he wrongly labelled it 'Sydney Gardens'.[6] This is unfortunate, as it is the most interesting of the three, and shows people using the A-frame swings by the river, exactly where they are shown on Harcourt Masters map of 1800. We know it must be Grosvenor, because a boat is sailing along the river in the background. The only watercourse in Sydney Gardens was the canal, which lay in a cutting. Very faintly – the watercolour has faded – a hillside is shown in the background, and, standing on the same spot today, in the winter when the leaves are off the trees, the same hillside can be seen.

Enticing though Eveleigh's description was, less enticing was the price of subscription. For £100, each subscriber received to a ticket – in the form of a metal token – which admitted two people to the gardens.[7] That equates to over £11,000 today. This was the same price as that for Sydney Gardens, but Grosvenor was much further from the centre of town. Subscribers were invited to see the plans, which still survive in Bath Record Office. The paper upon which they are drawn is now very fragile but the drawings have survived

The Taylor and Meyler map of 1793 shows Grosvenor's delights already clearly planned out

well, along with most of the explanatory text. Unfortunately they also gave the Pulteney shareholders ideas which a map of Bath from 1793 suggests they had not previously considered for Sydney Gardens. The map shows Sydney Gardens with a formal layout, whereas the map of Grosvenor is shown with winding paths and curvaceous shrubberies around circular spaces. Eveleigh's plan was very much in the picturesque style and, with its meadow, Alderney cows and rural walks, shows a nodding acquaintance with Marie Antoinette's hamlet at Versailles. Meanwhile, Spring Gardens went on much as before. With the competition gone, it was more successful than ever, with attendances of over 2,000 at both the King's and the Prince of Wales' birthday celebrations.

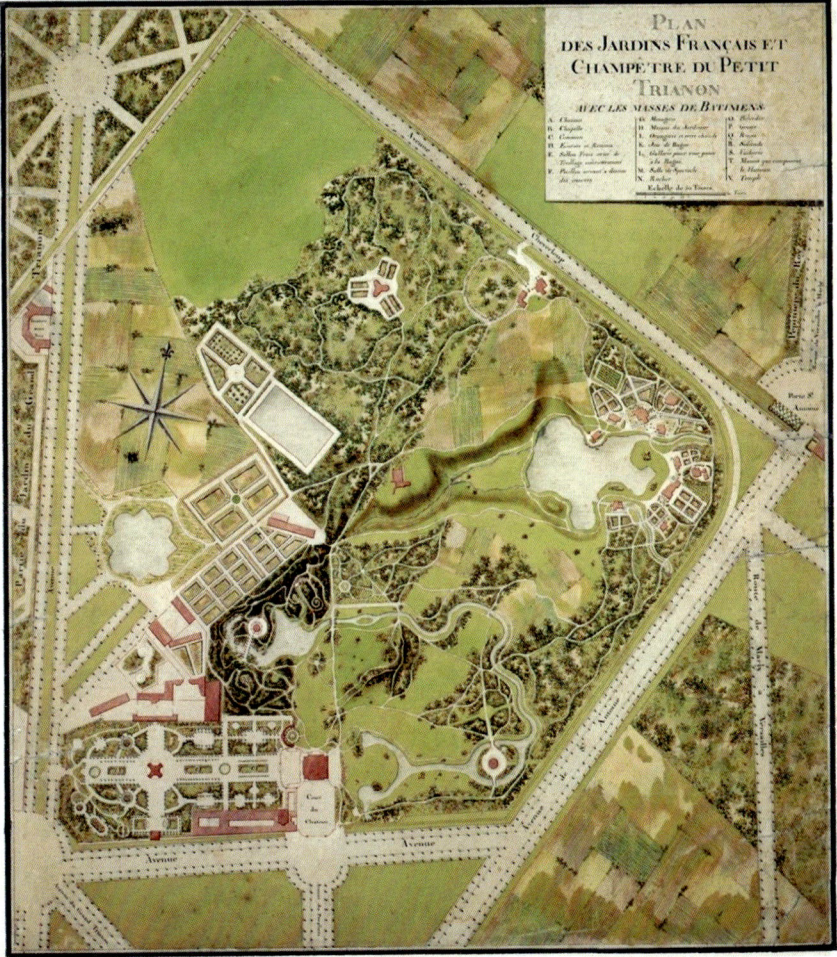

The gardens of Le Petit Trianon at Versailles, which were laid out in a naturalistic style in 1783, may have been another influence on Eveleigh. On this plan of the gardens, the winding paths at the bottom right seem to prefigure those at Grosvenor.

Sydney Gardens on Taylor and Meyler's 1793 map – a far more formal layout than that at Grosvenor. While such a design was consistent with the geometric design of the Pulteney Estate, it was already somewhat unfashionable, and, as plans for the gardens were still being formulated, they were altered to reflect the more naturalistic style espoused by Eveleigh.

Signor Invetto, now living in Frog Lane, was able to give his full attention to his fireworks. He even had a benefit evening at Spring Gardens with fireworks 'such as were never attempted before in these parts'. Spring Garden rolls, now called Sally Luns [sic] inspired someone calling himself Ensign Fun to send a strange and somewhat garbled poem to the *Bath Chronicle*:

To the incomparable Mistress of my Affections at Spring-Gardens near Bath

> In every age, and in every clime,
> The poets have chanted in good and bad rhyme
> The triumphs of LOVE and his mother;
> Complexion, eyes, lips, teeth, arms, legs, and noses,
> They painted as lilies, and glow of red roses,
> To kindle a flame hard to smother.
> Where the vertical sun emits his fierce rays,

And the soil is burnt up by continual blaze,
The beauties are black as a sloe;
Less intense, they become of a faint sable hue,
Still less by degrees, if historians say true,
Till at length they are as pallid as snow.

But justness of figure not always will prove
A trap for the heart, and incitement to love.
An elegant form strait and tall
Many hearts may ensnare, whilst a good winter piece
Many others prefer to the beauties of Greece,
In a mould fat and round as a ball.

Look around, Macaronies, this town is the test
Of the different source of true love in the breast,
From various forms, airs, and faces;
Each heart overwhelm'd by the fair, brown, or black,
Will think there's in others of beauty a lack,
Whilst *his* goddess alone has the graces.

Be these then *your* beauties, and think yourselves blest,
Whilst their eyes are implanting dire shafts in your breast,
But *I* their proud conquests defy:
The maid to my taste, can eradicate pain,
And by pressing her close, I my case soon regain,
But such as *your* love – 'tis my eye.

She's fair and she's brown, she's round and she's flat,
She is crusty and crummy, and luscious and fat
As a muffin, roll, or butter'd bun;
You may think this is fiction, and fabulous story,
But in ten minutes time she'll be smoking before ye,
And by name is y'clept SALLY LUN.[8]

Almost unnoticed, in August 1792, while Spring Gardens was enjoying some of its biggest crowds, Grosvenor Gardens opened. It appears very little was ready. The advertisement promised just tea and wines, but pleasure boats

NEW-INTENDED
VAUXHALL and RANELAGH GARDENS, NEW TOWN, BATH.

NOTICE is hereby given, that a General Meeting of the Subscribers will be held on Monday the 5th day of November, (being the first Monday in the said month) at the Spring Gardens, at 11 o'clock in the forenoon, in pursuance of a Covenant contained in the Articles of Agreement entered into by the said Subscribers.   NATH. BAYLY,

Bath, Oct. 23, 1792.   Clerk to the said Subscribers.

In 1792, advertisements for the rival schemes appeared in the *Bath Chronicle*. The first, seen above, alerted subscribers to the Sydney Gardens scheme that there would be a meeting – at Spring Gardens.

The second, seen below, described the future delights of Grosvenor Gardens. The plan which was available for inspection still survives, albeit in a very fragile state, and extracts from it feature on pages 128-29.

GROSVENOR GARDENS, VAUXHALL, AND HOTEL.

AS these delightful Gardens are already in so forward a state, that some idea may be formed of their future elegance and utility, those Ladies and Gentlemen desirous of becoming Subscribers to so promising an undertaking, on such a delectable site, are requested to send their addresses to EVELEIGH, Architect, 24, Cheapside, New-Town, Bath; in order that a Committee may be formed, and Trustees appointed, to manage this extensive concern.

The subscriptions to the above will be 100l. each, which will entitle each Subscriber to a ticket for admittance of two persons annually to these Gardens, containing near fourteen acres in fee, and consisting of a large and commodious Hotel, Saloon, with Organ, Mechanism, and Orchestras; Hot, Green, Succession, Fruiting, and Ice Houses; Conservatories, Pinery, Fruit, Flower, and Kitchen Gardens, with framing; Aviary, Temple with Chimes, Swimming Bath, two Bowling Greens, Labyrinth, Merlin's Swings and Cave, Grotto, Fireworks, Cannons, Accommodation for Angling, Fish-Ponds and Bason, Ferry and Pleasure Boats, Meadow for Alderney Cows, Alcoves, Boxes, Retreats, Pleasant and Rural Walks, with lamps, &c. &c. both for Summer and Winter Amusements.

Each intended Subscriber will be attended with the plan and particulars, and due notice sent of the time and place of meeting.

N. B. Each share will be transferable.   [8259

were already plying from a wharf at Cheapside, where Grove Street stands today. As the advertisement made clear, the opening was more by way of a viewing for potential subscribers, who were informed that 'these delightful gardens are already in so forward a state that some idea may be formed of their future elegance and utility'.[9]

However, a report in the *Bath Herald* was more up-beat:

> The annals of horticulture cannot produce an instance of so rapid a change from a common grass field to a luxuriant, highly cultivated spot, as is now displayed in Grosvenor Gardens. It is scarcely one year since the plan was first proposed, and in that time a row of elegant buildings has been erected; a complete garden has been made:– spacious walks well gravelled have been formed, and the whole of a plan so admirably projected, brought to such a state of forwardness, as to claim the admiration and wonder of the numerous companies who daily frequent it. Nothing but the greatest success can attend exertions so deserving the public patronage.[10]

When 1793 dawned, none of the subscribers to the competing gardens could have guessed what a calamity was awaiting the schemes. On 1 February, France declared on war on Great Britain. There was a run on the banks. Many provincial banks operated within very tight margins, and in Bath they had been loaning large sums to builders like Baldwin and Eveleigh, in the belief that the building boom would continue. The finances of such banks were always precarious, only secure if everything was going well. In the financial climate of 1793, they were simply unsustainable. First to go down in March was the Bath City Bank, which was holding the funds of the Sydney Gardens project. Fortunately for the subscribers, only the first payment had been deposited at the bank. Shortly afterwards, the Bath and Somersetshire Bank also went under. This was a disaster for both Baldwin and Eveleigh. Both struggled on bravely, however, with Grosvenor Gardens opening in May, and offering breakfasts as well as inviting subscriptions for walking, angling or bowling.

One high point of Spring Gardens' 1793 season came in June, when a Mr McDonnell performed a variety of the 'most admired' Scots and Irish music on the Irish pipes. His performance was divided into six acts, with four pieces

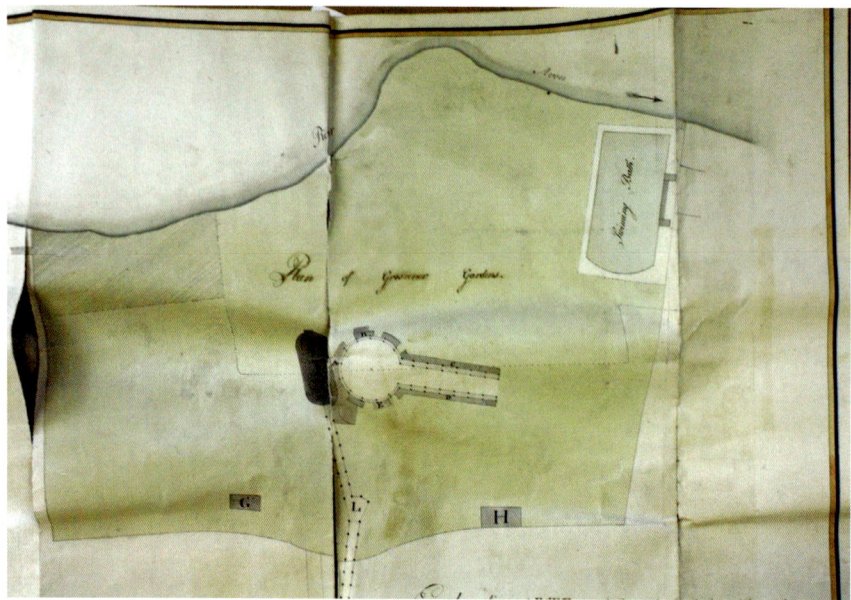

Eveleigh's plan of Grosvenor Gardens, oriented with south at the top, showing the circle of boxes, the saloon, and the bathing pool, which came complete with dressing rooms. G is a greenhouse and H a hothouse. L is a covered way from the hotel to the saloon, showing that Eveleigh had considered how the facilities could still be used in poor weather.

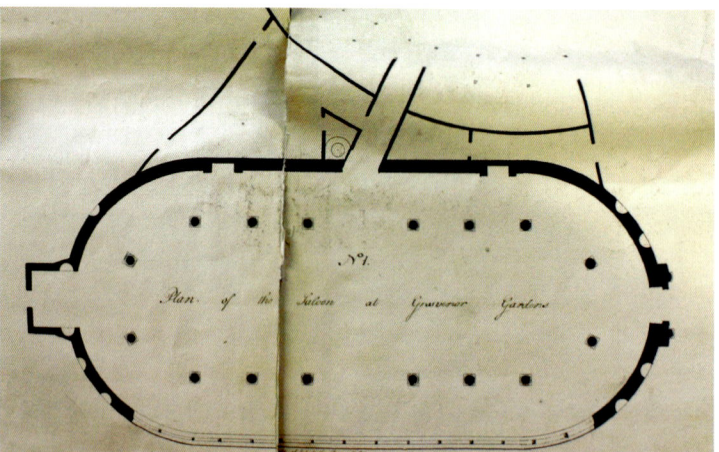

The plan of the saloon, showing another covered way leading out into the arena of dinner boxes. The area for fireworks was behind the saloon, so that spectators could watch in safety through the large windows. There was even a public convenience. Eveleigh was proud of his ability to supply patent water closets which could be installed anywhere 'without the least effluvia'.

BOLD IDEAS AND BROKEN DREAMS 129

Eveleigh's drawings of the elevations of the saloon, demonstrating his attention to detail. Noteworthy features include an ornamental fireplace, a musicians' gallery and the roof structure.

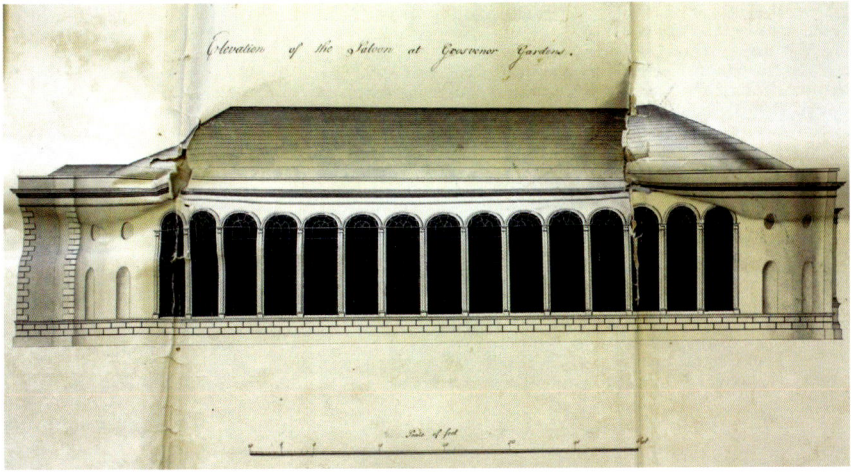

in each act. He was also prepared to play, between the acts, any favourite tune that may be desired by the company. This sounds to modern ears very much like an excess of pipe music, and perhaps the management of Spring Gardens had their doubts too, for they added that, after this, 'proper music will attend on the ladies and gentlemen who chuse to dance'. The following week, the company was perhaps relieved to hear that Signor Invetto would be putting on one of his superb firework displays.

In the midst of all this financial uncertainty, John Jelly of Elm Bank, attorney, and son of the architect and builder Thomas Jelly, decided to open a new horticultural venture, called Walcot Botanic Gardens. In September 1793, he announced in the *Bath Chronicle* that he proposed to open to the public a botanic garden in a nursery formerly run by a Mr Jones.[11] He revealed that, as the 'study of Botany has from childhood been the amusement of my leisure hours', he had built up 'a very large and expensive collection of plants, exceeded by very few in the kingdom'. Not only did he want to share it with the public, he thought it would be a worthwhile addition to the amusements of Bath. Small though it was, in some ways it was a return to the idea of a garden as a quiet retreat.

The advertisement also laid out the terms of subscription. An annual subscription would cost half a guinea, and allow the subscriber to walk in the gardens, inspect the plants, and also 'have use of a room and books', by which one assumes Jelly meant they could look at his library of botanical books and make notes. However, those who paid one guinea would also receive roots and

John Jelly advertises his new venture – the Walcot Botanic Garden

BOLD IDEAS AND BROKEN DREAMS 131

One of the tokens which admitted visitors to the Botanic Gardens

seeds, while really keen horticulturalists who wanted to chat to the gardener, James Eyles, had to pay two guineas. It seems odd that someone should be charged extra for being as enthusiastic as the owner, but, as the Bagatelle had demonstrated with its glasses of water, nothing came for nothing in Georgian Bath.

Like the proprietors of Grosvenor and Sydney Gardens, Jelly issued tickets in the form of tokens. The tokens for Walcot Botanic Gardens were very elaborate, and included a quotation from I Kings 4:33. On one side was depicted a gate in a wall with the phrase, 'He Spake Of Trees, From The Cedar Tree That Is Lebanon'. On the other the quotation continued, 'Even Unto The Hyssop That Springeth

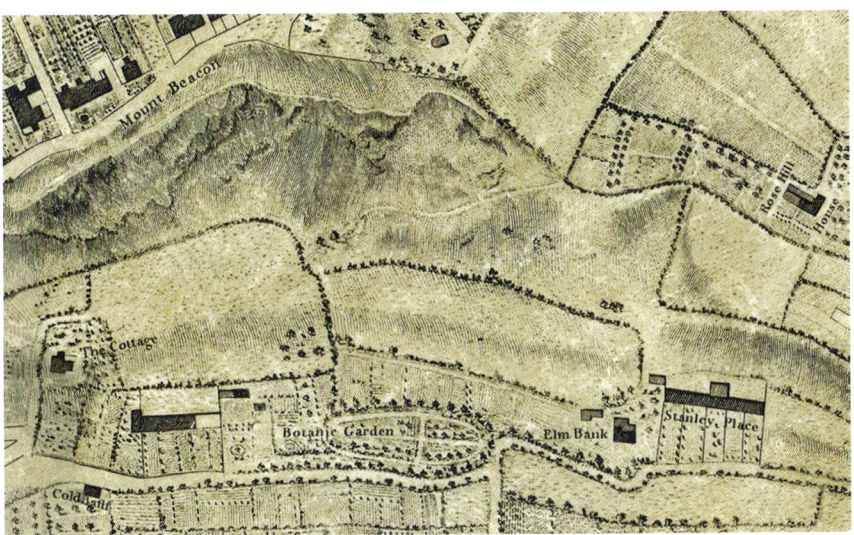

The Botanic Garden on Harcourt Masters' map of 1800. Today, the road below it is known as Camden Road, and Coburg Villas stand on the site of Elm Bank. The garden itself lies under the gardens of Prospect Place and the realigned Camden Road.

Out Of The Wall', and was accompanied by a depiction of a cedar tree and a romantic ruin with plants, presumably including hyssop, growing out of it.

For the large schemes on the Pulteney estate and at Grosvenor, meanwhile, the storm clouds were gathering. Even so, there was still optimism at Sydney Gardens in September, when the first tree was planted, cannons were fired from Spring Gardens and the customary barrel of strong beer was dispensed among the spectators.[12] In October, however, Baldwin was declared bankrupt, and his former pupil, Charles Harcourt Masters, was appointed as architect to Sydney Gardens in his place.[13]

The following month, the inevitable happened, and Eveleigh too was declared bankrupt.[14] The mortgagees of the Grosvenor project foreclosed on him and prepared to offer it for sale by auction. Lot 1 included the gardens, along with No 23 – described as 'the centre house of a certain pile of buildings, called GROSVENOR PLACE' – and its neighbour, No 24. The description

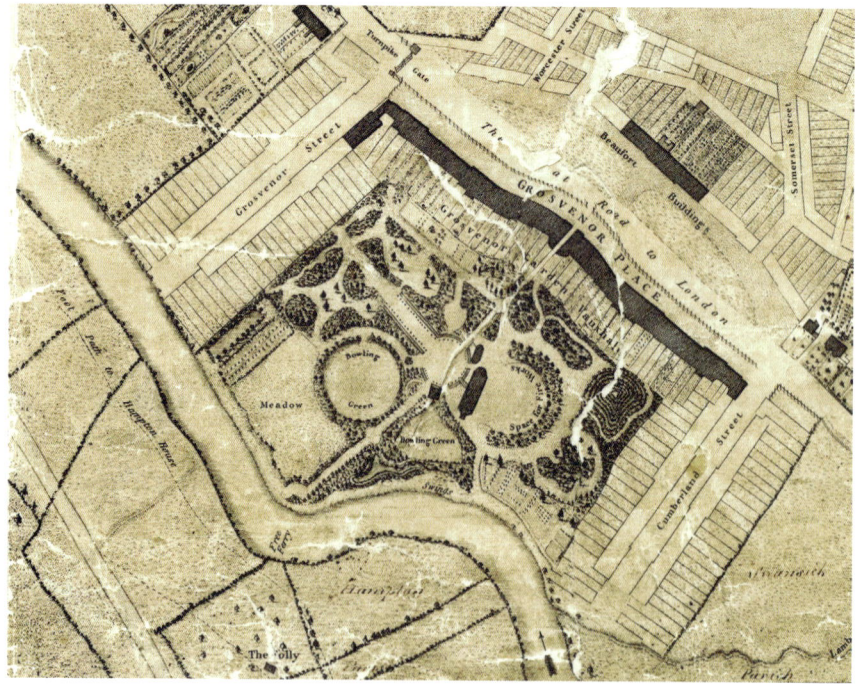

Grosvenor Gardens on Harcourt Masters' map of 1800, showing the planned side streets which were never built. All the facilities – bowling greens, swings, free ferry and 'space for fireworks' – are clearly marked.

of what was on offer is revealing, because it indicates what was built and what was not at this stage.[15]

No 23, which formed the entrance to the gardens, was described as having been 'intended for a TAVERN or HOTEL'. The saloon was similarly described as being 'intended for a banqueting house' – suggesting it had not been fitted out. The gardens had largely been laid out, but the pleasure bath was not yet built, and other 'ornamental improvements' were also described as 'intended'. The auction notice added, however, that the gardens had been much resorted to, and the walk from Laura Place beside the River Avon was a pleasant one. As we have already seen, there was no Advertising Standards Authority to oversee the truth or otherwise of what was published.

Seven more houses were offered for sale as individual lots – Nos 19-22 to the west and Nos 25-27 to the east. Like Nos 23 and 24, they were 'now building', being 'nearly covered in' and having 'commodious outlets'. If we look at the façade of the central house, we can see that, despite having been occupied for over 200 years, it has never been properly finished. Eveleigh's aim was to make it unlike anything Bath had seen before, throwing the architectural rule book out of the window to achieve the effect he wanted. The result is – or should have been – a sparkling, joyous piece of architectural exuberance appropriate for a grand entrance to pleasure gardens. The gardens were intended to be fun – a place of relaxation, titillation, excitement, entertainment, alfresco dining, swinging and swimming. This sense of fun is expressed in the curvaceous façade of the central houses, which was intended to include paterae featuring carv-

The grand entrance to Grosvenor Gardens

ings of birds and animals, with floral garlands around the pillars. Some carvings were finished, but several paterae remain blank, and the lowest set of garlands was never completed.

Eveleigh's collaborators in the scheme, the brothers William and John Townsend, silversmiths, and Richard Hewlett, carpenter, decided to try to rescue the scheme. In May 1794, the gardens finally opened properly, under the management of John Townsend. There was, however, still much to be done. In June 1794, an appeal for subscribers stated that the saloon was only partly finished and many of the other features, such as the hothouse, pleasure bath and archery ground were

only just begun. Eveleigh had spent over £7,000 on the development. The new proprietors and mortgagees had acquired it for £5,500, but estimated that a further £5,000 was needed.[16] All in all, the project would have cost, in modern terms, over £1,220,000. However, the gardens were staging lavish events, such as fireworks by Signor Invetto in July, even though he was also still working for Spring Gardens.

The proprietors of Grosvenor knew they had to get their act together fast. The Sydney Gardens scheme was progressing well, although the side buildings which Baldwin had designed as elegant exits from the garden were abandoned. This worked in the shareholders' favour, for, unlike Grosvenor, they were not

BOLD IDEAS AND BROKEN DREAMS   135

Left: The seven columns on Eveleigh's façade, breaking the strict Palladian rule that columns had to be grouped in even numbers. It can be seen that the lowest set of garlands were never carved.

Top right: Two of the three carved paterae, alongside two of the unfinished ones. Whatever was intended to appear to the right of the lion, room has been left for it to overhang the edge of the oval.

Centre right: The lion

Bottom right: One of the elaborate, garlanded Ionic columns. Whoever the stonemason was, he was a master of his craft.

Below: The unique curvaceous façade

A charmingly illustrated advertisement for fireworks at Grosvenor Gardens. Although Invetto's name is not mentioned, the event must feature one of his naval battle set pieces.

saddled with half-built houses to finish and sell.

In April 1795, Sydney Gardens opened for walking only, but was planned to be ready for the entertainment of the public by the beginning of May.[17] Since the shareholders were only now advertising for someone to take on the gardens until Christmas, this was an ambitious target, but, as we shall see in Part Three, there was somebody ready and waiting. As with Grosvenor Gardens, there still remained work to be done, and it would have been better to wait a year. However, the subscribers probably felt that, despite all the financial difficulties both schemes had experienced, they did not want to let Grosvenor Gardens become too established. Initially, however, Grosvenor felt little effect from the opening of Sydney Gardens. Townsend had left to take over Spring Gardens, so Grosvenor had a new manager, William Hewlett, a carpenter and brother of Richard Hewlett. One has a sense that William had drawn the short straw. When he announced in May that he had taken the gardens, he added that he wished to acquaint his friends that he continued in business as a carpenter, and would pay the utmost attention to orders.

Financial troubles did not just affect the major players. In February 1795, John Jelly, owner of Walcot Botanic Gardens, was declared bankrupt.[18] His house – that 'new-built, valuable and desirable messuage' with its hothouse and garden 'elegantly laid out' – was auctioned off, along with all his household furniture, fine prints, books, and plate. Even his harpsichord by Kirkman, one of the country's top makers, went under the hammer. The notice added that the moveable frames and stock of the botanic garden were to be sold immediately.[19] The evidence suggests that the garden was bought by Robert Jones, its original owner. In June 1796, an advertisement for the auction of a house on Beacon Hill advised those wishing to view the property to apply to Robert Jones at the Botanic Gardens, Beacon Hill. However, he did not advertise the gardens, and in the directory for 1800, he is described as nursery man and seedsman, so it seems that it reverted to what today we would call a garden centre.

Nevertheless, the parlous state of the economy did not deter another small entrepreneur from opening a pleasure garden. In July 1795, Peter Vivier, a French confectioner from Lodève in Hérault, who ran a shop in Brock Street, announced that he was opening a Glaciere Garden on the slopes of Lansdown, near Sion Hill.[20] This was, in effect, an outdoor ice-cream parlour, where, on payment of sixpence, or an annual subscription of one guinea, subscribers could walk in the garden and enjoy strawberries and cream, or ices. The following June, he placed an advertisement in the *Bath Chronicle* thanking 'the Nobility, Gentry, and Publick, for the ... favours he was honoured with at the Glaciere last summer'. 'Refreshments', he added, were 'kept constantly ready, made with the very best materials, in particular ICES of various kinds prepared on the spot by himself', and, by booking in advance, 'parties may be accommodate with Breakfast and Afternoon Tea'. The advertisement

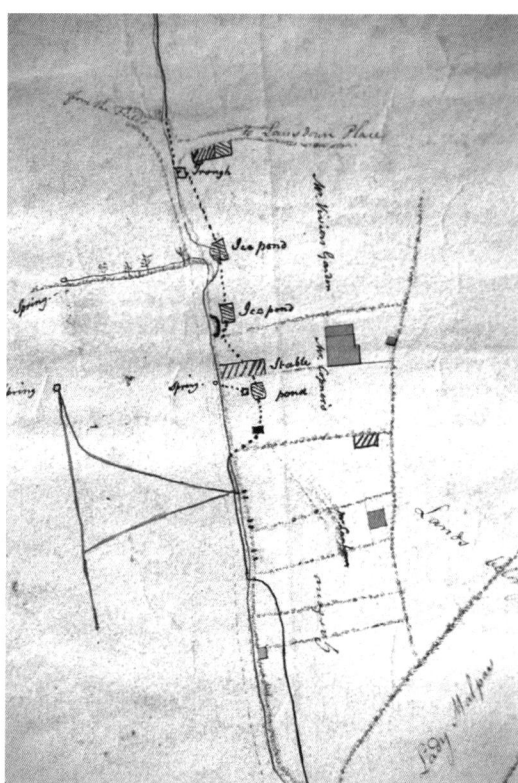

This plan of springs in what is now the Cavendish Road area of Bath dates from about 1790. High Common is on the left, with the site of the future Cavendish Place and Cavendish Crescent on the right. Vivier's Garden can be seen towards the top, just below the turning to Lansdown Place – now known as Lansdown Crescent.

concluded, however, on an ominous note, offering the Glaciere 'to be let for a Publick Garden'.[21] And that is the last we hear of it. Vivier died in 1803, and although his widow continued the confectionery business at the shop, there were no more attempts to revive it as a pleasure garden.[22]

With Sydney Gardens open, and building work in Great Pulteney Street progressing, albeit slowly, both Grosvenor Gardens and Spring Gardens were feeling the pinch. Spring Gardens went first. If Townsend thought he would be more secure at Spring Gardens, he erred. The astute Meshach Pritchard had left while the going was good. However, Townsend put considerable effort into providing entertainment. There had been a resurgence of interest in bowling – both Grosvenor and Sydney Gardens boasted two greens and there was another in the grounds of the Lower Rooms, which were now known as Mr Heaven's Walks. So in 1795 Townsend laid out a 'complete bowling green'.[23] It was completed by August, in time for the annual Prince of Wales' birthday celebrations, when Invetto's fireworks were promised to be 'particularly novel and magnificent'.

However, by August 1798, maps show that Johnstone Street had come right to the northern edge of Spring Gardens, and Townsend announced he was quitting.[24] Although he went out literally with a bang, presenting a 'Grand Gala Night with Illuminations and a Brilliant Display of Fire-works by the Ingenious Signor Invetto', the *Bath Chronicle* did even not bother to report the gardens' passing. On December 17, all the contents were sold, including mahogany tables and chairs, a large chandelier, paintings, and the lamps and transparencies for the illuminations.[25] Townsend himself went on to run a large inn in the Market Place called the Greyhound & Shakespeare. By 1800, the architect

Harcourt Masters' 1800 map shows the Pulteney estate encroaching on the former Spring Gardens. On the other side of the river, the former Harrison's Walks remained untouched by the changes in Bath's fortunes.

John Pinch had set up a yard and office in the former gardens.[26] In 1811, when the site was eventually put up for sale, it was described as

> all that substantial and convenient MESSUAGE, BUILDINGS, YARD, and PREMISES, being part of SPRING-GARDENS in the parish of Bathwick, and adjoining the river Avon; erected by, and for many years in the possession of, Mr John Pinch, architect, And also, a large and convenient YARD and PREMISES adjoining, now used as a timber-yard, and in possession of Mr Wm Watkins.[27]

It was a sad end for a garden which had given so much pleasure for over sixty years.

Grosvenor Gardens, meanwhile, was still hanging on desperately. By August 1796, the members of the rescue team were themselves declared

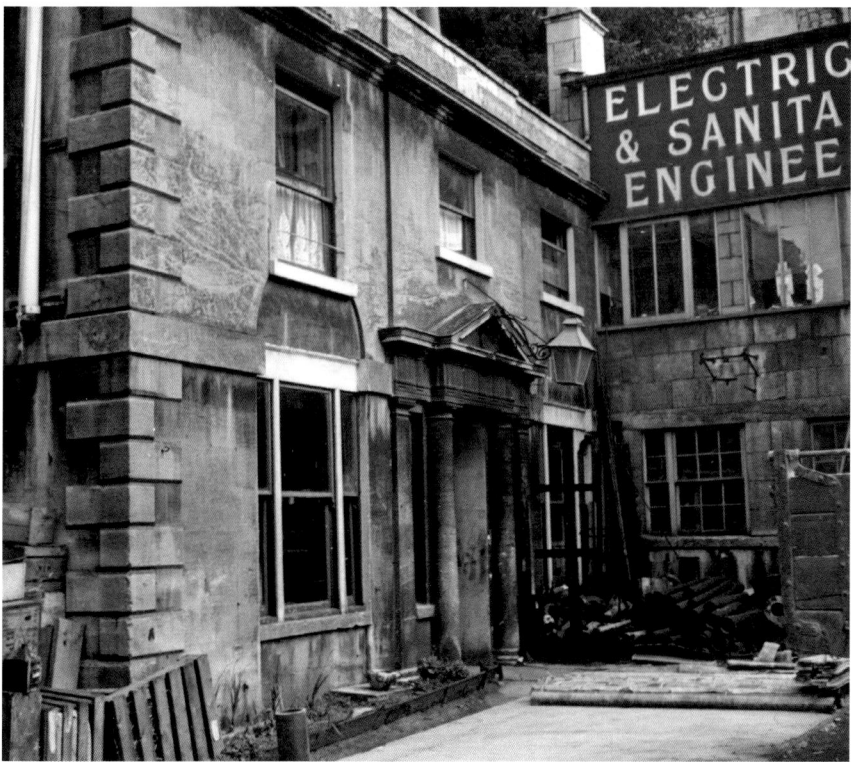

Spring Gardens House, built as offices by John Pinch on the site of Spring Gardens. Demolished around 1970, the Beazer Maze now covers the area.

GROSVENOR
Gardens Vauxhall.

On TUESDAY Evening next, August the 1st, 1797,
THESE GARDENS WILL BE OPENED

WITH A

Brilliant Illumination,

AND A

CONCERT

OF

VOCAL AND INSTRUMENTAL MUSIC

PRINCIPAL VOCAL PERFORMERS,

Messrs. Brown, Stanton, and Miss Bloomfield.

ACT I.	ACT II.
OVERTURE.	OVERTURE.
SONG, *(When Night and left upon my Guard)* Mr. STANTON.	SONG, Mr. STANTON.
Favorite SONG, Miss BLOOMFIELD.	COMIC SONG, Mr. BROWN.
COMIC SONG, Mr. BROWN.	SONG, Miss BLOOMFIELD.
SCOTCH SONG, Miss BLOOMFIELD.	COMIC SONG, *(the Tinker)* Mr. BROWN.
SONG, Mr. BROWN.	
OVERTURE.	OVERTURE—FINALE.

THE CONCERT TO BEGIN AT SEVEN O'CLOCK.

Tickets ONE SHILLING each,

To be had at the Bar of the Garden, which entitles the Bearer to Six-pence in Liquor.

COLD HAM, TONGUE, &c. IN SMALL QUANTITIES.

☞ The Labyrinth with Chair Swing is in good Order.——A Boat attends to convey Persons across the Ferry to the Garden *(gratis)*.

Gye, Printer and Bookseller, Market-Place, Bath.

The playbill for a concert at Grosvenor Gardens in 1797

bankrupt, and the proprietors advertised the gardens to let.[28] Early in 1797, Mr E Davis took it on, and laid out 'delightful and extensive' pleasure gardens.[29] The labyrinth was certainly planted by this time, for a poster for a concert in August 1797 included the information that 'the labyrinth with chair swing is in good order'. A free ferry was laid on to carry people across to the gardens, and those using it were 'requested not to give any gratuity to the person who has care of the boat'. Pleasure boats were 'provided for those who prefer going up by water, from the slip at Grove Street, near Laura Place'.

Davis was determined to make the gardens work, and put on several large events in 1797 and 1798. However, it seems that wild swimmers were something of a problem, for an advertisement for a grand gala night included this stern message:

> If any persons are seen bathing in the river near the Gardens, and shall behave themselves indecently in future, their clothes will be seized, and means taken to prosecute them for the offence.[30]

In May 1799, Davis brought in another Italian firework maker from Vauxhall, Signor Benelli.[31] Eveleigh had designed an area specifically for firework displays, and in July Invetto staged a display there whose centrepiece sounded very like his ever-popular sea battle between two ships, although this time it was meant to represent part of the Battle of the Nile.[32] With the saloon now in operation, concerts could be held indoors as well as outside. However, Davis also advertised part of the gardens to let, describing them as spacious and elegantly planted and suitable for use by nurserymen and gardeners.[33]

In June 1800, Signor Invetto hired the gardens to stage a benefit.[34] A week earlier, Invetto had also staged a display at a grand concert for the benefit of a musician called Thomas Shell.[35] This was the former Master Shell, who had performed at Spring Gardens and Villa Gardens. Even though he could not have been very old, a year later, Grosvenor Gardens held a benefit for his widow, at which his six-year-old son, also called Thomas, performed.[36] That same summer, Invetto held another benefit there, when he had to admit that he had suffered great losses and sickness for the last three years.[37] Despite all his hard work, he had not been able to 'gain half a subsistence by his business'. Life had certainly been cruel to him. He had lost his first wife in a terrible accident, and his second left him two years after they were married for a German jobbing painter. She also stole several of his shirts, six silver teaspoons, some money, and her child's bed-gown.[38] This child must have been their daughter, Sarah Mary, named after Invetto's first and second wives, who died in 1794. Mary Invetto must, however, have returned, for they had a son in 1799, and Mary was working with Invetto at the time of his death. But it seems sad that, after providing exciting entertainment for so many people for years, all his hard work was not enough to maintain a living wage in what were probably very hard times for everyone.

By this time, Grosvenor Gardens had changed hands yet again, and were being run by W and J Barrett.[39] They tried patriotic events, such as one for Nelson – who had lived in Bath for a time – to celebrate his return from the Battle of Copenhagen.[40] The performance was in the 'spacious saloon' which was advertised as being 'dry under foot'. This is a curious remark, and leaves one wondering how well laid the floor was. However, that November nurserymen and seedsmen were once again invited to take over the lease.[41] This time it was the whole of the gardens – 'variously planted with trees and shrubs, but having much room for cultivation' – which was on offer. It was suggested that anyone taking them on could charge for walking around the

An early twentieth-century postcard showing Kensington Meadows and Grosvenor Gardens flooded to allow skating in winter

gardens and keep open 'the Coffee House' – a building which curiously does not seem to have been mentioned before. There were, however, no takers.

Despite all its advantages – and Grosvenor did have advantages over Sydney Gardens, not least its saloon – it was defeated by being too far from the city centre and too close to the river. The mist often rises up from the Avon, and the Georgians were very suspicious of what they called 'the damps'. The gardens were low-lying, and in times of heavy rain they flooded. They were so prone to flooding that, during the late nineteenth and early twentieth centuries, Kensington Meadows and the site of Grosvenor Gardens were deliberately flooded in winter so that people could skate on them.

In 1803, several of the houses in Grosvenor Place were put up for sale, as well as 96 shares in what was described as 'that large divided property, Grosvenor Garden'.[42] It marked the end for Grosvenor Gardens' career as a pleasure garden. Later it became the nurseries and market gardens that the desperate shareholders had ultimately hoped for. Only one arch of the saloon remained standing, like some relic of an ancient civilisation. With the demise of Grosvenor, Sydney Gardens was the only pleasure garden left in Bath.

Eventually, as this sale notice shows, the collapse of the Grosvenor development was complete, as Richard Hewlett and his collaborators also went bankrupt

All that remained of the saloon by the twentieth century was this impressive arch – the doorway at the northern end

III

THE PROUDEST BOAST OF THIS EMPORIUM OF FASHION

THE STORY OF SYDNEY GARDENS

To those occasional visitors of Bath, who may be unacquainted with the localities of this elegant City, it may be necessary to state, that the eastern extremity of Great Pulteney-Street – a street the most spacious and magnificent perhaps in the world, certainly unequalled for the respectability and opulence of its inhabitants - is terminated by a grand Hotel, through the centre of which a spacious corridor opens to these extensive pleasure grounds – the proudest boast of this emporium of fashion, occupying an area of sixteen acres, which were originally laid out by Mr HARCOURT, and first opened to the public in 1795.

John Kerr, 1825

1

FIRST IMPRESSIONS

The Happy Accidents of the Swing

In December 1794, John Gale, who ran a hatter's, hosiery and haberdashery business at 3 Wade's Passage, announced to the public that he was selling up and quitting Bath.[1] However, in April 1795, after the proprietors of Sydney Gardens had advertised for 'persons desirous of taking the said Garden until Christmas next', he announced that he was selling, 'considerably under prime cost, the remaining part of the stock of Hats, Hosiery, Gloves, Black Lace, &c ... having taken Sidney-Gardens, Vauxhall'.[2] He may have thought that, as the lease was so short, it would give him chance to decide whether he should stay in Bath or not. Even so, he announced his arrival in grand style, declaring in early May that the gardens were 'now opened for breakfasting and afternoon tea, wine, &c', and stating his determination to conduct the business 'with the utmost Spirit and Liberality, by procuring every article of accommodation of the very best quality'.[3] He also expressed the hope, 'from the high encomiums already passed on the superior style in which this Garden is designed, that its visitants (and particularly Subscribers) will be so numerous, as to render the Refreshment not only in quality, but also in quantity, equal, if not superior to all other places of publick entertainment'.

Following Grosvenor's lead, a Merlin swing was intended but was not yet ready, although Gale promised it would be available by June. Two ordinary

Opposite: The Happy Accidents of the Swing, as painted by Fragonard. Note the young man gazing up enraptured – but what is he gazing at? And what of the man in the shadows, who is literally pulling the strings?

swings were already in place, but Gale stipulated that they could only be used on Sundays after 5.30 pm. Three weeks later, he decided on a total ban, announcing sternly:

> No swinging can be permitted on Sundays.[4]

This had nothing to do with irreligious exercise and everything to do with the development of women's underwear. Women did not wear drawers of any kind until the late Regency period, and it was not until late in the nineteenth century that knickers were joined up at the crotch. Fragonard's famous painting of a young lady on a swing, kicking her legs joyfully in the air, is usually known in Britain as *The Swing* but its real name is *Les hasards heureux de l'escarpolette* – 'The Happy Accidents of the Swing'. If you look at the picture carefully you will notice that it is not her face that the young man is admiring. Clearly this sort of thing could not be allowed on Sundays. Gale also stipulated that servants in livery would not be admitted, so that fashionable visitors could enjoy themselves without worrying that their servants might be spying on them. Many a servant had appeared as a witness in divorce cases.

Bath was used to pleasure gardens, but could the newly opened Sydney Gardens impress visitors? We are fortunate in having some first impressions, even though some of the authors chose to express them in poetry rather than prose. The first was published in the *Bath Chronicle* on 27 August 1795, and is in the form of a letter followed by a poem. As so often with newspapers at that time, it was anonymous, the writer using the pseudonym Palæmon:

> Though for these twelve-months I had heard much of Sydney-Gardens from persons in some taste, and from persons of no taste at all; yet I could not be prevailed on to walk even the length of Pulteney-street, to visit a place, which, within these two years, I remembered a mere barren uncultivated spot; such as, I imagine, the Esquilian [sic] Hill at Rome was, before Mecenas [sic] built a palace there, and made extensive gardens.
>
> I was last week however dragged to Sydney-Gardens by a very worthy friend; a man of good sense; yet whose *taste*, in this instance, I was disposed to question: – But I have seldom been more agreeably surprised than I now was, on entering the circular area; and on being

led from thence through the different walks and to the numerous seats and points of view; the variety, beauty, and commodiousness of which, in so small a spot of ground, is astonishing. The whole indeed is so artfully contrived, as to give it a very extensive appearance, and the particular objects are disposed and executed with so good a taste as to make it at least *equal* to anything of the kind about Bath. Nay, the rising ground and elevation of some part of it, and the beautiful prospects which that affords, give it a *superiority* to most of them.

The trees and shrubs have made surprising shoots in so small a time; and the foliage is so luxuriant, as to afford ample shade for ornament and use.

The principal pavilion on the brow of the hill is supported by Ionic columns of beautiful free-stone, and would do no discredit to Wilton or Stourhead, or any Nobleman's seat in the three kingdoms.

The ruin was in the form of a castle. This impression of it dates from about 30 years after the opening, when its newness had been masked by ivy and trees.

In short, the easy and agreeable approach to and from Pulteney-street, will, I doubt not, make it the constant resort, not only of gay parties in an evening, but of the studious and contemplative, and persons of leisure, in a morning, or for breakfast parties, or for a retired walk.

The water is prettily managed; and the ruin, though on a small scale, is proportioned to the place, – and when the rough stones are grown mossy by time, will have a very romantic and picturesque appearance.

On SYDNEY-GARDENS

> Would you enjoy fine views and breathe pure air,
> To Sydney slopes each morn and eve repair:
> Whate'er your taste, for prospects or good cheer,
> Cascades, or rural walks, you'll find them here.

> Whether you'd muse alone, be tête à tête
> With some fair nymph, you'll find a snug retreat.
> Ye gayer parties! Who'd have others see
> How *happy* and how frolic you can be;
> In open boxes brave the public eye,
> And laugh and romp, and saucy man defy!
> But if to matrimony you aspire,
> Ascend the swing, some amorous youth you'll fire:
> Shewn to advantage thus, your heighten'd charms
> Will surely tempt some Lover to your arms.
>
>   Ye Critics! If some faults you chance to find,
> Pray point them out, we'll take it vastly kind.
> But, let these scenes your wives and daughters view,
> Who, in this case, can judge as well as you.
> And, if *they* are not *charm'd* with Sydney-Garden,
> We'll give them back their money – every far'din.

This account suggests that giving Sydney Gardens time to develop before opening was worth it. Even to this observer, who was preparing to be disappointed, the plants were well-established and tall enough to provide shade. The pavilion at the top was complete, as were the sheltered seats. The water he refers to was an artificial rill, which ran down from a spring on the northern side of the gardens, creating little cascades. The ruin was in the form of a ruined castle, with a moat in front of it, supplied by water from a spring, and was often used as the venue for fireworks.[5] The poem invites a young lady to attract some amorous youth by ascending one of the swings – but not, of course, on Sundays.

A year later, another poem appeared in the *Bath Chronicle*.[6] Although light-hearted, it contained much interesting information, as did the footnotes, which were added by the Editor.

> Written in SIDNEY GARDENS
> SIDNEY! * thou boastedst that Arcadian plains
> Glow'd erst with maidens fair and artless swains,
> Who in sweet innocence were wont to rove,
> Enjoying nature's laws and pastoral love;

FIRST IMPRESSIONS   151

We do not know what the ordinary swings at the top of the gardens were like. Possibly they were simple A-frame swings, like those at Grosvenor, but there are other possibilities.

The painting by Watteau, on the left, depicts a simple swing suspended from two trees, with a young lady being pushed by her energetic swain.

The French print below, from the early nineteenth century, shows a young lady on a similar swing but ensconced in a comfortable chair.

At morn and eve they tripp'd the verdant mead
In simple figures to the oaten reed;
Rose with the lark, and when the setting sun
Proclaim'd approaching night, *their* day was done.
    Our Sidney spurns such silly rites as these,
But gives delights of richer zest to please;
We know no periods of the days we spend,
To *us* alike – the dawn, noon, eve, and end:
Ingenious Fashion rules throughout the whole,
Deceives the sense, and captivates the soul.
Here in the broiling sun we swallow tea,
Charm'd with the tweedledum and tweedledee; †
Cram down the muffin, and the butter'd bun,
And that eccentrick‡ dainty – *Sally Lun*;
Then take a puzzle in the verdant maze, §
Turning and twisting many different ways,
But with some fair one, form'd to make a wife,
Wish ourselves Hymen-rivetted for life.
    Arrah! By J-sus, cries a *Honey dear*,
How our *swate craters* grace this motley sphere –
They dance II, they sing, they play – ah, how they play!
And *chate* the long and tedious hours away.
BATH! whilst such raptures they amusements bring,
I'll bid adieu to care and *have my swing!* ¶

  * *Sir Philip Sidney who wrote the Arcadia*
  † *Horns and Clarionets*
  ‡ *Not made in the city, and to be met nowhere else*
  § *At present dry wattled hedges, but quick-growing plants and shrubs creeping up them*
  II *Many of the Irish ladies singularly accomplished in these elegant arts*
  ¶ *Merlin and other swings suspended for grown gentlemen and ladies*
  ☞ *The author supposes the proprietor's name Sidney.*

Thanks to the poet and the editor, we know what they had to eat while listening to horns and 'clarionets'. 'Sally Luns' were served here too, along with muffins

FIRST IMPRESSIONS 153

One likely candidate for the type of swings in Sydney Gardens is seen here in another French print from the 1770s, entitled La balançoire à Rambouillet. It certainly shows the young lady off to advantage.

and buttered buns, much as they had been at Spring Gardens, and from the description, it seems the rolls were made on site. The labyrinth was constructed of wattled hedges which had fast growing plants climbing up them while they were becoming established. Despite still being at an early stage of its development, it was seen as a romantic meeting place. And once again, the last word is reserved for the swings.

What neither account mentions is the hotel – the building that is now the Holburne Museum. The final design for it was still being decided late in 1794 and the foundation stone was not laid until November 1796. The first we hear of it being open is on 18 October 1798, when the gardens were advertised to be let, 'together with the elegant new-built tavern'.[7] It was not known as a tavern for long; when accommodation started to be provided it became known as an hotel. But, whatever it was known as, its opening marked the beginning of an extraordinary story, as Bath's grandest pleasure gardens went on to dazzle and delight visitors and residents alike throughout the Regency period and on into the reign of Victoria. Before tracing that story, however, we should take a closer look at what the gardens were like in their formative years.

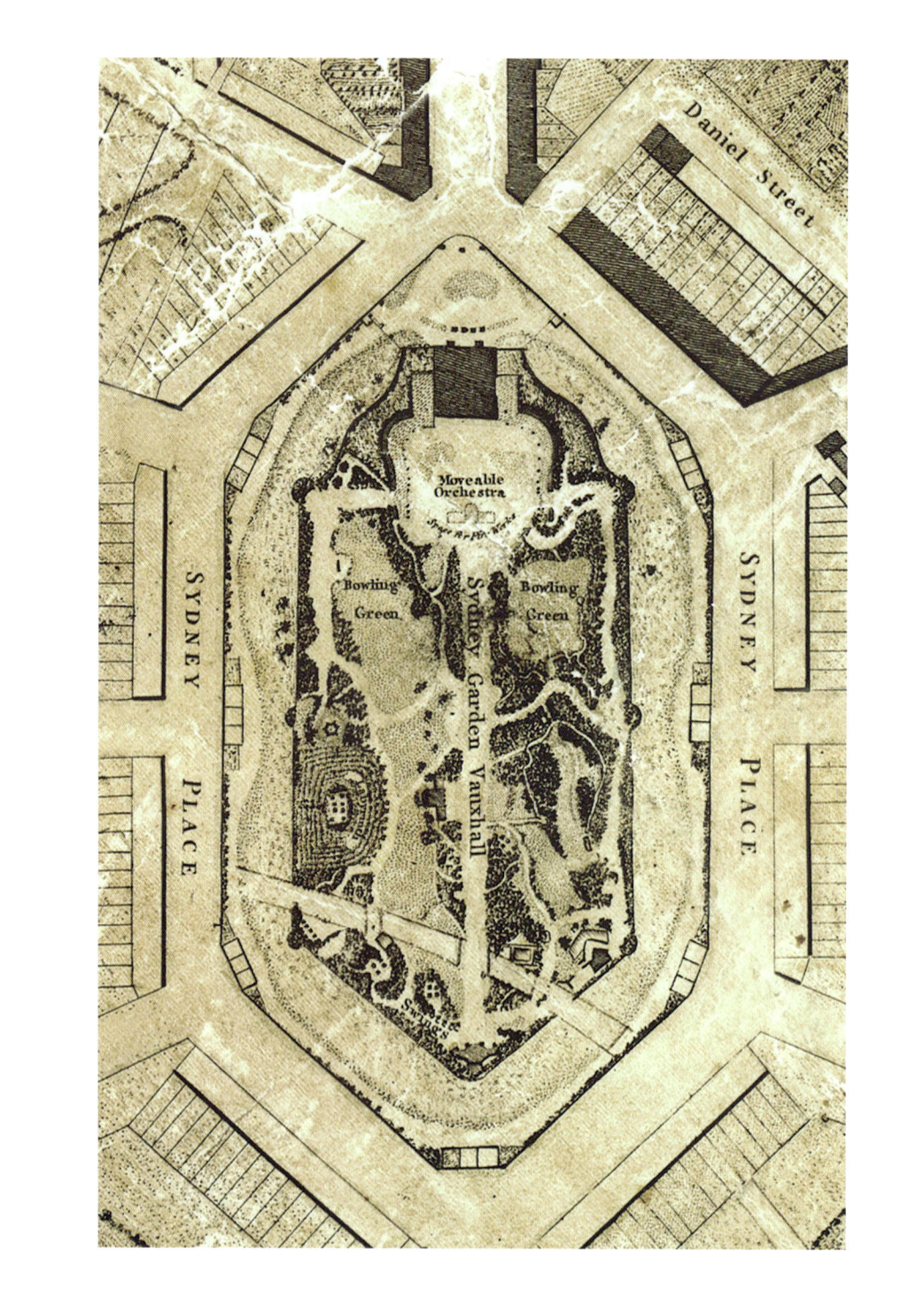

2

FIXTURES AND FITTINGS

Open for Business

When John Gale took the lease on the gardens in 1795, there was still much to do. It was not until 1799 that they could be described as a fully-functioning enterprise. Despite this, at the end of 1795, John Gale signed a new lease, to run for one year. Given the brevity of the lease, it was a brave decision. He may have felt that, despite all the financial difficulties, the gardens' location at what was intended as the centrepiece of the Pulteney estate would provide a captive audience.

When William Pulteney first decided to develop the Bathwick estate, he turned to his fellow Scot, Robert Adam. While Adam was a great architect, he was not always a practical one. Pulteney Bridge, though charming, is too narrow, as the Bath Corporation pointed out at the time. It was not the plan the council had agreed to, and they were upset by the idea of shops on the bridge. They said, with what would prove to be remarkable foresight, that 'the circulation of air will be prevented, that the smoke will greatly incommode the neighbourhood on each side of the river, that if a concourse of people constantly pass over it, which must be the case before the shops can be of any value, the dimensions of the bridge will then be too narrow to make the passage convenient'.[1]

The estate that Adam designed on the other side of the bridge was, in some ways, equally impractical. The designs which survive show a network

Opposite: Sydney Gardens on Harcourt Masters' map of 1800, oriented with south-west at the top

of streets and circular junctions but no grand boulevard. In fairness, he had suggested building another bridge in the place where North Parade Bridge was built 60 years later, but, having built Pulteney Bridge, he seemed uncertain how to lay out the streets leading away from it. In one plan he offered a choice of veering off in one of

Nothing demonstrates both the beauty and the impracticality of Pulteney Bridge better than this engraving. The entrance to the bridge looks wonderful but everyday traffic had to cross it, including, as this picture shows, herds of cows. The artist has reduced cows and humans to half size to minimise their impact. Full-sized cows would have shown up the narrowness of the roadway.

five directions; in another he offered a choice of carrying straight on or making a sharp left or right turn.[2] Neither solution was very satisfactory, nor were they in line with Pulteney's vision of creating a grand entrance to Bath. So he turned to the city architect Thomas Baldwin, who came up with a dramatic alternative. He started by drawing a line roughly a kilometre long, running north east from the bridge. He then divided the line roughly into tenths, the first of which formed Argyle Street. This allowed him unobtrusively to widen

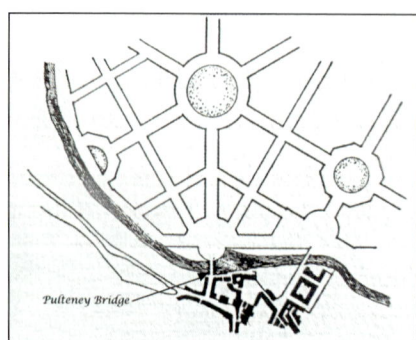 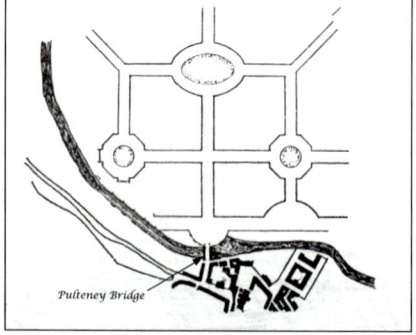

Two designs proposed by Robert Adam for the Pulteney estate.

the street from the narrowness of Adam's bridge to the broad expanse of Great Pulteney Street, further disguising the transition by interposing the wide open space of Laura Place. The remaining distance he divided into three. The first third formed Great Pulteney Street, while the final third was intended to be Upper Great Pulteney Street, and the central third was Sydney Gardens, at the heart of the planned estate. He also planned a crescent facing the river on the site now occupied by the Recreation Ground, and a square where Henrietta Park now stands. In 1792, no one knew that this grand design would never be completed, and today the breadth of Baldwin's vision is often forgotten.

But what dictated the direction of the line which formed the central spine? To discover that, you need to stand at the front gate of the Holburne and look

Taylor and Meyler's Map of 1793, showing the Pulteney estate as designed by Thomas Baldwin, with projected roads sketched in, along with a square, a crescent and rond-points

straight down Great Pulteney Street. Right at the far end, on the horizon, you will see a hill topped with trees. This is known today as Twerton Roundhill, although its original name was Barrow Hill or High Barrow Hill. It was thought to be man-made and John Wood believed it was the burial place of Bladud, legendary founder of Bath. From the top of the gardens, where the pavilion stood, there was a much better view of it, although today it is hidden by trees. So early visitors would have looked down the central avenue of the gardens and across the city towards a hill which enshrined a connection with Bath's mythical past. Although this may have been fortuitous, it seems far more likely to have been a deliberate attempt to link the modern city with its legendary founder.

The view of Twerton Roundhill – striking enough from the entrance to the gardens, but imagine it from 900 feet further back and 60 feet higher up

Looking north from the top of the gardens, early visitors had a view of the precipitous slopes of Beacon Hill which, before the trees grew up, created an echo. Even today, we find echoes enchanting and intriguing. Before technology made vocal reproduction commonplace, they were even more popular.

The view northward to Beacon Hill is today largely screened by trees

Dropping their gaze from the distant horizon to survey the gardens, it would have been clear to those early visitors that not all the planned features were ready. Had the subscribers not been dealing with a competitor who had stolen a march on them, it is likely they would have waited a further year before opening. From contemporary accounts, newspaper advertisements and by deduction, we can gain a clear impression of how the gardens must have appeared in their early years.

Tree planting had begun in 1793, and from contemporary reports we know that the pavilion at the top of the gardens was built by the time the gardens opened. It was then much wider than it is now. Its façade curved in a Hogarthian double line of beauty, and with slender Ionic columns and little cherubs on the top, it must have looked delightful.

As mentioned earlier, the sham castle was also there by 1795, although, as a ruin, it looked rather too new – as indeed it was. Eventually, ivy grew up it, and with its moat and shrubbery, it must have made a charming and unexpected addition to this corner of the gardens.

Although the swings were in position, south of the pavilion, two of the most popular features, the labyrinth and the Merlin swing, were not ready until August 1795. They do not seem to have formed part of the original

The pavilion at the top of the garden as it appeared in the early twentieth century, little changed since it was built, apart from having had a house added to the back of it

plan. The first reference to the Merlin swing came as late as May 1795, and it is likely that the idea to place it in a labyrinth was stolen from Grosvenor, which had such a feature at an early stage. There seem to have been teething problems with the Merlin swing in Sydney Gardens, however, for in October, two months after it was installed, an advertisement admitted that

> the Merlin Swing calculated for two or four people to swing sitting, which is now open, has lately undergone an improvement, which makes it work with the greatest ease and pleasure, and for the accommodation of invalids, who wish to use it for their health. Tickets 6d each through a curious grotto and 3d each through the gate of the labyrinth.[3]

There are numerous theories about what a Merlin swing was, but we can be fairly certain it was the fore-runner of the swing-boat. There is an eye-witness account of it by Frances Baroness Bunsen who, as an old lady, recalled a visit to Sydney Gardens in 1796, when the swing was new:

> One day I walked with my Mother & Aunt to the Sydney Gardens, as they were called: in one part were swings, & one in particular called a Merlin swing, in which the swingers sat two & two, opposite: those at the opposite corners pulling ropes alternately by which the swing was set in motion. Two gentlemen had joined the two ladies in their walk & acceded to their desire of mounting the swing: I & my little sister remained on the gravel walk with the maid, & saw the two gentlemen pulling, & the swing going high, to the great pleasure of my Mother & Aunt, until the countenance of one of them having become paler & paler, he had almost fainted, when the gardener stopped the swing & helped him out.[4]

The swing was the brainchild of John Joseph Merlin, a talented inventor and watchmaker, who created perhaps one of the world's most famous automata, *The Silver Swan*, held at the Bowes Museum in Barnard Castle. His catalogues included an amazing variety of inventions, ranging from the useful – such as chairs for invalids to wheel themselves about and a machine to allow a blind person to play at cards – via the entertaining – such as in-line roller skates and a mechanical organ – to the weird – such as two 'elegant

FIXTURES AND FITTINGS 161

This illustration from 1799 may show a Merlin swing. The date is right and the mechanism at the top looks like that of an Archimedes claw, on which Merlin based his design, and suggests it would have swung from side to side.

Left: John Joseph Merlin by Thomas Gainsborough. He is holding another of his inventions – a pocket balance for weighing gold coins, to check they had not been clipped.

Below: Merlin's Silver Swan. When wound up, the swan dips its head down to the water, which is made of rotating glass rods, and appears to catch a fish. The fluidity of the movement is extraordinary.

Antique busts placed at the extremities of the room' by which two people could converse without being overheard. He was also a talented musician, and built harpsichords, tuning devices, and a music desk for four musicians. The forerunner of the Merlin swing was something he called

> a portable Hygaeian Chair, in which the Nobility and Gentry may swing themselves with perfect Safety, so as to afford an easy Motion, and uncommonly pleasing Exercise. For the peculiar Advantages of this to Health, the Reader is referred to Dr Carmichael Smith's excellent Pamphlet on the Utility of Swinging in Pulmonary Consumptions and other Disorders.[5]

James Carmichael Smyth (not Smith) was a Scottish physician and medical writer whose pamphlet extolling the benefits of swinging was published in 1787. He based his theory on the proven health benefits of sailing, arguing that swinging was a viable alternative. Some doctors also felt that being seasick was good for you, although Smyth was dubious about this.

Merlin later developed the chair into what he called an escarpolet.[6] He made one in which two people could swing, and another which was portable so that it could be used in the house or garden. As already noted, the first commercial use of the Merlin swing seems to have been at Grosvenor.[7] A later description – not by Merlin himself – claimed that it was built on Archimedean principles.[8] This probably relates to its use of pulleys similar to those found in the device known as the Archimedean claw. Originally an instrument of war, designed to lift the bow of a Roman warship out of the water before dropping it and breaking it in two, it was eventually adapted to other uses. Merlin swings soon found their way into a variety of other venues – in 1821, for example, a team of horses bolted when they were terrified by a Merlin swing at a fairground.

The exit from the labyrinth was via a 'romantic subterranean passage' which led to a grotto. This became known as Merlin's grotto, and was described in 1825 as 'a rude excavation, which, supported by columns, and encrusted with shells, offers a representation of the abode of England's celebrated philosopher'. It is no longer in the gardens, and was long thought to have been lost when the railway came through. This is not the case, however, as it survived the building of the line. There is at least one reference to it still being there in

1847, and it was almost certainly rescued and reconstructed elsewhere when the part of the gardens in which it stood was later sold for building.⁹

The bar – which became known as the Middle Bar – was also in the gardens from the start. With the tavern at the entrance not even started, there had to be somewhere to serve refreshments, which, in the winter

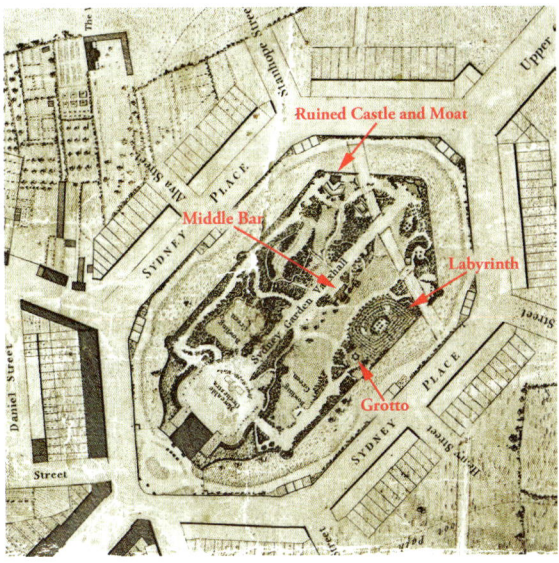

The location of the labyrinth, grotto, middle bar, ruined castle and moat indicated on Harcourt Masters' 1800 map

months, included gravy and pea soup. The bar also acted as the ticket office for the labyrinth and grotto, and provided the London and Bath newspapers for customers to read. In response to the growing popularity of bowling, two bowling greens were laid out, a large one to the right of the main promenade and a smaller one to the left, enclosed by shrubs. At the bottom of the promenade, a space was left for fireworks, but it was not the dedicated and perhaps safer space that Eveleigh had envisaged for Grosvenor Gardens.

Surprisingly, Sydney Ride, around the edge of the gardens, did not open immediately. The first time it was mentioned in an advertisement was in June 1796 when it was described as having a gentle incline, 'free from dust and commanding some of the most delightful and romantic views about Bath'.[10] It was for gentlemen and ladies on horseback only, and subscriptions were 10s 6d right through until Christmas, five shillings for three months and sixpence a time for non-subscribers. Servants attending their masters or mistresses were admitted to the ride free of charge. A year later, Gale was stressing its health benefits, claiming that it afforded 'a healthy and fashionable airing for gentlemen and ladies on horseback'. It is not clear what the surface of the ride originally consisted of – all we know is that it was 'free from the inconvenience of dirt in winter, or dust in summer, and not incommoded by carriages of any kind'. However, it was almost certainly spent bark from the tanning process, which gave a firm but comfortable surface for horses, protecting the fragile legs of thoroughbreds from injury, and was very popular for riding courses.

That leaves the entrance building, originally referred to as a tavern, but later known as Sydney House or Sydney Hotel. Although the foundation

The west front as designed by Thomas Baldwin, from the plans of 1794. Baldwin's signature can just be seen below the word 'Elevation'.

Great Pulteney Street with this design imposed, showing how Baldwin intended the street to appear.

stone was not laid until 1796, the proprietors had taken the trouble to license the gardens as early as 1794. The licensee was George Clark and the name of the gardens was given as 'Vauxhall Ranelagh'.[11] This meant that the gardens themselves were licensed, allowing alcoholic beverages to be served from the bar. The delay in starting work on Sydney House was partly due to Baldwin's bankruptcy in 1793. He had designed a light and airy building which would have closed off the view from Laura Place more effectively than what was eventually built. It was two bays wider – that is, it had seven windows across the front, instead of the five in the design produced by Harcourt Masters when he was appointed in Baldwin's place. Baldwin's design was also in the same neo-classical style as Great Pulteney Street, whereas Harcourt Masters reverted to a Palladian style for the façade, with a more delicate design for the back. Harcourt Masters' first design shows a delicate colonnade running right across the front of the building, with a walkway, protected by an iron balustrade, above it.[12] It is a great shame this was not built, as it was closer to Baldwin's original design and would have blended in better with Great Pulteney Street. What Harcourt Masters finally decided on was very like Baldwin's design for the Guildhall, with the central section pulled forward to create a porte-cochère. It was, however, less expensive than either of the earlier designs, indicating that cost was becoming an issue.

At the rear, Baldwin planned to reduce the height of the building to two storeys, and have glass doors leading into the gardens set in an Adamesque archway. Although Harcourt Masters followed this design, reducing the height of the building to two storeys, he set the doors in a less imposing archway. He also designed a semicircular bandstand (or orchestra) jutting out from the centre. Stretching out in a semicircular arc on either side of the building were supper or dining boxes, like those at Vauxhall. One might have assumed that these would have been built after the central part was complete, but the 1795 account mentions them, so at least some must have been built by then. Indeed, they would have had to have been erected, to give visitors somewhere to sit for the public breakfasts.

Baldwin planned an obelisk in front of Sydney House, on the spot where the front gate now stands, with a gate to each side. He also planned seven buildings arranged symmetrically around the perimeter of the gardens, which would have been divided into semi-detached villas, each with a private garden.

Harcourt Masters' original design of 1794

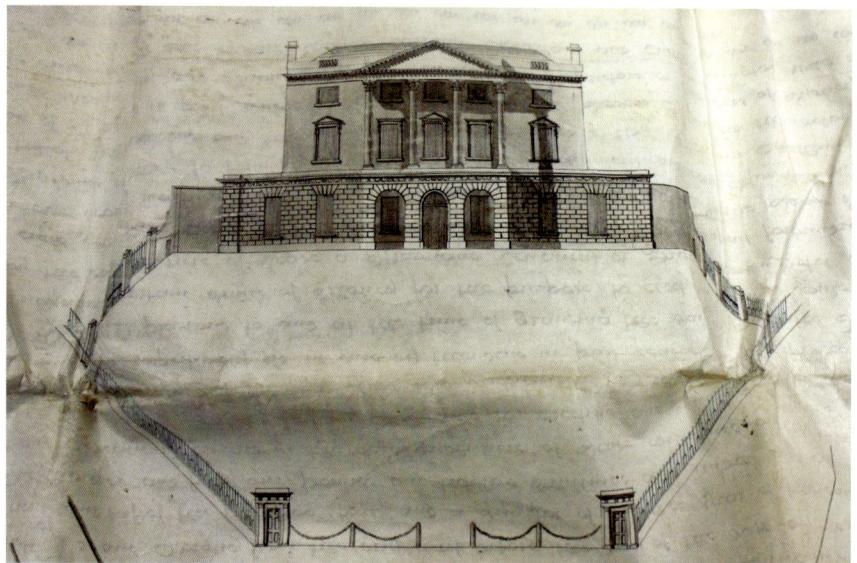

Harcourt Masters' final design, from a plan of 1811

Thomas Baldwin's design for the Guildhall – it can be seen how similar it is to Harcourt Masters' final design for the Sydney Hotel

FIXTURES AND FITTINGS 167

Baldwin's design for the entrance to the gardens from the hotel

A print by Jean-Claude Nattes shows Harcourt Masters' design for the garden front as finally realised. To each side are the supper boxes, some of which must predate the building.

The buildings would have had archways running through them, which would have served as an exits – or 'outletts' as Baldwin described them on the plans – from the gardens. The only entrance was at the front – obviously there could only be one because tokens had to be checked or money taken. This raises the question of how people entered the gardens when Sydney House was being built. Presumably, to avoid the building work, a section of wall had to be left open to serve as a temporary entrance.

So this was the realm that John Gale leased for three years in 1795. In 1798, his lease ran out, and when the gardens were offered to let that October, they included the 'elegant new-built tavern, containing a banqueting room, coffee and billiard rooms, elegant orchestra and every other requisite for genteel accommodation'.[13]

In John Gale, the proprietors had chosen the right man to get the gardens off to a good start. In the 1798 advertisement, the gardens were described as 'that justly celebrated and fashionable resort of pleasure'. However, the fates had decreed that the tale of Sydney Gardens

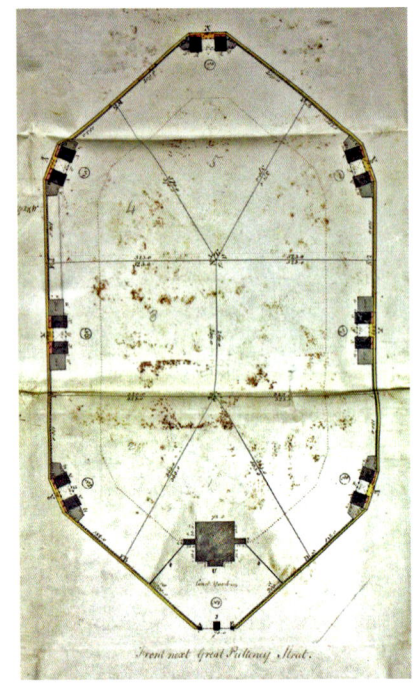

Baldwin's survey of the gardens, showing his careful measurements, as well as the position of what he called 'outletts' and the obelisk planned for the entrance.

The intended obelisk

FIXTURES AND FITTINGS   169

The street elevation of one of the 'outletts' intended for the centre of each side and the top of the gardens.

The outlett at the top was intended to have this façade overlooking the gardens.

The other outletts at the angles were intended to have this elevation to the street....

...while this was the intended garden elevation for all the outletts except the one at the top.

would be a rollercoaster ride of scintillating success alternating with debts and dereliction. Their survival today is simply a miracle, and there have been several times when they were almost lost to the people of Bath. In the end, it was their affection for the gardens that saved them for us today.

In the next chapter we look at their first fifty years. During that time the proprietors went from admiring and protecting their celebrated and fashionable asset to being so desperate for money that they welcomed Mr Brunel's new-fangled, smoky, noisy railway into their sylvan retreat.

A Sydney Gardens entrance token

3

THAT CELEBRATED AND FASHIONABLE RESORT OF PLEASURE

1796-1839

As we have seen, John Gale was the man whose energy and enterprise led to the rapid success of Sydney Gardens. He threw himself enthusiastically into providing what the public wanted. He also had the bright idea of making the gardens accessible all year round, tempting visitors with the prospect of a fashionable winter promenade and supplying hot drinks and other refreshments.[1] He kept the public in touch with what was happening, whether it was good news or bad. When the installation of the Merlin swing was delayed, he apologised and made sure people were aware, so that they would not turn up and be disappointed. He knew – and let the public know – that the gardens were still a work in progress, but assured them that, 'from the superior and novel style' in which they were designed, 'visitants, and particularly admirers of picturesque plantations, will be much gratified in contemplating [their] rising beauties'.[2]

Yet, when the proprietors advertised in November 1795 for someone to take the gardens on for one year when Gale's lease ran out, he may still have been hesitant about renewing it. It would be another month before they started advertising for contractors to build for the tavern, and the foundation stone would not be laid until the end of 1796. Without the tavern, accommodation for visitors was limited, acting as a deterrent for those who may have been tempted by Gale's advertisements. Nevertheless, in January 1796 Gale

Opposite: The back of the Tavern about 1800 showing the dinner boxes to each side and the orchestra raised up on what appears to be a temporary structure

announced that he had taken the gardens for another year, and in the event stayed on until March 1799. With his new lease in place, he began to organise the sort of events that had been so popular at Spring Gardens.

Royal anniversaries were an obvious opportunity to attract the crowds. That meant fireworks, and in Bath that meant Signor Invetto. Sure enough, in June, on the occasion of the King's birthday, there was a grand gala, with 'splendid illuminations', a concert and 'several capital pieces of fire-works by Signor Invetto'. Because the tavern had not been built, there was no room where the company could gather, such as those at Spring Gardens or Grosvenor. Gale therefore 'erected at very great expense, a most elegant Room ... called the Duke of York's Gallery', which would be 'superbly illuminated for Supper Parties'.[3] Unfortunately, the weather was not kind, and the event was postponed until the following Friday, when the *Bath Chronicle* reported that there were more than 4,000 people present.

In August, for the Prince of Wales' birthday, the illuminations consisted of 'upwards of 3,000 variegated lamps' and once again there were fireworks by Invetto.[4] For once, two entrances were open, one facing Great Pulteney Street and one capable of being negotiated by sedan chairs, facing Bathwick Street. This time over 3,000 people attended.

Staging these events was not cheap, and, on the King's birthday the following year, Gale apologised for the price of tickets, but said that, as he wanted to put on shows 'superior to anything of the kind ever given in this part of the kingdom', the expense of doing so meant that entrance to grand gala nights would cost two shillings. On all other gala nights, however, tickets would still be one shilling.[5] Two shillings in 1797 had a purchasing power of about £10 today, so that seems not unreasonable.

Gale was spurred on to further efforts the following year. At the grand galas, there were exciting attractions, such as the 'minute representation of the glorious action between Lord Duncan and the Dutch Fleet', which concluded with a hornpipe danced by a British sailor.[6] The machinery was by J Rebecqui, an Italian puppeteer, whose theatre was often a feature at Sydney Gardens and whose wife created the costumes for his puppets – or fantoccini, as they were known. Gale also supported local charities and organisations. He was thanked publicly by the Bath Loyal Volunteers for allowing them the use of the gardens for their parade and providing them with dinner.

THAT CELEBRATED AND FASHIONABLE RESORT OF PLEASURE 173

By Permission of the Worshipful the MAYOR.
In the GREAT ROOM,
AT THE
Golden Lion, Dale-street,
J. REBECQUI's New Italian and English
FANTOCCINI,
Under the Patronage of his Royal Highness the PRINCE of WALES.
This present Monday, Wednesday, & Friday next,
The 2d, 4th, and 6th of June, 1800.
Will be presented the following ENTERTAINMENTS.
A COMIC PIECE, CALLED
L'ERREUR DU MOMENT.
End of Act the First, the Favourite Song of "The Soldier's Adieu," by Mr. WEBBER.
To which will be added, the Grand Dramatic Romance of

Blue Beard,
Or, FEMALE CURIOSITY.
The Scenery designed and painted by Messrs. EDKINS and SONS, Bristol; the Machinery by J. REBECQUI, and the Dresses, &c. by Mrs. REBECQUI.
In the Course of which will be displayed,
An Oriental Procession of Blue Beard,
With his Band, Guards, Attendants, &c.
A Chain of Mountains, over which Blue Beard is seen to pass,
Being an exact representation of Eastern Magnificence of Travelling;
TURKISH WARRIORS.
STUPENDOUS ELEPHANT,
Bearing on his Shoulders a Canopy of Gold, under which is placed
BLUE BEARD.
The Blue Chamber, with rich Transparent Paintings.
THE GRAND PALACE.
The Grand and Magnificent Garden of Roses.
BLUE BEARD'S CASTLE,
From the Top of which ERENE discovers
AN ARMY OF TURKISH SOLDIERS,
Who rescue FATIMA, and accomplish the downfall of the Tyrant.
The whole to conclude with
The Sepulchre and the Skeleton Scenes,
In which Blue Beard had murdered all his Wives, and about to slay Fatima.
PART THIRD.
Mr. BRESLAW will Display a Variety of New Invented
Capital Deceptions and Experiments,
The Particulars of which are too numerous to insert.
The Doors to be opened at Half past Seven o'Clock, and to begin precisely at Eight.
The Room is commodiously prepared, that every Person may have a view of the Performance.
Admittance TWO SHILLINGS each Person.

A poster advertising a performance of Rebecqui's Fantoccini in London

Despite Gale's popularity, when the lease came up for renewal in March 1799, he decided not to renew it. Even though the tavern was now open, the date passed without a taker, and it was not until the following month that Thomas Holloway took over the lease.[7]

Holloway's first grand gala, which included Mr Nimroide, who gave imitations of birds, is famous – or perhaps notorious – because it was mentioned in two letters to Cassandra Austen by her sister Jane. In the first, dated 2 June, she wrote:

> There is to be a grand gala on Tuesday evening in Sydney Gardens, a concert, with illuminations and fireworks. To the latter Elizabeth and I look forward with pleasure, and even the concert will have more than its usual charm for me, as the gardens are large enough for me to get pretty well beyond the reach of its sound. In the morning Lady Willoughby is to present the colours to some corps, or Yeomanry, or other, in the Crescent.

On 19 June she wrote again to Cassandra:

> Last night we were in Sidney Gardens again as there was a repetition of the Gala which went off so ill on the 4th – We did not go till nine and then were in very good time for the Fire-Works which were really beautiful and surpassing my expectations- the illuminations too were very pretty.[8]

The event celebrated was the King's birthday, which so often seemed plagued with bad weather, although the *Bath Chronicle* report suggests Jane was being a little unfair about the first occasion. The illuminations were still lovely, even if the fireworks were less than exciting. Perhaps she had been put into a bad mood by the presentation of the colours, which went on interminably. The corps to which she refers so flippantly was the Frome Volunteer Association of Cavalry, led by a Captain James Wickham, which eventually marched from the Crescent to Sydney Gardens, and were given a public dinner at the Guildhall.[9]

In fairness to Jane, she was not alone in being disappointed by the original performance. Holloway himself confessed that the repeat performance was due to 'the Disappointment experienced by a great number of Ladies and

Gentlemen ... on account of the badness of the weather'. He went to great lengths to ensure they would not be disappointed again, replacing Mr Nimroide with Rossignol Jr, persuading Invetto to produce even more new and astonishing effects, and opening a 'new banqueting room' for supper parties.[10] Fortunately, on this occasion the heavens smiled on his endeavours and the weather was fine.

By the end of 1799 the gardens were once again to let and Holloway took them for another year. However, he had already been forced to raise his prices – it now cost two shillings for all gala nights, grand or otherwise. In 1799, work started on cutting the Kennet & Avon Canal through the gardens. This had been finally agreed in 1795, after strong objections from the proprietors of the gardens, and then only on payment of £2,100. The canal company also had to agree to provide ornamental bridges 'in the manner of the Chinese' and decorative tunnel entrances. Although this sounds expensive, it was still cheaper than tunnelling right around the southern edge of the gardens, which had been proposed at an earlier stage. While work was in progress, the shareholders and management committee of the canal often met at what was now being referred to as the Sydney Hotel. By 1800, the bridges had been erected by George Stothert, an ironmonger in Bath, who not only had interests in both the canal and the gardens, but was also an agent for the Coalbrookdale foundry, where the bridges were made. The tunnel portals, which could be seen from the gardens, were adorned

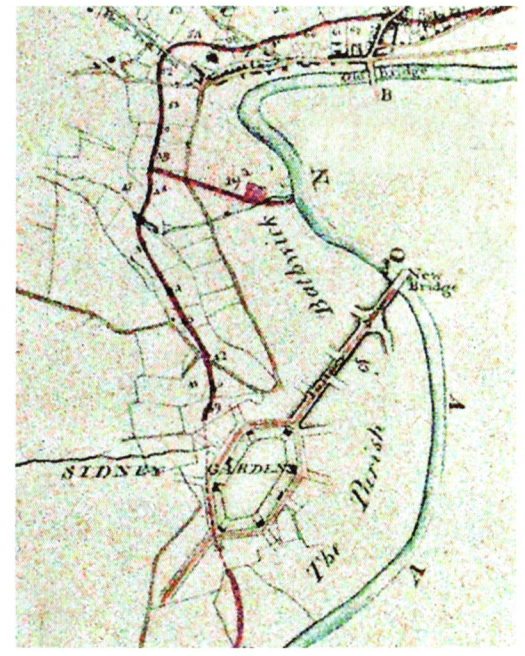

A plan showing the route originally surveyed for the Kennet and Avon Canal – drawn in red – including the tunnel which it have taken it to the south of Sydney Gardens

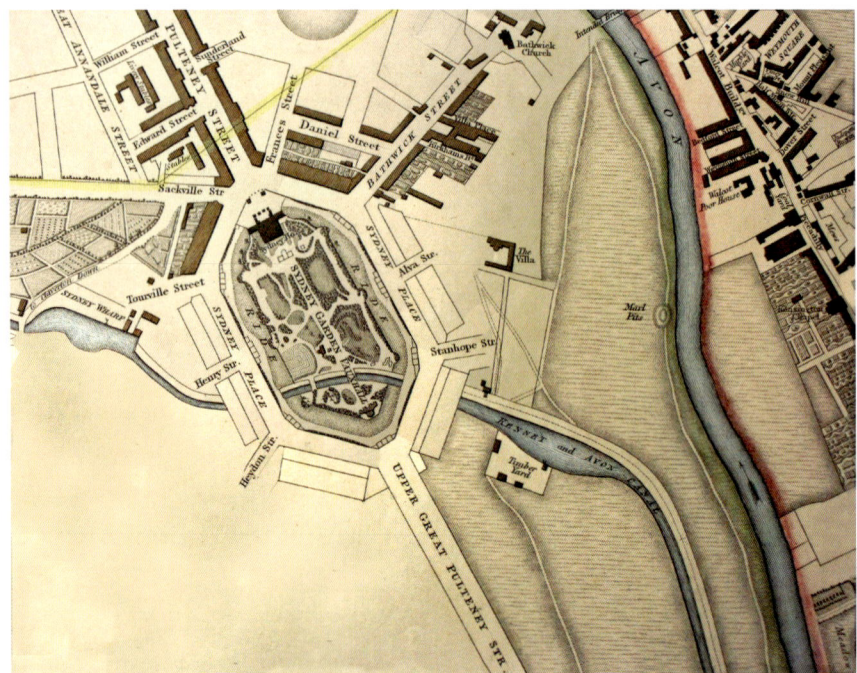

Above: The final route taken by the canal through the gardens from a map of 1810, with Sydney Wharf to the west and Darlington Wharf to the east

Left: The tunnel arches, with Old Father Thames at the east end of the gardens, and Sabrina, Spirit of the Severn, at the west

Below: One of the bridges 'in the manner of the Chinese', erected in 1800

THAT CELEBRATED AND FASHIONABLE RESORT OF PLEASURE 177

Two views of the canal shortly after it opened. The top one shows the pavilion, while the bottom one shows visitors crossing to a rustic shelter.

with carvings and flanked by empty niches to make them look romantically antique. In the centre of the garlands over either arch is a bust. The eastern one represents an old man and the western one a young woman. They are believed to represent Old Father Thames and Sabrina, Spirit of the Severn, signifying that the Kennet & Avon Canal links those two great rivers. No access was provided from the canal to the gardens, however. While visitors were happy to admire the canal from above, they had no wish to have canal folk intruding into their refined enclave.[11]

During 1800, when work on the canal through the gardens was 'finished in a durable and substantial manner', the canal proprietors held a general meeting at the hotel, before proceeding along the canal to Monkton Combe to see how work was progressing there.[12]

In March, Holloway announced that he was leaving, and his household furniture was put up for sale at the hotel.[13] Among the items were twenty

John Nixon's somewhat unflattering portrayal of fashionable society enjoying itself in the gardens about 1801. It is unclear whether the old lady on the extreme left is glowering in disapproval at the high jinks or the attentions of the raffish interloper beside her. On the extreme right, meanwhile, two children attempt to break up a dog fight.

good bedsteads, indicating that providing lodgings was part of his business. The new lessee had already signed in January – it was none other than John Gale, who this time had taken the gardens for what he described vaguely as 'a term of years'.[14] If work on the canal had deterred Holloway from continuing, Gale saw it as an advantage. He extolled 'the novelty of the Kennet and Avon Canal, which is carried through the garden and ride, and completed in the most handsome manner, with ornamental iron bridges &c. with various Improvements in the plantations'.[15] He also threw himself into promoting charity events. In April, one half of the receipts from public breakfasts went to a fund for the relief of the widows and orphans of the seamen who fell in the victorious Battle of Copenhagen. His donation, of £12 11s 0d from 251 breakfast tickets, was second only to that of the Bath Corporation. Gale also held a ball in the hotel's great room to celebrate Nelson's victory.[16]

Gale had discovered a winning formula, but he was not a man to rest on his laurels. In 1802, he engaged André-Jacques Garnerin, described in the *Bath Chronicle* as 'the celebrated aeronaut'. Gale also cunningly let people into the gardens to see the balloon being filled, which drew even greater crowds. When it was full, Garnerin and his companion Mr Glasfurd were towed to the top of the gardens and back, before making their ascent in perfect weather. The *Bath Chronicle* described this as 'the most sublime spectacle ever exhibited' in the gardens. As well as huge crowds in the gardens, hills, streets and rooftops all around were full of spectators. The balloon slowly disappeared over Bathampton Down, and finally landed at Mells. After the ascent, there were fireworks and a gala. Admission on this occasion was five shillings.[17] Three days later, the gala was

Garnerin's balloon landed at Mells Park, ten miles south of Bath, to the astonishment of the locals

repeated, and Garnerin made a night ascent in which, it was promised, the balloon 'would rise majestically and display the appearance of a luminous meteor'. Garnerin was also the inventor of the parachute, although he does not seem to have demonstrated it during his visit to Bath.

In 1804, the Royal Charlotte Packet began running along the canal from Sydney Gardens to Bradford on Avon three times a week. In order to allow access to the canal, a door was opened in the side wall to give access to the departure point on Darlington Wharf.[18] In the spring, there was a Grand Fête Champêtre organised by the Bath Harmonic Society for the ladies of Bath. Rowland Mainwaring, in his *Annals of Bath,* described this as

> a magnificent display of liberality and taste. Not less than 1,200 persons sat down to an elegant breakfast, consisting of all the delicacies which the season produced, provided by that excellent caterer, the renter of the gardens, Mr Gale.

Never was remembered such an assemblage of elegance and beauty as distinguished that Elysian scene, so novel and gratifying in its general arrangements. At this time, 'The Harmonic Society' was admitted to be perfect – certainly at its meridian.[19]

That same year, nearly 4,000 people attended the celebrations for the King's birthday. In September, the proprietors of the gardens revived the idea of the 'outletts'. They advertised fourteen plots for building, 'at present forming parts of the beautiful lawn surrounding those fashionable and delightful gardens'.[20] The plans were those drawn by Thomas Baldwin in 1793, although they were revised so that each building could, if desired, form a single house rather than a pair of semi-detached villas. No more was heard of this plan, however.

It may also have been in 1804 that the Sydney Tap was built. It was licensed in 1805, but its location is something of a mystery. We know from a contemporary advertisement that it was a detached building, and operated independently from the tavern.[21] A possible candidate is the now ruinous building in the gardens, to the right of the main avenue. Another building

Darlington Wharf became a regular departure point for passenger boats along the canal to Bradford on Avon. The Scotch Boats began operating in the 1830s.

The entrance to the gardens depicted by Jean-Claude Nattes in 1805. The words 'Sidney Tap' are inscribed on the wall to the right of the tavern.

immediately to the right of Sydney House has been suggested, but that does not appear on maps until much later. It would also have stuck out into the ride, and was still there after the tap was destroyed in a gas explosion. The words 'Sidney Tap' can clearly be seen in an engraving by JC Nattes from 1805, inscribed on the wall on the south side of Sydney House. It has been suggested that it had to be outside the gardens because a tap would have been used by servants, but that is not necessarily true. It could have been for the refreshment of thirsty gentlemen who did not want to sit down and chat over tea or coffee. Taps were places where beer was served directly from the barrel, and beer was popular with all classes.

In 1805, Gale decided to expand his empire and took on the Lower Assembly Rooms. Given that they were already struggling to compete with the Upper Rooms, this was ambitious and he does not seem to have had them very long.[22] However, all seemed to be going well at the gardens. Then, in July 1809, Invetto died, after a lingering illness. He was not an old man, but life had not been kind to him. His widow, the same Mary who had once left him for a travelling salesman, announced that she was continuing the business. Various mutual friends asked Gale to allow her to stage a benefit performance. It is clear that Gale had his doubts, for in the advertisement he said he had been induced to do so. However, the same advertisement had a note from Mrs Invetto appended to it, explaining that the performance was not going ahead and making it plain that Gale paid her off, for which she was grateful.[23] Perhaps he felt that it was too soon after her husband's death, or that she was not up to it. However, a year later, she did mount a display at the gardens, for the Prince of Wales' birthday.[24]

Two months later, in October 1810, she was dead. There was a massive explosion at the works in Ladymead, which destroyed her house as well as the adjoining one. Mary Invetto was killed instantly, and her assistant, who had dragged her body out in the hope she was still alive, died a few days later. Two children were orphaned, and the assistant left a widow and child.[25] There was often a terrible price to be paid by those in the business of supplying a moment's pleasure to the masses. Behind all the glamour and excitement of fireworks, there was darkness and danger for those who created the displays.[26]

New attractions installed in the gardens included a grand cascade in which the water, represented by tin sheets on belts, flowed past models of a windmill, a watermill and a village, and under a bridge across which walked groups of 'passengers'.[27] A similar cascade at Vauxhall, on which it seems to have been based, was described in *The Microcosm of London* in 1810:

> At the end of the first act of the grand concert, which is usually about ten o'clock, a bell is rung by way of signal for the exhibition of a beautifully illuminated scene, called the cascade. A dark curtain is then drawn up, which discloses a very natural view of a bridge, a water-mill, and a cascade; a noise similar to the roaring of water is also well imitated; while coaches, waggons, soldiers and other figures, are exhibited crossing the bridge with the greatest regularity. This agreeable piece of scenery continues about ten minutes.[28]

With both John and Mary Invetto dead, Gale hired Vincento de Mortram, 'engineer to the Prince Regent and artist in pyrotechnics at Vauxhall, London'.[29] Mortram specialised in what he called Chinese Fireworks and, in a programme from May 1811, gave a detailed description of a display in 'four divisions':[30]

First division
Signal rocket with lights and maroons
Battery of Maroons
Pyramid of Calcutta light
Rockets with comets and stars
Wheel of Boreas of various coloured fires representing the gustful winds of the Heathen deities
A metamorphosis wheel, with Prussian cross richly adorned with stars of knighthood
Flight of rockets

Second division
A discharge of sosissons
A grand horizontal wheel with a display of Egyptian spire fire which will discharge a flight of rattle-snakes
A discharge of tail-star rockets
A saxon wheel decorated with Chinese flyers
A girandole wheel which will discharge five pump stars etc
A flight of sosissons
Rockets

Third division
A vertical wheel representing small cannon with a rolling sun
A spiral wheel illuminated in silver fire
A flight of rockets
A regulating piece with a wheel in the centre of blue and gold fire; to conclude with
A Mosaic cross
Maroons
A flight of rockets

Fourth division
A magnificent Mosaic temple with Egyptian pyramids in gold and silver fire with Chinese spiral fountains and a representation of throwing red-hot shot: at the same time will discharge a flight of rockets, shells, chests of artillery etc etc

Left: A Chinese themed firework display at Vauxhall, probably devised by Mortram

Below: This Oriental bandstand in Vauxhall may have been similar to the 'Chinese Orchestra' at Sydney Gardens on the occasion of the Chinese firework display

All this was costing Gale money, but he was not prepared to let standards slip. Nevertheless, he was engaged in a precarious venture. Unlike Purdie, he had given up his day job – it would have been better if he had not. In 1812, when he mounted his final grand gala display, for the Prince Regent's birthday, all still seemed set fair, however. Although Mortram promised a representation of Mount Vesuvius, the theme was predominantly Chinese. The fireworks were Chinese, there were to be Chinese lanterns and the Sydney Gardens musicians were to play in a Chinese Orchestra in the centre of the gardens. A military band was also engaged to play during some of the events (although this was Irish and not oriental).

However, at the bottom of the advertisement for this extravaganza was a short paragraph informing the public that this was his last opportunity to provide amusement for the company, as he was leaving on Lady Day, the term of his lease having expired.[31] He added that the fireworks had been procured at vast expense, and it soon became clear it had all proved too much for him, for in April 1813 he was declared bankrupt.[32] In May, the hotel, but not the gardens, was taken on by Robert Lansdown – the same man who had taken over King James's Palace in an emergency 24 years earlier.[33] It is likely that he was called in to do the same thing for the hotel – he was not there very long but was a safe pair of hands. The gardens seem to have been taken over, for a short time, by Mortram, who mounted what was intended to be a spectacular display in June. As Rowland Mainwaring records, however, he probably wished he had not:

> The renter of Sydney Gardens seemed particularly desirous to produce something new on this enlivening occasion; and it is but justice to add, that at all times he used his utmost exertions to gratify the public by the variety of his amusements. The programme, in honour of the King's birth-day, certainly did present 'something new'; and, without doubt, the pyrotechnic ingenuity of Signor Vincento de Mortram was, on the present occasion, at its utmost stretch. We give a portion of the advertisement for the entertainment of our readers. It appeared in these words: –
>
> 'The grand scene will be truly classical, and so admirably contrived that the taste of everyone cannot fail to be gratified. It will exhibit the ivy tower in the ruins of the old castle upon whose turrets lowering clouds will gradually descend; and as they of necessity disperse, the heathen deities will be exposed to view, and commence their operations. Nothing in description can here be detailed to describe its magnificent effects – it must be seen to elicit the admiration which it must deserve. In conformity with the mythology of the ancients, Phaeton will descend in a fiery car, whose wheels, in rapid rotation, will set the world on fire; and the whole garden will appear in one mighty blaze! And as this impetuous youth is returning to the ivy tower, he will be struck with a thunderbolt by Jupiter, and hurled headlong into the

River Po!, whilst a cascade is playing through its Gothic battlements, producing a most impressive and wonderful effect.'

Now let us relate the sad termination of this grand mythological scene: – From some unknown cause, the wheels of Phaeton's car failed in their expected rapidity, and 'the world was not set on fire', (or the Thames either), but the whole apparatus fell (as predicted) into the 'swiftly-sailing Po!' without even a friendly push from the mighty thunderbolts of Jove. What became of Phaeton was never correctly ascertained, some supposed he was drowned, as the lights were extinguished, and perfect darkness followed. In short (as may be imagined), the whole was a complete failure; and the company retired, expressing, in no unmeasured terms, the most marked dissatisfaction.

Many personal squibs were let off on that occasion, of which the following may be selected as having less asperity than many others: –

> PARTURIUNT MONIES
> At Jupiter's ire,
> And Phaeton's fire,
> The people with wonder were big;
> But Jupiter Ammon,
> Proved nothing but *gammon*,
> And Phaeton's car a *mere gig*.[34]

This seems a little harsh – the *Bath Journal* was more forgiving, reporting that everything at the gala went well,

> excepting the grand scene at the gothic castle; unfortunately a total failure happened in the machinery; neither Jupiter nor Phaeton having condescended to appear in their celestial abodes to gratify the expectations of the numerous assemblage of mortals whose curiosity had been raised to the highest pitch! The whole of this pompous scene rather seemed to terminate in Tartarean darkness than to exhibit a magnificent display of Heavenly brightness, suited to a council of the Heathen Gods assembled on mount Olympus! The disappointment however, was received with much patience and good humour.[35]

This good humour did not extend to the proprietor of the gardens, who, as noted earlier, seems to have been none other than the firework maestro in charge of this extravaganza, Signor Vicento de Mortram. Greatly embarrassed by the debacle, and convinced he had been the victim of sabotage, he placed an exasperated advertisement in the *Bath & Cheltenham Gazette*:

> The Proprietor begs leave to return his most unfeigned acknowledgments to the very respectable and crowded Company who honoured him with their presence and patronage on FRIDAY EVENING, for which he shall ever entertain the most lively sense of gratitude. Particularly to those Ladies and Gentlemen who so warmly congratulated him on the brilliancy and liberality he displayed on the occasion, he returns his most sincere thanks; but with the deepest regret does he observe that the confusion accompanying the descending of the Car to let off the fireworks was occasioned by some malicious person unknown who wantonly set fire to one of the Fountains of Fire in the trees before the men appointed to execute the plan could possibly press through the crowd to their respective places from the Cascade and therefore the effect of the exhibition was lost.[36]

Mortram redeemed himself later that year, with a grand working temple, illuminated with silver fire and gold rays, as well as other spectacular fireworks.

For the next few years, the gardens and hotel went through various changes of lessees, although Mortram seemed to be a fixture with regard to the fireworks. To address the problem of riotous behaviour, watchmen's boxes had been built on either side of the entrance to the gardens about 1810, but in 1817, Mr G Farnham took the gardens and ran them without any problems for seven years.

One of the watchmen's boxes

In 1819, Pierce Egan visited the gardens and penned the following description:

> The entrance to Sydney Tavern and Gardens has to boast of much respectability; and the tavern is a capacious and elegant erection.
>
> Sydney-Gardens is one of the most prominent, pleasing, and elegant features attached to the City of Bath. The hand of taste is visible in every direction of it; and the plants and trees exhibit the most beautiful luxuriance. Upon gala-nights, the music, singing, cascades, transparencies, fire-works, and superb illuminations, render these gardens very similar to Vauxhall. The Orchestra is close to the back of the Tavern, neatly arranged and elevated, with a large open space before it, well gravelled. The gradual ascent of the principal walk, that leads to the top of the gardens up to a half-circular stone pavilion [sic], which is paved and covered in, with a seat round it, and supported by several stone pillars, upon a gala-night has a most brilliant effect, from the numerous variegated lamps with which it is ornamented. The walks are all well rolled and gravelled; and seats and places for refreshment are to be met with in various parts of the gardens. The view, when seated in the above pavillion down to the orchestra, across arches covered with lamps, gives it a very captivating appearance. Upon those nights set apart for promenading only, a military band attends; and music also enlivens the scene, when public breakfasts are given. There are also several swings, adapted for the ladies; and others for gentlemen. Numerous covered-in boxes; and several alcoves formed with much botanical taste, grottos, &c, render this promenade highly attractive during the summer evenings. In the most retired parts of the gardens one of these grottos, it appears, was once the happy meeting-place, and dedicated to the tender passion, with a sincerity and animation unrivalled, by one of the greatest geniuses that ever adorned this or any other country, but who is gone to that 'bourne from whence no traveller returns', following the superior, amiable, and affectionate object of his heart, who had also long been previously consigned to the icy tomb of death. The remembrance of the late Richard Brinsley Sheridan, Esq and his wife,

Miss Linley, (termed the syren and angel of the concerts at Bath,) must render this grotto a most interesting feature to every lover of talent, elegance, and virtue ...

Upon the whole, Sydney-Gardens must be viewed not only as a great ornament to Bath, but is another, among the numerous proofs of the great anxiety of the inhabitants to render the amusements of this elegant City, without a parallel in the kingdom! The Kennet and Avon Canal runs through the gardens, with two elegant cast-iron bridges thrown over it, after the manner of the Chinese; and the romantic and picturesque scenery, by which they are surrounded, is fascinat-

The elegant cast-iron bridges thrown over the canal

ing beyond measure. Great opposition, it seems, was originally made to the canal running through these gardens by the proprietor; but it gives such a variety to the walks, that its introduction is now viewed as a great addition. It would be a matter of some difficulty to point out a spot of ground so tastefully laid out as Sydney-Gardens. Vauxhall, it is true, may boast of its superiority for brilliancy, and number of lamps, and vocal performers; but, in other respects, viewed as a garden, the competition would be perfectly ridiculous. The Labyrinth, shown here at three pence each person, is an object of curiosity. The inducement to enter it is one of Merlin's swings, which appears not only very prominent, but easy of access. However, it might puzzle any cunning person, if left to himself and without a clue, for six hours, to acquire the much wished-for spot; and it is rather a difficult task when the explorer of the Labyrinth has the direction pointed out to him from a man stationed in the swing. The inns and outs necessary to be made, it is said, measure half a mile. When the swing is made, and the secret unravelled, the guardian of this sort of Fair Rosamond's bower conveys the visitor once more into the public walks; the variety of which, that continually meet the eye of the promenader are truly attractive. A most delightful piece of ground, like a bowling-green, enveloped with trees, and a small natural cascade from a spring, cannot be passed with indifference. The company, generally, are of the most respectable description; and upon some of the gala-nights, upwards of 4000 persons have paid for admission, which is 2s 6d each. In fact, the most fastidious observer cannot find fault with Sydney-Gardens, which have also another advantage to recommend them to the visitors of Bath, namely, in having a surrounding ride, for the accommodation of ladies and gentlemen on horseback, that commands beautiful and romantic views, and of being free from dust in the summer, and dirt in the winter. The terms of subscription for walking are for one month, each person, 4s; for three months, 7s 6d; and the season, 10s. If two in one family, each 7s 6d; ditto, if three or more, each 6s. Non-subscribers, for walking, 6d each time. Nursery maids with children in arms, one subscription. Gentlemen and families may be accommodated with elegant apartments at Sydney-House. The terms of subscription to the ride, one month, 2s 6d each person. Three months, 6s. Six months, 10s. The year, 15s. Non-subscribers, 6d each time.[37]

The swing seen in Nixon's sketch of 1801 may be the one built by Merlin, as the mechanism at the top conforms to that in his description. However, if it is the Merlin swing, Nixon used considerable artistic licence by omitting the labyrinth in order to show it.

From Egan's description, we can gauge how much the labyrinth had grown up. It now needed a man raised above the hedges to guide people through. Some idea of what it was like can be gained by visiting Glendurgan Gardens in Cornwall. In 1833, when it was fashionable to copy historic mazes, the Fox family who lived there decided to create a scaled-down version for their children to play in. The Glendurgan site is on a hillside, which must be why they chose the Bath labyrinth, which also stood on a slope.

The Glendurgan maze

Egan's list of the terms of subscription features a curious and rather worrying item – the inclusion of nursery maids with children in arms. The gardens were never intended to be for children – they were very much an adult pleasure ground. This is another sign that the gardens were not bringing in the money the proprietors had hoped for. From now on, the financial burden of the gardens would become increasingly onerous.

In June 1822, to celebrate the first day of Bath Races, there was a gala featuring a young American from what had been Astley's Circus but was by then Davies'. He performed on the slack rope, a feat which was becoming increasingly popular. For the first time, we also hear about the hermit in the hermitage. There have been various theories about him, but Farnham's advertisement makes it clear that he was not a real person but some kind of transparency.[38]

In June 1824, following complaints about trespassers, it was decided to raise the height of the boundary walls to seven feet.[39] Farnham had steadied the ship for seven years, but he had not introduced much that was new. Mortram was still supplying the fireworks, and Farnham had gone into business with him, acting as his agent in Bath. However, one attraction that must have caused excitement was a machine known as 'Russian Mountains', a forerunner of the roller coaster. It was invented in France, promoted in this country by Monsieur Graulhie, and erected in the gardens for 'exercise and recreation'. Described as 'long the boast and attraction of the capital of France', the mountains combined 'portability and flexibility' with an elliptical track about 400 feet (122 metres) and 80 feet (24 metres) high.

The advertisement in the *Bath Chronicle* on 22 January gave visitors an idea of what they could expect:

> Persons wishing to ride, enter their cars from the ground, and by gradually ascending, are prepared to [sic] the subsequent rapidity of their descent; and by these means a constant succession of rounds may be performed without once quitting the car.

A French view of Les Montagnes Russes or Russian Mountains

We are used to seeing fairground rides but back then it must have been exciting and even a little frightening for people in Bath unused to such a phenomenon. Somewhat alarmingly, however, the foreman of the machine met with an accident, so the opening had to be postponed. Once the season for galas began, the mountains were moved to another site, described simply as 'Pulteney Road', but which may have been a small pleasure garden visited by Pierce Egan:

> On quitting Bathwick Church the visitor proceeds along the New Road to Widcombe, in the middle of which, a path on the right, through the fields, leads to the Ferry. The venerable abbey is here seen to much advantage, and the elevated buildings on the other side of the City also add to the prospect. Pass Waterloo-Gardens, to view which, threepence is charged for an admission; it, however, may be engaged for select parties. The gardens are small, but contain some pleasing walks, and the use of a swing. In turning round from this place, the South Parade and the Old Rooms now appear to the eye of the spectator. On approaching to the river side, on the right is a walk alongside the Avon to Pulteney-Bridge. The surrounding view from this precise spot is extremely picturesque.[40]

If this is where the Russian Mountains moved to, it is not surprising that a French entrepreneur said they had gone to Pulteney Road than refer to the gardens by name.[41] Astonishingly, however, Egan's description is the only reference to these elusive gardens, and, even though he pinpoints their location fairly precisely, only one map – drawn by Harcourt Masters in 1800 – shows anything resembling a formal garden in this area. Admittedly, it would not have been called Waterloo Gardens until 1815, but this could have been a renaming.

In July 1824, there was a dramatic change at Sydney Gardens when William Bridle announced that he had succeeded Mr Farnham.[42] Bridle was a controversial character. From 1808 to 1821, he had been

Are these the elusive and short-lived Waterloo Gardens?

head gaoler at Ilchester Gaol. Unluckily for him, after the Peterloo Massacre in Manchester in August 1819, the main speaker, Henry 'Orator' Hunt, had been charged and sent to Ilchester. He accused Bridle of drunkenness, licentiousness with female prisoners, torture and corruption, and managed to get an investigation launched, as a result of which Bridle was sacked. Hunt even published an *Investigation at Ilchester Gaol, in the County of Somerset, into the Conduct Of William Bridle, the Gaoler, before the Commissioners Appointed by the Crown*, which contained an unflattering likeness of Bridle, armed with chains and a hanging rope. He also published *A Peep into a Prison, or the Inside of Ilchester Bastille,* which was equally condemnatory. Bridle was furious, not least because he could not afford to appeal, but he could – and did – write a riposte – *A Narrative of the Rise and Progress of the Improvements Effected in His Majesty's Gaol at Ilchester, in the County of Somerset, between July 1808, and November 1821, under the Governance, Suggestion, and Superintendance of Wm. Bridle, Keeper: being the First Part of his Exposition of, and Answer to, the Charges Lately Brought Against Him by Henry Hunt, a Prisoner Confined in the Said Gaol.*

An unflattering caricature of William Bridle from Henry Hunt's book

There are those who claim that this investigation made Hunt a great prison reformer, but, in fairness to Bridle, the prison he had taken on was a better place when he left than when he arrived. He separated the women from the men, and instituted workshops for the prisoners to occupy their time. Hunt dismissed these as 'an expensive toy', even though, in 1818, Thomas Fowell Buxton, a noted prison reformer, had reported that, because the prisoners were kept occupied, there was 'no filth, no disorder, no tumult', within the prison, nor anything that 'would disgrace the most quiet and well-regulated manufactory'. Buxton also rated Ilchester Gaol as 'excellent'.[43] One is left with the impression that Hunt treated Bridle unfairly. Bridle claimed all along that there was a political motive to Hunt's attacks, and he was probably right. In addition, the working class Bridle seems to have been angered that Hunt, a member of the gentry, was granted special privileges while in gaol.[44]

Whatever the rights and wrongs of the case, Bridle is the last man one would have expected to run pleasure gardens, but he took on the task with gusto. His advertisements were more eye-catching than Farnham's discreet notices, and, for his very first gala, he had new acts for people to enjoy.[45] These included 'the celebrated and inimitable Il Diavolo Antonio', who performed on the 'rope volante' or slack rope. His real name was Antonio Migasi, and his family would go on to found one of America's leading circuses. Monsieur Clyne, the 'Celebrated French Hercules', performed feats of agility, balancing and strength, including balancing a ladder on his chin, with a boy on the top. Mortram still provided the fireworks, and Bridle introduced a Pandean band, in which most of the musicians played pan-pipes – something which had already proved popular at Vauxhall. Bridle also promised that there would be additional police and

The Pandean Band at Vauxhall – Bridle brought a similar band to Bath

other officers on hand to 'preserve the strictest order'. There is a definite sense that the gardens had been sliding gently downmarket and Bridle seems to have decided that the best tactic was to accommodate this new audience.

About 3,000 people attended Bridle's first gala and he was obviously relieved to have got off to a flying start. He even went to the trouble of inserting a notice in the *Bath Chronicle* thanking people for turning up to his first two galas.[46] By the time the gardens opened for the 1825 season, Bridle had made several improvements. Almost as soon as he took over, he introduced a Cosmorama, which consisted of paintings, shown four at a time and changed frequently, of 'the most celebrated spots on the globe'. In today's world, where we can see what is going on almost anywhere in the world at any time, this is a sharp reminder how remote foreign countries were to most people less than two hundred years ago.

During the winter, the gardens had been replanted with evergreens, shrubs and flowers, and the ride was macadamised. This was not tarmacadam, which not invented until 1902, but a way of resurfacing roads pioneered by John McAdam in which two layers of finely crushed stones were bound together to create a firm surface. A small section of this surfacing seems to have survived and can be found on the north-west side of the gardens, west of the railway line.

This forsaken path may be all that is left of the ride, showing what may be Macadam's original surface. At time of writing, an archaeological investigation was being planned to discover more about it.

Bridle replaced the cascade with a theatre, and installed an aviary. He also employed John Kerr, 'author of numerous dramatic pieces performed in the London theatres', to write what he called a syllabus, which contained a plan of the labyrinth.[47] Kerr's grandiloquence did Bridle proud. On entering the gardens from the hotel, he informed his readers, 'the astounding beauties of the spot burst at once upon the view'. In the foreground was 'a spacious esplanade surrounded by tastefully decorated alcoves'. To the left of this was the theatre, in line with 'a cluster of neat and

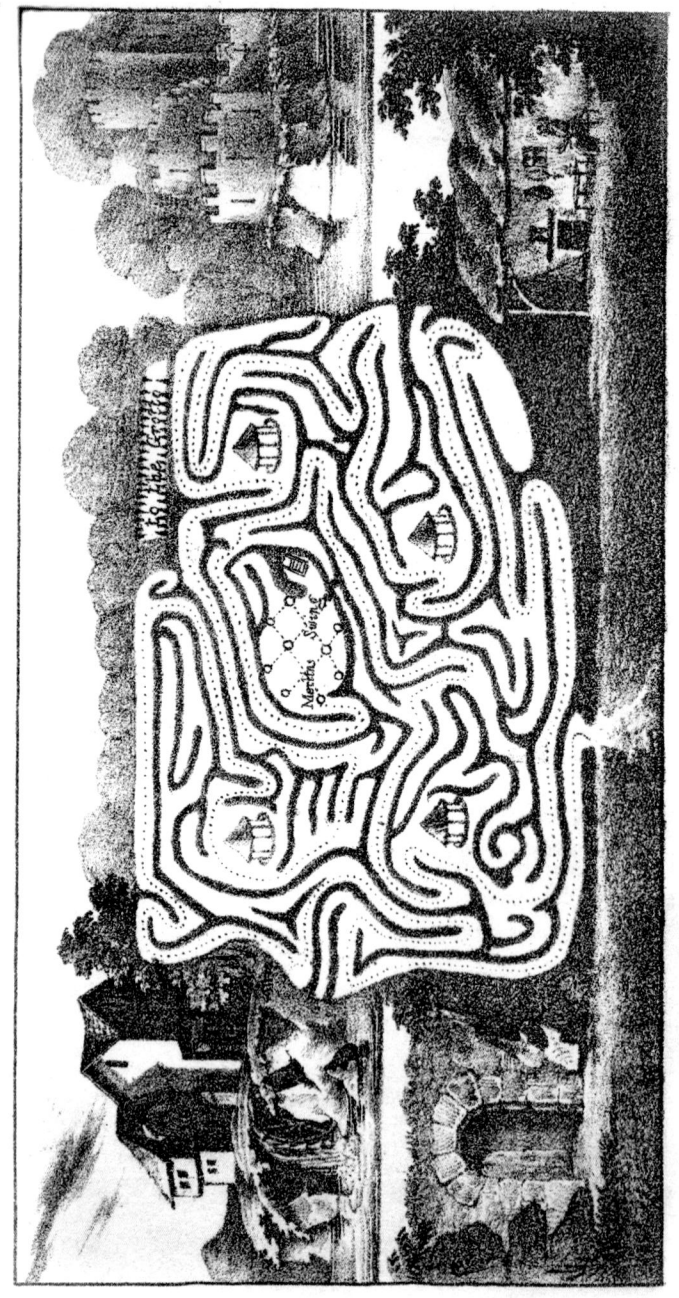

The Labyrinth in Sydney Gardens, Bath.
The dotted line denotes the path to be pursued.

The plan from Kerr's syllabus, showing (clockwise from top left) the miller's habitation, the 'ancient dilapidated castle', the hermit's cottage, and the grotto arch

appropriate alcoves, capable of accommodating six hundred visitors', at the end of which was the aviary. Kerr describes the cosmorama as standing opposite the theatre, 'at the extremity of a rising walk'. It has been suggested that the now ruinous building in the gardens was the cosmorama, but Kerr's description appears to rule out this out, since it is not on a rising walk or at the extremity of anything. However, several contemporary plans show a building right up against the ride, which does fit Kerr's description.

Kerr tells us that the ride had leaping bars, while from the pavilion there were views of the 'verdant promontories of the Barrow Hill'. Passing the swings, visitors would have seen, beyond a screen separating the ride from the gardens, some arched doorways leading into 'the extensive Reservoirs, from which Bathwick is supplied with water'. They can still be seen today. Today, however, we are used to having a constant supply of water. In those days, as the syllabus tells us, the pipes, which ran beneath the canal, were 'turned on and off daily, at stated periods, by an appointed engineer'.

The 'sombre rising bank' with the entrance to the reservoirs

One of the arched doorways

The ivy-covered castle had a hanging wood of lofty trees to its right, while its battlements were 'filled with artillery and thickly clustered with evergreens'. From the castle 'a fine verdant avenue' afforded 'a prospect of the larger Bowling Green, the vista being terminated by a screen of lofty trees and choice plants, in the midst of which the Cosmorama is distinguished'. This further suggests that the cosmorama was the building right against the ride, as it is the only one which fits the description.

Kerr described the canal as presenting, 'on its placid bosom, an ever-changing picture', while in every season it 'contributes to the variety and beauty of this enchanting spot'

A 'streamlet', issuing from the castle moat, was 'artfully directed through a close shrubbery', before gurgling 'with pleasing murmurs over several rocky promontories, and after giving motion to the Mill-wheel', flowing into an artificial lake. It then swept round the 'lesser Bowling Green' and terminated in a circular basin. A large stone which formed a bridge over the rill was 'worthy of observation' as it 'formed part of the lid of a coffin, discovered a few years ago in the adjoining enclosure', containing 'a skeleton in perfect preservation.' At first it was believed to be Roman, until someone noticed the figures 1000-600 carved into the lid. This, Kerr rightly informs us, ruled out it being Roman – whether he was right to interpret it as the year 1600 is another matter.

The labyrinth, according to Kerr, was 'designed and planted by an intelligent native of Scotland', and was nearly twice as large as the maze at Hampton Court. The exit was through a 'romantic subterranean passage', leading to Merlin's grotto, which, like Egan, Kerr erroneously identified as 'the favourite retreat' of Sheridan and Elizabeth Linley.

Below the labyrinth was the thatched hermit's cottage, affording 'shelter to the pious Anchorite, who appears quietly seated, perusing his homilies'. Kerr fails to mention that this was a transparency rather than a real person, but rather gives the game away by adding that 'the fire and latticed wicket, when rendered transparent, add greatly to the general rusticity'. This feature we know was introduced by Farnham, the previous tenant, but another attraction, the watermill with the miller's habitation, which stood on the other side of the gardens, is mentioned for the first time, suggesting that Bridle introduced it.

Kerr ends his description of the gardens by adding that the Hotel was 'commodious, the Apartments spacious, and Families are accommodated with Board and Lodging on economical terms'.

Bridle continued to attract interesting and unusual acts. Though he was unable to book the famous tightrope walker, Madame Saqui, he attracted her brother Baptiste Lalanne to the gardens for the 1827 season.[48] In May Lalanne made a 'grand ascension' from the gravel walks in the gardens to the top of the hotel.[49] There is no picture of Lalanne performing this feat, but it must have

Madame Saqui's brother must have replicated her feat of descending a tightrope when he came to Sydney Gardens. However, only illustrations of his more famous sister performing the feat survive.

been very similar to his sister's ascent and descent in Vauxhall. The same gala also featured 'the infant Mademoiselle Gravelet' whose 'exercises on the rope' formed 'one of the finest specimens of performance ever witnessed in this city'. As the season progressed, so the displays grew ever more daring. In August, Lalanne introduced 'many novelties, among which he will make the Grand Ascension without his Feet touching the Rope', as well as playing 'several Musical instruments while going through his exercises'.[50] During the same performance, Mademoiselle Gravelet danced, 'for the first time, the Gavot of M Vestris', while Monsieur Gravelet – presumably her father – danced on the 'Corde Volante in the manner of Signor Antonio'. Interestingly, the famous tight-rope walker Blondin's real name was Jean-François Gravelet but it has proved impossible to discover if she and her father were related to him.

There was another balloon ascent from the gardens in May 1829, by 'Mr Green the aëronaut', but, after climbing to about 1000 feet, the gas started escaping 'through some fissures in the silk' and the balloon descended rapidly, landing in the garden of a house in Kingsmead Terrace, just over half a mile away. The *Bath Chronicle* reported that 'a number of persons crowded round the balloon in its descent, and the gas escaped in such volumes that one poor boy was nearly suffocated'.[51]

The following year, Bridle announced that the gardens would open on 12 April with a 'royal salute of ordnance' from the tower. Scientific experiments, which would become a permanent feature, were introduced for the first time with a fountain displaying hydraulic experiments before the water descended into a rock-lined basin, filled with gold and silver fish.[52] Further scientific displays were scheduled for May, when Dr Wilkinson of Bath arranged with Bridle to demonstrate a new fire-resistant fabric called asbestos. The demonstration involved a man clad in a suit of asbestos walking safely through a fire 'of considerable extent'.[53] Unfortunately, the weather was poor on the day, and it was postponed to June, when it was advertised that the asbestos-clad man would hold masses of red hot iron in his hands.

Bridle introduced another innovation to the hotel. Realising that the waters of Cheltenham and Leamington Spa were eclipsing Bath's in popularity, he announced that the hotel would have a pump room, where the waters from those spas would be available from eight to ten o'clock in the morning.[54] He added that 'to guard against metallic impregnation only glass and porcelain' would be used to serve them. A correspondent in the *Bath Chronicle*, styling himself 'A Constant Reader', greeted this with approval, especially the early hours and the accompanying music. He considered it an 'adoption of those means which greatly contribute to the health both of body and mind'. Curiously, it was not only water from the spas of Cheltenham and Leamington that Bridle supplied. Visitors could also sample the delights of water from Gloucester, the result of a quixotic and short-lived attempt by that city to reinvent itself as a spa town to rival Cheltenham.

May was a busy month for the gardens. One public breakfast included a visit by the American-Siamese twin brothers, Chang and Eng, who were touring England. Their presence attracted a larger crowd than normal and, what with the setting and the fine weather, the event gave 'general satisfaction and delight'.[55]

Chang and Eng – the original Siamese twins

At the end of May, Il Diavolo Antonio, the slackrope walker and star of Bridle's first gala, returned from a three-year tour of the continent. Mortram having retired, fireworks were now being staged by the self-styled Chevalier Southby, who was also from Vauxhall in London.[56]

On 26 June 1830, George IV, who had been ailing for some time, died. From a professional point of view, Bridle would have been taking a keen interest in reports of his health. Had he survived another few weeks, his birthday, on the 12 August, would have been marked with the traditional gala. If, on the other hand, he had died at the height of the season, an extended period of public mourning could have led to cancellation of several major events, entailing significant financial loss. In the event, although the King's death was marked by the customary observances – the abbey bells tolling throughout the day, flags on public buildings flying at half mast – public mourning seems to have been muted, to say the least, and Bath's shopkeepers made no more than a token gesture by 'partially closing' for a few days, and Bridle only had to cancel one event.[57] The truth is that George IV had become very unpopular. By contrast, when William IV was proclaimed King, there was, despite the inclement weather, rejoicing, with a splendid parade, a banquet in the Guildhall, 'merry peals' from the abbey bells and guns fired in Sydney Gardens.[58]

At the end of July, the weather finally improved enough for Dr Wilkinson to carry out his experiment. The evening began with a demonstration of Davy's safety lamp, before a finger and then the head of the brave volunteer were covered in asbestos and exposed to fire. This done, he donned what Dr Wilkinson later described as 'a cap, coat, and pantaloons, of asbestos fabric', and

> courageously entered an avenue of near 24 feet in length, formed of faggots of wood, and when in active conflagration he walked deliberately through, backwards and forward, more than twenty times, and occasionally rested in those parts where the flame was most intense, constituting a scene terrific in beholding, but highly gratifying as to its results; most satisfactorily demonstrating that, by means of this protecting dress, lives and valuable property may be rescued, which otherwise must left to the mercy of this devouring element.[59]

On 21 September, Prince Leopold of Belgium arrived in Bath, on his way to Malvern to stay with his sister, the Duchess of Kent. The following afternoon, he visited Sydney Gardens, where he

> was received by Mr Bridle and a very full company with three hearty cheers. The Prince proceeded slowly through these beautiful and picturesque promenades, the effect of which was greatly heightened by the vast throng of fashionables present, and his Royal Highness, admiring the views, the distribution of the walks, and the general effect of this Elyseum, was pleased to say that he was surprised a city so abounding in beauties natural and artificial, was not selected as the general residence of the nobility of the country.[60]

Who could have imagined that Bridle would be greeting royalty, when only nine years earlier, his name was dragged through parliament as the epitome of cruelty and corruption? There must have been many in the city who felt that he deserved this royal seal of approval, as he had proved to be very charitable, entertaining the children from Bathforum schools as well as supporting many other local organisations.

Two events in October also indicated how Bath was changing. Early in the month, Bridle decided to mount an experiment to see if the gardens could be lit by gas. Bath had one of the earliest gasworks in the country, opened in 1818, but it took another twelve years for pipes to be laid across to Bathwick.[61] Bridle arranged for pipes to be laid to the Sydney Hotel and for a large star, seven feet in diameter, to be placed over the doorway and lit by gas.[62] It is hard for us to imagine how spectacular gaslight would have seemed to people, compared with anything they had seen before. Perhaps Sydney Smith summed up the excitement and wonder best when he wrote to Lady Mary Bennet in 1821, after a visit to Lord Durham at Lambton Hall:

> What use of wealth so luxurious and delightful as to light your house with gas? What folly to have a diamond necklace or a Correggio, and not to light your house with gas! The splendour and glory of Lambton Hall make all other houses mean. How pitiful to submit to a farthing-candle existence, when science puts such intense gratification within your reach! Dear lady, spend all your fortune in a gas-apparatus. Better to eat dry bread by the splendour of gas, than to dine on wild beef with wax candles!

The other event was a visit to Bath by the Duchess of Kent and her eleven-year-old daughter Princess Victoria on 28 October. Not that there was anything unusual in a royal visit to Bath, but during this one the duchess and her daughter visited the Bath Park Improvements, and the princess gave permission for the park to bear her name, in appreciation for the welcome she had received from the people of Bath.[63] Royal Victoria Park was only the second public park in the country, the first being Regent's Park. Pleasure gardens had been for the rich. If you could not pay, you could not go in. From now on, there would be more and more parks for the people. It was not good news for Sydney Gardens.

The gardens were used increasingly for political events. In December 1830 the radicals John Roebuck, General Charles Palmer and Henry Hobhouse held a well-attended meeting in the gardens to decide which two of them should stand against the Conservative candidate Colonel Daubeney at the next election.[64] On a lighter note, a few days after Christmas, Mr Bridle was given a cuckoo which had been removed, when young, from the nest of a hedge-sparrow, for his aviary.[65]

Bridle continued to introduce new attractions the following year, including an eagle chained in the ivy-covered tower and a bear which was 'quite secure' and would climb to the head of his pole when 'invited'.[66] In addition to the aviary, there was a pheasantry with gold and silver pheasants, while monkeys were disposed about the gardens to amuse 'juvenile visitors'. Bridle was quietly changing the face of the gardens, and widening its audience appeal. He laid on concerts, bazaars and masquerades as well as public breakfasts. One unintentionally comedic event took place in the summer when the young men of the Second Somerset Militia, were ordered to Bath for 28 days training. Due to government economies, no new uniforms had been supplied, so the clothes fitted where they touched. In addition, these were young men more used to farming than marching. The results were predictable. Rowland Mainwaring takes up the tale:

> Sydney-gardens was appointed for their drilling parade, while they usually assembled for muster in the area in front of the hotel. Their clothing and accoutrements had been supplied from old military stores, of at least five-and-twenty years standing; and the antiquity and grotesque appearance of these habiliments, drew many smiles from the good-humoured countenances who wore them, as well as from those who, from curiosity, had assembled to witness their evolutions.
>
> The 'marching and counter-marching', the 'right and the left-about', the 'mark-time', and the 'double quick', of the impatient drill-serjeant, contrasted with the calm endurance and unconscious mistakes of the more patient recruit, produced such a series of unpleasant concussions, and such a jumbling of pirouettes and confused whirlings, that the greatest merriment was afforded to the spectators, and (as far as was consistent with military dignity), enjoyed

by themselves. Upon the whole, as a military body, they certainly wore a very whimsical and amusing appearance; and, doubtless, they were not a little rejoiced when the time arrived to return to the tillage of their native soil.[67]

Even though all seemed to be well at the gardens, with new attractions being added, Bridle was struggling financially. No wonder, then, that he lost his temper with the council over illuminations for the coronation on 8 September 1831, when the council upstaged his coronation gala.

When the mayor had said there would be no public illuminations, Bridle saw the chance to attract the public and mounted a grand celebration gala with expensive illuminations. The mayor promptly changed his mind, causing Bridle financial loss, as he indignantly complained in a letter to the *Chronicle*.[68] Despite this, he was still opening new attractions in the gardens a year later, including an archery ground and a quoits ground. He also continued to hire celebrated performers, such as Herr Davide Joel, the famous German siffleur, who would converse with the nightingales 'and other winged choristers'.[69] But the proprietors had already advertised the gardens, hotel and Sydney Tap to let, adding that gardens could be converted to 'zoological or botanical purposes'.[70]

By June 1832, Francis Norrison was in charge. A few months later, he declared that the hotel had undergone a thorough repair and every room was newly furnished. He was making a virtue of necessity – in June that year everything Bridle possessed had been put up for auction – even the trees and shrubs. The auctioneer declared that 'without pretensions to the vacillating opinion of taste' the furniture 'may be recommended as possessing the more sterling properties of substantiality and usefulness; and, therefore, the less subject to peculiar appearance by the fluctuation of Fashion'. This sounds like a roundabout way to avoid saying it looked a bit dated. It was described as a peremptory sale, and it does seem to have been arranged in haste.[71] Only a week before it was announced, Bridle had advertised a gala to celebrate the passing of the Reform Act. He was desperately trying to stave off bankruptcy and in that he seems to have succeeded.[72]

Norrison took the gardens on in troubled times. In the election that year Bath elected a Whig and a Radical, to the disgust of the *Bath Chronicle*, a staunchly Tory paper. No wonder that it gleefully reported an argument between Roebuck, the Radical candidate, and Mr Foster, a supporter of Hobhouse, the Whig candidate. It took place at the polling station in Sydney Gardens, and what began as an exchange of insults ended with Roebuck striking Foster.[73] Norrison, meanwhile, wisely kept on his other business as landlord of the Three Cups Inn in Northgate Street. He appears to have considered making the Sydney Hotel a coaching inn, publishing details of road connections to the gardens and advertising lock-up coach-houses, excellent horses and careful drivers. He also advertised that the hotel supplied coaches to all parts of the

Brunel's proposed route for the Great Western Railway took it through the middle of Sydney Gardens

kingdom. Such a scheme would have seemed preposterous a few years earlier, but, thanks to the newly-opened Cleveland Bridge and the new Warminster Road, then in course of construction, Sydney Gardens was now ideally poised to attract custom from coaches and private carriages running from London and Portsmouth to Bath.[74]

What nobody appreciated, however, was that, thanks to a young man who would become increasingly well-known in Bath, the coaching business would soon come to an abrupt end. In March 1833, Isambard Kingdom Brunel was appointed to survey the route of a railway linking Bristol and London. Known initially as the London and Bristol Railway, by 1833 it had been renamed the Great Western Railway (GWR), and the route he chose through Bath cut Sydney Gardens in two.

At first, Norrison seems to have been unaware of these plans, and life went on much as before. Il Diavolo Antonio returned with two young Diavolos in tow.[75] People wrote to the newspapers insisting that the plans for the railway would come to nothing. But, in the gardens, the clientele now included shop workers, some of whom caused a fracas.[76] Norrison decided to quit, and in January 1834, the gardens were put up to let again.[77] A meeting, held in the gardens on 31 January, led to the foundation of the Bath Floral and Horticultural Society. No one could have foreseen that this society would ultimately be the saviour of the gardens, but so it would prove.[78]

That was still in the future when William Chatterton, while keeping on his chemist's business in Argyle Street, took on the lease in April 1834. He announced, in a disdainful tone, that 'a variety of circumstances ... has in some measure tended to diminish the attractions of these gardens', but was confident that he could restore their respectability. To this end, he planned to convert the hotel to 'a private lodging house, reserving only the coffee room for the accommodation of visitors to the gardens'.[79] The proprietors seemed to have vetoed this idea, opting instead to extend the hotel. They advertised for an architect, and John Pinch the Younger, surveyor to the Pulteney estate, was awarded the contract, which included giving the building an extra storey. The proprietors let out the Middle Bar separately, while Mr Chatterton, unable to carry out his plans for the hotel, held various events including a course of lectures.[80] He also renamed the gardens Royal Sydney Gardens, perhaps as a riposte to Royal Victoria Park.

The building after Pinch's alterations, with an added attic storey

On 1 August 1834, to celebrate the abolition of slavery in the British Empire, the friends of emancipation met in the gardens to establish a society for the universal abolition of slavery.[81] Whether or not those who arranged the meeting were aware of it, their choice of venue was deeply ironic. William Johnstone Pulteney, who had established the gardens, owned slave plantations in Tobago, Dominica and Grenada, which were acquired by Britain from France after the Seven Years War. The construction of plantations in these new British colonies were the focus of intense slave trading and financial speculation in the 1770s – the same period that he was starting the development of the Bathwick Estate.[82] These, however, were overshadowed by his interests on the American mainland, where he acquired an estate of over one and a quarter million acres in western New York, worked by slave labour, in 1792. As Whig MP for Shrewsbury he opposed the abolition of the slave trade, and in his last major speech in parliament, on 28 February 1805, he said that abolition would be tantamount to abandoning the cultivation of the West Indies: much eloquence, he thought, but little judgment had been applied to the subject. When he died in 1805, his daughter Henrietta Laura Pulteney, inherited his property empire along with a personal estate worth over £400,000. Despite the abolition of the slave trade in 1807 she maintained the plantations in the West Indies until her death the following year. They remained as part of the trust established by her will until the end of slavery in 1834.[83] Her estate was inherited by William Harry Vane, Earl of Darlington and later Duke of Cleveland, who, when compensation was awarded to slave-owners following the abolition of slavery in 1834, received £4854 16s 9d for 233 slaves on the Lowther estate in Barbados.[84]

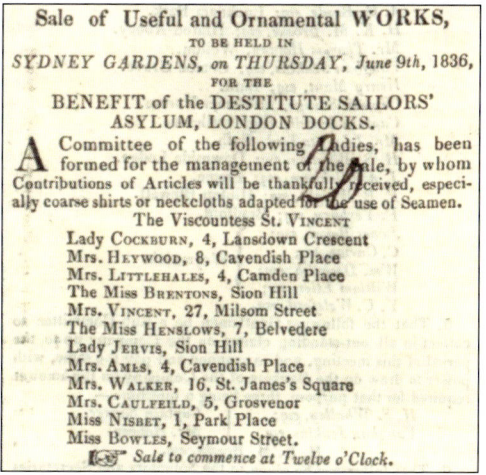

Among the events in the gardens in 1836 was a sale for the benefit of the Desitute Sailors' Asylum. The print below, on which it is described as a Fancy Fair for the Relief of Distressed Seamen, shows the stalls set up in the dinner boxes.

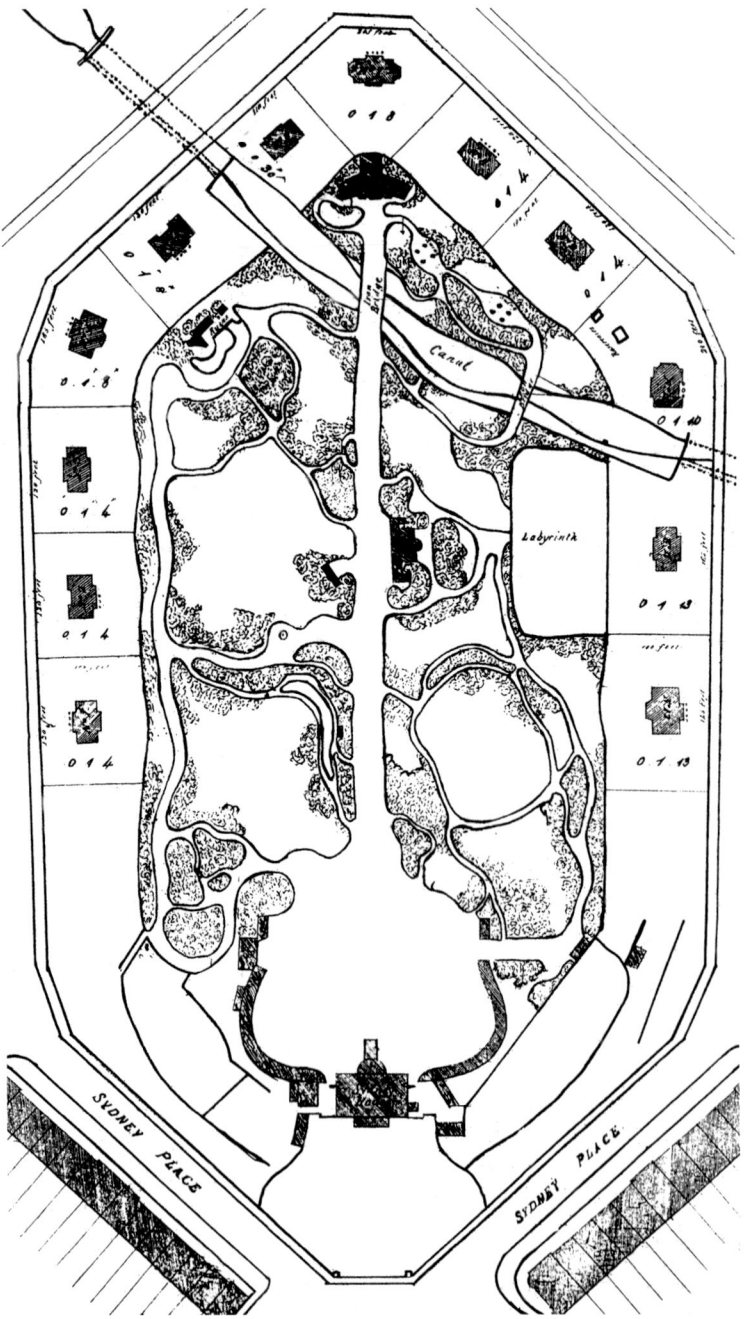

John Pinch's plan of 1837, with parts of the ride marked out as building plots

The gardens were now entering another period of uncertainty. Chatterton gave up in September 1835, and no new lessee was sought while work went on to extend the hotel.⁸⁵ However, the Bath Royal Floral and Horticultural Society, as it now styled itself, was holding frequent events, which attracted large crowds. Prominent among the exhibitors was General Augustus Andrews, who lived in a newly-built house across the road, called Vellore.

In July, Henry Seymour, of the Pittville Pump Room in Cheltenham, announced he had taken the gardens.⁸⁶ His first gala was greeted with enthusiasm and attracted 'upwards of two thousand persons'.⁸⁷ Towards the end of the year, the building work on the hotel was finished, and in December Seymour announced that he was now lessee of the building, which he renamed the Pulteney Hotel.⁸⁸ The additions were described as extensive, and a plan of about 1837 shows several newly erected buildings near the hotel, which may have been extra stables, for Seymour had also decided to run it like a coaching inn, offering 'Posting, Flys, Stabling, and Lock-up Coach Houses'. The plan also shows parts of the ride marked out as building sites. One house, joined to the pavilion at the top of the gardens, had already been built

> **ROYAL SYDNEY GARDENS and PULTENEY HOTEL, Bath.**
>
> H. SEYMOUR has the honour respectfully to announce to the Nobility, Gentry, and the Public, that the above Establishment will be OPEN for their reception on TUESDAY, Dec. the 6th.
>
> The extensive additions and improvements made to the Hotel, enable H. S. to offer such accommodations that, he trusts, will conduce to the comfort of those Families who may honour him with their patronage, and whose continued support it will be his constant endeavour to deserve.
>
> *Wines and Spirits of superior Quality.*
>
> Posting, Flys, Stabling, and Lock-up Coach Houses.

Henry Seymour offers 'Posting, Flys, Stabling, and Lock-up Coach Houses' in an advertisement from 25 May 1837

Terms of subscription explained in an advertisement from 25 May 1837

> **PULTENEY HOTEL AND ROYAL SYDNEY GARDENS, BATH.**
>
> H. SEYMOUR has the honour respectfully to announce to the Nobility, Gentry, and Public, that the above Establishment is NOW OPEN for their reception. The extensive additions and improvements made to the Hotel, enable H. S. to offer such accommodations that he trusts will conduce to the comfort of those families who may honour him with their patronage, and whose continued support it will be his constant endeavour to deserve.
>
> **WINES, SPIRITS, POSTING, &c.**
>
> The GARDENS will be opened to Subscribers and the Public from seven o'clock in the morning until dusk in the evening, upon the following TERMS OF SUBSCRIPTION:
>
> | FOR A FAMILY. | | FOR ONE PERSON. | |
> |---|---|---|---|
> | The Season ..... £1 1 0 | One Month ...... 0 7 6 | The Season ...... £0 12 6 | One Month .. 0 5 0 |
> | Two Months .... 0 12 0 | One Week ..... 0 3 6 | Three Months .. 0 7 6 | One Week .. 0 2 0 |
>
> Admission for Non-Subscribers, 6d. each time of entering the Gardens.
>
> A Family paying £1 11s. 6d. may have the privilege of introducing to the Gardens those friends who are visiting at their houses — Subscribers' Tickets not transferable.
>
> It is understood that the subscription for the season terminates with the year, and does not include admission to the Gardens during any public entertainment, nor the entrance to the labyrinth.

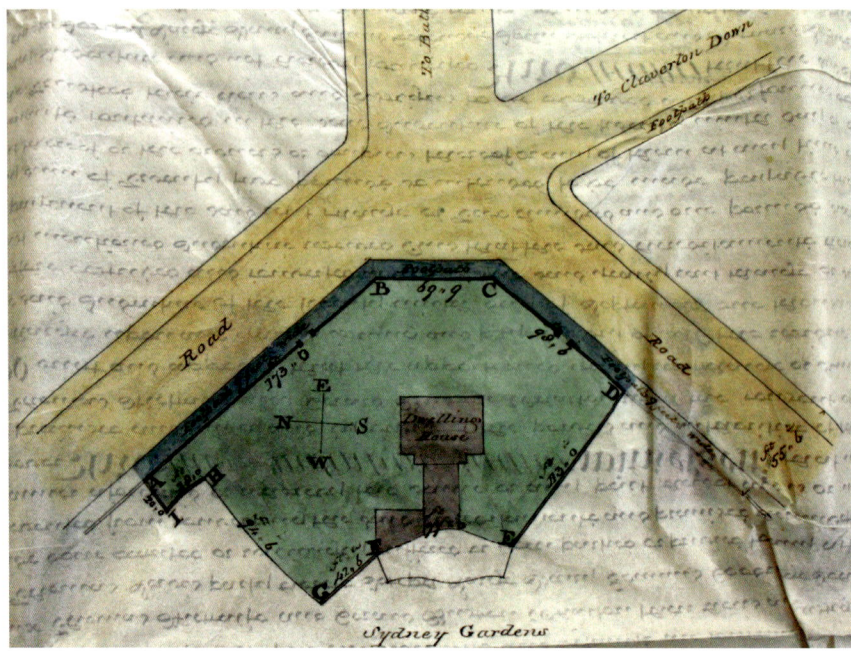

The plan from the deeds for Sydney House, showing the pavilion attached to it

A print of the gardens in the early 1830s, with stars ready for a firework display attached to two of the trees, and the newly-built Sydney House just visible through the trees

in 1834. The owner, John Stone, called it Sydney House, and, as it lay across part of the ride, this meant that the ride was now defunct.

Meanwhile, as the railway between Bath and Bristol neared completion, the day when work would start on the section through Sydney Gardens loomed. In view of their resistance to the canal, it might be thought the proprietors would have fought Brunel every inch of the way. On the contrary, they were delighted. The gardens were struggling, and only being kept going by the Horticultural Society. The reason for the proprietors' enthusiasm was that the GWR had agreed to pay them substantial compensation. In March 1839, when they held their annual dinner, it 'not only comprised every delicacy in meats and vegetables that the season could supply, but was served up with that taste which has ever distinguished this hotel since it has come under the management of Mr Seymour'. Among the guests was George Frere, the resident engineer on the Bristol to Bath section of the line, who received a toast of 'success to the Great Western Railway'.[89]

Even as the proprietors and their guests enjoyed the dinner, plans to bring the railway through the gardens were being drawn up and work began later that year. The days of Sydney Gardens as a Georgian pleasure resort were over. The last of George III's sons, King William IV, had died in 1837 and the Victorian age had dawned, bringing with it Victorian technology. The question was, could the gardens find a new role?

4

THE AUTUMN OF A FORM ONCE FINE

1839-1891

Sydney Gardens' glittering career as one of the glories of Georgian Bath was now over. The passing of time had left the Georgian era behind, along with its decadence and scandal, to be replaced by the sedate, respectable Victorian age. But Sydney Gardens did not die, although its survival is little short of a miracle. After 40 years of irreverent fun, with balloons, galas, fireworks and public breakfasts, the new age intruded roughly into the gardens. They could so easily have been destroyed completely. Yet trying to find out what was happening to them as the navvies of the GWR marched in is almost impossible.

Anyone reading the *Bath Chronicle* during the years when the railway was being constructed east of Bath station would have had little idea of the disruption caused in Sydney Gardens. There seems to have been a conspiracy of silence. It requires considerable detective work to discover that all was not well. This silence has led people to assume that most of the features of the Georgian pleasure gardens were swept away by the railway. In fact, as we shall see, a surprising number survived. They only went later, when the financial strains of the gardens led to them being sold off by the proprietors.

However, in 1839, one of the earliest pieces of news relating to Sydney Gardens concerned not the railway but William Bridle. The *Bath Chronicle* – to whom Henry Hunt had been anathema – had a soft spot for Bridle, and the tone of the report was sympathetic:

> Opposite: Track-laying in Sydney Gardens. This print by JC Bourne shows the series of bridges as the line passed through the gardens and under Bathwick Hill. It also shows how much lower the line was then than it is now.

Among the instances of reverses of fortune there may be some more remarkable, but few more deserving our sympathy, than that of a former lessee of Sydney Gardens – Mr Bridle. He is at present in the Bath Hospital, and being in the lowest degree of poverty before entering that establishment, will, on his discharge, be without the means of procuring the common necessities of life. He has tried various means of obtaining some charitable aid, but has generally been unsuccessful.[1]

Meanwhile, the present incumbent of the gardens, Mr Seymour, must have been worrying about his future. Not only was the Pittville estate in Cheltenham, where he was still running the Pump Room, in financial difficulties, there were serious problems in Bath too. In addition to the disruption caused by the railway, and several events being a wash-out due to the appalling weather, the members of the Horticultural Society had begun to fall out among themselves about where they should hold exhibitions and whether they should have a garden of their own.[2] Eventually, one faction announced they had acquired

Work on the Great Western Railway between Bath station and Sydney Gardens. This print by JC Bourne gives some idea of the work that would have been in progress in the gardens at the time.

the Victoria Cottage and gardens in Royal Victoria Park, and hoped to extend the gardens into the ground originally intended for a zoo. Another faction considered this a waste of money which would spread their resources too thinly. Finally, in November that year, there was a split in the society. Seymour sided with the splinter group which wanted to stay in Sydney Gardens. They called themselves the Bath Horticultural Society and made an agreement with Seymour to hold six exhibitions a year. This must have been a blow to the other faction as Seymour was secretary of the Cheltenham Horticultural Society, based at Pittville, which had an established reputation.

Using contacts he had made though running Pittville Spa, Seymour was doing his best to attract the crowds, and in July 1839 proudly announced that he had entered into an engagement with Mr Van Amburgh, 'who, with his celebrated menagerie of lions, tigers, and leopards, will shortly have the honour to appear at' Sydney Gardens.[3]

Van Amburgh – an American whose Native American grandfather had adopted this European sounding name – was an animal tamer, amazing the crowds with acts involving big cats. The Queen was entranced with them, and saw him perform on several occasions. However, his training was based on

Van Amburgh in a dramatic pose. Unfortunately for him and his employees, this sentimentalised view is misleading. The big cats did not always take kindly to his treatment.

what the *Bath Chronicle* later described – accurately – as 'abominable cruelty ... which no rightly constituted mind can contemplate with any feeling other than that of disgust'.[4] Although Seymour managed to book him for Pittville, he would not appear in Bath until 1842, for while appearing in Paris in 1839, he was badly injured by one of the animals, and could not perform for several months.

Despite the weather, some galas did go ahead, with fireworks now provided by John George D'Ernst. He, like previous pyrotechnic experts in Bath, worked at Vauxhall, and, like many of the others, he came to a tragic end in 1842, when his factory in Lambeth exploded, killing him along with his sister-in-law and two workmen.

In November, the *Bath Chronicle* published a long and rather sad letter from William Bridle asking for charity.[5] He was living in a tenement in Hot Bath Street, a destitute cripple and unable to support himself. He reminded the people of Bath that his efforts to extend the season, for example by introducing archery at Sydney Gardens, had been applauded, and that when the Dowager Queen Adelaide visited Bath, she declared her time in Sydney Gardens would be 'reckoned amongst the most pleasant and agreeable hours of her life'. But in doing all this for the public, he had lost everything he possessed. He hoped Bath would prove charitable. Sadly, it appeared it did not. Bridle went from disaster to disaster. Still trying to clear his name after Hunt's allegations in 1842, he visited the Home Office to submit a petition about his treatment before smashing a window, saying he was prepared to go to prison because he was penniless and starving, and had nowhere else to go. Five years later, both Bath newspapers, even the normally radical *Bath Journal*, joined together appealing for aid. Bridle, who was living in White Lion Street, Pentonville, was described as being in a starving condition. The journalists appealed to his friends as well as to those who, however mistakenly, believed he deserved the verdict against him. What became of him is unclear, although a William Bridle of Islington is recorded as having died in the workhouse there in 1851, aged 72, and the likelihood is that this was him.[6]

Evangelistic groups such as the Lord's Day Observance Society would doubtless have drawn a moral from this sad story, had they not been preoccupied with a more pressing concern – the railway. Not only was the GWR planning to run services on a Sunday, but their navvies were working on a Sunday as well. As thousands of navvies descended on the city as work progressed, beerhouses sprang up to cater for their thirst and it is likely that the Sydney Tap did a roaring trade. In Sydney Gardens, the amount of work involved must have been enormous. You only have to stand on the bridge in the centre of the gardens and look down to see the amount of earth that had to be moved to make this cutting. Then there are the bridges – one at either end, and two in the gardens, including one made of iron. Yet, if the Bath newspapers are to be believed, events in Sydney Gardens continued imperturbably. There are, however, clues to what was really going on.

Early in January 1840, Brunel made a sketch of a little building in a vaguely Chinoiserie style for Sydney Gardens. What he intended it for is a mystery. Possibly it was a tea-room to replace the Middle Bar which was swept away by the railway. As he drew it with steps leading down to the line, however, it has been suggested it was planned as a wayside station. Another possibility is that he had ideas about running the gardens himself or as an attraction owned by the GWR. As we will see later, this is not such a fanciful idea. It may also have been that the Bath Horticultural Society asked him to design them an exhibition hall. However, as their secretary was Edward Davis, a highly skilled architect, they turned to him instead.

An enigmatic sketch by Brunel on squared paper showing the mysterious Chinoiserie building, with steps leading down to the line

Davis had been the architect selected to transform Crescent Fields and Bath Common into the ornamental grounds which became Royal Victoria Park. Much of his work was inspired by Sir John Soane, whose pupil he had been, but, as can be seen from Park Cottage in Royal Victoria Park, he was quite capable of producing designs more reminiscent of John Claudius Loudon. So, when he was commissioned to build a rustic pavilion for the society, it might have been assumed that he would turn again to Loudon for inspiration. What he came up with was described by the 1843 *Original Bath Guide* as 'a very elegant Rustic Temple', while the *Bath Chronicle* called it a

The cottage Edward Davis designed for Royal Victoria Park in the style of Loudon

splendid Rustic Pavilion ... a light and elegant erection, constructed of unbarked wood, in the form of an octagon and surmounted by a lantern of similar shape and construction, with apertures for the admission of light in each of its sides.[7]

Perhaps surprisingly, the influence was clearly that of Soane. Drawings from Soane's office, now held at the Sir John Soane Museum in London, show several lodges and cottages with rough wood columns, as well as an octagonal dairy. Davis was also almost certainly responsible for what is known as the gardener's lodge in Sydney Gardens, although so far no one seems to have been able to fix a date for it. However, its Soanian style, in particular its deep eaves and plain columns, shows a distinct resemblance to some of Davis's other buildings in Bath. If it was by him, it must have been built by 1842, when he resigned from the Horticultural Society.[8] The 1843 *Original Bath Guide* has a map which, although inaccurately drawn, includes certain details missing from other maps. It appears to show something roughly on the site of the lodge, and this would fit with information gleaned from other maps. We know that the lodge was not there in 1840, for example, when the tithe map was drawn, but had appeared by 1852/3 when Cotterell & Spackman carried out their surveys.

THE AUTUMN OF A FORM ONCE FINE

No image of the Rustic Pavilion seems to exist, but it sounds very like this one, from a salted paper print of 1854, in another spa town – Eaux-Bonnes, in France

The gardener's lodge (above left) is much more in the style of Soane and of Davis's other work in Bath. It shows a distinct similarity to the park gates in Royal Victoria Park (above right), also by Davis.

Below the rustic pavilion was a rockery, in the centre of which was the fountain Bridle had installed in 1830 to display hydraulic experiments. We can be fairly certain that it was Bridle's fountain because

The Rustic Pavilion stood on this raised site above the rockery which formed part of the fountain

it was constructed by Blanch and Son of New Bond Street, who had made the gas illuminations for him. At the first horticultural show in April it only threw out seven puny jets of water, possibly because the railway works had disrupted the supply of water. In June, however, after it had been refitted by the company, it was a very different story:

> It was, on this occasion, an object of very general attraction, being so constructed as to represent a variety of pleasing figures, and to throw up water in some very curious forms. Of these, that which created the greatest interest was a single jet thrown perpendicularly to the height of five or six feet from the centre of a large basin. In this basin swam a small hollow golden globe, which, being carried about in the eddy formed in the basin by the falling spray, was at length caught up by the ascending stream, and appeared to climb the liquid pillar as though attracted by the influence of some invisible power. When it reached the top, it would for some time remain stationary, causing the water to curl back like the leaves of some gracefully spreading plant, till owing to an inequality of volume in the uprising stream by the admission of air (the stream, on such occasions, invariably diverging from the perpendicular) the ball was thrown into the basin beneath to climb and fall anew.[9]

Even in our sophisticated times, that sounds quite enchanting.

In addition to the pavilion, there were four handsome Venetian tents, each 95 feet in length. All this must have gone a long way to hiding up the work that was going on in the gardens, but occasionally real life intruded. In March, a messenger with a parcel for the Sydney Hotel came up the footpath by the canal. He asked two young men he met on the path for directions to the hotel, but they asked him his business. They then demanded the parcel, before knocking him down, and, when he cried out, running off with it. The newspaper report of the incident stated they looked like railway labourers, and as the navvies wore a very distinctive style of clothing, they would have been easy to identify.[10]

Six months later, two navvies were working near the gardens when earthworks collapsed on them. One was buried but survived, despite having a dislocated hip and bruises, while his companion suffered a broken thigh.[11]

A year later, on 28 June, just two days before the opening of the line, Sir Frederick Smith, Government Inspector of Railways, went over the line. He found it far from ready. In Sydney Gardens the balustrade had still to be built and some of the copings of the bridges were not in position. Some bridges were not even finished. Not unnaturally, Smith was concerned about public safety. At 3am on 30 June, Smith went over the line again and found most of the work had been done. Brunel promised that the rest would be complete before the line opened. Just over four hours later, the first train left Bath for London. Sydney Gardens, like Bath, would never be the same again. Mr Seymour had had enough, and gave up both the Pittville Pump Room and the Pulteney Hotel to start a new life in New Zealand, where he eventually became a member of the newly-formed legislative council.

The report of the Bath Horticultural Society in February 1841 indicates that by now it was the society that was keeping the gardens going. Over the previous year, nearly 12,000 people had attended their shows.[12] In May, when Seymour left and the hotel and gardens were once again advertised to let, however, they must have wondered what the future held.[13] Even so, their show in July 1841 was an unqualified success, partly thanks to railway providing an added attraction. The *Bath Chronicle* reported that

> the gardens presented even a more beautiful appearance than ever, the late genial weather having considerably improved the beautiful

foliage with which they abound. The cutting of the railroad through the upper part of the grounds, which it was at first supposed would materially injure their appearance, has had a contrary effect. A noble arch has been thrown across the centre, and a beautiful stone parapet runs along the side. The former was crowded with different groups of visitors throughout the afternoon, who watched with pleasurable anxiety the passing of the trains.[14]

It has been a long cherished belief of local historians that the GWR destroyed the best-loved Georgian features of the gardens, but it is a myth. Most of the losses, as we will see, occurred much later. Indeed, there is evidence to suggest that Brunel tried to make the most of the existing features. So what was lost and what remained?

As already mentioned, the Middle Bar went, and it seems possible that the castle moat was affected, but the Ordnance Survey map of 1886 shows what appears to be the outline of the castle. It matches almost perfectly the outline

This print shows the depth of the railway cutting. It also reveals that what is now a muddy lineside path was laid out as a gravelled promenade where people could enjoy viewing the trains.

on the plan of 1837. The railway also just missed the shelter by Baldwin opposite the Middle Bar. But what of the grotto and labyrinth? Expert after expert has stated that they disappeared. The architect Eric Parry, in his book *Context: Architecture and the Genius of Place*, states firmly that the labyrinth was obliterated. But the experts are wrong. The grotto, labyrinth and Merlin swing survived the coming of the railway. There is plenty of evidence to prove it.

If the route of the railway is drawn onto Pinch's 1837 survey, it can be clearly seen that the line missed them. Then there is Brunel's iron bridge, which crosses the railway at an odd angle, and is not in line with the central avenue or the other bridges. It appears that Brunel built it like this to preserve a view of the grotto from the back of the hotel. Finally, there are several accounts which specifically refer to the labyrinth and grotto after the railway came through.

In 1927, an elderly resident recalled seeing the labyrinth in the gardens as a boy. He was not born until after 1840, so he knew that it must have survived the coming of the GWR. The notion that it vanished with the railway was by then well-established, so he wrote to the paper to refute it.[15] He estimated that it was still there until the early 1850s, which, as we will see, was accurate.

There are also contemporary accounts. Before the gardens opened for the season in 1845, it was advertised that the labyrinth had been restored, presumably after suffering damage during the building of the line.[16] The advertisement failed to mention the grotto, however, which could suggest that it had fallen victim to the railway. Fortunately, a publisher called Charles Knight regularly printed a series of books called *The Land We Live In*, and Volume III, printed in 1847, contained a description of Sydney Gardens. It was by a Victorian journalist and poet called Andrew Winter, and, although it is very much of its time in its sentimental tone, is worth quoting in full. Not only does it accurately describe the gardens, in the very last sentence it also mentions the grotto. Clearly the proprietors were still propagating the erroneous theory that it was the grotto where Sheridan had secret assignations with Elizabeth Linley:

> The prospect, as we proceed up Great Pulteney Street, is one of the sights of Bath. It resembles Portland Place, London, in width and architectural effect; but it is a full third longer than that street, and

it is terminated by the very handsome Sidney [sic] Hotel, which, besides serving its ordinary purposes, forms a noble entrance to the Sidney Gardens, – a place of great resort to the citizens of Bath and Bristol: it was, indeed, for a long time the Vauxhall of the two cities, pyrotechnic exhibitions taking place here nearly every week. Having been planted above half a century, the trees have grown up to a stately altitude, and assume all the wild luxuriance of a forest. A thousand beautiful effects meet the eye at every turn, and one cannot help contrasting the charming effect of these gardens with the trim, cold, bare appearance of the Victoria Park. For some time past, however, it has been a melancholy solitude: no gay lamps now hang between the trees: 'Glitt'ring like fire-flies tangled in a silver braid'. The pathways are deserted, the flower-beds neglected, and the arbours rotting; and the whole domain looks forgotten and abandoned, with the exception of two lines of life which traverse it in the shape of the Kennet and Avon Canal, and the Great Western Railway. Handsome terraces skirt and overhang the iron-way, and ornamental bridges span it, whilst the Canal forms quite a piece of ornamental water to the Gardens, adorned as its margin is with weeping-willows. Standing between these two great arteries of the west, the Past and the Present seem pictured to us at a view. Along the Canal comes a barge, 'The Sylph of 70 tons' – for it is a curious fact that the heavier the tonnage and appearance of these vessels, the lighter and more aerial is the name given to them – a string of horses, or perhaps men, towing it slowly along. It moves so gently that the ripples scarce curve from its bows; the helmsman moves the helm sleepily with his jutting hip, the blue smoke from the little cabin creeps upwards in an almost perpendicular thread, and the whole seems a type of the easy-going world that is departing. Then on a sudden a rumble is heard in the distance, where the traffic-brightened rails, like lines of light, vanish in a point; a speck of black is seen: it grows up to us in a moment, rushes past, and we stand gazing at a long thread of white cloud, painted distinctly against the green background of trees; and ere it has broken up and drifted into fantastic fragments, the train, with its long freight of thousands, is lost in the mist of the distance:

> 'Men, my brothers, men, the workers, ever reaping something new;
> That which they have done but earnest of the things that they shall do.
> Not in vain the distance beacons : Forward, forward, let us range,
> Let the great world spin for ever down the ringing grooves of change.'[17]

However much the material aspect of the world might alter, the emotions of the heart never do; and we read with as much delight the love-tales of times long past as those of our own immediate day. Along these garden-walks, Sheridan once rambled with his beloved, and the grotto is pointed out in which they used to sit.

Although this description is faintly melancholy, it does make it clear that the grotto was still there. So if the grotto and the labyrinth survived, what of the Merlin swing? In 1883, in a book called *Historic Houses in Bath, and their Associations,* the author REM Peach recalled visiting the gardens with Louis Napoleon (later Napoleon III) when he was staying at the Pulteney Hotel:

> In 1846, Prince Napoleon, after his escape from Ham, resided in it for many months, and during that period he acquired a certain kind of popularity. His habits were dignified, but he affected none of that reserve and mysteriousness which have commonly been imputed to him. Several of his friends, including Lady Blessington, Count D'Orsay, and Prince Jerome Napoleon, and others, visited him at this time. We remember on one occasion, we were strolling in the gardens, near a large double swing, set up between two parallel quickset hedges; one of the daughters of the lessee (Mr Barnard Watson) was in the swing, which 'wobbling' violently threw her out. The Prince, being on the upper side, at once sprang through the hedge, caught her up, and finding her not hurt, gently chided her for her temerity, and then led her into the house to her father.

A swing between two quickset hedges sounds very like a swing in a labyrinth. Moreover, it was a double swing, and one which you sat in rather than on

– in other words, exactly like the Merlin swing. As we shall see, in an act of folly by the proprietors, these features were lost to the gardens in 1853 – but it was not the fault of Brunel and the GWR.

The account from *The Land We Live In* was perhaps pessimistic. It is true the ride was defunct, with Sydney House blocking it at the top, and part of it converted to a nursery by Edward Tiley, who ran a florist's on Pulteney Bridge. However, events were still being held in the gardens. There were regular flower shows, and in 1842 Van Amburgh returned to set up his splendid marquee in the gardens. He arrived in the city in grand style, at the head of a 'grand procession', 'driving in hand his eight beautiful Cream-coloured horses, accompanied by his Band of first-rate Musicians'.[18] He made a return visit two years later.[19]

Even though trains had started running through the gardens in 1841, it seems that work on the line continued for some time afterwards. This may have been because of subsidence or to finish off work left incomplete because of the rush to get the line open. All we know is that, over two years after the grand opening, a man described as 'an excavator employed on that portion

Louis Napoleon as he would have appeared when in exile and staying at the Pulteney Hotel

As he appeared after being declared Emperor Napoleon III

of the railway passing through Sydney Gardens' was still at work there. The reason he appeared in the columns of the *Bristol Times & Mirror*, however, is because, on 23 September 1843,

> he met with a serious accident, by walking upon the parapet of one of the bridges crossing the line, whilst in a state of intoxication, when he fell, and alighted across the rails below, the height from which he had fallen being upwards of thirty feet, whereby he sustained a severe fracture of the thigh, besides breaking several of his ribs, and receiving other sever contusions. He was taken to the Hospital, where he still remains in a very dangerous state.[20]

Meanwhile, the hotel had become a hydropathic establishment. Early in 1843, it was reported that a Mr Jenkins of Liverpool had taken the gardens and hotel as 'an institution in which "the cold water system" is to be practised on a large scale'.[21] In April it was announced that the water cure establishment would be run by Dr AE Mastalier and that well known Bath figure, Dr CH Wilkinson, who seems to have given his name to the establishment as a seal of approval.[22] The general management of the building was to be under the care of Barnard Watson and his wife, who corresponded with would-be residents. It was advertised in many newspapers, as well as respected London magazines. On 24 April 1843, the *Sherborne Mercury*, in an article featuring places where the 'German Water Cure' was available, reported that

> of these Establishments, the most prominent is that at Sydney Gardens, near Bath, situated at the foot of the Claverton Hills, and supplied with water from the famed springs in the neighbourhood, which, for purity, cannot be exceeded. This Establishment is fitted up with a variety of Douches and other appliances of the Water Cure, and is under the medical superintendence of Dr. Mastalier, a German physician of eminence, who has practised the Water Cure in Germany for a number of years, with success only equalled at Grafenburg – and whom report speaks of as a person of particularly mild, gentlemanly deportment.

Mild and gentlemanly Dr Mastalier may have been, but this did not ensure the success of the hydropathic establishment. The last advertisement for the water cure at the Sydney Hotel appeared in October 1844, by which time Mr Watson was already running entertainments in the gardens.[23] A year later, Watson was firmly in charge, and it was during his time at the hotel that Louis Napoleon came to stay at the hotel. It is often claimed that Lord Street in Southport, where he also stayed, inspired his plans for the rebuilding of Paris, but Great Pulteney Street, down which he would have gazed every morning, must also have influenced him. He demanded that his new boulevards should be uniform in height and style, faced with cream-coloured stone, and preferably end in a viewpoint. Lord Street does not have the architectural regularity of Great Pulteney Street, it is not built of cream-coloured stone, nor does it have a viewpoint at the end, unlike Great Pulteney Street which looks towards Barrow Hill. However, it is probably fair to say that both Bath and Southport contributed in their own way to Louis's vision for Paris – and other French cities – which was interpreted so successfully by Baron Haussman.

In addition to restoring the labyrinth, which had afforded so much amusement to visitors in former years, Watson erected what was known as the Gothic Hall. This was a prefabricated wooden building, 70 feet long and 40 feet wide, which could seat up to 800 people. It was the meeting place that the gardens had long needed, but would eventually prove to be too little, too late. The building was described as being 'of the florid Gothic order, with a roof supported by rich tracery, and other beautiful embellishments,

A stage set by Thomas Grieve. Presumably his decorations in the Gothic Hall would have been just as dramatic.

and stained glass windows'. It was decorated by Mr Grieve, a theatrical scene-painter, famous for his panoramas at Covent Garden and Drury Lane.[24] It was lit at night by gas and 'gothic lanterns' and was almost immediately pressed into use, with a comic pantomime by the Boleno Family, followed a few days later by the Distin Family Quintet playing silver saxhorns. This was quite a coup for Watson – the Distin Quintet were so famous that they were depicted on Parian-ware jugs. Their horns were based on those invented by Adolph Sax, and they went on to become one of Britain's foremost brass instrument makers and players.[25]

They were so well received that Watson booked them for three more concerts. He must have hoped that the hall would make his fortune, even though it had cost him about £1000. But trouble was looming. When he sought to renew the licence for the theatre, people living in Sydney Place objected, as did the Theatre Royal in Bath.[26] The residents complained about the noise of afternoon rehearsals and crowds in the evening. Mr Watson pointed out, with justification, that there had been crowds attending Sydney Gardens before the houses in Sydney Place were built. He had gone out of his way to make the part of the gardens nearest Sydney Place more attractive by creating walks and planting shrubs, and added that Lord William Powlett, representing his brother, the 2nd Duke of Cleveland, who had inherited the estate, was happy with the building. The theatre's solicitor said that they would withdraw their objection if dramatic performances were confined to the summer months. Watson replied he did not intend to stage regular dramatic performances at all. The residents were

The Distin family on tour in America

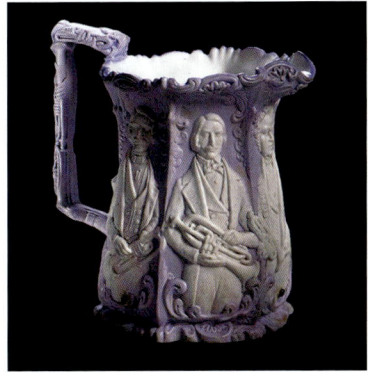

As depicted on a Parian ware jug

then left high and dry when it transpired they had been unaware that this was the renewal of a licence, not an application for a new one. The licence was granted.

The concerts continued, including one by Louis-Antoine Jullien, a well known French musician who had made a name for himself in London, with large orchestras and a dramatic style of conducting. The fireworks continued too, under the direction of Henry, another member of the Mortram family. Although there was a fire at their factory, the Mortrams, unlike most firework makers at that time, managed to escape injury and death.

Louis-Antoine Jullien at his dramatic best. He was so famous that WS Gilbert included 'the science of Jullien, the eminent musico' as one of his ingredients for a Heavy Dragoon in Patience, 20 years after the musician's death.

Mr Watson was true to his word about not staging dramatic performances in the winter. Instead, in November, he ran a series of lectures.[27] The hall was also used by the Horticultural Society for a chrysanthemum show, in December.[28] In the same month the Royal Lilliputians – the smallest family in the world – staged a performance. The tallest was Henrick Brockstedt, at 36 inches, them came his sister Maria at 32 inches, and finally, the fourteen-year-old Christian at 28 inches.[29] They were the European response to General Tom Thumb, who was touring Britain at the time.

Under Barnard Watson's guidance, everything seemed to be going well. The list of people staying at the Pulteney Hotel was impressive, the concerts attracted well-known stars, and Watson kept announcing improvements to the hotel and gardens. There were more balloon ascents, firework displays and Saturday morning assemblies 'crowded with the leading fashionables now in Bath', including Louis Napoleon. People must have been a trifle surprised to learn that Watson did not assume sole control of the property until December 1846, when he announced that all *al fresco* amusements except music would be abandoned, the hotel would be extended and the gardens laid out with 'beautiful parterres, containing the finest floricultural specimens, and improved by ornamental arbours and walks'. The *Bath Chronicle* wished every success to 'the admirably regulated establishment which his judicious and indefatigable exertions have raised to so high a standard of excellence and reputation'.[30] The glory days of Sydney Gardens seemed to be returning and throughout 1847, it looked as though business was booming. As late as November 1847, Watson was being thanked for his generosity in allowing a church group to hold a meeting in the Gothic Hall and heating it for them at his own expense. Unfortunately, he was keeping the show on the road by not paying his bills.

The first sign that all was not well came in December, when the hotel was advertised to be let, along with the gardens, which were described as being 'laid out in lawns, promenades, a curious labyrinth, waterfalls, fish ponds, with many rustic arbours, and other buildings, with a large and productive kitchen garden'.[31] The advertisement added, somewhat disingenuously, that 'income was insured from the subscription of residents and the admission of visitors'. So it was, but, as the sorry trail of financial disasters that marked their history indicated all too clearly, it was never likely to be enough to keep the gardens going.

By January 1848, three tradesmen in Bath – a wine merchant, a tea dealer and a silversmith – finally ran out of patience and forced Watson into bankruptcy.[32] The contents of the hotel and gardens, including the Gothic Hall and a panorama of the Isle of Wight, right down to the birds in the aviary and the goldfish in the ponds, were put up for sale.[33] Watson was also being pursued by the Commissioners for Paving in Bathwick for not having paid his rates.

The proprietors of the gardens bought the Gothic Hall, and for a short time ran the gardens themselves, with a certain amount of success. The dancing at galas went on until midnight, which further upset the residents of Sydney Place, and outside caterers were brought in to provide food. There were more balloon ascents and the gardens were illuminated by outside contractors, but the hotel remained dark until September 1849, when it was taken by James Ivatts of Ivatts' Hotel in Clifton.[34] He renamed it the Royal Pulteney Hotel, and announced that it had been newly furnished and redecorated throughout.

Meanwhile, Messrs Hervey and Kirkham took over running events in the gardens.

But, as the gardens moved into the 1850s, even though many of their original features survived, they had reached a point where they could so easily have been lost. In April 1850, the *Bristol Times and Mirror* published an account of Bath by a German visitor, which included a reference to Sydney Gardens:

> Bath is ... not exclusively for the fashionable world: it possesses also sufficient sources of contentment for people of less pretention. For them the Sydney Gardens are a peculiar attraction, lying at the top of the beautiful Pulteney-street, of which a beautiful view is afforded from the hotel belonging to the gardens. These are an elegantly laid out little park, through which flows the Kennet and Avon Canal, and under it the Western Railway (from London to Bristol) is carried. Besides a labyrinth formed by the ingenious windings of a hedge (which entertains the people constantly, and to an incredible degree), they also afford various amusements, à la Vauxhall, rural concerts, air balloons, fireworks, &c, &c.[35]

This account reveals that the gardens, formerly so fashionable, and lauded for their spaciousness, were now regarded as 'a little park', frequented by 'people of less pretention'. In November 1850, one long-standing feature of the gardens met its end in a singularly dramatic way. On the morning of Monday the 11th, Mr Harford, the licensee of the Pulteney Hotel Tap (as the Sydney Tap was now known), noticed a smell of gas. He entered the bar parlour to find out where it was coming from, and there was an immense explosion. The windows in the parlour and the adjoining room were blown out, the ceiling collapsed and he was knocked down, his hair singed and his hands blistered. It was thought that boys who had been drinking beer in there on Sunday night had turned off the gas to steal the pipe, causing a leak.[36] Whether the building was rebuilt is not known, but the tap never re-opened.

Mr Ivatts did not stay at the hotel very long (perhaps wisely), and, before it was let again, local residents tried to hold a meeting with Lord Powlett, but he was unexpectedly called from Bath so it was postponed. They were complaining about the noise 'and other nuisances arising from the exhibitions and entertainments' and wanted to take on the lease themselves.[37] They were unsuccessful, and in May 1851, John Davis announced he had taken it over.[38] Despite the outraged voices of the residents, the circuses, balloon ascents, fireworks and galas continued. However by November, Mr Davis announced he was selling up, shortly before being declared bankrupt.[39] He challenged this, saying that part of his debt had been paid. He was still in control in the following January, when he was summonsed for assaulting a young man, although a witness, Samuel Bevey, testified that the reason Davis ejected him from the gardens was because he, along with some of his friends, had deliberately damaged the plants and shrubs. When Bevey had remonstrated with them, they told him to mind his own business.[40] It was not Davis's only appearance in court that month. He was also charged with allowing bad characters into the gardens, and in particular into the Gothic Hall. Seventeen young men and nineteen young women had been discovered there in the early hours of the morning. Fifteen of them were known as disorderly characters – in other words, prostitutes were now using the gardens. Davis tried to argue that he did not know who they were and that the gardens had been a place of public amusement for the last 150 years – which was a gross exaggeration. The magistrates were not impressed, but, as he promised to do something about it, they reduced the fine.[41]

By now, the proprietors were getting desperate, and in February 1852 they considered an offer from the Bath General Hospital (known today as the Mineral Water Hospital) to take over the entire site.[42] The Hospital Committee considered that 'the building in Union Street has, for a long time, afforded insufficient accommodation; the heart of a bustling town is a bad site for a hospital; and the total want of airing ground has, probably, seriously retarded the recovery of the patients'. They therefore proposed taking over the Pulteney Hotel, where they would be able to 'discontinue the practice of sending the patients into the streets to take exercise', and converting the old hospital to shops. Even though the plan entailed piping the hot water from the springs to the former hotel, an agreement was reached and a price of £1,540 was settled on. There was just one more person's consent required – Lord Powlett (who, as well as representing his brother, the 2nd Duke of Cleveland, owner of the Bathwick Estate, was Lord of the Manor of Bathwick). But the residents of Sydney Place had been busy, and had canvassed Lord Powlett to stop the sale going

> BATH GENERAL HOSPITAL.—We understand that the Committee of the Bath General Hospital are now engaged in maturing a plan for the purpose of extending the usefulness of that excellent charity. The building in Union Street has, for a long time, afforded insufficient accommodation; the heart of a bustling town is a bad site for a hospital: and the total want of airing ground has, probably, seriously retarded the recovery of the patients. At all events, the Committee feel that it will be desirable if it be possible to remove the Institution to a more airy situation, and to discontinue the practice of sending the patients into the streets to take exercise. They, therefore, propose to purchase the Sydney Hotel with its grounds, and to convert it into a Hospital. The negociation, we hear, is already considerably advanced, a sum having been offered for the property, which, it is probable, the proprietors will accept. The consent of the manorial authorities is, however, necessary, and it will be requisite to obtain an alteration of the terms of the original grant of the land, which provides that the grounds attached to the hotel shall be kept open for the public recreation. Should these obstacles be overcome, the hotel would be enlarged to meet not only the present, but prospective demands on the hospital; while the building in Union Street would be converted into shops, and, thereby, might materially assist in providing the funds required for effecting the alteration. The hot water would, of course, be conveyed to the new Hospital in pipes to be laid down for the purpose.

Plans to move the Mineral Water Hospital to Sydney Gardens, from the *Bath Chronicle* of 19 February 1852. It was lack of consent from 'the manorial authorities' and the opposition of local residents that scuppered the idea.

ahead. He took their side, agreeing that it would 'entail a great nuisance in that locality', and adding that there must be airier situations to be found in Bath.[43] So that was the end of that plan.

Meanwhile, the residents had formed a society to make the gardens popular again. This, though, was very much popularity on their own terms, for the right sort of people. The *Bath Chronicle* noted, a trifle waspishly, in its report on the initiative, that 'we need scarcely add that all entertainments of a questionable character will be rigidly excluded'.[44] But one can hardly blame the residents. There had been pickpocketing, throwing stones at trains, and other antisocial behaviour. However, the Horticultural Society shows continued, and regular summer concerts were held in the gardens. These proved highly successful, despite an exceptionally wet summer. There was also an equestrian show in a tent – a variation on the circuses of previous years.

Then, in August 1852, the Bath architect James Peacock came forward with a plan for a Crystal Palace for Bath – a miniature version of the one built in London in 1851.[45] The Horticultural Society appears to have had something to do with the idea as the plans were exhibited at one of their meetings. It was promoted as 'a great addition to the amusements of the city, forming, as it might in the summer, the scene of horticultural and other exhibitions, and in the winter a promenade and garden'. Peacock said he contemplated 'several works in connection with the building, such as fountains in front of Sydney Hotel, the formation of a museum, to which the Gothic Hall would be appropriated, and generally the renovation of the Gardens'. Sadly, these plans would never materialise. By November that year, Peacock was in financial trouble and by March 1856 he was confined in Kingsdown Lunatic Asylum, where he died in January 1857 of influenza, at the age of just 52.[46] However, he left his imprint on Sydney Gardens in the form of the two houses called Lonsdale and Pulteney Villa, the latter now called Ravenswell. They are often attributed to Henry Edmund Goodridge, because his name appears on the deed transferring the land to John Vaughan, the builder. It is only there, however, because he was a trustee of the gardens. The deeds of Lonsdale make it clear that James Peacock was the architect.[47]

For the gardens, this development was a disaster. While selling part of the ride may have been a good idea – it was, by now, virtually dead ground – it is hard to know what possessed the proprietors to sell part of the gardens as well. It seems even more bizarre that they agreed to the sale of an area containing about half of the labyrinth, as well as the grotto and the swing, which were still popular features. The grotto does not seem to have disappeared, however. Over the years, various people have suggested that the grotto in the gardens of Vellore House – now the Bath Spa Hotel – just across the road, might have come from Sydney Gardens. The idea has been dismissed, sometimes quite angrily, by others, on the grounds that it did not appear in the gardens of

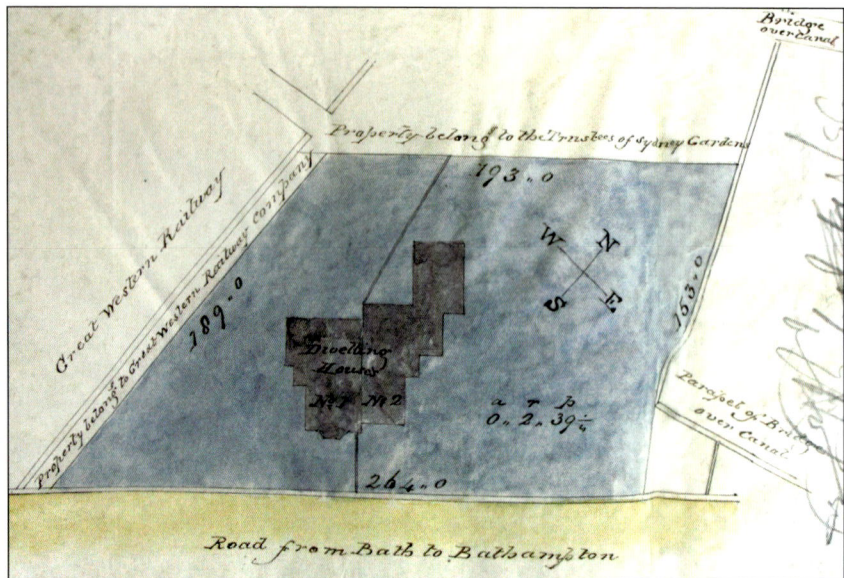

The plan attached to the deeds of the land sold to John Vaughan shows how deeply it cut into the gardens. In the amended version of the plan, below, the labyrinth and grotto, taken from Harcourt Masters' map of 1800, are superimposed to indicate how they fell victim to the building work. The rest of the area bought by Vaughan, between the labyrinth and the road, originally formed part of the ride.

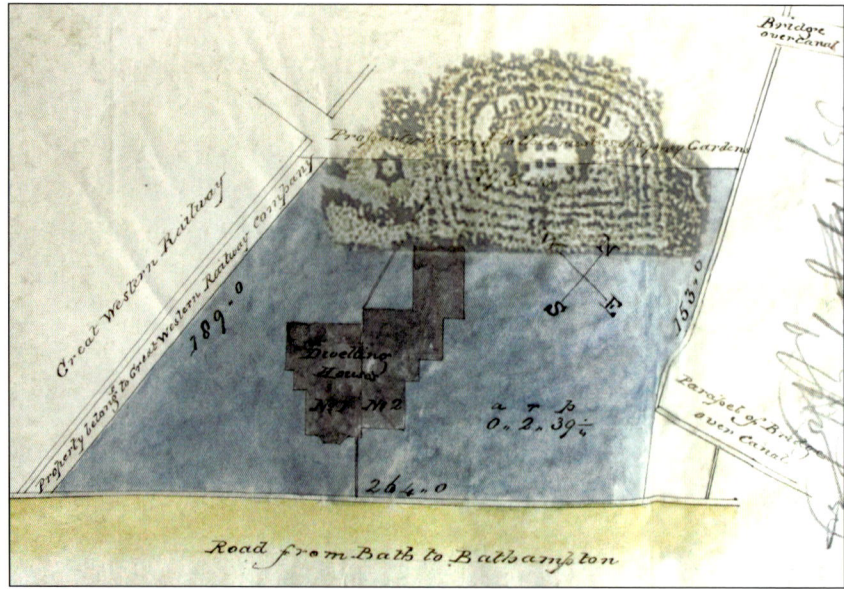

Vellore until the mid-1850s.[48] Where, they demand, was it between 1840 and then? The answer is that it was still in Sydney Gardens, where it had always been.

There are a number of reasons for suspecting that the Vellore grotto came from Sydney Gardens. Firstly, it is very much in the style of Josiah Lane of Tisbury, who designed numerous grottoes, including those at Bowood, Wardour Castle and Fonthill. It is not known who created the grotto in Sydney Gardens, but, if it was not Lane, it was someone using his grottoes as a model. We have a detailed description of it from Kerr's *Syllabus* of 1825:

MERLIN'S GROTTO

A rude excavation, which, supported by columns, and encrusted with shells, offers a representation of the abode of England's celebrated philosopher. A mossy seat circumscribes the cell, which serves as a truly desirable retreat in the summer.[49]

The grotto at Vellore has lost any shells it might have had, but it certainly appears to have a seat around the inside, and is supported by columns. Like the one in Sydney Gardens, it is circular, and the size matches. It is built of tufa, as late eighteenth-century grottoes were. Pieces of tufa still remain scattered around Sydney Gardens. If this were a genuine mid-nineteenth-century grotto, you would expect to find Pulhamite, a fake rock, which was cheaper than the real thing. There is none, and this grotto was not cheap at all.

Vellore House was, as we have seen, the home of General Augustus Andrews, who had been a leading light of the Horticultural Society from the beginning. A keen gardener himself, he always allowed his gardeners to claim the credit when they won prizes at the shows. By 1853, when the grotto in Sydney Gardens had to be removed, he was extending his grounds. Standing by the entrance to Vellore House today and surveying the gardens, one has to wonder if he was trying to recreate Sydney Gardens. There is a Doric Temple to one side, there are ponds and fountains, and the layout of the gardens is not dissimilar.[50] Andrews would surely have seized the chance to acquire the original grotto when it had to be demolished. However, taking down such a structure, and carefully labelling it to allow its reconstruction would have been expensive, and we know that the general's grotto was very expensive. He died in 1858, and when the house, grounds and contents were put up for

An early twentieth-century postcard of the grotto in the grounds of Vellore House, before ivy had been allowed to hide its details

The grotto today

Above left: The buttresses on the Vellore grotto are consistent with those indicated on the Sydney Gardens grotto on Harcourt Masters' map of 1800

Above right: The grotto arch

Left: The entrance to the grotto

Below: A grotto built by Josiah Lane at Wardour Castle in 1792

The steps leading down into the gardens from Vellore House, with the outlying stones of the grotto just visible in the distance. Although now largely hidden by trees and undergrowth, when first installed the grotto would have been far more prominent. A striking feature of these gardens is the sound of running water, a sound which would also have filled Sydney Gardens before the rill was diverted when the railway was built.

sale, the grotto was described as 'lately erected at a cost of upwards of £1000'. Today, that would probably equate to over £100,000. It would be pleasing to think that the Sydney Gardens grotto had survived.[51]

Lonsdale and Pulteney Villa were on sale by August 1853, and Lonsdale sold almost immediately.[52] Also up for sale that year was the Pulteney Hotel, which was purchased to be used as a school. The previous year, a committee of 20 clerical and lay gentlemen had set up the Bath Proprietary College 'for the education of the sons of gentlemen'. All they needed were premises. Although they had promised to build new ones, with a military school and playground attached, in the end they settled on the old Pulteney Hotel. However, they did not need it until August, so for a time during the spring of that year, it was used as a base for the 2nd regiment of the Somerset Militia, who trained there for a month, with their band playing in the gardens.

Although the college also leased the gardens, they could not stop people using them as subscribers had the right of entry. The gardens did become much quieter, however. In June the committee running the gardens an-

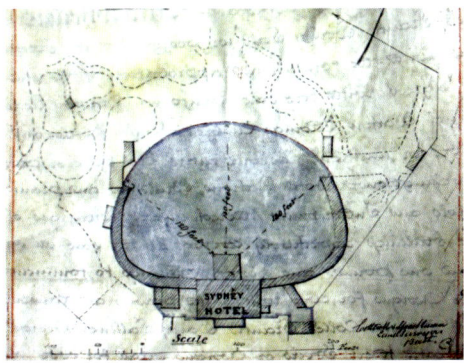

A plan showing the extent of the area acquired by the Bath Proprietary College

nounced that they were starting an archery club, and band concerts continued to be held. But one venue vanished. The college had no need of the Gothic Hall, which they put up for sale in August. Being prefabricated, it could easily be moved, but, with it gone, the committee of the Horticultural Society decided they could no longer hold their shows in the gardens, and moved to Royal Victoria Park. Sadly, this move was not a success, and in January 1855 the society was wound up due to financial difficulties.[53]

However, a new group, comprising the Hanoverian Band committee and some other concerned citizens, stepped into the breach.[54] They wasted no time in organising a Grand Horticultural Fête, held on 30 May, which the *Bath Chronicle* declared to be 'the best show ever seen in Bath, both in extent, variety, and excellence, and, moreover, in the number and character of the

The former hotel as the Bath Proprietary College

attendance'.[55] The *Chronicle's* report also records the transformation which had overtaken the gardens:

> The grounds ... have been greatly changed since we last visited them, and certainly for the better. Their somewhat straggling dimensions having been curtailed for the purposes of the school by which the house is occupied; a garden-like look has been imparted to them, and it is well maintained by the neat trim turf, clean walks, and rustic seats scattered about, now under the shade of some spreading tree, now where a glimpse is caught of the transient railway trains, or a peep of town and country. The beauty of the ground was heightened on this occasion by classical figures, displaying poetry in its most beautiful forms disposed with much taste on the greensward, and amongst the shrubs ... The company began to arrive at one o'clock, and, until five, the stream of visitors never ceased to flow. We are informed that 4,000 people passed the gates. What is more, everybody was delighted – high and low alike; and let us express the pleasure we felt in witnessing the mingling of all classes ... The crowds streamed along the winding paths in living garlands, collected on the turf like animated bouquets, or it was massed round the band spangled and coloured like a large parterre of flowers. Picturesque groups filled the alleys, fringed the bridges, decked the shrubs with colours as they were seen flitting by on the other side, and endued every nook and corner of the grounds with life and motion ... The youngsters found out the archery butts and the swings, half hid amongst the trees – aye and the confectionery and ices too, spread amidst florid wreaths in the Swiss cottage.

Despite the overblown style, this conveys a real sense of what this auspicious occasion must have been like – although that Swiss cottage is something of a mystery. Was the writer referring to the rustic pavilion, perchance? In any event, he was mightily impressed, expressing the hope that this would be 'the beginning of a better future'.

Its success may also have inspired another entrepreneur, James Aust, to open tea, pleasure and aquatic gardens on the old Villa Fields site, which he cheekily advertised as being near Sydney Gardens.[56] Sadly, these would go the same way as many of the previous pleasure gardens. Within two years, Mr

Aust's property, including his boats, his illuminations, and some more ill-fated goldfish, would go under the hammer to pay his creditors.

The Hanoverian Band, however, went, from strength to strength. They organised another fête in August and by the following year had come to an agreement with the proprietors to hold two horticultural fêtes a year and to play twice a day in Royal Victoria Park and in Sydney Gardens for twenty weeks. The date chosen for the 1856 spring fête was Wednesday 28 May, which turned out to be the day before the National Celebration of Peace at the end of the Crimean War. Accordingly, the committee arranged to continue their fête on the following day 'in order to add to the enjoyment of the Peace Holiday'.[57] For the Peace Holiday Fête, as the additional day's festivities were called, the Hanoverian Band were augmented by the band of the North Somerset Yeomanry. On this occasion, subscribers were not admitted to the gardens gratis, but, at the suggestion of the mayor, children from Bath's charity schools were allowed to view the show for two hours before the public were admitted at 11 o'clock.[58]

By this time, the college had been fenced off from the gardens. A few years later, the *Bath Chronicle* described the palings as 'unornamental', so they were clearly no asset to the gardens.[59] As a result, the side gateway was made into a formal entrance to the gardens, with a thatched lodge where entry money or tickets could be collected.[60]

An extensive programme of improvements was also carried out. The old winding paths were grassed over, shrubs and small trees were removed, and the lawn, where people gathered for the band concerts, was extended. One cannot help but feel that this was a determined effort to obliterate the past. Perhaps this was the right decision – within two years, Vauxhall Gardens in London, the forerunner of all these

The new ticket booth. This photo was taken in the late 1880s, by which time the original thatch had been replaced by tiles.

gardens, would close – but Sydney Gardens survived. Even so, many lamented the changes that had overtaken the gardens, not least the *Bath Chronicle,* which in 1857 published – in stark contrast to their enthusiastic review of the changes a couple of years earlier – a wistful account of what had been lost:

> We never visit the Sydney Gardens without being struck with the sad havoc which has been made of the picturesque by modern improvements. Moated by the canal, trenched by the railway, the great promenade truncated by the college, the edges eaten away by residences – the Gardens are a poor shadow of themselves. They are, indeed, one of many proofs of the fact that we do not value blessings until we have lost them. When the Gardens possessed long alleys, a labyrinth, a ruin, delicious grassy glades enclosed within trees, and formed a superb wood, then they were neglected; but now that they are shorn of these attractions, and have become 'cabinned, cribbed, confined', the citizens are trying to make the most of them. What they are now remind us of what they might have been – a region where could be realized all the charms of the poet's land – contemplation in shady alleys, rest on mossy banks, the music of birds, and delicious quiet amidst a population of trees.
>
> Yet the Gardens are still beautiful – 'the autumn of a form once fine'. There are still broad patches of soft green turf, sloping green banks, and masses of foliage sufficient to give that air of rurality which the imagination delights in, above all things, at this time of hot weather.⁶¹

Looking into the gardens from the new entrance

During the spring fête in 1857, as a treat, some boys from the workhouse were allowed to sit on the banks of the canal, 'listening to the music in the Sydney Gardens and watching the gaily dressed groups parading up and down the walks'. Many people stopped to look at them and one lady gave a police officer a shilling 'to get some buns and throw amongst them'. Others followed suit, and the delighted boys ended up with a bun each, at which they gave three cheers for the Hanoverian Band Committee.[62]

In July, Jullien returned to perform at the gardens, attracting a crowd of over 9,000. But like so many in the entertainment industry in the past, he was in deep financial trouble. In 1859, he was imprisoned for debt. Released temporarily, he attempted suicide to escape his creditors, which led to his re-arrest and incarceration in a lunatic asylum, where he died in March 1860. Yet in his day, he had been so famous that there were Staffordshire pottery figures of him. He was a showman whose exploits foreshadowed those of Liberace – he even conducted with a jewelled baton – but he was also a dedicated musician, who introduced some of the greatest European music to an English audience.

Jullien may have been labouring under his financial woes, but the Hanoverian Band's success continued. In 1859, for the first horticultural fête of the season, over 10,000 people thronged along Great Pulteney Street to the gardens. Another new gateway, opposite New Sydney Place, had been opened, allowing improved access into the gardens, and the paths had been widened. Nevertheless, the tents were so full, it was reported that the plants were almost inaccessible. The *Bath Chronicle* waxed positively lyrical – the 'snowy canvas' of the tents contrasted 'strikingly with the emerald sward', ladies were 'arrayed in every adornment that art and skill can produce', and the bands of the Grenadier Guards and the Hanoverian Band 'were in the highest degree gratifying, and well deserved the eulogiums passed upon them by the company'. The fêtes became so popular that shops closed for the half day, church bells rang, and excursion trains came from all round the area.[63]

It seemed the Hanoverian Band Committee could do no wrong. In 1860, the *Bath Chronicle* went so far as to claim they had 'a charmed existence'.[64] Even when the day of a fête began gloomily, the weather soon cleared up. The proprietors placed advertisements in the newspapers with details of what trees and shrubs were in bloom, and in May, when the nightingales were singing, kept the gardens open until dusk. There were were also 'gymnasium swings' and an archery practice ground. In July, a national archery meeting was held at Sydenham Ground on the Lower Bristol Road, and to entertain visitors a

Fête Champêtre was held in Sydney Gardens. As well as a fire-eater, singers, and a band of young musicians, there were illuminations, with miniature lamps twined among the trees. There was even a firework display, with 'blazing rockets, insinuating blue lights, flaming Roman candles, whirling fiery wheels, and hundreds of grand gorgeous pyrotechnical designs'.[65]

The following year, the Hanoverian Band Committee bravely decided to become lessees of the gardens. They built a bandstand, overlooking the central lawn, during excavations for which a stone coffin containing the body of a woman, thought to date from the twelfth or thirteenth century, was discovered. The bandstand, designed by Charles Phipps, a local architect, was described by the *Bath Chronicle* as

> a light and elegant structure remarkably well adapted for sound, and in harmony with the lovely scenery of the gardens. The woodwork burnishing, and the painted ornamentation of the interior have been well carried out, the colours having been artistically chosen.[66]

The college also held their sports days in the gardens. One notable event in 1861 was a sack race, for which the boys were sewn into the sacks, resulting in 'bounds, tumbles and shuffles', to the entertainment of the crowd.[67]

The bandstand, with seats laid out on the new band lawn

Other organisations held fêtes in the gardens with entertainment provided by the Hanoverian Band. In August 1864, the Working Men's Committee of the Bath United Hospital held a gala which opened at 2pm and went on into the evening, when the gardens were lit with gas illuminations, thanks to the gas company, who laid pipes virtually free of charge. Fire balloons were released, and scientific electrical experiments were carried out by Mr Rudge.[68] Among his other devices was a miniature electric train, which ran along an electrified rail. This was fifteen years before Werner von Siemens, usually regarded as father of the modern electric train, demonstrated his engine. The evening concluded with a display of fireworks, witnessed by over 10,000 people.

Although the gardens settled down into a period of unprecedented stability, there was the occasional incident. In 1868, a visitor to the gardens caught a child throwing stones at trains. When he remonstrated with him, he replied that he didn't think he had hit them – and prepared to throw another. This was reported to the police, and the child appeared before the magistrates. Described as 'a diminutive urchin', his name was William Woolf. Although he was only nine years old, his parents did not appear in court. The magistrates were concerned at his neglected condition and sent him to the Somersetshire Industrial School for seven years. The discipline at the school would have been strict, but he was doubtless better off there than he would have been with his neglectful parents, as he was fed, clothed, received an education and taught a craft.

In the same year, the Hanoverian Band extended their fêtes to two days, though they soon reverted to one day. Attractions which would have been familiar to visitors in earlier years, such as acrobats, illuminations and scientific experiments, still featured. However, it seems that attendance figures were dropping, despite new events being introduced. The fête in May 1874 was not so well attended as usual, despite good weather, which may have been why the committee announced that the autumn fête would be combined with the Bath Grand Poultry, Pigeon and Caged Bird Show. This proved so successful that for a short time it became a regular feature of the autumn fêtes. By 1877, rabbits were being exhibited as well, and the college allowed the livestock show to be held in the space behind the college building. However, in 1879, the poultry show committee, claiming that attendances had diminished, declined to take part in the autumn fête that year. It was a decision they may have rued, when good weather led to the floral fête being well attended.

Although they were fortunate on this occasion, however, the Hanoverian Band was beginning to suffer from the same problem as previous organisers of events – the weather. They had been famous for having good weather, but their luck was deserting them. Moreover, there was occasional criticism of the quality of their music, one critic saying they sounded too German. Given that most of the bandsmen came from Germany, this is hardly surprising. By 1882, however, financial concerns and increased sniping meant that the band not only sought aid from the council, but decided to employ more musicians, with a greater variety of instruments. The organising committee also changed its name to the Floral Fête and Band Committee.

While all this had been going on, there had been major changes afoot at Bath Proprietary College. In 1878, it had been taken over by a group of people who wanted to establish a college in Bath on the lines of Clifton College in Bristol.[69] The new college was called Bath College, and the plan was for it to occupy the Proprietary College until a more suitable building could be made ready. The building they had in mind was Vellore, the former home of General Andrews, which had been bought by Charles Kemble, Rector of Bath Abbey in 1860. Kemble had died in 1874, and his widow sold the house to the college in 1878. Before the college could move in, extensive alterations, including an extension, were needed, but, even after these were complete, the old Proprietary College continued in use, while they considered the question of what to do with it.

In 1880, however, the lease of the college and gardens came up for renewal. The band committee were keen to renew, but others also had their eyes on the property. In 1881, Albert Alfred Hare tried to reopen it as an hotel, which, in keeping with the spirit of the age, he planned to call the Imperial Hotel. One of the proprietors of Sydney Gardens, Mr Inman, wrote to him enthusiastically, revealing that an offer had been made to open it as a reformatory, but this had been turned down as being 'a disadvantage to the neighbouring houses'.[70] Nearby residents were no more enamoured of the proposal to return the building to its former use, however. Despite Mr Inman warning that, 'if those interested in opposing the opening of another first-class hotel are successful, it is highly probable that arrangements may become necessary by which the beautiful gardens will be cut up into building plots', Mr Hare was not granted the lease, and the building which had once rung with music and laughter was left empty and unloved.

On a brighter note, Mr Inman's dire prognostications concerning the gardens failed to come to pass, and the fêtes and concerts continued. The Temperance Association, however, having discovered, possibly as a result of Mr Hare's abortive attempt to obtain a licence, that alcohol was on sale at the floral fêtes, begged the committee to stop the practice. The request seems to have been ignored, and with good reason. Selling alcohol was a major source of income, especially with attendances like that in September 1879, when 19,000 people visited the gardens during a two-day fête.[71] Fêtes continued throughout the 1880s, and one was even held by the Temperance Society. In 1883, the tessellated pavement and other remains from the Roman Villa discovered at Box were displayed 'during the hours of the band concerts'.[72] In August that year there was a Feast of Lanterns: 'Chinese Lanterns in large numbers were placed on the borders of the paths, and when darkness set in the appearance of the gardens was very attractive'.[73] The fireworks that night were by Brock's, a company which survived until 1987.[74] The whole event was so popular it was repeated a few days later and soon became an annual event.

In 1885, after over twenty years of frequent use, the bandstand was in need of renovation, which

> was placed by the Floral Fête and Band Committee in the hands of Messrs Cotterell Brothers, of this city and Bristol. It has been painted and decorated by them in a manner exactly adapted to the purpose for which it is used, and the position it occupies. Surrounded as it is by foliage of various shades of green, it was natural that the 'eye of art' should suggest the complementary colour of terracotta. And that this should not be too rigid a contrast, it has been tempered down to a harmony – no less correct in colour than in music – by the introduction of Wedgwood blue and shades of cream; the columns, the gallery and spandrils supporting the roof, being bronze tipped with gold. On one of the panels of the sounding board, and on the canopy, are displayed the musical insignia of the harp, the victor's palm, and some other appropriate designs.

The report in the *Chronicle* concluded by declaring that Cotterell's had produced 'a specimen of art creditable to themselves, and at the same time a small compliment to their city'.[75]

Around the same time, swings and seesaws were introduced to attract children with young families. By and large, life went on very much as before, with floral fêtes, rose shows, temperance rallies and so on. There were balloon ascents, a circus featuring Monsieur and Madame Langslow, known as Blondin's rivals, and Ohmy, the flying man.[76] In August 1888, electric lights replaced the gas lighting in the gardens, so successfully that several businesses in the city centre switched to electricity as well.[77] Another new attraction was a troupe of actors called the Woodland Players, run by Mr Ben Greet, who performed Shakespearean plays such as *A Midsummer Night's Dream*, along with excerpts from other plays.

Sydney Gardens also received two royal visits – from the Duke and Duchess of Connaught in 1881 and Princess Helena, Duchess of Albany, in 1889. In both cases, a station was built in the gardens. This was because of what the *Bath Chronicle* called the 'inconvenient and somewhat restricted space of the railway station', which had been the object of criticism from

A train on the down line passing the spot where the royal visitors would have disembarked. Note the mixed gauge lines, which shows the picture was taken before 1892, when the broad gauge rails were removed.

the early 1860s.[78] Sydney Gardens was deemed a more attractive place for them to arrive, especially as it meant they would drive down Great Pulteney Street – always intended to be the grand entrance to Bath – instead of along Manvers Street, which was lined with timber yards. To make way for the station, part of the stone balustrading was removed, and a temporary platform was erected. Brunel's puzzling picture of steps down to the line in this spot, and of a mysterious Chinoiserie building, suggests this may always have been intended here. However, on each occasion the train had to pass through Sydney Gardens on the down line, before the royal carriage was detached at Bath Spa Station and coupled to another engine which brought it back on the up line to the temporary platform. When Princess Helena visited in 1889, the corporation also went to the trouble of laying a carpet along the gravel path which ran parallel with the line.

Taken all in all, the fifty years following the coming of the railway probably was the most settled and successful period the gardens had ever enjoyed, but there were storm clouds on the horizon. Behind the scenes, the trustees of the Holburne of Menstrie Museum had been trying to persuade the shareholders of Sydney Gardens to allow them to move into the former Bath Proprietary College – or Sydney College, as it was now generally known. The museum, which was in premises in Charlotte Street, had been established in 1882 under the will of Mary Anne Barbara Holburne, whose brother, Sir William Holburne, had made a collection of paintings and objets d'art. Under the terms of her legacy, this collection was to form the basis of a museum for Bath. Negotiations had not gone smoothly, however. Some of the proprietors of Sydney Gardens had initially refused to part with their interest in them. After this hurdle was overcome, the trustees encountered another legal difficulty, when the Court of Chancery ruled that the will did not allow them to pay a ground rent. This effectively put paid to their plans.

The council then came up with the idea that the building would be suitable for an Art and Science Institute. At first all went well, but then negotiations ground to a halt. Rumours abounded, one being that the GWR had its eye on the building. This may not have been far from the mark – it is possible the company had always toyed with the idea of taking it over, and this was the reason for Brunel's lineside scheme. The stumbling block to all these plans was the 4th Duke of Cleveland, who had inherited the Pulteney estate in 1864.

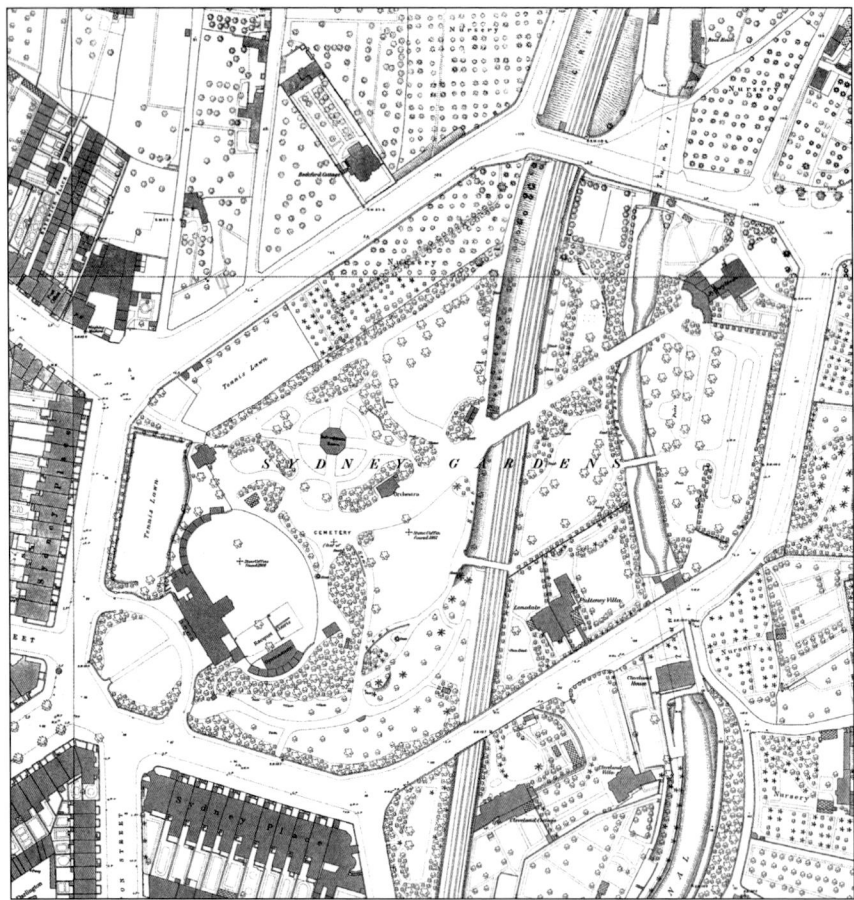

A Ordnance Survey Map of 1886, showing the changes in the gardens

He was now in his late eighties and proving very difficult to approach. This probably had less to do with his advancing years, however, than with the terms under which the proprietors held the gardens. Although few people seemed aware of it, time was running out for Sydney Gardens.

On 30 September 1794, the proprietors had signed a lease with Henrietta Laura Pulteney, for a term described very precisely as '97 years less 6 days'. This meant that on 24 September 1891 the lease would run out. It slowly became apparent that the duke had his eye on making as much money as he could from the site. He already had experience of dealing with developers. In 1889 he had been in negotiations with a company to build a mammoth hotel on the site where Recreation Ground now stands, which was then known as Pulteney Meadows. One of the main objections to this, made in an editorial in the *Bath Chronicle*, was the very one that many are making about the proposed stadium on the Recreation Ground today:

> The Pulteney Meadows form part of and heighten the effect of one of the most charming views of our city. The scene from the North Parade or the Grove, with its broad expanse of meadows, its clustering trees, between which the graceful tower of St Mary's can be seen, and the wood-crowned declivity to which these form the harmonious foreground, is the admiration of every visitor, the like of which, as the fringe of a commercial centre, it is not easy to find. And this beautiful prospect is to be blurred and obscured by the erection of gigantic pile of doubtful utility, and which, from the lack of success, might become a positive eyesore.[79]

Fortunately, this scheme fell through, but the idea of reopening Sydney College as an hotel gathered pace. By the time the site went up for sale in April 1891, a syndicate had been formed to promote the plans for its future.[80] It was reported that it had been sold to a Mr Wilkins of Bradford on Avon, but later reports indicated that there had been difficulties in negotiations.

On 21 August, less than five weeks before the expiry of the lease, the Duke of Cleveland died. But there was no respite for the gardens. In November, a petition seeking the winding-up of the Society of the Proprietors was published, and, as the year drew to a close, it became clear that the story of Sydney Gardens was at a turning point.

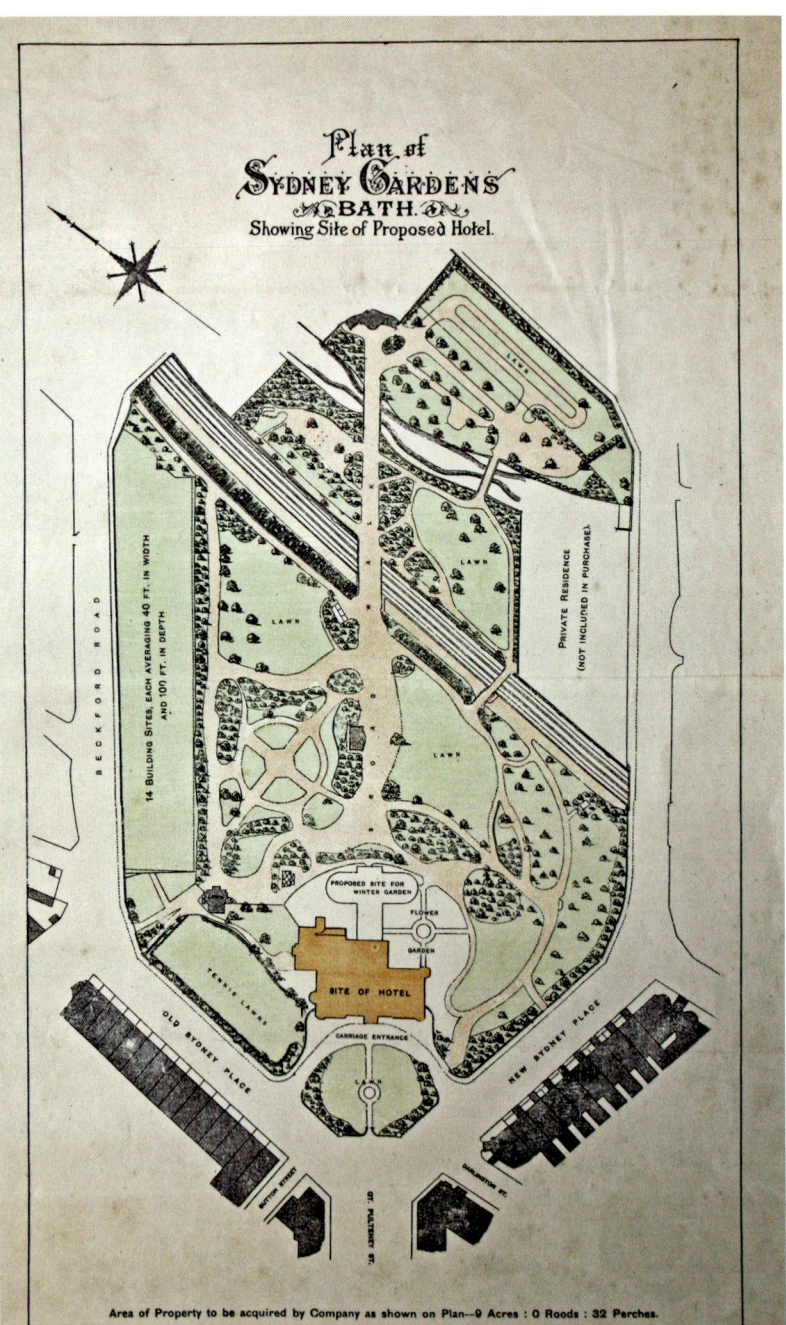

5

FROM PRIVATE PARTIES TO PUBLIC PARK

1892 onwards

The century which had passed since the plans were first drawn for Sydney Gardens had seen changes which, in 1791, would have seemed literally revolutionary. By 1891, over 60% of working men had the vote. Trade unions were decriminalised in 1867, and in 1871 the trade union movement was formally recognised. A form of state education was now widespread, although there was concern about school boards, which were seen as wasting taxpayers' money by giving extra classes to promising children. Nevertheless, it was a very far cry from the educational policy formulated by Hannah More, who declared around 1790 that, 'I allow of no writing for the poor. My object is not to teach dogmas and opinions, but to form the lower classes to habits of industry and virtue.'[1] Overall, the rate of literacy was much higher. The Crystal Palace Exhibition of 1851 had shown that the masses were eager to be entertained in a way which would also further their education. Nor were they 'the great unwashed'. They turned up in their thousands, dressed in their best clothes, and had a wonderful time. In general, even working people had more free time, and public parks were where this time was often spent.

Bath had been one of the leaders of the public park movement. Royal Victoria Park opened in 1830, while Bathwick Park, also called Henrietta Park, opened about ten years later.[2] Hedgemead Park was established by

Opposite: A plan of 1896 showing a proposed – and vastly enlarged – hotel with a winter garden at the back. The paths through the gardens, along with buildings and other features, are clearly drawn, while the parts of the gardens already lost to development are immediately apparent. On the north side, the former ride is also earmarked for '14 building sites'.

1890, after a landslip, and Alexandra Park opened in 1902 to celebrate the coronation of Edward VII and Queen Alexandra. The notion of a park where people had to pay an entrance fee or subscription was looking increasingly outdated. However, the thought that Sydney Gardens might be lost to the city caused alarm in many circles, especially during the period between 1892 and 1908, when their fate hung in the balance.

This proved to be a worrying time for the Floral Fête and Band Committee. The band was now usually known as the Summer Band, as a more sophisticated orchestra was hired to play at the various concerts during the winter season. The Summer Band received grants from the council, but this seemed to have been an excuse for many councillors and aldermen to make gratuitously rude remarks about it. While quibbling over the funding, they complained that the band was not big enough, not good enough, and did not give enough free concerts. Some argued that it was not loud enough, others that it was too loud. The band's defenders pointed out that if you kept a band starved of funds, it could not employ more musicians and would struggle to improve, or indeed exist at all. If it was forced to give more free concerts, it would also earn less money. Common sense usually prevailed but often only after the situation had been carefully explained to some councillors. In 1897, after Henrietta Park was donated to the city as part of the Diamond Jubilee Celebrations, one alderman suggested that the band could play there – in fact, he thought that was what they had agreed to do. It was tactfully pointed out to him that there was no bandstand in Henrietta Park, and he had confused the venue with Hedgemead Park, where another band already provided the music.

One thing which hit the band's income was a dwindling interest in floral fêtes, while the weather was so often a dampener on these events. Then there were the residents around Sydney Gardens, who were all too ready to complain, with the *Bath Chronicle* not far behind, despite the paper's support for the gardens.

In 1894, a *Bath Chronicle* journalist complained about the former rustic pavilion, by then marked on maps as the refreshment room. Not only did it rarely fulfil that function; the structure was 'suggestive of the Robinson Crusoe hut of pantomime'.[3] It appears that Edward Davis's building had not worn well. In July that year, someone styling himself 'Paterfamilias' wrote to the paper with an unusual complaint. While congratulating the committee on the 'exquisite beauty and excellent taste in the arrangement of the recent rose and orchid show', he felt that the fireworks started too late. He liked his family and servants to enjoy them. Rather charmingly, he liked to send two or three servants to the show, and if the fireworks started late they would have already had to leave, as he lived some way out of town. He also felt that starting at ten o'clock was not a good idea because it was not 'desirable for young persons' to be out so late.[4] But that was nothing to the complaints after the August Bank Holiday Floral Fête in 1895. Although it was successful, it was the addition of a 'Great Dog and Poultry Show' which caused the trouble. There had been poultry shows (which included rabbits) before, but the dog show was a new departure. While dog-lovers may have enjoyed it, there were complaints about the noise of the dogs barking, which echoed all round the gardens, as well as the fact that most of the dogs seemed to be terriers. Given the excitable nature of most terriers, no one should have been surprised about the barking.[5]

The following year, the poultry fanciers were told there were to be no more dogs – so they replaced them with cats. Other attractions on this occasion included shooting booths. Unfortunately, a young man called Frederick Toose, working at one of them, was shot in the thigh by someone firing at the targets.[6]

Despite it all, the committee managed to keep the entertainments coming. One popular attraction was Ben Greet's Woodland Players, who often returned to present their pastoral plays. By this time the troupe was becoming famous and toured America several times. They even performed on the lawn of the White House for President Roosevelt. Ben Greet – whose real name was Philip Barling Greet – was knighted in 1929. So this was something of a coup for the gardens. Military bands often visited, the most popular being the Band of the Royal Marines, Portsmouth. Since contemporary postcards show that, even in their home town, they could command crowds simply by marching down the street, it is not surprising that they were recalled to Sydney Gardens on several occasions.

Queen Victoria's Diamond Jubilee in 1897 was a high point for Sydney Gardens. Although the autumn fête was a complete washout, the Jubilee celebrations were a different matter. Sydney Gardens hosted the concluding events of the city's festivities, with a concert and firework display, which ended with a representation of Sham Castle illuminated. The *Bath Chronicle* not

A poster for Ben Greet's players during their American tour. Judging by the variety of costumes the poster suggests they were putting on selections from Shakespeare's plays, which they also performed in Sydney Gardens.

only rated the display as 'unusually good', but noted that 'the illumination of the Gardens, with fairy lamps, Chinese lanterns, etc, was greatly admired, particularly the festoons of lanterns over the central lawn'. The gardens were also the venue for Bathwick's own jubilee celebrations, which lasted all afternoon and evening, and ended with dancing, when coloured fires were lit along the upper wall of the railway, illuminating the trees.[7]

One of the more unusual events in the gardens occurred in 1898, when there was a lifeboat parade through the city, using the former Ilfracombe lifeboat, and a demonstration of life-saving at Sydney Wharf. This was to be followed by a Venetian fête in Sydney Gardens, but once again the weather was unkind. Although the lifeboat was successfully launched into the canal at Sydney Wharf, the fête was postponed till a few days later, when it went off very well. One popular attraction was a musical bicycle ride, with the young lady riders all dressed as sailors, and the handlebars of their cycles decorated with national flags. Members of the Bath Rowing Club took people for rides in the lifeboat, which was illuminated with Chinese lanterns.[8]

However, throughout these years, the main anxiety for the band committee was uncertainty over the future of Sydney Gardens, and the problem of renewing their lease. The prospect of Sydney College once again becoming an hotel which could control access to the gardens was a constant worry, not just for the band, but for the city itself.

There had been some surprise, given the collapse of the scheme to build a large hotel on the old Spring Gardens site, that a similar scheme should have been mooted for Sydney Gardens. However, the Duke of Cleveland had resolved that either the college should be returned to its former role as an hotel or he would leave it empty. The *Bath Chronicle* gave this news a cautious welcome, as it might mean the gardens would get the long-anticipated Winter Garden, as well, it was suggested, as a covered tennis court.[9] However, further uncertainty ensued when the duke died in August 1891, and Captain Francis Forester inherited the estate.

Nothing definite had been decided by August 1892, when the Society of the Proprietors of Sydney Gardens was finally wound up.[10] In 1893, the whole of Sydney Gardens, including the former hotel, was put up for sale by auction at the Grand Pump Room Hotel.[11] It now became apparent that Walter Hill, the proprietor of the Royal Station Hotel, had made a secret deal to buy the gardens from the duke, at a very low price. Having bought them as a speculation, he had decided to offer them for sale, in the hope of making a quick profit. To tempt potential purchasers, a licence was obtained from Captain Forester, permitting 'the building of an Hotel on the site of the Sydney College, and detached and semi-detached Villas on certain portions of the grounds, comprising 16 Valuable Building Sites'. Fourteen of these were on the former ride, fronting Beckford Road, and the remaining two were at the top of the gardens, where the ride had been replaced by turf banks. As this was where the fête committee erected one of their large tents, there was considerable alarm and dismay at the news. Mr Hill, however, said, somewhat disingenuously, that he felt that it would a calamity if the gardens were built on, and hoped they would not fall into the hands of a speculator.[12]

The GWR tried to throw a spanner in the works by claiming that it owned the land beside the railway and the ground on which the bridges stood. Mr Hill said there were no documents to back up this claim, and no one had heard it made before. There was still a restriction governing the use of

CITY OF BATH.

To Investors, Speculators, Hotel Companies, Company Promoters and others.

Sale of the Valuable and most excellently situated FREEHOLD PROPERTY, recently known as the "SYDNEY COLLEGE," the extensive and very beautifully laid-out Pleasure Grounds at the rear (with a separate entrance thereto) known as the "SYDNEY GARDENS," together with 16 Eligible BUILDING SITES.

H. C. WANSBROUGH
(Of Bristol),

Begs to announce his instructions from the Owner, to OFFER FOR

SALE BY PUBLIC AUCTION,

At the GRAND PUMP ROOM HOTEL, Bath,

ON TUESDAY, JUNE 13, 1893,

At THREE for FOUR o'Clock in the Afternoon,

In one or more Lot or Lots as may be decided on, and subject to Conditions of Sale, obtainable as mentioned below,

THE HIGHLY-VALUABLE AND INTERESTING

FREEHOLD PROPERTY

KNOWN AS THE

SYDNEY GARDENS
ESTATE,

Containing a Total Area of 10a. 2r. 3p.

Or thereabouts, and comprising the commodious and thoroughly well-built RESIDENCE erected many years since for the purposes of an Hotel, but more recently used as a Scholastic Establishment, and known as the

SYDNEY COLLEGE.

The Building, which is in the Classic Style, and has a most substantial appearance, contains—On the BASEMENT—Kitchen, Two Small Rooms, very Extensive Cellarage. GROUND-FLOOR—Large Dining-room communicating with Room at back, Sitting-room, Lavatory, Pantry, Housekeeper's-room, Kitchen, Scullery,

The sale of the Sydney Gardens Estate advertised in 1893

the grounds, which stipulated that they had to be public pleasure gardens – although they were only public in the sense that the public was admitted at a fee. As the auctioneer said, no admission fee had been laid down, and the purchaser could charge £50 a head if he wanted. It was pointed out that the gardens were still held by the Bath Floral Fête and Band Committee 'for the purpose of holding out-door concerts, fêtes, flower shows, firework displays, and similar entertainments, and also as pleasure grounds, open daily to the public on payment of a small sum'. However, their lease would run out in September 1893, after which the purchaser could take over the gardens.

Despite all these assurances and blandishments, and a large attendance at the auction, the gardens did not sell. When asked if they would be sold as separate lots, the auctioneer, Mr HC Wansbrough, said they would go as one lot or not at all. There was considerable alarm at the thought of houses being built on the gardens, but no one was prepared to be a public benefactor and buy the gardens to prevent this happening.

Within a week, however, news was circulating that the gardens had passed into the hands of a stranger, and the band committee had been given notice to quit. In September, there was an ominous indication about the intentions of the new proprietor. The Floral Fête and Band Committee were still being kept in the dark about their future, and had packed up all their belongings ready to move out at Michaelmas, if need be. It was proving impossible to ascertain what rent the new owner would accept, but he told the committee that, if he ran the gardens as a business, he would 'leave no stone unturned in order to seek a profit on his investment'.[13] This statement naturally caused alarm to the residents, and there must have been considerable relief when it was reported in November that the committee had been able to sign a lease for another year.[14]

Meanwhile, the new owner of the hotel, now revealed as Mr Davey Jones of Bristol – described as a man of 'high respectability' – was seeking to be granted a provisional liquor licence for the hotel he planned to build on the site of the old college.[15] It was not intended to have a bar – the licence was just so that hotel residents could order drinks. The architect would be John S Whittington, who, in 1889, had been commissioned to enlarge a former private school in Weston-super-Mare, transforming it into the Grand Atlantic Hotel. A similar extension scheme was proposed here, with 75 bedrooms, as well as separate accommodation for servants. Lifts and electric light would be installed and, 'as far as is possible', it would be fireproof.[16] After a three week delay so that the magistrates could inspect the plans, the licence was granted. However, voices were already beginning to raise concerns about the future of the gardens. The Floral Fête and Band Committee were granted another year's tenure, but the increased rents they had to pay to Mr Jones merely added to their other woes.

Despite various complaints, most Bathonians still cherished Sydney Gardens and were concerned about their future. This is clear from numerous letters published in the *Chronicle*, whose editor was critical of the council for not having purchased the gardens when it had the chance, and feared it was now too late to save them.[17] Meanwhile, the war of attrition between Mr Jones and the Fête and Band Committee continued. The band announced that they had received notice to quit at Michaelmas and this time would go. After some negotiation, however, they decided to sign a new lease, albeit at an increased rent.

There were signs that work was about to start on the new hotel. In April 1896, HC Wansbrough placed an advertisement offering the tennis lawn, which faced Old Sydney Place, to let with immediate possession, and, in another advertisement, asked for builders to submit tenders for building work.[18] However, there was no mention of the mysterious Mr Jones. It would later transpire that, like many previous occupiers of the Sydney Hotel site, he was running out of money. The well-established Bath building firm of Hayward and Wooster did not know that, however, when they carried out some work on the site. Since they had taken their instructions from Mr Wansbrough, they were probably not alarmed when, in November, a notice about a prospectus for a new hotel company – Sydney Gardens Hotel (Bath) Limited – appeared in the *Bath Chronicle*. Mr Jones' name did not appear, but Mr Wansbrough was to be company secretary. Several well-known Bath citizens were among the directors, including Percy Stothert, a member of the family who had been involved with Sydney Gardens from the start. The manager of the Ilfracombe Hotel – then considered to be one of the finest establishments of its kind in the country – was to be a consulting director.[19]

Contained within the prospectus was the news that the company had yet to purchase the gardens from 'the vendor'. It also included the design for

The Ilfracombe Hotel, built in 1867, greatly expanded in the 1880s, and demolished, after a long period of decline, in 1976. In its heyday, before the First World War, however, it was considered one of the finest hotels in the country, so it is hardly surprising that developers were keen to build a similar hotel in Bath.

The extraordinary design conjured up by John Whittington for the Sydney Gardens Hotel. The original building can just be made out in the centre, almost smothered by Whittington's additions, not least the baroque porch he intended for the entrance.

the hotel. To our eyes, it is simply hideous, but the Victorians were deeply influenced by Baroque architecture. You only have to look at the extensions to the Guildhall of about the same date to see that the elegance and refinement of late Georgian architecture was out of favour. Captain Forester had insisted that the old building be retained, but the architect, John Whittington, had done his very best to obscure it. He had done something very similar to the school at Weston-super-Mare, but that, at least, had been a rather undistinguished mid-Victorian building, not part of a larger Georgian scheme. The plans for the rest of the site were also ambitious and once again held out the possibility of a Winter Garden. By now the number of bedrooms had risen to 94, exclusive of servants' rooms.

By the end of the year, it is evident from correspondence in the newspapers that concern was mounting. By early 1897, demands were growing for the gardens to be purchased, and the former college building converted to an art gallery. People were at last coming forward and offering donations – some quite substantial – to make such a scheme a reality. One correspondent suggested that the gardens should be purchased as part of the jubilee celebrations, claiming that they were still on the market. This must have come as a surprise to those who did not know that a further sale was contemplated, but by July it became common knowledge that the Gordon Hotel Company had been negotiating to buy it.[20]

At last, this sounded like a serious proposition. The company had been founded by Frederick Gordon, who became known as 'the Napoleon of the Hotel World'. Entering the hotel trade in 1869 to assuage his grief at the loss of his wife, he proved to have the golden touch. By 1897, hotels such as the Grand in Trafalgar Square, and Metropole hotels in London, Brighton, Cannes and Monte Carlo were part of the chain. The architect appointed to look at the Sydney Hotel was Alfred Waterhouse, who had designed the Metropole in Brighton. However, the company made it clear that arrangements should be made for Bath's mineral waters to be pumped along Great Pulteney Street to supply the hotel. This was a tactical error – some of the other hotels, especially the Lansdown Grove Hotel, were unhappy about the proposal, and understandably so. At this point, Major Charles Edward Davis, nephew of Edward Davis and Surveyor of Works for the council since 1863, said that he thought that the council 'were absolutely debarred from doing anything of the kind, but if they wanted a loophole they could say that they really had not sufficient water'.²¹ It was agreed to continue talks with the hotel company, and in December the *Bath Chronicle* announced that work would soon commence, adding that a representative of the hotel company had been handed the keys.²² This last claim, at least, was true. But the story was to take an even stranger turn, in which the real reason for Major Davis's advice would become apparent.

Davis by now was 70 years old. His relationship with the council had frequently been a stormy one. Although his claim to have discovered the Roman Baths was dubious – the existence and extent of the Great Bath had been estimated accurately in the eighteenth century – he had battled tenaciously with the council to uncover more of the site, and his stewardship of it has been described by an eminent present-day archaeologist, Professor Barry Cunliffe, as 'immaculate'.²³ Nevertheless, he was cheated out of building the Pump Room extension to protect the baths – now he was about to wreak his revenge on the council. As well as protecting Sydney Gardens, with its connections to his uncle, he planned to achieve a lifelong ambition.

Major Davis, photographed at about the time the battle of the hotels was in progress

In March 1898, the council received a letter from Alfred Holland, who had hitherto been manager of the Gordon Hotel Company. Unbeknown to anyone in Bath, he had left Gordon Hotels and joined Spiers and Pond, the pioneers of mass catering. He told the council he had been talking to Major Davis and understood there was another site suitable for an hotel in Bath, at Boatstall Lane. Not only was he keen to develop the site, he promised the council that, if they gave him the go-ahead, he would build a new road linking Orange Grove with Pulteney Bridge. Enticing though this prospect was, his offer was met with consternation. One alderman asked if this meant that the Sydney Gardens hotel scheme was 'knocked on the head'. The mayor replied he did not know. Confusion reigned.[24]

The first indication that the Sydney Gardens scheme was to be dropped came when the provisional licence for the hotel was not renewed. When this was brought to the attention of the magistrates, the mayor caused considerable surprise by announcing that the Gordon Hotel would not be coming to Bath. He added that one of the directors had told him that Mr Gordon had never liked the idea, and it was Mr Holland who had promoted it. Almost immediately, however, this claim was rejected, and when Samuel Hayward, an accountant in Bathwick Street, wrote to the company to ascertain the situation, the company secretary replied that it was still under consideration.[25]

However, with Major Davis pushing the scheme through for Mr Holland, the result was inevitable. When asked by a council member if it – or something like it – was not his pet project, Major Davis cheerfully replied, 'since the days that I sucked. I have pursued it to the end'.[26] He just lived long enough to see the Boatstall Lane Hotel – called the Empire – open before his death in 1902.

Meanwhile, the Sydney Hotel stood silent and shuttered. Some work had been done for Mr Jones, because Hayward and Wooster had to sue for payment. They chose to pursue Wansbrough, who thought this unfair as he was just an agent, although the court thought otherwise. Indeed, what his role had been in the hotel saga is something of a mystery. All this uncertainty was, however, a real headache for the Floral Fête and Band Committee. With such short leases, it was difficult for them to make improvements, although they introduced some new attractions. In August 1899, they held a waltzing competition, with excellent prizes. It attracted a large audience, though not many competitors. The report in the *Bath Chronicle* noted that 'the coker nut [sic] and shooting ranges were well patronised, The Bioscope also received its mead of support.'[27]

Towards the end of 1899, however, something rather strange happened. In September, the Floral Fête and Band Committee announced that they only had three weeks of their lease left to run.[28] Then, suddenly, with no more talk of rent rises, or fears of being ejected from the gardens, the committee seemed to be firmly in control. Whatever official disclaimers were coming from the Gordon Hotels group, this was surely an indication that they had given up.

The Sydney Hotel – silent and shuttered, with broken windows and plants growing out of its walls, while negotiations continued

In September 1900, the committee leased out the gardens to a group of pierrots, who proved so popular that the Roman Baths Committee complained that they had lost revenue to them. The chairman of the Roman Baths Committee said that 'he did not like to use strong language, but he did not think it was very good taste on the part of the Floral Fête Committee in having the Pierrots at the Sydney Gardens during September, seeing that their committee allowed the Summer Band to play in the Roman Promenade every wet day in the summer'. Mr Seers, of the Floral Fête Committee, said they simply let out the gardens to those who wanted them when the committee was not using them.[29]

Pierrot shows were extremely fashionable at the time, with almost every seaside resort boasting a troupe. However, the ones in Sydney Gardens were not a local company, but the Adeler and Sutton troupe, who had virtually introduced the pierrot craze to this country. Edwin Adeler and WG Sutton had started as seaside performers in 1894, moving on to Harrogate, where they introduced the pierrot shows. These became so popular, they eventually set up the Summer Entertainments Syndicate Company. It was estimated that, by 1902, there were over 30 pierrot troupes operating throughout the country, the majority run by the Syndicate.[30] The troupe which came to Bath included Sutton himself, and Erroll Stanhope, one of the first women to be employed in such a troupe, who became famous as 'England's Lady Whistler'. Both, by this time, were well known. Although only 80 people attended the first performance, the second attracted 1,400, and 1,700 turned up the following weekend.[31]

The relief of Mafeking is announced in Bath

With celebrations for the relief of Mafeking and events to coincide with the Bath and West Show, which was held on Beechen Cliff in June 1900, the gardens suddenly seemed to be undergoing a resurgence. The fête on the final day of the Bath and West Show was 'thoroughly enjoyed by many thousands of pleasure seekers', with music, singers and 'other sources of popular entertainment'. In addition to the shooting gallery and 'cocoanut shies', there were also roundabouts.[32] These later became a source of complaint, but, initially at least, they proved popular with all. The festivities went on 'until a late hour ... and very much later tired, but still merry, and sometimes very merry, parties of jolly holiday makers were to be seen making their way homewards through the streets of the city, usually so very quiet'.

A few days later, the *Chronicle* shed some light on the lavatorial facilities these revellers would have experienced, following a report by the council's Medical Officer of Health. In May, a group of children from the Band of Hope in Weston-super-Mare had visited the gardens. After lunch, when they had been given milk to drink, they visited various places in the city, during which time they purchased and ate cherries and sweets. On their return to the gardens about 50 children and a few adults were taken ill. The Medical Officer and a veterinary inspector examined the farm where the milk had come from and checked the milk itself, and in the end decided that a combination of the train journey, excitement, buns, cherries and sweets had set off one or two children vomiting, and the rest had followed. However, he also examined the sanitary arrangements in the gardens and was not impressed:

> With regard to the sanitary arrangements at Sydney Gardens, there are two so-called earth closets set aside for females and children, but the automatic arrangements for discharging earth does not act. In another part of the Gardens are two trench closets and some urinals for men, similar to those usually put up for temporary use out of doors. These, if used by a large number of persons, must become very offensive, and I think there may be some reason in the complaints which have been made as to the closets; but at the time of my visit they were in a cleanly condition.[33]

This gives a revealing insight into what passed for public conveniences at the time. They sound even less satisfactory – cleanly or not – than the ones at Spring Gardens described by the Rev John Penrose nearly a century and a half earlier. How they would compare with the facilities at some present-day music festivals, however, is another matter.

Apart from this, life went on much as before for the next five years. In 1902, the Woodland Players returned again after a 'highly successful' season in London. In September that year, there was a balloon ascent to celebrate the centenary of the first ascent from the gardens by Garnerin.[34] Among the crowd was a flamboyant American Wild West showman called Samuel Franklin Cowdery, who had changed his name to Cody, and moved to England about 1890.

The guests at the centenary of the Garnerin ascent. Samuel Cody is the flamboyant character in the centre with wide-brimmed hat and prodigious moustache

He had always had an interest in manned flight, and went on to build man-lifting kites and aircraft, some of his inventions being adopted by the Admiralty and the Army.

In August 1903, the pierrots returned, although the following month they lost the waterproof awning to their tent when there was a tremendous gale. Sydney Gardens also suffered badly. No trees were uprooted, but chestnuts, beeches and elms were all severely damaged, and 'a large maple ... was so low dismembered that the pathway to the luncheon pavilion was impassable'.[35] This seems to be the last reference to Davis's rustic pavilion, and as it disappears from maps around this time, it probably did not survive the storm.

In July 1904, a 'rubber of living whist' was played 'by 60 ladies and gentlemen in appropriate costumes' at a special fête. This was a craze that had swept the country, and a similar event had been held at a carnival in Royal Victoria Park the previous month. Lit by 'electric arcs and the soft glow of innumerable Chinese lanterns', the players 'underwent the process of shuffling, or rather of being shuffled', after which 'the rubber got under way'. The *Bath Chronicle* described it as

The balloon being filled

Flying high above the city

> a most picturesque game. One of its most charming features appeared to be a graceful minuet, which some irreverent onlooker was heard

to call 'the goose-step', and which others suggested should be turned into a cake-walk or the two-step as a variation.³⁶

That same year there was a piece of news which would have repercussions for the gardens – Frederick Gordon, the owner of Gordon Hotels, and Sir John Maple's partner in the Maple furniture business, died in Monte Carlo. In its obituary, the *Bath Chronicle* said that the Gordon Hotel Company still owned the gardens along with the old Sydney College.³⁷ Gordon's death

The participants in the game of Living Whist

prompted the company to offer the whole site for sale a year later, at a price which, the *Bath Chronicle* reported, 'would justify the Corporation in purchasing the Gardens for the benefit of the city, a step which should have been taken some years ago'. The report raised the spectre of the gardens being sold to a developer and houses being built on the site of the ride if the council did not make the purchase.³⁸

There was no further news until March 1908, when the *Chronicle* reported that 'it is stated in well-informed local circles that the question of the Corporation purchasing the Sydney Gardens is again taking definite form'. The editor, after reminding readers that the property 'must be maintained as pleasure gardens', added that,

> if the Gardens were purchased by the city there would be the natural consequence of them being thrown open to the public. They could hardly be purchased with the ratepayers' money and the present charge for admission retained.³⁹

This painting by Samuel Poole conveys the charm of events in the gardens about 1904, with Chinese lanterns strung from tree to tree, the bandstand illuminated, and crowds of fashionably-dressed visitors strolling about or listening to the music

By June 1909, negotiations between the owners and the council were well advanced.[40] One stumbling block had been the old college. The trustees of the Holburne collection had tried to buy it, but the Gordon Hotel Company would not sell it separately. The obvious way round this was for the council to buy the whole site and then, subject to agreement from Captain Forester and the High Court, sell the building and some surrounding land to the Holburne trustees. When this was put forward, it did not go down well with members of the Ratepayers' Association, who held a noisy meeting in the Sawclose to oppose it. Cllr Valentine Evans, who was often long on rhetoric but short on facts, asked what the council was going to do with the old college building once they had bought it, apparently unaware of the arrangement with the Holburne.[41] By November, the deal with the Holburne was virtually agreed, although there was still talk of building houses on the site of the old ride. It was also suggested that a school could be built fronting Sydney Place, where there was plenty of room for a playground.

While politicians wrangled, most Bathonians were preoccupied with a much more pleasurable event, for 1909 was the Year of the Bath Pageant. Although the pageant itself was held in Royal Victoria Park, there were

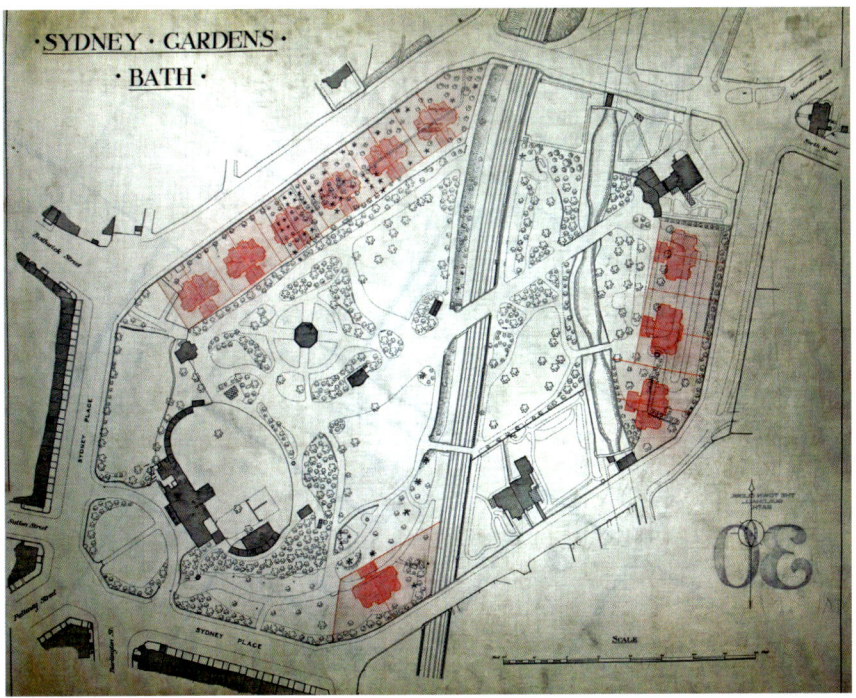

As late as 1909, there were still plans for houses to be built on the site of the ride. This scheme was for 20 semi-detached villas.

numerous fringe events, most of them held in Sydney Gardens. On Monday 19 July, there were 'gorgeous illuminations', a display of fireworks by J Pain and Sons 'on a scale never before attempted in Bath', and a Band and Promenade Concert.[42]

The *Bath Herald* reported that

> probably never before have the gardens been so crowded as they were last evening (at one time the queue formed to the entrance of the grounds stretched as far up Pulteney Street as Pageant House), and a more fascinating scene has certainly never been witnessed there. Thousands of tiny electric lamps of a variety of delicate tints had been specially installed by Messrs R Kendall & Sons. They were used chiefly to line the paths, nestling among the luxuriant foliage of the trees, and under these novel and entrancing conditions, visitors were able to admire the natural charms of the beautiful grounds to the utmost … From the

> **D**URING Pageant Week Bath will be en Fete, and the Entertainment and Fancy Dress Ball Committees have made the following Evening Arrangements:
>
> MONDAY—GORGEOUS ILLUMINATIONS, DISPLAY OF FIREWORKS ON A SCALE NEVER BEFORE ATTEMPTED IN BATH, AND BAND, SYDNEY GARDENS, AT 8 P.M., 6d.
>
> TUESDAY—BESSES O' TH' BARN BAND CONCERT, SYDNEY GARDENS, AT 8 P.M., 6d.
>
> WEDNESDAY—CHILDREN'S FAIRY PLAY & BAND, SYDNEY GARDENS, AT 8 P.M., 6d.
>
> THURSDAY—LIVING CHESS AND ANIMATED PICTURES OF THE PAGEANT, SYDNEY GARDENS, AT 8 P.M., 6d.
>
> FRIDAY—FANCY DRESS BALL AT ASSEMBLY ROOMS, TICKETS (INCLUDING SUPPER), 10/6, PIERROTS AT SYDNEY GARDENS, AT 8 P.M., 6d.
>
> SATURDAY—GREAT BATTLE OF FLOWERS, DECORATED MOTOR CARS. (PRIZES FOR BEST DECORATED CARS.) BAND, SYDNEY GARDENS, AT 8 P.M., 1/-. PAGEANT PERFORMERS IN COSTUME HALF PRICE.
>
> **FESTIVAL SERVICES** with Special Preachers are being arranged at Churches of all Denominations both for the Sunday previous to and after the Pageant. The Lord Bishop of Bath and Wells will preach in the Abbey on Sunday, July 18th, 11 a.m.
>
> **A HOUSING COMMITTEE** has been formed, whose sole function is to arrange for the comfort of Visitors to the Pageant. Applications for apartments should be addressed to: **THE SECRETARY, HOUSING COMMITTEE, PAGEANT HOUSE, BATH.**
>
> **THE AUDITORIUM** is designed to accommodate about four thousand persons.
>
> **REFRESHMENTS** will be supplied on the ground by Messrs. FORTT & SON, Confectioners, Bath; and Chocolates by Messrs. BONNET & SON, Bath.
>
> Ample accommodation for carriages, motor cars and horses will be provided. The Committees hope that in the event of any of the Pageant Performers wishing to be Photographed, they will avail themselves of the services of the Official Photographers, Messrs. LEWIS BROS., Seymour Street, Bath, who will have a studio on the ground.

Details of events in Sydney Gardens from the official guide to the pageant

brilliantly illuminated bandstand the Bath Military Band, conducted by Mr WFC Schöttler, discoursed an excellent programme of music, while in another part of the grounds Mr Carl Fredricks' Costume Concert Party catered for hundreds of appreciative listeners with song and dance and patter. The party have returned from their seaside tour with quite a number of new items which were very popularly received. Elsewhere a tent was provided for dancing, and there were many who availed themselves of the opportunity, the music being provided by a string orchestra, supplied by Mr Schöttler. The country fair amusement grounds were under the management of Messrs Fredricks and Larcher, and throughout the evening they were thronged with crowds of people. The electric switchback, and the 'slipping the slip', a novelty which caused a good deal of merriment, seemed to be especially popular … Late in the evening there was a gorgeous display of fireworks by Messrs Pain, and for half an hour the sky was brilliantly illuminated and the foliage of the trees assumed a variety of lovely tints. There were several novel features in the display. One was like a fairies' maypole – a revolving horizontal wheel, with dangling ropes of many colours

As ever, the music was provided by the Bath Military Band, under their talented conductor, Mr WFC Schöttler

crowned by a fountain of fire; and another fascinating spectacle was the outline of a burning house, with a fire engine madly working close by, and the firemen playing on the building with their hose.[43]

On the following evening, the star turn was the Besses o' th' Barn Brass Band from Lancashire, founded in 1818 and still going strong today. The review in the *Bath Herald* seemed to imply that brass bands were something of a novelty in Bath. 'The instruments are wholly of brass,' it informed its readers, 'and for every one present who missed the softening influence of reeds there were scores who revelled in the astounding effects the composition of the band rendered possible.'[44]

On Wednesday, girls from Harley Street School performed a play, *In My Lady's Garden*, written by their headmistress. So popular were they that 3,000 people turned up to see them, and they could easily have packed out another performance. In a prologue, it was explained that the girls have formed a fairy garden to while away an hour':

> My lady and her maid attend and exact loving homage from the assembled flowers, tended by the Spirit of the Flowers, and before her

they pass through a floral alphabet, so that there are some 31 'speaking parts', after which the second chorus of much smaller children appear as butterflies with their Spirit. In due course the Spirit of the Night sends all to sleep, and the Spirit of the Past speaks an epilogue which brings the play to an all too early conclusion.[45]

On Thursday there was Living Chess and a film – described as 'animated pictures' – of the pageant, as well as a band concert.

On Friday a Fancy Dress Ball was held in the Assembly Rooms, while for those unable to attend, there were pierrots in Sydney Gardens. But the greatest spectacle was reserved for Saturday night, when between eleven and twelve thousand people crowded into the gardens. The *Bath Chronicle* described the build-up to the festivities:

> In the crowded streets, figures clad in all the varieties of garbs of the past nineteen centuries, jostled one another, while on the pavements and grouped at the corners of the principal thoroughfares, staid citizens in more sober raiment watched the progress of this strange mingling of many generations. Cab ranks were deserted, and down Pulteney Street there was a continuous, steady procession of every kind of vehicle. All roads led to Sydney Gardens, where a wind-up to the week's festivities was promised in the shape of a magnificent fête of unprecedented brilliancy … The Sydney Gardens have been the scene of many a gorgeous gathering, but never has it been thronged with such a mass of colour and movement as on Saturday night. Pageant performers, in costume, and everybody else were there. The proceedings commenced with a parade of the decorated vehicles … Undoubtedly the most popular of the exhibiting vehicles were the motor cars, which had been garnished in every conceivable way. Probably the most effective and novel was that above which a swing was erected, a young girl occupying the seat, and gently swaying to and fro as the car proceeded … Unfortunately the crowd was so dense that a comparatively small number of people were able to see the competitive vehicles.

The parade over, some of the characters who had taken part in the pageant in Royal Victoria Park over the preceding days 'entertained the spectators in a

The Canadian and American representatives with Lady de Blaquiere as Mother Bath – dignity and grace personified, until it was time for the Battle of the Flowers

novel manner'. As the band struck up, 'a continuous circle of Anglo Saxons in their war paint, Romans in their armour, and a number of literary and other characters kept up an impressive parade in front of the bandstand, while the Elizabethan ladies held a revel round the car'. This was the prelude to the main event of the evening, the arrival of ladies from other towns and cities called Bath in North America, along with the great and the good of Bath. After they took their seats 'in the orchestra', prizes were awarded for the decorated vehicles, then 'five calls were sounded on a bugle'. This was 'the signal for the battle of flowers to commence':

> The ladies on the bandstand accordingly began to pelt everyone near at hand with the flowers, mostly made of paper, the American girls seeming to particularly enjoy this form of mimic fighting. Soon the firework display was in full swing, the whole concluding with a fine set piece, wishing 'Prosperity to the American Baths'.[46]

To say these events were popular is an understatement. Far more people attended them than went to the pageant in Royal Victoria Park. Sadly, it was the last stand for Sydney Gardens in their role as private pleasure gardens, but at least they went out triumphantly.

In August 1910, the bill was passed giving the council the go-ahead to buy Sydney Gardens. Arrangements were made for the Holburne trustees to acquire the building, although the legal claims of the Bathwick Estate held matters up. However, the trustees had already engaged someone to convert it to an art gallery. This was the eminent architect Sir Reginald Blomfield, who was no fan of Georgian architecture. He was one of the leading proponents of what became known as the 'Wrennaisance' – a revival of the Baroque style of the seventeenth century. In Bath, Mowbray Green's ground-breaking book *The Eighteenth Century Architecture of Bath*, published in 1904, was only just beginning to persuade people of the virtues of Georgian architecture. Unfortunately, Blomfield was not persuaded. He thought Georgian architecture was frigid and set out to make the hapless old building more ornamental. Although Pinch the Younger had added an extra storey to it, the exterior had otherwise survived almost unscathed, but Blomfield soon put paid to that. Behind the façade, the building was ripped apart, its old rooms removed to create a gallery. This was understandable – it had already been altered internally, and it has to be said that he created a well-designed space for the Holburne collection. It was what he did externally that was so heavy-handed. At the front, he removed the two wings and curtain walls which had been there from the beginning, replacing them with a colonnade, upon which he set urns and balustrading. Another balustrade was added to the roofline, and the first floor windows were lengthened, destroying their proportions. The small attic windows above them were removed and replaced with oval medallions, draped in garlands – not delicate husks like those on Baldwin's buildings opposite, but heavy branches – alternating with tablets. In the outer medallions two inappropriate, seventeenth-century style faces, of a man and a woman, were carved.

Harcourt Masters' Palladian façade had always sat rather uncomfortably as a *point de vue* at the end of Baldwin's delicate neo-classical Great Pulteney Street, but at least the Corinthian columns on the porte-cochère had lightened its severity. Now Blomfield created something which looked heavy and overbearing, but very Queen Anne, satisfying his aesthetic prejudice. It could have been even worse. Blomfield's drawings show that he planned to top it off with a dome of monumental ugliness. Domes were very much in fashion – Brydon, who had designed the Guildhall extensions in 1893, inflicted a

Blomfield's final design for the western façade of the Holburne Museum

This fragile blueprint shows the same design with an added dome

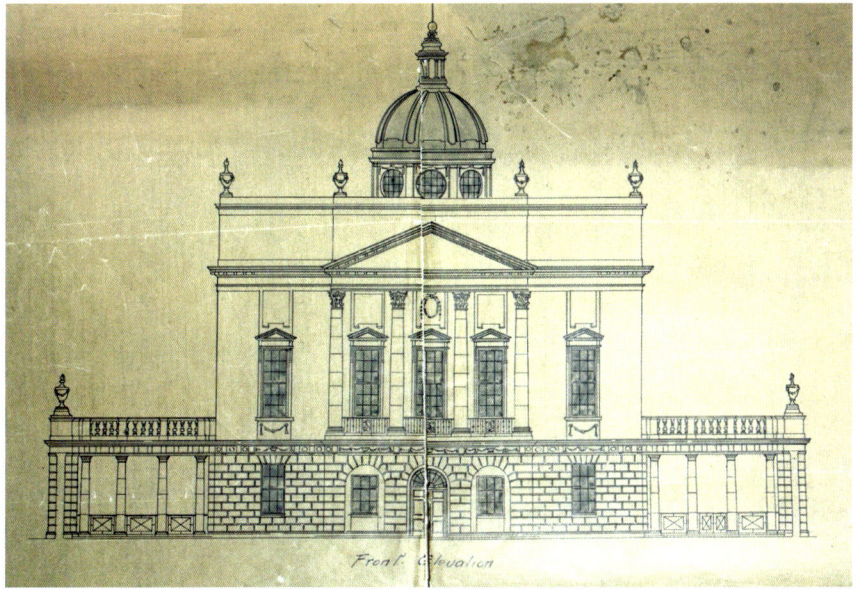

dome on the top of Baldwin's original building. One critic described it as looking like 'a toadstool great in girth and flat', giving the impression that 'St Paul's had come to Bath and pupped'. Blomfield's dome certainly was not flat; reminiscent of the dome Yeoville Thomason had incorporated into his design for Birmingham's Council House and Art Gallery 30 years earlier, it was aggressively assertive. Fortunately, the Holburne trustees rejected this final touch, although Prebendary Boyd, the chairman of the trustees, recorded his deep regret at its abandonment.

Once the council had taken on the gardens, there was considerable work to be done. Several rather scrubby trees and shrubs were felled, and ivy cleared off the walls. The Floral Fête and Band Committee also had some ideas, one of which was to build a pavilion – a plan which was placed in abeyance and never revived. The Bath and District Rifle Association wanted to erect a rifle range, but the Bathwick Estates objected on behalf of the residents, so it was suggested there should be a bowling green. Eventually, late in 1912, the Floral Fête and Band Committee decided to terminate the lease of the gardens, a decision which was triggered by the sudden death of their band leader, WFC Schöttler, in November 1912. He had literally worked himself into the grave, with an endless round of concerts, teaching and solo work. Despite being in the throes of a chill, he had returned from a day's teaching at Downside, and then determinedly set out the same evening to conduct the orchestra at the Theatre Royal. Within twenty four hours, he had collapsed and was discovered to be suffering from pneumonia. Despite being rushed to hospital, within a week he was dead. The loss of this inspirational figure seemed to have knocked the stuffing out of the band committee. At this point, the council decided it would take over management of the gardens, the task falling to the Parks and Cemeteries committee.

As discussions about renovation of the gardens, provision of facilities and programming of events got under way, the problems of them being run by a council committee began to emerge. Civic finances, party political differences and councillors with conflicting agendas – included those who wanted to spend the absolute minimum on the gardens – all made for lengthy discussions. So through the years, as councillors did their best to keep the park going and supply essential services, they took some dubious decisions and occasionally some downright disastrous ones.

One of the first decisions to be taken in 1913, albeit not without opposition, was that the entry to the gardens should be free.[47] Cllr Stone of Oldfield Park was one of those who objected, arguing that the charge should remain, and the gardens be reserved for visitors to the city. It was pointed out, however, that it was asking too much to expect the ratepayers to pay for the upkeep of the gardens but not be allowed into them. It was agreed, however, that they could be closed on special occasions, and that there should be an enclosure in front of the bandstand where a charge could be made for people listening to the band.

At the same meeting, Percy Jackman, the chairman of the Parks and Cemeteries Committee, reported that 'the Gardens were in such a hopeless state when they took them over that it had been necessary to have three or four men there'. Many of the structures were in urgent need of maintenance. The bandstand was in particularly bad shape, and the temple – as the councillors described the pavilion at the top of the gardens – needed its ceiling match-boarded. Nearly all the seats in the gardens were in poor condition, and required a coat of paint – a job which some councillors felt that the Floral Fête and Band Committee should pay for. There was also a prolonged argument over the stone vases, which had adorned the side entrance to the gardens. When the council discovered that these had been quietly sold, they confronted the Floral Fête committee, who replied that, as they had bought and installed them, they were at liberty to dispose of them. They also described them as weather-worn, although photographs taken a few years earlier suggest otherwise. The Town Clerk pointed out that, as they were fixtures and fittings, they should not have been removed. The Holburne trustees then joined in and said that they had anticipated that the vases would remain. Eventually, the council paid £10 for the remaining fixtures and fittings, and the Great Vase Row, which had rumbled on for months, quietly died away. Meanwhile, other facilities and improvements were added, including tennis courts, though at first they were grass rather than hard courts.

Almost immediately, the council contrived to get itself embroiled in another controversy over the Temple of Minerva, which was Bath's exhibit in the Festival of Empire at the Crystal Palace in 1911. At the time it was suggested that, after the festival, it should come back to Bath and be re-erected either in Royal Victoria Park or the Institution Gardens – the former Harrison's Walks.

However, once the exhibition was over, Bath Corporation simply left it where it was. In 1913, however, they were told that it was in the way of the forthcoming Anglo-German exhibition, and, if they wanted it to stay there, they

The Temple of Minerva from the 1911 Festival of Empire was re-erected near the bandstand in Sydney Gardens

would have to pay. After much wrangling, it was agreed to bring it back to Bath and re-erect it in Sydney Gardens. As King Edward VII had died in 1910, it was suggested that it could form Bath's memorial to him, but it was felt that, since it had been an advertisement for Bath, this smacked of *lèse-majesté*. The Pageant Committee then suggested that it could commemorate the pageant, and offered to pay for a plaque. This was a sound idea, as one of the two stage

It was intended to be a copy of the Roman temple beneath the Pump Room

sets erected for the pageant in Royal Victoria Park had indeed represented the Temple of Minerva. At the time, everyone in Bath would have been aware that, although the pageant had not taken place in Sydney Gardens, they had played a major role in the pageant festivities and had hosted the final event. Over time, however, memories of the pageant faded, and today the temple causes confusion for the general public and local historians alike: the public being led to believe that the pageant took place here, while some historians claim that the gardens had nothing to do with the pageant at all.

While the councillors argued long and hard over whether or not the temple should return to Bath, once that was decided – which was not until 1914 – its position within Sydney Gardens was agreed unanimously. It would take the place of what was dismissively described as 'the old shelter'. Indeed it was old – it was one of the original features of the gardens, and presumably designed either by Baldwin or Harcourt Masters. Yet not even the fledgling Old Bath Preservation Society – a forerunner of the Bath Preservation Society – raised its voice in protest against its destruction. Although the shelter may have been in a bad state, the stone was in sufficiently good condition to be re-used to build a store for the gardeners on the east side of the gardens, 'near the wall adjoining Sydney Road'.[48] This structure – now known as 'the bothy' – still survives immediately to the south of the entrance to the canal tunnel.[49]

This strange little building, known as the bothy, contains the remains of the original shelter which previously stood on the site of the temple. It is planned to convert it back to public use.

In contrast to the lack of concern over the loss of the shelter, when the council announced plans to erect 'iron conveniences', voices were raised in dissent. One councillor claimed that 'the beautiful old gardens' had been 'laid out with a lot of architectural skill' (as indeed they had) and the conveniences should be built of Bath stone.[50] It was decided, however, to commission William Farrer of the Star Works in Birmingham to install an iron public convenience, serving both ladies and gentlemen. A year later, it was suggested that more conveniences should be provided, but the Sydney Gardens sub-committee said they absolutely could not support such an idea.

Along with the conveniences, a new drinking fountain was purchased, and electric light installed in the bandstand and the lower part of the gardens. A new entrance to the gardens, facing Bathwick Street, was opened, replacing the one which led into the grounds now owned by the Holburne. It was equipped with turnstiles and a paybox, designed by the city architect, AJ Taylor, for use when a charge was made for entry to special events.

The first of the iron loos. It was originally for both ladies and gentlemen.

The paybox designed by City Architect AJ Taylor

The Temple of Minerva was unveiled on 15 June 1914. Unbeknown to everyone at the time, just over seven weeks later Britain would be at war with Germany. When war came, Sydney Gardens took on a new role. The affection Bathonians had for the gardens is apparent from a letter Trooper William Piles, serving in France with the Dragoon Guards, wrote to his wife back in Widcombe in October 1914. Like many others, he still thought the war would be over by Christmas, so was in an understandably upbeat mood:

> I have been in the fighting line, and I shall be pleased to be up there again, because you get a good run of sport, and, being a cavalry man, I get plenty of dashing about seeing life. It is just your luck if you get hit, but still you don't think of such a thing. It is all the world like

being in Sydney Gardens watching the fireworks, only there is a little more noise.⁵¹

But it was not over by Christmas. In June 1915, the mayor opened the bowling green in the gardens and the bowling club invited wounded soldiers to use their facilities.⁵² The *Illustrated London News* also published a photograph showing wounded soldiers listening to a band in the gardens.

Wounded soldiers, in their hospital uniforms, sit and enjoy the sunshine and the music in the gardens in 1915

Two soldiers stand near the gardener's lodge – perhaps they had come to play bowls

In 1916, a large war hospital opened at Combe Park (on the site where the Royal United Hospital stands today), and ambulances were needed to take patients to the baths in the city centre for treatment. At a Licensed Victuallers' Association meeting, the decision was taken to purchase an ambulance for the Red Cross when one of their members announced he could get his hands on one for £127. It was presented to the Red Cross in June 1917 at the start of a three-day fair in Sydney Gardens, opened by Lady Waldegrave. Attractions included dancing, bowling competitions, and a 'mechanical theatre' in the pavilion – now referred to as the 'loggia' – in which the coronation of George V was represented by marionettes. The *Chronicle* described some of the other entertainments:

> On the old swings site there were exhibits of conjuring and mysticism by Mr Frederick Vallance, who is also a ventriloquial humorist. Miss Adair and Miss Poppy Ford appeared in the one-act play 'Emery Brown' and Miss Ford recited 'The Reflections of a Penny'. There were 'burlesque' impressions by Mr S C Hoskins (late of the Duke of Cornwall's Light Infantry). The scholars of St Luke's School ... gave an exhibition of Egyptian calisthenics ... Among the smaller amusements was one held in connection with the Temple of Minerva booth, known as a puffing competition. A number of rubber balls had been painted to represent the features of various ladies of the VAD, and bore their Christian names. Each ball had a hole cut into it for the insertion of a cigarette, and the contest consisted of squeezing the ball so as to exhaust the cigarette, the quickest to accomplish this winning the prizes.[53]

Over 20,000 people attended the fair and £3,000 was raised.

Another three-day 'holiday carnival' was held the following year, although the *Bath Chronicle* admitted that 'this June the carnival would have lapsed but for the public spirited action of Mr WS Pearce, the popular lessee of the Palace Theatre, in offering to promote another such comprehensive effort'.[54] The opening ceremony was attended by the Marquis of Bath and Lady Kathleen Thynne, who were greeted by a guard of honour of wounded soldiers at the entrance to the gardens. In a speech before the festivities commenced, the mayor, Dr Preston King, 'alluded to the presence in the Gardens of a kiosk where recruits for Queen Mary's Auxiliary Army could enrol. Women had

Callisthenics by schoolchildren at the 1917 Red Cross Fair

done splendidly,' he continued, 'but many more were wanted, especially for the land, to get in the harvest.' A fanfare of trumpets then sounded, after which Lady Thynne declared the carnival open. The entertainments included a lady's tug of war, the Top Notes Concert Party, resplendent in pierrot costumes, and a sale in which fifteen sheep, donated by 'tradesmen of the city', were auctioned off. It was explained that 'they could not be sold for slaughter, but could be delivered to the Red Cross'. A few weeks later, the *Chronicle* reported that the fete had raised £2,769 – with more still to come in – which would be divided among the Royal United Hospital and Red Cross Hospitals around Bath.[55]

Just over four months later, on 11 November, the war ended, although peace was not formally declared until the signing of the Treaty of Versailles on 28 June the following year. To celebrate, the government decreed that 19 July should be Peace Day, and in Bath, as elsewhere, 'a very elaborate programme of entertainments' was drawn up. These included 'the Mayor's Garden Party at the Sydney Gardens for Bath men who had served and their wives or lady friends'. Unfortunately, as so often in the past, the weather was against them. The rain

> fell incessantly, though not heavily, and it was impossible to do more than stroll about on soaked turf or muddy paths and listen to the

concerts. Most of the musical arrangements were carried through, and an excellent tea was enjoyed, but the conditions were a great disappointment to those who had worked so hard to organise a good afternoon. That the idea would have been a great success, was obvious from the interest taken and the fact that some 5,000 guests faced conditions that would have deterred most, emphasised what an afternoon would have been spent if the weather had been kind. The many guests, however, did the gracious thing, and greatly cheered their disappointed hosts by the cheery way they accepted the conditions and made the best of things ... Some of the men created a diversion on their own by dancing on the lawn in the rain, to the great interest of the remainder. They 'carried on' indeed, with the true spirit of the British Army, and the garden party was worth holding despite the difficulties. One could not help realising that dry weather and sunshine would have transformed the afternoon into one of the most memorable spent in the Sydney Gardens.[56]

During the afternoon, the mayor, Alfred Wills, gave an official welcome to his guests from the bandstand:

Referring with regret to the way the rain had spoilt the city's attempt to entertain them, the Mayor said that when he saw the weather that morning his heart was in his boots, but he was very much 'bucked' when they came marching up Bridge Street with their band playing 'Pack up your troubles in your old kit bag' ... The gathering gave three hearty cheers for the Mayor, who then ... proceeded to the Queen of the West Lawn, where he planted a promising young oak to commemorate the celebration of peace. Arrangements had been made for a bowls competition, but the weather prevented it ... It was a tribute to the attractive nature of the programme that notwithstanding the drenching rain, several hundred people remained standing before the brilliantly illuminated bandstand until the Gardens closed at ten ... When the band played a selection of favourite ditties, the audience took up the refrain with gusto. 'Give me a cosy corner' was especially popular, though assuredly no such spot could be found in the Gardens on Saturday night. After the National Anthem, 'God Bless the Prince of Wales' was sung, and then the well-known hymns 'O God our help' and 'Abide with me'.

The Peace Oak planted by Alfred Wills was rededicated in 2003, with another ceremony in July 2019 to mark the centenary of its planting.

The spirit of cheerfulness in the face of adverse weather conditions may have done credit to all concerned. Less commendable was the council's refusal to allow Twerton Co-operative Society to hold a Children's Fête in Sydney Gardens, on the grounds that they were 'an exceedingly dangerous place for children and that the flower beds would be injured'.[57] Reported in the same edition of the *Chronicle* as that which carried coverage of the Peace Day celebrations, it demonstrated, perhaps more clearly than anything else, how little some deep-rooted attitudes and prejudices had been shaken by the war.

By 1920, as the popularity of the gardens increased, the conveniences installed in 1914 proved ever more inadequate for the needs of visitors. The Sydney Gardens sub-committee relented, and agreed to another iron convenience, for ladies only, which was installed by the famous Scottish iron founders, Walter Macfarlane, on a foundation built by the council.

Above: The iron Ladies Loo of 1921, awaiting restoration and a new use

Right: The paint peeling off the panels has revealed the decoration. It is likely they were painted cream, to merge in with Bath Stone, with the raised pattern probably in dark green.

In 1921, it was decided, when a fête was held for the Mayor's Hospital Fund, to make another new vehicular entrance at the top of the gardens, because they wanted to have roundabouts. Formerly, the roundabouts had been at the bottom of the gardens, but there were now tennis courts on the site. The proposal was warmly supported by councillors, as roundabouts brought in a great deal of revenue. They reckoned without the residents, however. It did not take long for complaints to start rolling in. In 1923, a councillor seriously claimed that Sydney Gardens was not the place for fêtes. By a majority vote, the members of the Parks Committee over-ruled the supporters of the residents, but within a few days of the British Legion Fête, it was reported that the residents of Great Pulteney Street and Sydney Place were up in arms, and had signed a petition against allowing roundabouts into the gardens. Still the council was adamant they would be appearing.

The residents were now furious. Led by the rabidly anti-Socialist Sir Muirhead Collins, who saw merry-go-rounds, swings, and similar amusements as an invasion by the working classes, these entertainments were described as noisy, damaging to the gardens, and – worst of all in the minds of those in Sydney Place – lowering the tone of a quiet residential neighbourhood. There was no one now who dared to point out that the gardens had been there longer than the houses and were intended for amusement, although not all councillors were sympathetic to the plight of the residents. As the gardens now included such facilities as a bowling green, a putting green and hard tennis courts, the member for Widcombe could not see why roundabouts should not be in the gardens as well. In the end, it was decided that the hard courts took up so much room that roundabouts could no longer enter the gardens. This seems a rather feeble excuse, but the killjoys had won, and the stage was set for the once glorious gardens to sink into a quiet retirement. The only good thing to come out of this fiasco was that the gate at the top of the gardens which had been made for the roundabouts was thrown open to the public.

Bit by bit, the historical character of Sydney Gardens were being nibbled away. Although the area around the college had been fenced off from the gardens for over 65 years, there was a gate through the fence through which people could come and go as necessary. In 1922, however, the Holburne Trustees decided to replace what they described as a 'wooden hoarding' bounding the site with a wall seven foot high, abandoning Sir Reginald

Bloomfield's carefully considered garden scheme for the rear of the museum. The council complained, on behalf of the residents, that there were fears it would look unsightly from the gardens. The trustees replied that the council had been misinformed – not about the height but about the unsightliness. The wall was, 'in the opinion of the trustees, of a decidedly more artistic character than the ordinary type of wall', and, 'so far from diminishing the attractions of the gardens, it will add to them'. In the end, it turned out to be less than seven feet high, but was rather poorly built, the Gardens Committee describing it as 'quite loose, with many of the stones easily removable'.[58] Its construction also meant that, for the first time, not only the house but a part of the former ride on either side of the museum was cut off from the gardens it was intended to serve.

In 1928, Cllr Smith said it was time to get rid of all the old guns in the gardens. No one asked where they had come from or what they were doing there. They were almost certainly the cannon which had been acquired for the city by Beau Nash and originally stood in Spring Gardens before being moved to the miniature sham castle in Sydney Gardens. Yet it was declared they were worth nothing.[59] People were more concerned about the German gun at the top of the gardens which was a relic of the Great War. The subject was dropped, but raised again in 1937 when prices for scrap gun metal were good. They were described as being 'no good and in the way' and so they were sold. The German gun was spared, however, at the request of Cllr Hopkins, who argued that, if it was sold, 'the boys will have nothing to practice with', adding that 'it is a great source of delight to the boys in the park'.[60] Three years later, in 1940, the German gun would go as well, to be melted down for the war effort.

At the same time that the councillors were discussing the cannon, it was noted that

> both the colonnade and the pavilion in Sydney Gardens were in need of renovation. The parks superintendent said provision had been made in the estimates. The chairman suggested the City Engineer (Mr FP Sissons) should ascertain what work was required, and give an estimate of the cost at the next meeting. This course was agreed to. When Councillor E White remarked, 'We must see we have enough

money,' the chairman rejoined, 'we must get on. We shall have all this old gun metal money.' (laughter).⁶¹

Little did anyone know it then, but herein lay the seeds of a controversy which would land the council in deep trouble. The estimate proved to be £1,400 – about £80,000 today. Clearly that was a substantial sum, but this was one of the original features of the country's only surviving Georgian pleasure gardens. Give its historic importance, the councillors might have stopped to ask themselves whether they could seek help with its restoration, or take advice on what should happen to it. They did not. They commissioned a cheaper alternative from a local builder, and went blindly ahead with it. The result is the lumpen, graceless block we see today. In the council's defence, it has to be said that the views once enjoyed from it had long vanished. Viewpoints were essential to Georgian gardens – there is, for example, a contemporary map of Stourhead with the viewpoints clearly delineated. But trees had grown up without being trimmed to preserve the view. Some may even have been deliberately planted to obstruct them. What is more, the gardens were, as some councillors claimed, little used, although that was largely their own fault. Apart from providing facilities for tennis and bowls, they had done little to encourage their use, yielding to pressure from residents who complained bitterly about anything they thought noisy or likely to lower the tone.

Almost as soon as the work was finished, the complaints began. One correspondent, Mr Crawford of Larkhall, described it as municipal vandalism. The most devastating attack came from Sir Ambrose Heal, the renowned furniture maker and head of the famous West End firm of Heal

A sketch of the pavilion before the 'restoration' of 1938, supplied by Sir Ambrose Heal to the *Bath Chronicle*

and Son. His letter, which was published in the *Bath Chronicle* on 3 September 1938, remains a model of how to express extreme anger while remaining icily polite. Unfortunately, he had been away when the decision was made – a decision which had been kept from Bath Preservation Trust – so he was too late to try to stop it. Now he pulled no punches in saying what he thought of the work:

> Sir, – It is impossible to understand on what ground there can be any defence for pulling down a delightful example of eighteenth- or possibly early nineteenth-century architecture and putting in its place a mutilated version of the original shorn of all the grace and distinction which characterised the old building.
>
> Through the neglect of those who should have preserved the Sydney Gardens loggia, it had been allowed to fall into decay; the woodwork was rotten and the whole structure had got into a bad state. Had the long overdue repairs been faithfully carried out the shapely form of the old loggia could have been retained in its entirety and a perfect restoration carried out. Mr GJ Long attempts to defend the new erection as (1) 'an intelligent and not overdone renovation'; and (2) 'as a most suitable reconstruction'. It is incorrect to say that the old loggia has been reconstructed, for only a portion of it has been retained, about two thirds of it has been destroyed. Whether this constituted an 'intelligent renovation' is very questionable – that it is 'not overdone' is certain. It is but half done.
>
> The old pavilion had charm and elegance; it was beautifully proportioned. The suave flowing lines of its delicately moulded cornice, gently bowed in the centre and sweeping away to the incurved ends, formed a delightful terminal to the garden vista. In its simple way it was a little architectural gem.
>
> In this so-called 'suitable reconstruction' the perfect proportion of the whole has been ruined. Only the centre bay has been preserved and the form of that has been spoilt. Instead of the subtly shaped lines of the front we now have a bald semi-circular erection, slavishly echoing the bow window above it, but entirely out of scale with the whole façade of Sydney House, from which it merely bulges. Where once

swept the graciously curved wings of the old pavilion are now stark, blank walls faced with cement! Between this bleak expanse of cement and the loggia stand two ironic (this is no printer's error) columns. The two dear little amorini, who used to play so prettily against the sky-line, are gone – presumably to some builder's scrapheap. What has become of them?

If all this is 'Restoration', what word does Mr Long use to describe 'Destruction'? Unfortunately I can find nowhere a photograph of the old loggia as it stood only a month or two ago, but I happen to have a clever etching which will serve as a pathetic reminder and, if the Editor will oblige with a reprint of the photograph of the new portico, which he recently published, to place alongside my etching we may join with the accusing Hamlet:

> 'Look here upon this picture and on this,
> A counterfeit presentment ...
> Could you on this fair mountain leave to feed
> And batten on this moor, Ha, have you eyes?'

Mr Long has applied the phrase 'ill-informed criticism' – by which I take it he means criticism with which he is not in accord – to Mr Green-Armytage's protest against this piece of vandalism. He goes so far as to assert, somewhat callously, that Members of the Council do not take such criticism seriously 'unless it suits their purpose'. This is an ominous saying which, in fairness to the Councillors, I am reluctant to accept for truth. If the criticism referred to is to be stigmatised, according to Mr Long's standards of culture, as 'uninformed', then I am content that mine should fall into the same category.

AMBROSE HEAL 3, Marlborough Buildings, Bath

The councillors were outraged, and, it has to be said, baffled and bemused by the censure. They thought it looked very nice, and that this was ill-deserved abuse. In retrospect, the failure to preserve the loggia can be seen as the first warning pebble in what would eventually become the avalanche of destruction known as the Sack of the Bath. The loss of the little cupids, or amorini, was needless. They were found, broken and damaged, on a heap of rubbish by the

'We now have a bald semi-circular erection, slavishly echoing the bow window above it, but entirely out of scale with the whole façade of Sydney House, from which it merely bulges.'

entrance to the gardens. Yet it seems they were very old. One writer suggested they originally adorned the old Hart Lodging in Stall Street, while another said they came from the Melfort Cross in the Cross Bath. Either could be true. The old Hart Lodging was pulled down about the time that Sydney Gardens was being planned, while at least one cherub from the Melfort Cross was saved and stands in a niche at the bottom of Milsom Street, Baldwin overseeing both these pieces of work.

A columnist for the *Bath Chronicle*, who called himself 'The Bellman', came to the councillors' rescue, and harrumphed that there was a good deal of unnecessary fuss being made about the reconstructed loggia. He asked if it really mattered if, 'in reconstruction, the architectural form of the original was not strictly copied'. However, there was a sting in the tail. He said that those who objected were asking why it should not have conformed to the original, and he himself could see no good answer to that. But he still thought it was a storm in a teacup.[62]

It was beginning to seem as if the council did not want people to enjoy themselves in the gardens. In December 1940, when Mr Adams of Edward Street asked whether the disused bandstand could be used as a shelter, where people could sit and enjoy the winter sun out of the wind, the council replied that it was too dangerous.[63] Although the Parks Committee was prepared to spend money on the bandstand in Royal Victoria Park, they were quietly allowing the one in Sydney Gardens to fall into disrepair. This was despite a visiting bandmaster telling the people of Bath that it was one of the best bandstands he knew, with a superb acoustic. At one time, the council had even made alterations to the bandstand in Royal Victoria Park to match it.

However, the need for wartime amusements brought a change of heart – provided someone else was paying. In April 1942, it was agreed that gramophone music could be played in the gardens for dancing on the band lawn. A few months later, Eileen's, the plantsmen and florists, who had long had a shop in Northumberland Place, decorated the bandstand for a concert, and a collection was made for the Mayor's Air Raid Relief Fund.[64] Some things, however were still not allowed. In February that year, four men were charged with gaming in Sydney Gardens on a Sunday. Their heinous crime, which was spotted by a passing police officer, was throwing a threepenny bit in the air and seeing which side it came down. They were each fined £1.[65]

Northumberland Place in 1970, with Eileen's Seed & Garden Shop – much-loved and much-missed – on the left

Sydney Gardens was provided with an air raid shelter during the war. It was a trench shelter, dug out of the lawns, and could accommodate 153 people. The gates of the gardens, which had always been locked at night, were kept open for the duration of the war, so that people could get to the shelter. Although its exact location is not recorded, one local resident believes it was near the Bathwick Street entrance, where her aunt and uncle lived. They recalled running down towards the park, helping a heavily pregnant woman to reach the shelter while dodging machine-gun fire.[66]

An Air Raid Wardens' post was also built in 1939 behind the portico on the south side of the Holburne Museum. Soundly constructed, albeit of poor quality brick, it proved too useful to demolish after the war, but remained something of an eyesore until the Friends of the Holburne held a competition to suggest ways of smartening it up. The winner was Sidney Blackmore, who proposed giving it a Regency Gothic facelift, and so successfully was the idea carried out that visitors may be forgiven for assuming it dates from the time of the

The former Air Raid Wardens' post, reinvented as a Regency Gothic garden house

gardens' inception. In 1983, it opened as a tea room and remained a popular and much-loved facility until it was supplanted by a new facility in the refurbished museum. It is now used by volunteers at the museum.

One recurring criticism of Sydney Gardens was ease of access to the railway line. An ever present danger was vandalism. During the summer of 1943, a terrible accident was only averted by the extraordinary courage and quick-thinking of an eleven-year-old girl. Two boys, aged ten and eight, had placed a large stone weighing 23lbs on the line, along with some branches. Rita Sartain, realising the danger to an oncoming train, climbed over and removed it. She knew she was risking her own life, and she only just escaped in time. The police stated that the train would have been derailed if it had hit the rock. Contributions for her rolled in, and she received an award. The story came to light because she was the prosecution witness.

Rita Sartain, looking remarkably unfazed by her fame

In October 1943, two thirteen-year-old boys stole cash from a container in the gentlemen's toilets. There was a more serious incident a year later, when nearly every seat in the park was damaged, with four or five being thrown in the bushes. A bed of dahlias was also trampled down. Nor did peacetime bring relief. In May 1946, 68 tulips were stolen from one of the beds. In 1950, it was reported that seats were continuing to be vandalised and were sometimes even thrown onto the railway or into the canal. This was despite the gates again being locked at night to protect the lawns from damage while they were being reseeded.

The council committed its own act of vandalism in 1948 by finally demolishing the bandstand, after hearing it would cost £450 to repair.[67] A correspondent to the *Bath Chronicle* pertinently asked why it had been allowed to fall into such a state, and reminded the council once again that it was acoustically superior to any other bandstand in the city.[68] It had been hoped that the steelwork in the bandstand could be used to build a new one, but it was deemed 'unrealisable'. Curiously, it was still deemed realisable enough to be used in other building work. The demolition cost the city £70.[69]

Sydney Gardens was to enjoy one last flowering of fun, however, possibly inspired by the Festival of Britain. In August 1952, the Spa Committee

By the 1950s, the Kennet and Avon canal was looking unloved and unkempt

announced that they were taking 'the opportunity of creating artistic illuminations which will give pleasure to many'. The illuminations were designed

> to show, to the best effect at nightfall, the beauty of trees and flowers and, at the same time, introduce something of particular interest to children – the illumination of animals and various kinds of bursary rhymes.

As well as firework displays, a lawn was set aside for dancing to a 'gypsy orchestra' and 'light and licensed refreshments' were 'tastefully served from 8pm till 10.30.[70]

It did not take long for dissenting voices to be raised once more. Once again the local residents were up in arms, and the trustees of the Holburne considered the festivities would be vulgar and bring disrepute on Bath. Undeterred, the Spa Committee did not just repeat the shows, but made them bigger over next four years. In 1953, various illuminations were floated on the canal, to the disgust of LA Edwards, Honorary Secretary of the Inland Waterways Association:

> The frolics of the Sidney [sic] Gardens, totally obstructing the navigation, is a breach of statute and should not be allowed. The maintenance boat all lit up with fairy lights under the footbridge illustrates how scandalous this state of affairs is.[71]

Lady Noble wrote from the Olympian heights of Royal Crescent, saying that these 'vulgarities and error of taste' was 'as remote from Jane Austen's day as can well be imagined'. In fact, Jane Austen herself could be fairly vulgar herself when she chose, and, given her appetite for laughing at people taking themselves too seriously, one cannot help but feel she would rather have enjoyed these apoplectic responses to a spot of innocent frivolity. As if to show the critics that they didn't care, the next year the Spa Committee dreamt up something even more splendid:

> The Sydney Gardens illuminations season opened at Bath on Saturday last with a programme of vastly wider scope then that of previous years. The Gardens are a veritable fairyland of colour and excitement.

The Loch Ness Monster, the delightful Dutch Mill and dancers, the children's corner, the fountain and waterfalls, and the lovely flower basket were some of the illuminated set-pieces which helped to provide a delightful picture. There are to be displays of fireworks each Saturday until Sept 25th. In addition to the illuminations, there are side-shows as well as competitions for which valuable prizes are offered; a greasy pole to be walked for the traditional prize of a leg of mutton; and dancing on the lawn to the music of a gipsy orchestra.[72]

The naysayers may have been unhappy but everyone else was having a great time, and by 18 September the 37,000th visitor of the season passed through the turnstiles, to receive a prize from the Mayor of Bath. The following year, 'a lovely illuminated and coloured figure of Mary, Mary Quite Contrary, surrounded by her silver bells and cockleshells' was one of the principal attractions, along with ships on the canal, and horticultural competitions for the longest carrot, largest parsnip and heaviest marrow. There was also a King and Queen Competition for old age pensioners, and, on August Bank Holiday, prizes for knobbly knees, slim ankles, and handsome men, plus 'many other comedy events'.[73]

The illuminations on the canal in 1956. In the distance is the tunnel at the west end of the gardens, on the left is 'The Little Old Mill', while illuminated water lilies float on the canal.

Could it get any better? In the opinion of the Spa Committee, which was running these events, it could. Once again, a reporter from *Wiltshire Times and Trowbridge Advertiser* was on hand to describe the start of the 1956 season:

The first of nine Saturday night displays at the Sydney Gardens, Bath, last week, revealed an illuminated 'fairyland' ingeniously set among the lawns and flower beds. The illuminations, which also provided a Bank Holiday Monday attraction, are the most ambitious to date. Settings and figure which hitherto have been confined to the colourful pages of a child's book of nursery rhymes, are presented in the most realistic manner possible ... On Saturday the Continental trapeze artist Leone gave a daring performance on the top of a 75ft mast in the centre of the gardens, and 20 girls paraded for the first heat of the £100 beauty queen competition.

The most spectacular innovation this year, the fifth season of the illuminations, is the children's corner, in which 15 episodes from 'Alice in Wonderland' are depicted in brilliant colours. Dominating the tableaux is a 35ft high fairy castle shimmering against the night sky, with a foreground of softly-coloured trees and a sparkling fountain.

Something new has been arranged for each Saturday, and a fireworks display will be included in each programme.[74]

The 1956 Illuminations also featured one of the travelling versions of the Guinness clock which had been such an attraction at the Festival of Britain. Delivered by one of Sparrow's cranes – a local firm which became an international concern – via the Bathwick Street entrance, the clock stood on the left nearly opposite the water fountain, and is remembered with affection by many residents.

One of the travelling Guinness clocks

During the week, over 100 girls took part in the eight preliminary heats of the Bath Beauty Competition, from which 17 finalists were selected for the final parade on Saturday night. Entries had come from a wide area, and the final parade included girls from Birmingham and London.[75] The Grand Finale also included an 'Extra-Special Firework Display' and 'Open Air Dancing to Sydney Jones & his Orchestra', as well as something that would have been totally new to most of those attending – the 'Barbadian Steel Band'.⁷⁶ Originally founded by Hallam Ifill in Barbados in the early 1950s, he brought the band over to the UK after emigrating and settling in Bath. Based at the YMCA in Broad Street, its first major public performance was at the Pavilion on Boxing Day 1955. In the late 1950s, after Osman Clarke and members of other bands joined forces with Hallam's band, it was renamed it the Barbados All Stars. Later, as some of the original members retired or returned to the West Indies, Hallam, together with Osman's son Toussaint, developed and restructured it as the Rainbow Steel Band. Still based in Bath, it has gone on to win national and international acclaim, and is now one of the oldest steel bands in the country.

Despite the success of the illumination festivities, financially they were a failure. The 1956 Illuminations were the last, and Sydney Gardens sank

The gateway providing access to the canal was opened up in 1983, and, like the railings beyond it, was awarded Grade II-listed building status in 2010. Because the towpath is now much busier, occasionally the gateway has to have a warning notice.

into a genteel retirement, the most exciting events being competitions at the bowling club. It was all a rather sad finale.

By the 1980s, the gardens were little visited, and almost forgotten except by those who lived locally. In an effort to tempt more people into them, a gateway was opened up between the canal and gardens in 1983. The railings beyond it, designed to stop people falling into the canal, were originally very utilitarian, but were later replaced by railings in a more ornamental style – a happy afterthought which seems to have persuaded Historic England that, like the bridges, they date from 1800 and should be listed accordingly. Although the gateway improved access, it also meant that the secret nature of the canal as it flowed through the gardens was lost.

However, in the run-up to the bicentenary of the opening of the gardens in 1995, Glenn Humphreys, the enthusiastic Heritage Parks Manager for Bath & North East Somerset Council, tried to assemble enough information to submit an application for Heritage Lottery Funding. On that occasion, it was not possible to carry the project through, though he later secured funding for the restoration of Royal Victoria Park. However, the seed had been sown.

The canal, especially in its quieter moments, remains a superb asset to the gardens, and forms part of a green corridor running through the heart of the city

From the front the Holburne Museum looks very much as Blomfield left it

At the back is the Eric Parry extension, for which permission was granted in November 2007

Before any more work on the restoration of the gardens went ahead, the Holburne received planning permission for an extension by the architect Eric Parry. Although the development was controversial, it opened up a gateway between the gardens and the building designed as the entrance to them, restoring something of the integrity of the original layout. Today, the Holburne Garden Café serves refreshments as the Tavern and Middle Bar did over two centuries ago. As part of the extension, the garden behind the Holburne was also redesigned. In 1919 Reginald Blomfield had drawn plans for the garden, including what he described as a 'hemicycle laid to lawn' – in other words a

One of the greatest benefits has been the reforging of the link between the gardens and the building designed as the entrance to them – a link which had been severed for over 150 years

semicircular lawn – with a raised flagged or gravelled terrace at the edge, and shallow steps leading down to it. In 2015, something very similar to this plan was finally carried out. However, the lawn was sensibly altered to a flagged area, and, although the steps were installed, ramps were added on each side to allow access for wheelchairs and pushchairs. The Holburne Museum has occasionally curated art installations in this garden involving illuminations, most notably the Field of Light at Christmas 2011.

The Holburne has often used its grounds for events, and in 2011 the old notion of illuminations using 'variegated lamps' was revived in the Field of Light, an art installation by Bruce Munro

Another installation, weaving through the columns at the front of the building, was this evocation of a starling murmuration, created from willow by Laura Ellen Bacon in 2015

Meanwhile, behind the scenes, the Parks Department had been working away on plans to restore the gardens, but needed financial assistance. In 2017 funding of £332,000 was secured to develop a Heritage Lottery Fund (HLF) bid through the Parks for People grant programme to restore and revitalise the Gardens. An application to the HLF for a £2.7m grant was made in August 2018.

As I was putting the finishing touches to this book, the exciting news came that the Bath and North East Somerset Council's Park Service had been awarded the HLF grant, resulting in the £3.7m restoration scheme being fully funded from the beginning of 2019. It has been a long time coming – plans and grant applications to restore the park had been in development for 25 years. The restoration will take three years, alongside a partnership programme of activities and events.

Historic features including the loggia, Minerva's Temple, and the Edwardian public conveniences will be restored. Flower gardens

The improvements to the gardens will also bring benefits to its wildlife

will be replanted, and viewpoints and wildlife habitats improved. In addition, the plans include 'a new café kiosk and toilets in the play area with highly accessible toilets for people with additional needs, which will be part funded by Bath City Forum'. Refurbishment of existing buildings will see the toilet block adjacent to the gardener's lodge become a community pavilion, and the bothy at the top of the gardens become an 'artist/craft workshop space'. Four tennis courts will be refurbished, a new play and activity zone for all ages will be created and a horticultural training programme set up for volunteers and those on work experience placements.

Sadly, a full restoration of the loggia is not included. There have been several pleas in the *Bath Chronicle* over the years for a generous donor to step forward to save the gardens, and from time to time, money was forthcoming. It would be a wonderful gesture if a local benefactor could step forward to restore this, the oldest feature in Sydney Gardens.

Whatever happens, Sydney Gardens is a remarkable survival from the days of Regency Bath. It has changed, but its ability to change has preserved it. Now it is destined to change once more to be a pleasure garden for 21st-century Bath.

POSTLUDE

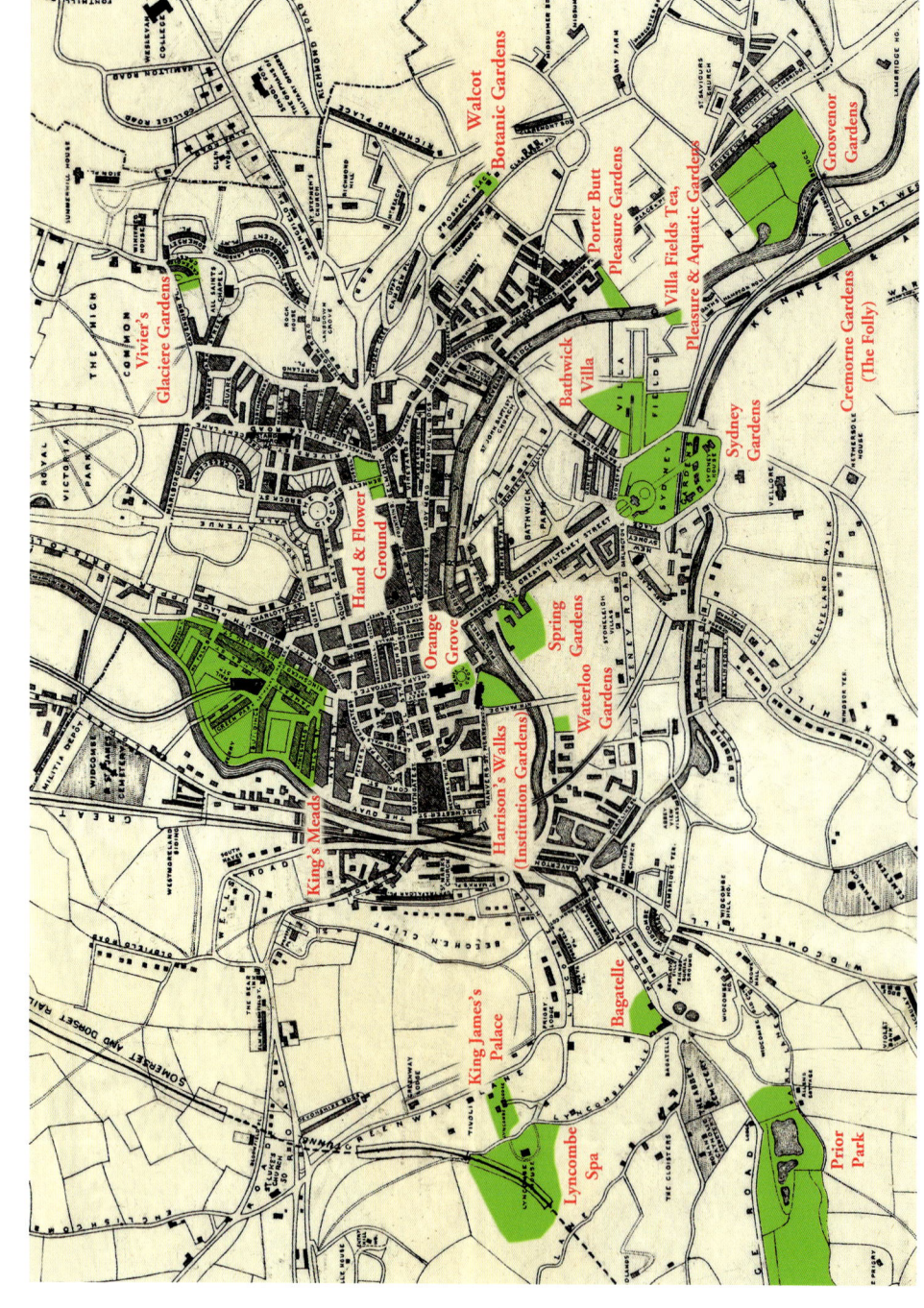

1

LOST PLEASURES

The Fate of Bath's Georgian Pleasure Gardens

Although Bath advertises itself as 'the Georgian City', little remains of the pleasure gardens which formed such an important part of its social life. Even those that survive in some form have changed out of all recognition. Some have continued to evolve as public spaces, some have been built over, while others have become private gardens. This gazetteer of lost pleasure gardens examines their fate.

The **King's Meads**, where Celia Fiennes walked, covered a large area, although how much of it could be described as pleasure gardens, as opposed to fields where visitors walked and took the air, is unclear. The area outside the west gate, where celebrations for Princess Amelia's birthday were held in 1728, disappeared shortly afterwards when Kingsmead Square (seen on the left), Kingsmead Street and Avon Street were built. By 1800, most of the meads had disappeared under housing, leaving just the odd fragment, like the

Opposite: A map of Bath, originally published by Spackman & Cotterell in 1852, revised in 1876, and further amended to indicate the approximate location and extent of Bath's Georgian Pleasure Gardens, as well as two later gardens – Cremorne Gardens (or the Folly) and the Porter Butt – which feature in the following chapter.

small park in front of Green Park West, to remind us of their open expanses. Kingsmead Square also survives as a popular meeting place, due in no small part to the large London Plane at its heart, which shades visitors during the heat of the day and at night is lit by dozens of lights. In March 2019, as part of plans to enhance the area, it was announced that work was underway to make the square more pedestrian-friendly.

As this photograph from around 1905 shows, the plane tree in Kingsmead Square has long been a prominent landmark

Orange Grove retained its trees until 1834, when they were felled 'preparatory to the construction of a new road'. On 4 September, the *Bath Chronicle* reported that the work had

> commenced on Tuesday, and in a day or two, there will not be a vestige of those old inhabitants of the spot. In the centre of the cleared area it is intended to enclose with iron railings a space of ground which is to be planted with ornamental shrubs.[1]

Two years later, when JC Loudon surveyed the changes that had overtaken Bath, he found that

> the Orange Grove has been remodelled, the old trees cut down, and a carriage road made round the inside; the obelisk in the centre is now surrounded by a circular grove planted with shrubs. The Abbey is thrown open by the adjoining houses being pulled down; and a fine view may be obtained from the Guildhall steps of the rich old Abbey, and the neat Gothic structure of the new St. Michael's Church, forming a striking and beautiful contrast.[2]

The Orange Grove as it appeared after the changes of the 1830s

The Orange Grove around 1905, with the Empire Hotel built, but two houses still standing on the east side

In 1912, with the houses gone, work started to round off the corner into Grand Parade and build a balustrade

In 1900, most of the buildings on the east side of the Orange Grove were demolished, including Nassau House, which, according to legend, had been occupied by the Prince of Orange during his stay in Bath. At the same time, the buildings to the north of them were removed to make way for the Empire Hotel and for a new road linking the Orange Grove with Pulteney Bridge. The construction of the new road, called in true imperial style the Grand Parade, entailed stopping up access from the Orange Grove to the river, which eighteenth-century visitors had used to take the ferry across to Spring Gardens. Two houses remained on the east side of Orange Grove, however, blocking the view eastward and standing in the way of plans to improve access to Institution Gardens. They were eventually demolished in 1912 so that work to round off the corner and build a balustrade could proceed.

The Orange Grove already had one Dutch connection, but in 1945 it acquired another when Bath 'adopted' the war-ravaged city of Alkmaar, raising money to send essential supplies.[3] Alkmaar responded by sending tulips to Bath, which were planted in the Orange Grove.[4] In 1949, a plaque was erected in the Orange Grove, 'dedicating the garden' to Alkmaar. A further plaque was erected in 2003 when a rededication ceremony was held to commemorate 'the bond of friendship between the two ancient cities of Bath and Alkmaar'.

Today, the Orange Grove, although surrounded by roads, is a green oasis in the heart of the city, with four trees and a floral display in summer. On hot days the grass is strewn with people taking time off from trekking round Bath.

As for **Bath Abbey**, where Celia Fiennes described people walking in wet weather, that option for healthy exercise was removed between 1863 and 1874, when George Gilbert Scott 'restored' the church. Some work was desperately needed, but one of his changes was to fill the nave full of dark oak pews, so its spaciousness was lost. It was certainly no longer possible to walk around it easily. Fortunately, a recent restoration has swept most of them away, though not without controversy. The change will once more allow visitors to stroll around and admire the abbey's beauties unimpeded.

Harrison's Walks still exist, though very much altered. Although their star faded with the rise of Spring Gardens, they were still visited, with part adapted to a bowling green by 1770. The Lower Rooms burnt down in 1820, but the

Bath Royal Literary and Scientific Institution, which was built on the site, took over a section of the gardens and renamed them Institution Gardens. Map evidence suggests it was probably about this time that the summer house on the river bank, already ruinous, was demolished. The first encroachment on the land, which also affected North Parade, came in 1836, when North Parade Bridge was built. JC Loudon describes its impact:

> One half of the North Parade has been made a carriage approach to the new iron bridge by widening the outer side for a footpath; the bowling-green in front, with the gardens of the Literary and Scientific Institution, have been laid out in fanciful walks and flower-borders; and, on the other side of the river, are raised arches along the meadows to the Pulteney Road. The bridge will command a picturesque view of the hills, Pulteney Bridge, the Abbey, and various streets; and of many picturesque places on the hills.[5]

However, a large part of the old gardens remain and form what today we call **Parade Gardens**. They are made up of several plots of land. The first piece to come into council ownership was that known as Institution Gardens, in

Looking down on Institution Gardens, about 1920. The circle of the bowling green can clearly be seen and survives today. To the right, on the site of the Lower Assembly Rooms, is the Bath Royal Literary & Scientific Institution.

1863. These were purchased from Earl Manvers with a subscription raised by a committee led by Jerom Murch, seven times Mayor of Bath between 1863 and 1892, and presented to the council. The land acquired also included a garden occupied by Mr Henry Bright.

The council also hoped to acquire, by means of another subscription, the riverside walk, but this was purchased in 1874 by Alfred Ridout, a master builder who had built Stanley Road, on the west side of Manvers Street, as a speculative venture, and lived in a four-storey building called Gable House at the far end of it. He had also carried out the carpentry work for the Grand Pump Room Hotel in Stall Street. Given the susceptibility of the low-lying ground beside the river to flood, it is far from clear what sort of development Ridout had in mind, and the council viewed the prospect with some alarm. However, in 1879 he died, aged just 44, and the council was able to acquire the land by subscription as before.[6]

This left the area which John Wood, on his plan of 1735, described as St James's Triangle. Although this forms the bulk of the gardens, it still does not belong to the council, which explains why Parade Gardens is the only park in Bath not open freely to the public. After Cam Gyde had taken over the Lower Rooms in 1771, he laid out a bowling green here, which survived until well into the nineteenth century. In 1836, after it had fallen into disrepair, Earl Manvers sold it to William Colborne Towers, of Laggan House, Lansdown, who planned to lay out the ground in front of North Parade 'ornamentally'.[7] However,

The triangle of land which was lost to the gardens when the Institution was demolished, the road layout altered and underground toilets constructed. This picture shows the area in 1933, just after the work was complete. The builders were FS and C Toogood – their board can be seen leaning against the balustrade.

this did not happen, and in 1864 the owners and occupiers of the houses 'in the vicinity of North Parade' adopted five 'resolutions', the first of which was 'that the present condition of the North Parade Garden, or Ancient Bowling Green, is discreditable to the City and injurious to the owners of property in the neighbourhood'.[8] Their interest in the garden arose not only from their proximity to it, for, as well as paying ground rent for their properties, they paid an additional rent which gave them access to the garden in perpetuity. When they presented the resolutions to Towers, who was described as lord of the manor, they proposed raising donations and subscriptions to organise the management and supervision of the garden. He was not only amenable to the suggestion, but even made a donation. This marked the beginning of a resurgence in the gardens' fortunes, as they became popular with residents and visitors alike, enjoying band concerts and other events.

When Towers died in 1866, the owners of the houses continued to manage the land, a role it seems the current owners still fulfil today. However, the houses at the western end of North Parade lost their access to the gardens in 1933, when the old Institution was pulled down, to be replaced by a new road layout with public conveniences in the former Institution cellars. With the Institution gone, it was deemed necessary to rename the gardens. Four

Parade Gardens today – its flowerbeds bright with colour, and people relaxing in the sunshine

names were considered – North Parade Gardens, Grand Parade Gardens, Spa Gardens and Weir Gardens – but in the end it was decided to call them simply Parade Gardens.⁹ The new layout also entailed the loss of part of the original gardens. Another part of the gardens to which access had long been closed off was the riverside path south of North Parade Bridge. Delia's Grotto, which stood alongside the path, still survives, however, on the terrace of a restaurant, while the path beyond it forms part of the restoration of the garden of 14 South Parade. Given their age and the fluctuations in their fortunes, however, the gardens are a remarkable survival, despite being incomplete. With their entrance fee, concerts and other events, they remain closest to the spirit of the Georgian Pleasure Gardens.

Spring Gardens are completely lost. Part of them lies under Johnstone Street, another section lies under the Beazer Maze, and their southern edge lies under the club house and north end of the pitch of Bath Rugby's leasehold land on the Recreation Ground.

The northern part of Spring Gardens once covered this area. In the foreground is the Beazer Maze, the only part of the former Spring Gardens site where people can still wander freely. Behind it is Johnstone Street, construction of which was held up for a considerable time during the war with France. The difference in building styles between the earlier houses and those built after several years' abeyance is clearly visible. The map on page 138 shows that the gardens came right up to where the two sets of buildings met.

Left: Looking north over the site of Spring Gardens, it can seen that work stopped on Johnstone Street after only a few houses had been built and was never resumed. The southern boundary of Spring Gardens was roughly where the halfway line of the rugby pitch is today.

Below: Looking east over the Recreation Ground about 1900, with Johnstone Street on the extreme left

Looking across the river to the Recreation Ground during the floods of November 1963. Similar floods occurred during the eighteenth century. In March 1774, for example, 'so great a flood ... as has never been but once exceeded in the memory of the oldest inhabitant' saw river levels rise more than twelve feet. Much of the lower part of the city was inundated and the bridge at Newbridge was swept away. Yet, although Spring Gardens would undoubtedly have been affected, no mention of it was made in the *Bath Chronicle* and the gardens opened for the season two months later.

The **Hand and Flower** ground on Lansdown Road was built over in the 1770s. It occupied a site between Alfred Street and Julian Road, with Saville Row and Russell Street marking its approximate western boundary. The Hand and Flower public house stood roughly where the corner of Alfred Street and Oxford Row (seen left) stands today.

In Widcombe, the **Bagatelle** is now private gardens.

Lyncombe Spa is the junior school for Prior Park College. During the nineteenth century, it came into the hands of the Moger family, who made their money from banking. From them it passed into the hands of the Sacred Heart Convent, then Lyncombe School, and then the Paragon School. While it was still the Paragon School, the groundsman Bill Rose uncovered many of the walks and, with a team from Green and Carter, who had solved the water supply problems at Heligan Gardens, restored the gravity-fed fountain. The original pond is now the football pitch.

Above: Lyncombe Spa House, now Prior Park Junior School

Right: Lyncombe Spa remains a watery place. This area is known by the children as 'Sloppy Swamp'

Below right: The spring which fed the spa now runs down to a gravity-fed fountain

Bottom: From there, it joins other springs before gushing out of the wall and flowing away

Opposite the former Lyncombe Spa is the site of **King James's Palace**, now houses and private gardens.

The largest Widcombe gardens – the grounds of **Prior Park** – are now run by the National Trust and progressively being restored to their eighteenth-century glory.

Water features were central to the design of Prior Park. The Serpentine Lake and the Cascade have both been restored by the National Trust in recent years.

To the east of Bath lie the old **Bathwick Villa** grounds. After the gardens closed, the house and grounds were acquired by the eccentric cleric Dr Trusler, while the fields became a patchwork of gardens, nurseries and orchards. Bit by bit, people built what were at first little shanties on them, often replacing them with more permanent houses. It must have been with some concern that they read, in 1830, the following item in the *Bath Chronicle*:

> We understand upon very good authority that the whole of the tenants occupying gardens, cottages, &c. under the Marquis of Cleveland, from the bottom of Grove-street to the extremity of the Villa fields, have received notice to quit, and that it is intended to dispose of this

entire tract of ground into elegant plantations and walks, similar to those of the Bath Park.[10]

However, the authority was not as good as the editor thought. In 1847, when James Tunstall, in his *Rambles about Bath and its Neighbourhood,* passed through Bathwick, he found that

> a large portion of the industrious population of this parish inhabit a primitive and sequestered spot, denominated the Villa fields, which lie between the railroad and river. Its cottages are detached, built each in its own plot of ground, apparently just as the whim of the settler suggested; for we have heard that this curious suburb resembles, in a great degree, a colonial settlement. In its centre is situated Bathwick Villa, which was inhabited, during a portion of the last century, by the Rev Dr John Trusler, a man noted for his eccentricity of character, who dedicated one of his works to the rising generation, by some of whom, however, he was so disrespectfully treated, that it not unfrequently happened that, on his return from the city, he would find his full-bottomed wig bristling with butchers' skewers, placed therein, without his knowledge, during his progress through the market.[11]

The settlement which grew up around the villa after Trusler died in 1820 had its own pub and even a lecture room, as well as warehouses and a boatyard. The villa itself retained an air of respectability, but Villa Fields was a different proposition. Although many of the inhabitants were respectable tradesmen, there were thefts and the odd outbreak of violence, more often than not caused by disputes over boundary fences. The residents were re-

Nestled between twentieth-century houses, the only surviving building of the settlement that grew up around Bathwick Villa in the early nineteenth century

garded by the council with suspicion, and they had to fight, complain, and campaign to get such amenities as street lighting, decent roads, sanitation and the vote. However, in December 1887, the Duke of Cleveland's agent, Frederic Farwell, announced that part of the site was to be cleared to make way for new brick cottages built on

Above: This blocked-up doorway on Powlett Road led from Villa Fields into Bathwick Meadows

Right: Two of the houses in Powlett Road, built in 1887 at the behest of the Duke of Cleveland

Below: Rockliffe Road, built in 1898 after Captain Forester had inherited the Bathwick Estate

what would become known as Powlett Road. The first ones to be built went to those whose houses were demolished to make way for them. By 1895, after Captain Forester had inherited the estate, the rest of the tenants were given notice, and Bathwick Villa was demolished about 1898. Forester's idea was to replace what in the worst cases were little more than hovels with a range of decently built houses. Incredibly,

> **Villa Fields.**
> The origin of the name "Villa Fields" is obscure. One idea is that the famous Barbara Villiers was connected with the family of the owner of the estate in her time. A well-known author of a work on Bath gives as his contribution the fact that a large villa, "Bathwick Villa," stood here, and the grounds were later used as a pleasure resort, something presumably of a combination of the amenities of the Sydney Gardens and the old Cremorne or Vauxhall Gardens at the extreme eastern end of the area between the Kensington Bridge and the canal. There is, however, some probability that the name comes down from feudal times, and that here were the dwellings of the serfs or villeins of the estate, or the "vill" of the freemen or frank pledges, from which terms we get the word village.
> W. O.

Above: By 1941, the origin of the name Villa Fields had been forgotten. A contributor to the *Bath Chronicle's* Notes and Queries column gave this confident – and entirely erroneous – explanation, while dismissing, a touch scornfully, the real reason.

Left and below: Two of the curious ornaments – thought to have come from Bathwick Villa – which adorn the porches in Forester Road

one of the little houses survived the redevelopment, and can be seen near the railway line. Meanwhile, some of the porches of the houses in Forester Road, which stand on the site of the villa, were adorned with strange gargoyles, pinnacles and urns, which are thought to have been rescued from the demolition rubble. At least one keen gardener in a house standing almost precisely on the site of the villa has also unearthed remnants of carved rubble.

Another survivor from Villa Fields is Bathwick Boating Station, which in 1855 James Aust was running as **Villa Fields Tea, Pleasure and Aquatic Gardens**. After Aust's bankruptcy, the property was acquired by Edward Maynard, a waterman originally from Lambeth, who kept the boat-building and boat-hire business going. At the age of 80, he agreed to hand control to the various boating clubs who used the boating station, and Bath Boating Company was formed. Maynard's manager

James Aust's pleasure garden still survives as Bath Boating Station. It has changed very little since this photograph was taken in the early twentieth century.

and caretaker, Frederick Fisher, was employed to run the boating station, and it is his descendants, the Hardick family, who still run it today.

Across the river, **Grosvenor Gardens** experienced a similar fate to Villa Fields. Most of the site was taken over by nurseries, but a number of cottages were also built. There was also a large house called Chestnut Cottage, which was renamed Nightingale House when Nightingale Nurseries opened in the early twentieth century. The swimming pool survived as a pond until the 1950s, and is still a damp area with towering willows even today. Another feature which survived into the twentieth century was the saloon – or rather, the outline of its walls, and its doorway, which stood like a Roman triumphal arch amid the nurseries (see the photograph on page 144). During the Second World War the level of the adjacent Kensington Meadows, was raised – it is

Above: Grosvenor Gardens after nurseries had been established and houses built on parts of the site, with much of it, however, left undeveloped because of the risk of flooding. To the right is Thomas Shew's suspension bridge.

Left: A close-up showing the ruined archway of the saloon to the left of the two trees, surrounded by other walls which once formed part of the building

Below: The back of Grosvenor today, with Ringswell Gardens built on the raised area

believed that much of the rubble from buildings destroyed in the Bath Blitz was dumped here. After the war, in the late 1940s and early 1950s, the levels at Grosvenor were also raised, covering the former nurseries, and a housing estate called Ringswell Gardens was built on the north side. However, the riverside walk is at the old level, and it is possible to find the spot where the drawing of the swings was sketched, as well as the wetland area which indicates the site of the swimming bath. In 2019, following a public consultation, work started to improve access to the meadows, plant trees, establish areas of wild grassland and carry out other improvements.

Much of Vivier's Glaciere Garden disappeared under Cavendish Crescent

Vivier's Glaciere Garden was built over by the 1820s, disappearing under Cavendish Place and Cavendish Crescent.

Waterloo Gardens has also disappeared without trace, although not under houses, but under Bath Cricket Club Ground. On the evidence of Egan's description and Harcourt Masters' map (see page 194), the high wall at the western end of Ferry Lane may mark its former boundary.[12]

The possible site of Waterloo Gardens

Walcot Botanic Gardens suffered the same fate by 1825, with the eastern end of Prospect Place built on the site of the gardens. The house at Elm Bank was superseded by three villas. One of them, Claremont Villa, still exists, but the other, semi-detached pair disappeared around 1900, to be replaced by Coburg Villas.

Finally, **Sydney Gardens** triumphantly survives, much altered, but with the original layout still just about detectable, as well as its later layers of history. However, the idea of gardens where people could have fun, relax and enjoy themselves with refreshment at hand was a popular one, and, as we shall see in the final chapter, it was pub landlords who took the idea and developed it with a variety of sports and entertainments for the public.

Coburg Villas stand on the site of Elm Bank House, while Claremont Villa, on the left, was built on part of Walcot Botanic Gardens

The eastern end of Prospect Place was also built on the site of the gardens

Sydney Gardens – still a garden for all seasons, just as John Gale, its first tenant, intended

2

WELCOME TO THE HOUSE OF FUN

How Pleasure Gardens became Fun Parks

One by one, the Georgian pleasure gardens vanished, but the idea of gardens where people could have a good time did not die. Almost immediately, new entrepreneurs dreamt up variations on the theme, and first on the scene were pub landlords.

For centuries, public houses and beerhouses, unlike inns and taverns, would have seemed fairly grim to us. They slowly got better as living conditions improved during the nineteenth century, and working people began to have more leisure time. There was also mounting concern about children on licensed premises. The Metropolitan Police Act of 1839 stopped children under 16 from drinking on the premises, and the ban was extended to the whole country in 1872. If publicans were to attract families, they needed to offer something different. Many looked to their pub gardens to see if they could make them as attractive and as much fun as the old pleasure gardens.

Pressing the gardens of pubs into service was not a new idea. The Hand and Flower ground on Lansdown had been used for many events. King James's Palace at Widcombe may well have started off as a drinking den. Even Bath's Spring Gardens were initially more pitched towards refreshment than entertainment.

Almost as soon as the day of the pleasure gardens was over, pubs in Bath began to step in. One of the earliest attempts to add a pleasure garden to a

Opposite: Twilight falls over the Folly, aka the Grosvenor Brewery, aka Cremorne Gardens, as a Bath-bound train steams past

pub, at the Porter Butt on the London Road, was a failure, however. In 1841, the pub had a new landlord, Daniel Giller, who, after improving the stabling facilities, set about organising events in the grounds, which backed on to the river. One of the earliest was a rowing match for a silver cup. By September, he was staging galas with fireworks. Unfortunately, these seem to have attracted some shady characters. While watching one display, Mr Ford, a tailor from Upper Borough Walls, felt someone trying to steal his handkerchief. This proved to be a well-known criminal called George Williams, who was given a three-month sentence for his audacity.[1]

Giller planted out the garden with trees and other plants. However, in March 1842, an ox being driven down the London Road became frightened and stampeded off. Some children standing in front of the pub ran inside to escape the animal, but it followed them. It knocked down an old lady in the kitchen, smashed up furniture, and got into the garden, where several of the new trees and shrubs were torn up. By the following year, Giller had decided to call it a day, and the garden became a skittle ground. Events continued to be held, however, and in June 1879, when the Shepherds' Fête and Gala were held at 'the Porter Butt Pleasure Grounds', 'the attendance was moderately large and the display of fireworks was a satisfactory one'.[2]

The Porter Butt in 2002 still advertised a 'family garden', but by now its days were numbered. It closed in 2009 and more recently flats have been built on what remained of its pleasure grounds.

The pub that put the most effort into turning itself into a house of fun, however, was the Folly, which lay on the border between Bathwick and Bathampton. Curiously, it may have had a connection with genuine Georgian pleasure gardens – at Grosvenor.

The Folly first appears as an unnamed building on Thorpe's 1742 map of Bath. It is also clearly delineated, though still unnamed, on the Pulteney estate map of 1770, where it is shown surrounded by an orchard, suggesting it was simply a farmhouse. However, it was already known as the Folly by 1786, when Richard Pierce inserted a notice in the *Bath Chronicle*:

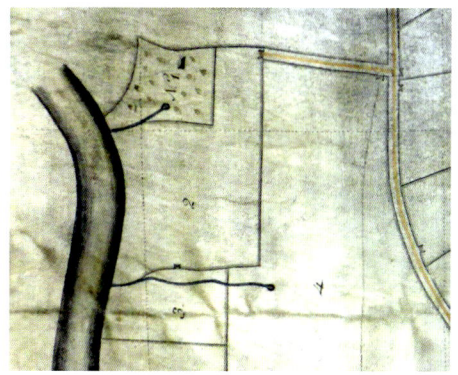

The Folly marked as No 1 on the Pulteney estate map of 1770

> Whereas the river in the Manor of Bathwick, extending from Dolemead to the Folly now rented by me, has been frequently robbed of Fish: I do hereby give notice, that whoever shall in future fish without my permission, or commit any trespass on that part of the River, shall be proceeded against as the law directs.[3]

Nothing is known of Richard Pierce, nor do we know who christened the building the Folly, or why. Perhaps the Pulteneys designed it as an eye-catcher, in imitation of Ralph Allen's Sham Castle, by embellishing the farmhouse. Taking an old building and turning it into something more picturesque by adding Gothic details or castellations was a well-established practice. The early landscape gardens of Rousham and Stowe both had working buildings – a mill and a farmhouse – converted in this way. Just as Ralph Allen had enlivened the western face of Bathampton Down with his Sham Castle, so perhaps the Pulteneys chose to brighten up the northern side. We may never know.

We next come across the building on Harcourt Masters' 1795 map of Bath, where it is clearly marked as the Folly, with a free ferry linking it to Grosvenor Gardens. By about 1795 it was being leased as a dairy farm by William Hulbert, who may well have provided refreshments to visitors while they waited for the ferry. The canal cut across the land at the back of the Folly in 1800, bringing a steady stream of vessels past this previously remote spot. Some of them were pleasure boats carrying sightseers, while the towpath became a popular walk for those wanting to enjoy some rural scenery, and a tea garden may have opened in the grounds of the Folly around this time to cater for them.

In 1830, Thomas Shew, who lived at the eastern end of Grosvenor and owned the land at the back, constructed 'a neat and commodious suspension bridge' over the Avon. This meant that a pleasant walk from Walcot to Bathampton and back along the river and canal was now possible – which would have made the Folly tearooms busier than ever.

In 1839, Matthew Hulbert, William's son, entered into an agreement with the Duke of Cleveland, who owned the land on which the Folly stood, to 'take down, remove or alter the messuage or tenement and buildings standing on the said plot of ground and also erect and build one good and substantial messuage or dwelling house with proper offices'. In other words, the Folly was redeveloped at precisely the time the railway was about to be built on a high embankment in front of it, cutting off the view across the river. If the Folly had been Gothicised or castellated, those decorations would presumably have been lost when the work was carried out.[4]

At first, Matthew Hulbert just served teas in the garden during the summer months. It is not clear when the Folly became a public house but it is tempting to

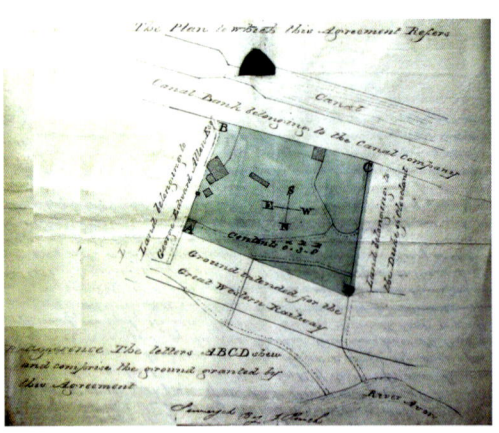

A deed of 1839, between Matthew Hulbert and the Duke of Cleveland, shows the buildings on the site

think that this coincided with the building of the railway, when there was an army of thirsty navvies to serve. However, Hulbert's main business at this stage was still farming. On a tragic note, in June 1839 Thomas Shew hanged himself in his house at Grosvenor.[5] His bridge, however, remained open, although only for pedestrians, as Matthew Hulbert had agreed not to build a carriage road to it.

The first reference to the Folly as a pub comes on 8 April 1847, when the *Bath Chronicle* reported that a drowning woman had been pulled from the river, after the alarm was raised by 'the son of Mr Hulbert of the Folly Public House'. Having been rescued, the victim was taken to the Folly to recover.[6] The Folly soon acquired a dubious reputation, however, and by 1852 the Watch Committee described it as a 'harbour for loose characters'. However, when it was put up for sale in 1854 it was described as an

> *Excellent FREEHOLD PUBLIC-HOUSE & GROUNDS,*
> *being the well-known Premises called*
> 'THE FOLLY'

> Delightfully situated near the bank of the Canal about one mile from Bath, with capital Brewery with never-failing Spring of Water, and Brewing Plant; large Lawn, Garden, Rustic Arbours, excellent Skittle Alley and 2 Pieces of Superior GARDEN-GROUND

> The FOLLY is most delightfully situated, and, being within a very moderate distance of the City, has been long known and highly appreciated by the Public as a summer resort for healthful recreation and amusement.

> The House contains, on the Ground Flour, a good Bar with superior Fittings; large Bar Parlour and Taproom; a Bakehouse with Oven; capital Kitchen and Washhouse, with all requisite Fittings; and the whole of the Premises have a never-failing supply of Pure Water. There are excellent Sitting and Bedrooms above. The Brewery is detached, and affords every facility for carrying on an extensive and lucrative trade; it is fitted up with a large Boiler, under-back Coolers &c upon the best construction, with Cellarage, Malt and Hop Rooms, &c. There is a neat Flower Garden, and the Lawn and Pleasure Grounds are very attractive, and, as a respectable summer resort, cannot be surpassed in the neighbourhood. There are stone and rustic Arbours, and one of the best Skittle Alleys in the City. A stable with Loft over, and 2 Pieces of GARDEN GROUND adjoining.

> The Brewing Plant and Fixtures to be taken at a a valuation in the usual way. The Tenure of the whole of the Property is Freehold. The House is subject to an Annual Ground-rent of £15, and the two pieces of Garden Ground to a Ground-rent of £16 6s 3d a year.

A succession of landlords ran the Folly for the next few years, until, in 1862, Thomas Osmond, from the Theatre Tavern in St John's Place, took over and attempted to give it a new image by renaming it the Cremorne Pleasure Gardens. The original Cremorne Gardens, off the Kings Road in Chelsea, had opened in 1845. They seem to have been inspired by the old gardens at Vauxhall, and like them, they developed a fairly bohemian reputation. Although the Folly was much smaller, Thomas Osmond aimed to offer the public entertainment similar to that on offer at London's Cremorne Gardens. There was a fountain, dancing, brewing from the Hampton Springs and the longest, most comfortable bowling alley in Bath, as well as gala nights lit by Vauxhall lamps. Despite Osmond being president of the Bath Licensed Victuallers Association, it retained a somewhat shady reputation, and in 1871, the magistrates nearly refused it a licence. By a strange quirk of fate, the original Cremorne Gardens in London were refused a licence that very year.

In 1881, Thomas Osmond was involved in trying to get a licence for the proposed Imperial Hotel at the former Sydney College, on behalf of Albert Alfred Hale. The magistrates suspected, however, that it was Osmond who really wanted to get his hands on Sydney Gardens. Shortly afterwards, it was rumoured that the GWR was trying to acquire Sydney Gardens. Although they failed, in 1887 they bought the Folly, suggesting that they may have had plans to run their own pleasure gardens. By now its official name was the Grosvenor Brewery, although it was still known as the Folly and as Cremorne Gardens. Over the years, licensees came and went and, with lack of investment, the pub slowly became somewhat run down. At the same time, it sloughed its raffish reputation, acquiring a new role as a family-friendly establishment, with swings and other diversions for the amusement of children. Many older resi-

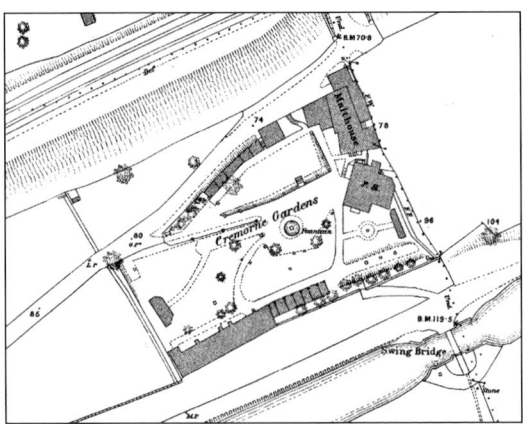

Cremorne Gardens on the 1886 Ordnance Survey map

dents of Bathampton recall with great pleasure being taken there by their parents.

At last, one fateful night in 1942, a stray German bomber brought the Folly's long if chequered history to an abrupt end. The report on the condition of the building stated that, although the damage was considerable, the building was still usable. But, given its dilapidated state, it was decided to let it slip gracefully into oblivion. It was not long before the remains of what had once been the imposing set of buildings seen on page 334 was no more, with much of its brick and Bath stone presumably disappearing for use elsewhere. It was not until 1958, however, that its licence was transferred to the Richmond Arms in Richmond Place, which until then had only had a beer licence.

The only known photograph of the Folly – or, as it was officially known, the Grosvenor Brewery. Taken around 1930, it was loaned to us by a descendant of Alfred Burgesss, the Folly's last landlord.

Today, the site of Bath's Cremorne Gardens is very overgrown, having been neglected by its previous owners, Railtrack and then Network Rail. However, the ground is now once again in private ownership, and, bit by bit, the

Slowly, the remains of the Folly are being uncovered by its new owners

The Retreat, set behind high walls in a hidden garden

The Larkhall Inn in the 1940s

owners are clearing the ground and discovering the remains of the building and other lost features.

Another Bath pub remembered with great affection by many is the Retreat, which lay at the top of a footpath from Summerhill Road to Primrose Hill. Here too, its garden is what most people recall. Unlike the Folly, there was no scandal or revelry attached to it. Hidden behind high walls, it really was a quiet and almost secret retreat from the outside world. It survived until 1975.

One pub still very much in business is the Larkhall Inn, which was described as having delightful gardens as early as 1840. They hosted a wide range of activities, from political meetings to village celebrations. But the heyday of the gardens came in the 1950s when Tom Harper ran the pub. In 1953, Tom and a friend built a model railway and village in the garden. Later, to protect it, it was moved under cover and a fairy house was added. In 1978, a subsequent landlord, Doug Wooten, won a prize for the best pub garden in the West of England, which he admitted to spending up to 40 hours a

Mary and Thomas Harper playing in the model village at the Larkhall Inn in 1953. The village was built by their father, Thomas Harper, and a friend and customer, Mr Walt Morgan, who worked on the railways.

The village, which featured a model of the Larkhall Inn, was later moved under cover.

week working on. Today, the gardens at the Larkhall Inn still provide pleasure for locals and visitors alike, with colourful flower beds in summer and lights hanging from the trees in the run-up to Christmas.

Today, pub gardens are as popular as ever, and come in all shapes and sizes. Some are simply beer gardens, but many have play equipment for children. The garden at the Hare and Hounds, famous for its magnificent views over the Charlcombe valley, even had a thatched Wendy House as late as the 1980s. But pub gardens are not the only way in which the spirit of pleasure gardens lives on. Opening a stately home to visitors has a long and honourable tradition, but in today's world the owners have to make their estates work hard just to keep the old houses going. Making use of the grounds to generate an income has become big business. Setting up attractions such as the wildlife park at Longleat is one way, but opening gardens to the public, providing refreshments and holding events and concerts is as popular today as it was in the Georgian period. At Prior Park, the National Trust runs events throughout the year, some, such as garden tours, aimed at adults, others, such as Easter Egg Hunts, aimed at children. Although Prior Park was never a true pleasure garden, visitors flocked there to admire its beauties, and continue to do so in even greater numbers today.

Parade Gardens and Sydney Gardens – pleasure gardens for the 21st century

In Parade Gardens – the former Harrison's Walks – there are band concerts, festivals and fêtes, just as there were in the past. With funding secured for the restoration and revitalisation of Sydney Gardens, the first and the last of Bath's Georgian pleasure gardens both face a bright future.

NOTES

Prelude

1. Eventually a fountain was added to Spring Gardens, but despite claims it was introduced in Elizabethan times as a trick fountain, the reliable *British History Online* website says there is no evidence to suggest it was there before 1614.

Part I, Chapter 1: The Company Goes Walking

1. Originally Bath's popular season was in the summer, but for most of the eighteenth century the popular times were spread over two seasons. The first was from just after Christmas until the end of May, at which point most visitors departed. During July and August, Bath can often be humid, so many in society took themselves off to the more countrified air of Tunbridge Wells. Events in Bath started again with the second, autumnal, season, which ran from September until late December. Local businesses, aided by the pleasure gardens, did their best to attract summer visitors, but as late as 1794, when the composer Joseph Haydn visited in August, he commented that the city was empty, 'for the people taking the baths don't come till the beginning of October, and stay through half of February'.
2. Celia Fiennes, *Through England on a Side Saddle in the Time of William and Mary* (London, Leadenhall Press, 1888), p. 109.
3. Fiennes, *Through England on a Side Saddle*, pp. 14-17.
4. They are faintly marked on Gilmore's map of 1697.
5. Edward Ward, *A Step to the Bath: with a Character of the Place* (London, J How, 1700), p. 13.
6. Ward, *A Step to the Bath*, p. 14.
7. Ward, *A Step to the Bath*, p. 16.
8. Daniel Defoe, *A Tour through England and Wales* (1724-27) (London, JM Dent and Co, 1928), II, p. 35.
9. John Macky, *A Journey through England: Letters from a Gentleman here, to his Friend Abroad* (London, J Pemberton, at the Buck and Sun against St. Dunstan's Church in Fleet Street, 1722) II, p. 128.
10. John Wood, *A Description of Bath*, 2nd edition (London, W Bathoe in the Strand & T Lownds in Fleet Street, 1765), I, p. 225.
11. *Farley's Bristol News-Paper*, 1 June 1728.
12. Wood rejected the name Mitre Green. His interest in matters pagan meant it suited him for it to be called the Grove. In 'The Making of Orange Grove' (Trevor Fawcett & Marta Inskip, *Bath History* 5, they too reject the name Mitre Green, believing it to be a corruption of Outer Green.
13. Wood, *A Description of Bath*, II, p. 342.
14. Bowling greens were not like the immaculate greens we see today. They were part of the social scene and associated with pleasure gardens. So fashionable were they that even at remote Brockley Combe, south-west of Bristol, there was a hilltop bowling green, equipped with buildings to supply visitors with chairs, tables and refreshments for their picnics. The artist Samuel Hieronymous Grimm visited it and made drawings, in which we can see people enjoying themselves in the enclosure next to the green, while watching the players. Fragments of the green survive today in the woods, along with the yews which were planted to protect the green from the winds blowing across the formerly bleak hillside.

Part I, Chapter 2: Riverside Pleasures

1. Public lavatories were constructed beneath road level in the mid 1930s as part of a Bath Improvement Scheme. After they closed they were converted to a night club, but the space has been abandoned for many years now as props have had to be installed to support the road.
2. Mary Chandler, *The Description of Bath: A Poem, Humbly Inscribed to Her Royal Highness the Princess Amelia* (Bath & London, J Leake and J Gray, 1734), p. 15.
3. Quoted in Trevor Fawcett, *Voices of Eighteenth-Century Bath* (Bath, Ruton, 1995), p. 178.
4. Quoted in Fawcett, *Voices of Eighteenth-Century Bath*, p. 51.
5. Thomas Harrison's will. Harrison's death is often given as January 1734, but at that time the year did not change until 25 March – the registers of Bath Abbey make it plain he died in what we would call 1735, and would often have been written at the time as 1734/5.
6. A kilderkin is a cask containing 18 gallons or 68 litres.
7. *Bath Journal*, May 1749; 'spaw waters' are those from Spa in Belgium.

Part I, Chapter 3: Out of Town

1. Walter Ison, *The Georgian Buildings of Bath*, revised edition (Bath, Kingsmead, 1980), p. 156.
2. The engineer John Padmore constructed the tramway for Ralph Allen about 1730. The crane, which was installed by 1733, included several important improvements to a style of crane already in use, known as a Rat's Tail. Little is known of Padmore himself. He was born in the late seventeenth century and died in 1735, in Bristol.
3. *Bath Chronicle*, 12 November 1761.
4. Bennet's mill still survives as a car showroom.
5. Wood, *A Description of Bath*, I, p. 79.
6. Information on King James's Palace was supplied to the Moger family of Lyncombe Spa by the holder of the deeds of The Cottage (as King James's Palace was then known) in the early twentieth century.
7. Wood may still have been smarting from a similar disappointment he suffered at Wicksteed's Machine. Wicksteed accepted a plan from Wood to house his machine, subsequently altering the plans to reduce the cost of the work. According to the aggrieved Wood, this so wrecked his design, he took his drawings back and never parted with them again. Widcombe was not a lucky place for Wood.
8. 'Diary of an Unknown Traveller', 1743, quoted in Fawcett, *Voices of Eighteenth-Century Bath*, p. 103.
9. Dr Richard Pococke, *The Travels through England of Dr Richard Pococke, successively Bishop of Meath and of Ossory, during 1751, 1752 and Later Years*, ed. James Joel Cartwright (London, Camden Society, 1889), II, p. 32.
10. Both springs are still identifiable today, producing the two different deposits and maintaining the temperature measured by Hillary.
11. W Hillary MD, *An Inquiry into the Contents and Medicinal Virtues of Lincomb Spa Water near Bath* (London, 1742), p. 61.

Part II, Chapter 1: A Most Delightful Spot

1. Frog Lane was replaced by the grander, more elegant, New Bond Street in the early nineteenth century.
2. *Bath Chronicle*, 26 April 1764.
3. Tobias Smollett, *The Expedition of Humphrey Clinker* (1771) (Ware, Hertfordshire, Wordsworth Classics, 1995), p. 35.
4. Carried out on the orders of William Johnstone Pulteney on behalf of his wife Frances. She inherited the Pulteney estates in 1767, after the death of General Harry Pulteney, who had inherited them from the first Earl the previous year. During discussions in the House of Commons in April 1769 about the Act of Parliament to permit the building of Pulteney Bridge, there was disagreement between the Pulteneys and the Corporation of Bath which was finally resolved in 1770. This survey shows the watercourses, one of the subjects which was an area of concern to the council.
5. *Bath Chronicle*, 8 October 1772.

6   Christopher Anstey, *The New Bath Guide*, (1766) (Bristol, Broadcast Books, 1994), Letter XIII, p. 93.
7   Rev John Penrose, *Letters from Bath: 1766-1767*, ed. Brigitte Mitchell & Hubert Penrose (Gloucester, Alan Sutton, 1983), pp. 96-98.
8   Despite the claims of the modern eponymous establishment that Sally Lunn sold her cakes in Bath in the late seventeenth century, it is unlikely that such a person ever existed. The first reference to a Sally Lun – the usual earlier spelling – is in a poem about Dublin in the *Caledonian Mercury* of 1776. There is, in the Dublin-based *Hiberian Journal* of 1776, a curious reference to 'The Poetic Criticism on Sally Lun being an insult to Majesty' and hence not printable. The first reference linking Sally Lun with Bath occurs in Philip Thicknesse's *Valetudinarian's Bath Guide* of 1780, in which he finds it

> astonishing that men, especially after the heigh-day of their youth is over, will go on loading their bodies with distemper, pain, and sorrow, till life is not worth accepting, and then repair to Bath, as if the aid of these fountains, without their own, were capable of working miracles, and yet I daily see people who professedly come to Bath for these purposes, first drink three pints or a quart of the bath waters, and then sit down to a meal of Sally Luns or hot spungy rolls, rendered high by burnt butter! Such a meal, few young men in full health can eat without feeling much inconvenience, and I have known and seen it produce almost instantaneous death to valetudinarians. (p. 23)

This sounds like the fare at a public breakfast. Thicknesse also recorded that his brother had died from eating a surfeit of Sally Luns (p. 12).
9   *Bath Chronicle*, 28 June 1770.
10   Anstey, *The New Bath Guide*, Letter XIII, pp. 94-96.
11   *Bath Chronicle*, 7 May 1767.
12   Simpson granted the main Lower Rooms to Cam Gyde in November 1771, who then closed the former Wiltshire's Rooms a year later, due to competition from the New Rooms.
13   The glass armonica was invented by Benjamin Franklin. He met Marianne Davis in London when she was seventeen. She was a musical prodigy, and became famous as an exponent of the glass armonica.
14   Reported in the *Bath Journal*, 21 November 1746.
15   'Argret' must be a spelling error for aigrette, a firework which looked like an egret's feather – egret's feathers were popular in head-dresses at the time. A 'tourbillion' was a type of star that spun in the sky and gave off large quantities of gold, silver or white light. A 'caduchet' rocket spiralled as it ascended. A 'wheatsheaf' was a large firework which was fixed to the ground and created an effect like a wheatsheaf. In this context, an 'air balloon' was almost certainly what today we would call a Chinese lantern which floated into the sky and seems to have had fireworks attached. 'Double Line rockets' were fired so as to run along a wire. A 'yew tree' was created from a yew-shaped framework with fireworks attached to it.
16   *Bath Chronicle*, 30 July 1761.
17   *Bath Chronicle*, 21 November 1765.
18   *Bath Chronicle*, 21 November 1776.
19   *Bath Chronicle*, 21 August 1777.
20   *Bath Chronicle*, 4 September 1777.

Part II, Chapter 2: Winners and Losers

1   Penrose, *Letters from Bath*, pp. 90-91.
2   Vaccination – using cowpox against smallpox – was unknown until Edward Jenner introduced it in 1796, although Benjamin Jesty, a farmer from Yetminster, had in 1774 experimented successfully on his wife and sons by inoculating them with cowpox. Inoculation was introduced into this country from Turkey by Lady Mary Wortley Montagu in 1721, but it involved using a live virus taken from someone who had only had a mild attack of the disease. Hence the insistence by councils that places for inoculation be away from the centre of cities.

3   *Bath Chronicle*, 25 June 1767.
4   *Bath Chronicle*, 13 July 1769.
5   *Bath Chronicle*, 1 March 1770.
6   *Bath Chronicle*, 6 June 1771 and *Bath Journal*, 1 and 22 June 1772.
7   *Bath Chronicle*, 9 September 1773; after an animated discussion on Twitter among historians about the meaning of 'proepilogical', Dr Leone M Jennarelli pointed out that, in Ancient Greek, 'proepi' exists as a sort of intensification of 'pro', and could be translated as 'beforehand'. So 'proepilogical' should mean: songs 'with a reflection consideration beforehand' ie a 'prologue' just made more intense by 'epi'. This appears to fit its use here precisely.
8   Guillet was a carver and gilder from London, of Huguenot origin. He came to Bath about 1771, and lived at Axford's Buildings. More information about this interesting family can be found at the National Portrait Gallery's online *Directory of British Picture Framemakers, 1600-1950*. There is, however, no mention of James's involvement in the Bagatelle.
9   *Bath Journal*, 30 October 1775.
10 *Bath Chronicle*, 20 June 1776.
11 *Bath Chronicle*, 30 October 1777.
12 *Bath Chronicle*, 19 February 1778.
13 *Bath Chronicle*, 23 December 1779.
14 *Bath Chronicle*, 3 August 1775.
15 *Bath Chronicle*, 19 June 1777.
16 *Bath Chronicle*, 23 April 1778.
17 Edmund Rack, *The Journal of Edmund Rack: An Enlightenment Gentleman's Observations on Georgian Bath* (Bath, Bath Royal Literary & Scientific Institution, 2018), p. 40 (18 February 1780).
18 Quoted in Andrew Swift & Kirsten Elliott, *Awash with Ale: 2000 Years of Imbibing in Bath* (Bath, Akeman Press, 2004), pp. 79-80.
19 *Bath Chronicle*, 30 November 1780.
20 *Bath Chronicle*, 2 November 1780.
21 *Bath Chronicle*, 18 March 1784.
22 *Bath Chronicle*, March 1792.
23 *Bath Chronicle*, 17 November 1791.
24 Montagu was on the panel at the Court Martial which acquitted Keppel. He was also local, his family coming from Lackham, near Chippenham. Harland was a friend and colleague of Keppel.
25 Frances Burney, *The Diary and Letters of Frances Burney*, revised & edited by Sarah Chauncey Woolsey (Boston, Little-Brown & Co, 1910), I, pp. 99-100 (4 June 1780); Richard Tattersall was the founder of the bloodstock auctioneers, still the leaders in the trade in Europe today, selling 10,000 horses a year. Tattersall named his new-built house at Ely Highflyer Hall after his most famous horse.
26 *Bath Chronicle*, 7 March 1782.
27 *Bath Chronicle*, 1 May 1783.
28 Also spelt Marret in some accounts, but Marrett is the spelling in legal documents.
29 *Bath Chronicle*, 5 December 1782.
30 See *Bathwick: A Forgotten Village* (Bathwick Local History Society, Bath, 2004), p. 47.
31 The word 'orchestra' here means a bandstand.

Part II, Chapter 3: Fireworks and Birdsong

1   Juvenile performers were extremely popular with eighteenth-century European audiences, Mozart being the outstanding example.
2   James Woodforde also recorded that he 'went and saw the "Dwarf Man" in Norwich, who goes by the name of James Harris from Coventry. He is exactly three feet high and very well proportioned in every respect' (James Woodforde, *The Diary of a Country Parson*, ed. John Beresford (London, Oxford University Press, 1926), II, p. 161 (entry for 17 November 1784).
3   *Bath Chronicle*, 10 June 1784.
4   *Bath Chronicle*, 12 May 1785.

5 *Bath Chronicle*, 7 June 1785.
6 *Bath Chronicle*, 16 Feb 1786.
7 *Bath Journal*, 1786.
8 *Bath Chronicle*, 3 August 1786; the box pictures at Vauxhall were painted by Francis Hayman at the suggestion of William Hogarth. One, *The Milkmaids' Garland*, survives in the Victoria and Albert Museum, and another, *The Seesaw*, is in the Tate Collection. Both can be viewed online.
9 Benjamin Milgrove, organist at the Countess of Huntingdon's Chapel and owner of a toy shop in Bond Street. Miss Poole's decision to switch allegiance to the Villa may have been due to Milgrove, who wrote music for Rauzzini, her tutor.
10 The word 'he' probably refers to Meshach Pritchard of the Parade Coffee House, who married Charlotte Purdie in 1774. This explains why tickets for Spring Gardens were sold there. It is noticeable that several of the advertisements refer to the proprietors in the plural; Pritchard took over running the gardens officially in 1790.
11 *Bath Chronicle*, 17 August 1786.
12 *Bath Chronicle*, 17 August 1786.
13 *Bath Chronicle*, 24 August 1786.
14 His name was actually Giovanni Antonio Invetto. The British newspapers struggled with these names, so for several years he called himself Signor Invetto, then tried Johannes, before Anglicising his name to John Anthony Invetto about 1784.
15 *Hampshire Chronicle*, 20 March 1786.
16 *Bath Chronicle*, 23 August 1787.
17 *Bath Chronicle*, 7 August 1788.
18 *Bath Chronicle*, 14 August 1788.
19 *Bath Chronicle*, 9 October 1788.
20 *Bath Chronicle*, 18 June 1789.
21 *Bath Chronicle*, 20 June and 17 September 1789.
22 Philip Astley was generally regarded as the founder of the circus ring. A skilled horseman and soldier, he turned his skills to good effect by learning to do trick riding, and building a team of other performers. There are several books and websites about this fascinating, resourceful man.
23 *Bath Chronicle*, 10 June 1790.
24 *Bath Chronicle*, 30 June 1791.
25 In early references to Johnstone Street, it is called Johnson Street, despite it being named after William Johnstone Pulteney.
26 *Bath Chronicle*, 16 June 1791.
27 *Bath Chronicle*, 2 June 1791.

Part II, Chapter 4: Bold Ideas and Broken Dreams

1 *Bath Chronicle*, 23 June 1791.
2 The newspaper report (*Bath Chronicle*, 30 June 1791) clearly says 143 houses. This is either a misprint for the 43 houses in the terrace facing London Road or includes the projected houses in the side streets, to be called Grosvenor Street and Cumberland Street.
3 Sydney Gardens were named after Thomas Townshend, 1st Viscount Sydney, one of Pulteney's political associates.
4 *Bath Chronicle*, 10 May 1792. A pinery is a hothouse for growing pineapples. This system had been invented in nearby Devizes in 1769 by Adam Taylor. This advertisement seems to be the first reference to the use of a Merlin swing as a public facility.
5 These are in the Victoria Art Gallery's collection.
6 Although Nixon painted a picture of Sydney Gardens (see page 178 for a black and white print of it), the original held in the British Museum has full colour palette and it is not a sketchy cartoon, like the Grosvenor Gardens ones.
7 Metal tokens were widely used in the eighteen and nineteenth centuries, and are highly collectable today. Usually of brass or occasionally of copper, proprietors' tickets were often of silver.

8   *Bath Chronicle*, 19 April 1792.
9   *Bath Chronicle*, 23 August 1792.
10 *Bath Herald*, 12 May 1792. The Editor of the newly founded *Bath Herald* was William Meyler. He was a admirer of Charles Fox, William Pitt's arch-rival, particularly after Fox achieved the repeal of Pitt's hated Shop Tax, which Meyler had vigorously opposed. As William Johnstone Pulteney was a supporter of Pitt, this may explain Meyler's support for the Grosvenor scheme.
11 *Bath Chronicle*, 12 September 1793.
12 *Bath Chronicle*, 19 September 1793.
13 *Bath Chronicle*, 10 October 1793; deeds and plans held in Bath Record Office show Harcourt Masters took over almost immediately, as they bear his signature.
14 *Bath Chronicle*, 7 November 1793.
15 *Bath Chronicle*, 7 November 1793.
16 *Bath Chronicle*, 12 June 1794.
17 *Bath Chronicle*, 9 April 1795.
18 *Bath Chronicle*, 12 February 1795.
19 *Bath Chronicle*, 23 April 1795.
20 *Bath Chronicle*, 9 July 1795.
21 *Bath Chronicle*, 16 June 1796.
22 *Bath Chronicle*, 24 November 1803.
23 *Bath Chronicle*, 13 August 1795.
24 *Bath Chronicle*, 23 August 1798.
25 *Bath Chronicle*, 13 December 1798.
26 *Bath Chronicle*, 4 December 1800.
27 *Bath Chronicle*, 21 February 1811.
28 *Bath Chronicle*, 4 August 1796.
29 *Bath Chronicle*, 4 May 1797; E Davis never gives his full name but it is possible he was Edward Davis, the landlord of the Griffin Public House in Monmouth Street. He was there in 1792, but had gone by 1800.
30 *Bath Chronicle*, 14 June 1798.
31 *Bath Chronicle*, 23 May 1799.
32 *Bath Chronicle*, 25 July 1799.
33 *Bath Chronicle*, 28 February 1799.
34 *Bath Chronicle*, 19 June 1800.
35 *Bath Chronicle*, 5 June 1800.
36 *Bath Chronicle*, 11 June 1801.
37 *Bath Chronicle*, 27 August 1801.
38 Advertisement inserted in *Bath Chronicle*, 8 March 1792 by Invetto, notifying the public he would not pay her debts.
39 *Bath Chronicle*, 26 March 1801.
40 *Bath Chronicle*, 11 June 1801.
41 *Bath Chronicle*, 8 October 1801.
42 *Bath Chronicle*, 17 November 1803.

Part III, Chapter 1: First Impressions

1   *Bath Chronicle*, 18 December 1794.
2   *Bath Chronicle*, 9 April 1795; 23 April 1795.
3   *Bath Chronicle*, 7 May 1795.
4   *Bath Chronicle*, 28 May 1795.
5   On the agreement Harcourt Masters signed with William Johnstone Pulteney to protect the springs on the land and create reservoirs for the estate's waterworks, a spring is shown in this location.
6   *Bath Chronicle*, 19 May 1796.
7   *Bath Chronicle*, 18 October 1798.

Part III, Chapter 2: Fixtures and Fittings

1. Quoted in Jean Manco, 'Pulteney Bridge', in *Architectural History*, 38 (1995, pp. 129-45), p.132.
2. The plans are held in the Sir John Soane collection.
3. *Bath Chronicle*, 15 October 1795.
4. This account rules out the theory, which is still current, that it was a forerunner of the Ferris wheel.
5. John Joseph Merlin, *Merlin's Mechanical Exhibition: Catalogue of the Different Pieces of Mechanism Exhibited at his Great Room* (n.d.), p. 7.
6. He appears to have anglicised the French word *escarpolette*, which is specifically a swing, rather than *balançoire*, which could be a swing or a seesaw. Had it been a type of Ferris wheel, he would have called it a *roue*.
7. Originally it was called more correctly Merlin's Swing but the apostrophe 's' was soon omitted.
8. John Kerr, *Sydney Gardens Vauxhall, Bath: Syllabus, or Descriptive Representation of the Numerous Productions of Nature and Art, Presented in this Extensive Establishment* (Bath, Meyler, 1825), p. 8.
9. This reference and its implications are discussed further in Part Three Chapter 4, pp. 327ff.
10. *Bath Chronicle*, 23 June 1796.
11. Bathforum recognizances 1794. On the plans drawn by Thomas Baldwin, the building is referred to as Vauxhall and Ranelagh House. George Clark was a builder, so it seems likely that he was the one appointed to carry out the building work, and additionally to ensure the gardens were licensed.
12. Deeds held in Bath Record Office.
13. *Bath Chronicle*, 18 October 1798.

Part III, Chapter 3: That Celebrated and Fashionable Resort of Pleasure

1. *Bath Chronicle*, 15 October 1795.
2. *Bath Chronicle*, 27 August 1795.
3. *Bath Chronicle*, 2 June 1796.
4. *Bath Chronicle*, 11 August 1796.
5. *Bath Chronicle*, 1 June 1797.
6. *Bath Chronicle*, 31 May 1798.
7. *Bath Chronicle*, 18 April 1799; although the *Bath Chronicle* calls him J Holloway in this advertisement, this must be a misprint – his name was Thomas Holloway.
8. Jane is inconsistent in her spelling of Sydney.
9. *Bath Chronicle*, 6 June 1799. Was the officer the inspiration for George Wickham in *Pride and Prejudice*?
10. *Bath Chronicle*, 13 June 1799.
11. The present gateway from the gardens was only granted planning permission in 1983.
12. *Bath Chronicle*, 12 June 1800.
13. *Bath Chronicle*, 12 March 1801.
14. *Bath Chronicle*, 29 January 1801.
15. *Bath Chronicle*, 19 March 1801.
16. *Bath Chronicle*, 30 April 1801.
17. *Bath Chronicle*, 9 September 1802.
18. *Bath Chronicle*, 9 August 1804; the packet station building is still there today, having recently been restored.
19. Rowland Mainwaring, *The Annals of Bath from the year 1800* (Bath, Mary Meyler & Son, 1838), p. 35.
20. *Bath Chronicle*, 20 September 1804.
21. *Bath Chronicle*, 10 May 1832.
22. *Bath Chronicle*, 31 October 1805.
23. *Bath Chronicle*, 24 August 1809.
24. *Bath Chronicle*, 9 August 1810.
25. *Bath Chronicle*, 25 October1810.
26. For those seeking more information on pyrotechnics, the expert in Britain is Rev Ronald Lancaster, author of *Fireworks, Principle and Practice*, 4th ed. (Palm Springs, California,

Chemical Publishing Co, 2005).
27 *Bath Chronicle*, 24 May 1810.
28 Rudolph Ackermann, *The Microcosm of London* (London, R Ackermann, 1810), III, p. 206.
29 His real name was Zachariah Mortram. His wife was Ann Pain, from the famous firework makers still in operation today.
30 *Bath Chronicle*, 30 May 1810: a sosisson is a type of firework made from a paper or canvas tube filled with gunpowder.
31 *Bath Chronicle*, 6 August 1812.
32 *Bath Chronicle*, 1 April 1813.
33 *Bath Chronicle*, 27 May 1813.
34 Mainwaring, *Annals of Bath*, pp. 138-40.
35 *Bath Journal*, 7 June 1813.
36 *Bath and Cheltenham Gazette*, 9 June 1813.
37 Pierce Egan, *Walks through Bath* (Bath, Meyler & Son, 1819), pp. 182-86; unfortunately for Egan, the grotto was not the one where Sheridan and Elizabeth Linley left notes for each other. That distinction went to Delia's grotto on the Lower Room's Walks, but this claim for the Sydney Gardens Grotto was still being repeated years later. Elizabeth Linley Sheridan died in 1792, three years before the gardens opened.
38 *Bath Chronicle*, 20 June 1822.
39 *Bath Chronicle*, 3 June 1824.
40 Egan, *Walks through Bath*, pp. 100-101.
41 *Bath Chronicle*, 3 June 1824.
42 *Bath Chronicle*, 8 July 1824.
43 Thomas Fowell Buxton, *An Inquiry, whether Crime and Misery are produced or Prevented by our Present System of Prison Discipline,* 2nd ed. (London, John & Arthur Arch, Butterworth & Sons, and John Hatchard, 1818), pp. 149-50.
44 See also the account of Bridle's trial in 1822 in *Bath Chronicle*, 22 August 1822, when he was acquitted of one charge of cruelty but found guilty of a charge of unlawful punishment. There was such a strong feeling in the court that the prosecution was unfair that his lawyers refused to take their fees and the jury pressed for mercy. Several magistrates in Somerset spoke warmly in Bridle's favour.
45 *Bath Chronicle*, 8 July 1824.
46 *Bath Chronicle*, 22 July 1824.
47 Kerr, *Sydney Gardens Vauxhall*.
48 *Bath Chronicle*, 12 April 1827.
49 *Bath Chronicle*, 31 May 1827.
50 *Bath Chronicle*, 16 August 1827.
51 *Bath Chronicle*, 21 May 1829.
52 *Bath Chronicle*, 8 April 1830.
53 *Bath Chronicle*, 6 May 1830.
54 *Bath Chronicle*, 13 May 1830.
55 *Bath Chronicle*, 20 May 1830.
56 *Bath Chronicle*, 24 June 1830.
57 *Bath Chronicle*, 1 July 1830.
58 *Bath Chronicle*, 8 July 1830.
59 John Murray, *Practical Observations on the Phenomena of Flame and Safety Lamps* (London, Holdsworth & Ball, 1833), p. 11; *Bath Chronicle*, 29 July 1830.
60 *Bath Chronicle*, 30 September 1830.
61 *Bath Chronicle*, 6 May 1830.
62 *Bath Chronicle*, 7 October 1830; similar illuminations can be seen in the Museum of Bath at Work, Julian Road.
63 This safely dispenses with the myth that she was offended by a comment about her legs and did not visit Bath again.

64 *Bath Chronicle*, 18 December 1834. At this time, Bath sent two MPs to parliament. The Tory Party had recently changed its name to Conservative, but was still widely known as the Tory Party – as it still is today.
65 *Bath Chronicle*, 30 December 1830.
66 *Bath Chronicle*, 31 March 1831.
67 Mainwaring, *Annals of Bath*, pp. 361-62.
68 *Bath Chronicle*, 8 September 1831.
69 *Bath Chronicle*, 19 April 1832.
70 *Bath Chronicle*, 22 March 1832.
71 *Bath Chronicle*, 21 June 1832.
72 It is often said that Bridle was declared bankrupt and ended up in Ilchester gaol as a prisoner. As will become evident, this was not the case. There is no record of his bankruptcy in *The Gazette*, and the only William Bridle in Ilchester Gaol at this date is a much younger man.
73 *Bath Chronicle*, 20 December 1832.
74 *Bath Chronicle*, 18 October 1832.
75 *Bath Chronicle*, 13 June 1833.
76 *Bath Chronicle*, 30 May 1833.
77 *Bath Chronicle*, 9 January 1834.
78 *Bath Chronicle*, 6 February 1834.
79 *Bath Chronicle*, 24 April 1834.
80 *Bath Chronicle*, 10 April 1834 and 24 July 1834.
81 *Bath Chronicle*, 7 August 1834.
82 Laurence Brown, *The slavery connections of Marble Hill House* (English Heritage, 2010) p. 11 (Online at: historicengland.org.uk/images-books/publications/slavery-connections-marble-hill-house/slavery-connections-marble-hill-house).
83 Brown, *The slavery connections of Marble Hill House*, p. 48.
84 Information from the Legacies of British Slave-ownership website (www.ucl.ac.uk/lbs).
85 *Bath Chronicle*, 17 September 1835.
86 *Bath Chronicle*, 7 July 1836.
87 *Bath Chronicle*, 21 July 1836.
88 *Bath Chronicle*, 1 December 1836; although the name continued to be used, it also continued to be known as the Sydney Hotel. On 4 May 1865, after it had been converted to a college, the *Bath Chronicle* referred to 'the Pulteney or Sydney Hotel, as it was indifferently called'.
89 *Bath Chronicle*, 28 March 1839.

Part III, Chapter 4: The Autumn of a Form Once Fine

1 *Bath Chronicle*, 31 January 1839.
2 The rainfall in the summer and autumn of 1839 was about double the seasonal average.
3 *Bath Chronicle*, 25 July 1839.
4 *Bath Chronicle*, 1 September 1842.
5 *Bath Chronicle*, 7 November 1839.
6 Parish registers for St Mary's Islington, burials, 24 November 1851.
7 *Bath Chronicle*, 30 April 1840.
8 It is not known why Edward Davis resigned. There may have been differences of opinion. In February 1841 there was a cryptic message in the *Bath Chronicle* from the Bath Horticultural Society stating that JF Goodridge 'is advised by his friends that it is quite unnecessary for him to notice anything emanating from Mr Edward Davis'. James Goodridge was a solicitor. Davis may simply have resigned because, when the two societies linked up again (see below), the joint society did not need two secretaries, or perhaps because he was getting more commissions as an architect.
9 *Bath Chronicle*, 4 June 1840.
10 *Bath Chronicle*, 19 March 1840.
11 *Bath Chronicle*, 10 September 1840.

12　*Bath Chronicle*, 4 February 1841.
13　*Bath Chronicle*, 13 May 1841.
14　*Bath Chronicle*, 29 July 1841.
15　*Bath Chronicle*, 13 August 1827.
16　*Bath Chronicle*, 1 May 1845.
17　A quotation from 'Locksley Hall' by Tennyson. The short-sighted Tennyson mistakenly thought that the railway lines were grooves – hence 'the ringing grooves of change'.
18　*Bath Chronicle*, 11 August 1842.
19　*Bath Chronicle*, 13 June 1844.
20　*Bristol Times & Mirror*, 30 September 1843.
21　*Bath Chronicle*, 26 January 1843.
22　*Bath Chronicle*, 20 April 1843. Charles Hunnings Wilkinson was a remarkable polymath and expert on galvanism. His lectures at the Kingston Pump Room, and experiments showing how an electric current could make the muscles of dead animals react, may have given Mary Shelley, then living just around the corner in Abbey Church Yard, inspiration for her novel *Frankenstein*.
23　*Bath Chronicle*, 31 October 1844.
24　*Bath Chronicle*, 17 July 1845.
25　Their music can be heard on a CD called *The Celebrated Distin Family* by the Prince Regent's Band.
26　*Bath Chronicle*, 24 August 1845.
27　*Bath Chronicle*, 27 November 1845.
28　*Bath Chronicle*, 4 December 1845.
29　*Bath Chronicle*, 4 December 1845.
30　*Bath Chronicle*, 31 December 1846.
31　*Bath Chronicle*, 23 December 1847.
32　*Bath Chronicle*, 13 January 1848.
33　*Bath Chronicle*, 17 February 1848.
34　*Bath Chronicle*, 27 September 1849.
35　*Bristol Times & Mirror*, 20 April 1850.
36　*Bath Chronicle*, 14 November 1850.
37　*Bath Chronicle*, 3 April 1851.
38　*Bath Chronicle*, 22 May 1851.
39　*Bath Chronicle*, 13 November 1851 and 18 December 1851.
40　*Bath Chronicle*, 29 January 1852.
41　*Bath Chronicle*, 15 January 1852.
42　*Bath Chronicle*, 19 February 1852.
43　Roger Rolls, *The Hospital of the Nation: The Story of Spa Medicine and the Mineral Water Hospital at Bath* (Bath, Bird Publications, 1988), p. 28.
44　*Bath Chronicle*, 1 April 1852.
45　*Bath Chronicle*, 5 August 1852. The newspaper incorrectly calls him John Peacock, instead of James.
46　Information on Peacock's death from Ancestry.co.uk.
47　Seen when the house was the Sydney Gardens Hotel in the 1980s.
48　The grotto is not shown on the map drawn by Spackman & Cotterell in 1852/3, but was there by the time of General Andrews' death in 1858.
49　Kerr, *Sydney Gardens Vauxhall*, p. 8.
50　The Doric temple may be later. It is not shown on the 1853 map, although the pond is, and the sale catalogue says that near the fishpond was a rustic summerhouse. The other possibility is that it, too, was rescued from Sydney Gardens and was awaiting reconstruction when Andrews died.
51　After the death of Andrews, Vellore was bought by Lady Morrison, who attempted to dispose of it immediately, but lived there until about 1861, when it was bought by Charles Kemble, Rector of Bath Abbey.
52　*Bath Chronicle*, 4 August 1853.

53 *Bath Chronicle*, 18 January 1855.
54 This band was formed by a group of Germans, notably three brothers whose surname was Koop, and some of their friends. Having made their way to Britain, they began playing at Weston-super-Mare about 1853, but soon moved to Bath. In its early years, all its members were German.
55 *Bath Chronicle*, 31 May 1855.
56 *Bath Chronicle*, 25 June 1855.
57 *Bath Chronicle*, 8 May 1856.
58 *Bath Chronicle*, 15 May 1856.
59 *Bath Chronicle*, 16 May 1861.
60 *Bath Chronicle*, 14 May 1857; according to the report, it was very neatly thatched by Mr Sims of Bathampton who executed his task in a most creditable manner.
61 *Bath Chronicle*, 16 July 1857.
62 *Bath Chronicle*, 21 May 1857.
63 *Bath Chronicle*, 12 May 1859.
64 *Bath Chronicle*, 10 May 1860.
65 *Bath Chronicle*, 12 July 1860.
66 *Bath Chronicle*, 16 May 1861.
67 *Bath Chronicle*, 26 September 1861.
68 This was John Arthur Roebuck Rudge. He eventually worked with a Bath photographer called William Friese Green, and invented the Rudge Projector or Phantascope. He is widely regarded as the father of moving pictures.
69 *Bath Chronicle*, 18 April 1878.
70 *Bath Chronicle*, 29 September 1881.
71 *Bath Chronicle*, 11 September 1879.
72 *Bath Chronicle*, 7 June 1883; this was by permission of M Stier & Sons, watchmakers of 19 New Bond Street, Bath. They had bought the pavement, boxed it up and were offering it for sale, from Mr Stier's house at 14 Sydenham Terrace.
73 *Bath Chronicle*, 8 August 1883.
74 The present Brock's Fireworks have no connection with this family.
75 *Bath Chronicle*, 7 May 1885.
76 *Bath Chronicle*, 17 May 1888.
77 *Bath Chronicle*, 23 August 1888; the man behind this scheme, HG Massingham, was a remarkable pioneer in electricity supply. A boot and shoe dealer by trade, with a shop at 18 High Street and 1 The Corridor, he eventually founded the company in Dorchester Street which became known as the City of Bath Electric Lighting and Engineering Co Ltd.
78 *Bath Chronicle*, 21 July 1881.
79 *Bath Chronicle*, 30 May 1889.
80 *Bath Chronicle*, 23 April 1891.

Part III, Chapter 5: From Private Parties to Public Park

1 Quoted in Martha More, *Mendip Annals; or A Narrative of the Charitable Labours of Hannah and Martha More in their Neighbourhood, being the Journal of Martha More*, ed. Arthur Roberts, 2nd ed. (London, James Nisbet & Co, 1859), p. 6.
2 Royal Victoria Park was not owned by the council but supported by private subscription. The two names for Bathwick Park seemed to coexist almost from the time it opened, before finally settling down as Henrietta Park, although the name Bathwick Park lingered on into the early twentieth century.
3 *Bath Chronicle*, 9 August 1894.
4 *Bath Chronicle*, 19 July 1894.
5 *Bath Chronicle*, 29 August 1895.
6 *Bath Chronicle*, 6 August 1896.
7 *Bath Chronicle*, 1 July 1897.

8   *Bath Chronicle*, 6 October 1898.
9   *Bath Chronicle*, 16 April 1891.
10 *Bath Chronicle*, 18 August 1892.
11 *Bath Chronicle*, 8 June 1893.
12 *Bath Chronicle*, 15 June 1893.
13 *Bath Chronicle*, 21 September 1893.
14 *Bath Chronicle*, 2 November 1893.
15 *Bath Chronicle*, 27 September 1894.
16 *Bath Chronicle*, 6 and 27 September 1894.
17 *Bath Chronicle*, 5 September 1895.
18 *Bath Chronicle*, 16 and 30 April 1896.
19 *Bath Chronicle*, 5 November 1896.
20 *Bath Chronicle*, 22 July 1897.
21 *Bath Chronicle*, 22 July 1897.
22 *Bath Chronicle*, 9 December 1897.
23 Barry *Cunliffe*, 'Major Davis: Architect and Antiquarian', *Bath History* 1 (Gloucester, Alan Sutton, 1986, pp. 27-60), p. 56.
24 *Bath Chronicle*, 31 March 1898.
25 *Bath Chronicle*, 25 August and 8 September 1898.
26 *Bath Chronicle*, 9 February 1899.
27 *Bath Chronicle*, 10 August 1899.
28 *Bath Chronicle*, 7 September 1899.
29 *Bath Chronicle*, 8 November 1900.
30 *The Welsh Coast Pioneer and Review for North Cambria*, 11 July 1902; see also Pete Faint, *Jack Hylton* (Peter Faint, 2014).
31 *Bath Chronicle*, 13 September 1900; 20 September 1900.
32 *Bath Chronicle*, 7 June 1900. The *Bath Chronicle* had shifted from their earlier spelling of 'coker nut' to 'cocoanut.' They finally used the modern spelling in 1917. Both versions existed previously. The first coconut shies appeared in this country around the mid-nineteenth century.
33 *Bath Chronicle*, 14 June 1900.
34 *Bath Chronicle*, 11 September 1902.
35 *Bath Chronicle*, 17 September 1903.
36 *Bath Chronicle*, 4 August 1904.
37 *Bath Chronicle*, 31 March 1904.
38 *Bath Chronicle*, 1 June 1905.
39 *Bath Chronicle*, 26 March 1908.
40 *Bath Chronicle*, 24 June 1909.
41 *Bath Chronicle*, 8 July 1909.
42 *Bath Chronicle*, 1 July 1909.
43 *Bath Herald*, 20 July 1909.
44 Andrew Swift & Kirsten Elliott, *The Year of the Pageant* (Bath, Akeman Press, 2009), p. 661.
45 Swift & Elliott, *Year of the Pageant*, p. 661.
46 *Bath Chronicle*, 29 July 1909.
47 *Bath Chronicle*, 11 January 1913.
48 Minutes of the Bath Corporation Sydney Gardens sub-committee 8 September 1913.
49 It was later converted to an electricity sub-station, and it has been claimed that this is what it was built as. However, the council minutes show that this was clearly not the case. It later reverted to being used by the parks department, although plans for the regeneration of the gardens include converting it to an 'artist/craft workshop space'.
50 *Bath Chronicle*, 1 November 1913.
51 *Bath Chronicle*, 31 October 1914.
52 *Bath Chronicle*, 12 June 1915.
53 *Bath Chronicle*, 16 and 23 June 1908.

NOTES 357

54 *Bath Chronicle,* 29 June 1918.
55 *Bath Chronicle,* 27 July 1918.
56 *Bath Chronicle,* 26 July 1919.
57 *Bath Chronicle,* 5 and 26 July 1919.
58 Committee Minutes, the Holburne Trustees, 18 October and 6 December 1922.
59 One councillor said he understood they were naval guns. Each weighed 8¾ cwt (about 445 Kg), which is rather heavy for Georgian naval guns, so it is unlikely, though not impossible, that they were.
60 *Bath Chronicle,* 20 March 1937.
61 *Bath Chronicle,* 24 April 1937.
62 *Bath Chronicle,* 22 October 1938.
63 *Bath Chronicle,* 21 December 1940.
64 Eileen's continued being public spirited for many years. Northumberland Place became famous for its floral displays in summer, many provided by the shop.
65 *Bath Chronicle,* 21 February 1942.
66 Information about the site of this shelter came from Jayne Williams. Other details came from Jim Warren of the Bath Blitz Memorial Project, who obtained his figures from an Air Raid Precautions booklet, published in 1941 by Mendip Press.
67 *Bath Chronicle,* 18 September 1948.
68 *Bath Chronicle,* 25 September 1948.
69 *Bath Chronicle,* 20 November 1948.
70 *Wiltshire Times and Trowbridge Advertiser,* 2 August 1952.
71 *Wiltshire Times and Trowbridge Advertiser,* 22 August 1953.
72 *Wiltshire Times and Trowbridge Advertiser,* 7 August 1954.
73 *Wiltshire Times and Trowbridge Advertiser,* 30 July 1955.
74 *Wiltshire Times and Trowbridge Advertiser,* 11 August 1956.
75 *Wiltshire Times and Trowbridge Advertiser,* 22 September 1956.
76 *Wiltshire Times and Trowbridge Advertiser,* 29 September 1956.

Postlude, Chapter 1: Lost Pleasures

1 *Bath Chronicle*, 4 September 1834.
2 JC Loudon, ed., *The Architectural Magazine, and Journal*, Vol. III (London, Longman, Rees, Orme, Brown & Longman, 1836).
3 *Bath Chronicle*, 7 April 1945.
4 *Bath Chronicle*, 11 May 1946.
5 Loudon, *The Architectural Magazine, and Journal*, III.
6 *Bath Chronicle*, 21 February 1931, 18 May 1940 and 3 April 1879.
7 *Bath Chronicle*, 14 April 1836.
8 *Bath Chronicle*, 17 March 1864.
9 *Bath Chronicle*, 10 February 1934.
10 *Bath Chronicle*, 7 October 1830.
11 James Tunstall, *Rambles through Bath and its Neighbourhood* (London & Bath, Simpkin, Marshall & Co, 1847), pp. 107-108.
12 Egan, *Walks through Bath*, pp. 100-101.

Postlude, Chapter 2: Welcome to the House of Fun

1 *Bath Chronicle*, 2 September 1841.
2 *Bath Chronicle*, 12 June 1879.
3 *Bath Chronicle*, 9 February 1786.
4 Andrew Swift & Kirsten Elliott, *The Lost Pubs of Bath* (Bath, Akeman Press, 2005), p. 337.
5 *Bath Chronicle*, 27 June 1839.
6 *Bath Chronicle*, 8 April 1847.

BIBLIOGRAPHY

I used the following sources extensively:

Newspapers, in particular the *Bath Chronicle*, first published in 1760 (and now available online via the British Newspaper Archive: www.britishnewspaperarchive.co.uk), and the *Bath Journal*, first published in 1744. Other regional newspapers, accessed mainly via the British Newspaper Archive, were also used.

Directories consulted for Bath included: Gye's *New Bath Directory* (1792), Robbin's *Bath Directory* (1800), Brown's *New Bath Directory* (1809), Wood & Cunningham's *New Bath Directory* (1812), Gye's *Bath Directory* (1819), Keene's *Bath Directory* (1824, 1826, 1829), Silverthorne's *Bath Directory* (1833, 1837, 1841, 1846), Hunt's *Bath Directory* (1848), Clarke's *Bath Directory* (1849), Erith's *Bath Directory* (1850), Vivian's *Bath Directory* (1852, 1854), Robinson's *Bath Directory* (1856), Lewis's *Post Office Bath Directory* (published biannually from 1858 to 1892, and annually from 1894 to 1927, and thereafter in 1932, 1933, 1938, 1938 and 1940), Kelly's *Directory of Bath & Neighbourhood* (published in 1929, 1930, 1931, 1934, 1935, 1936, 1937, 1947, 1950, 1952, 1955, 1957, 1959, 1961, 1963, 1965, 1967, 1968, 1969, 1970, 1971, 1972).

Comprehensive collections of Bath directories are held in Bath Record Office and Bath Reference Library. Bath directories for 1846, 1852, 1864, 1876, 1884, 1895, 1902 & 1911 can also be consulted online at the University of Leicester Special Collections website (http://specialcollections.le.ac.uk/).

Other works consulted:
Bathwick: A Forgotten Village, Bathwick Local History Society, Bath, 2004
Bathwick: Echoes of the Past, Bathwick Local History Society, Bath, 2008
The Original Bath Guide, Bath, Meyler and Son, 1843
Ackermann, Rudolph, *The Microcosm of London*, Volume 3, London, R Ackermann, 1810
Anstey, Christopher, *The New Bath Guide* (1766), Bristol, Broadcast Books, 1994
Atkinson, Peter, *Sydney Gardens and the Development of Eighteenth Century Pleasure Gardens in Bath* (dissertation submitted to the Architecture Association as part of the Graduate Diploma in the Conservation of Historic Landscapes, Parks and Gardens, June 1989)
Brown, Laurence, *The slavery connections of Marble Hill House*, English Heritage, 2010 (online at: historicengland.org.uk/images-books/publications/slavery-connections-marble-hill-house/slavery-connections-marble-hill-house)
Burgess, Glenn & Matthew Festenstein, eds., *English Radicalism, 1550-1850*, Cambridge, Cambridge University Press, 2007
Burney, Frances, *The Diary and Letters of Frances Burney*, revised & edited by Sarah Chauncey Woolsey, 2 volumes, Boston, Little-Brown & Co, 1910

Buxton, Thomas Fowell, *An Inquiry, whether Crime and Misery are produced or Prevented by our Present System of Prison Discipline*, 2nd ed., London, John & Arthur Arch, Butterworth & Sons, and John Hatchard, 1818
Chandler, Mary *The Description of Bath: A Poem, Humbly Inscribed to Her Royal Highness the Princess Amelia*, Bath & London, J Leake and J Gray, 1734
Chapman, Mike, '*Kensington Meadows Local Nature Reserve, Bath: A Desk Based Historical Assessment'*, January, 2010 (www.bathnes.gov.uk/sites/default/files/kensington_meadows_historical_study_copyright_bnes_and_mike_chapman2.pdf)
Cunliffe, Barry, 'Major Davis*:* Architect and Antiquarian', *Bath History* 1, Gloucester, Alan Sutton, 1986, pp. 27-60
Defoe, Daniel, *A Tour through England and Wales* (1724-27), Volume 2, London, JM Dent and Co, 1928
Drake, Peter, *The Memoirs of Capt. Peter Drake*, Dublin, S Powell, 1755
Dunn, Mary, *A Very Pleasant Situation: The History of Lyncombe House and the Paragon School*, Bath, Paragon School, n.d.
Egan, Pierce, *Walks through Bath,* Bath, Meyler & Son, 1819
Elliott, Kirsten, *Queen of Waters*, Bath, Akeman Press, 2010
Eyles, William E, 'Electricity in Bath 1890 –1974 (Part I)', Supplement to *Histelec News* (The Newsletter of the Western Power Electricity Historical Society), December 2005 (wpehs.org.uk/histelec-news)
Faint Pete, *Jack Hylton*, Peter Faint, 2014
Fawcett, Trevor and Marta Inskip, 'The Making of Orange Grove', *Bath History* 5, Bath, Millstream Books, 1994, pp. 24-50
Fawcett, Trevor, 'Bath City Council Members, 1700-1835', (historyofbath.org/images/documents/a8b02716-6797-4897-a5ca-040e894f0512.pdf)
Fawcett, Trevor, *The Bagatelle and King James's Palace: Two Lyncombe Pleasure Gardens (with notes on Lyncombe Spa and Wicksteed's Machine)*, Bath, Trevor Fawcett, 1998
Fawcett, Trevor, 'William Street: an Apothecary's Progress', in *The Survey of Bath and District: The Journal of the Survey of Old Bath and its Associates,* 23 (October 2008), pp. 38-41 (historyofbath.org/images/documents/6bd46612-d5c9-45fd-90ba-744938e1a592.pdf)
Fawcett, Trevor, *Voices of Eighteenth-Century Bath*, Bath, Ruton, 1995
Fiennes, Celia, *Through England on a Side Saddle in the Time of William and Mary*, London, Leadenhall Press, 1888
Foyle, Andrew Foyle & Nikolaus Pevsner, *The Buildings of England: Somerset,: North and Bristol*, New Haven & London, Yale University Press, 2011
Grieves, Kevin, 'A Literary Entrepreneur: William Meyler of Bath', *Bath History* 12, Bath, Bath Preservation Trust, 2011, pp. 81-93
Hammond, Cynthia Imogen, *Architects, Angels, Activists and the City of Bath, 1765-1965: Engaging with Women's Spatial Interventions in Buildings and Landscape*, Aldershot, Ashgate, 2012
Hare, Augustus, *The Life and Letters of Frances Baroness Bunsen*, London, Routledge, 1879
Highfill, Philip H, Kalman A Burnim & Edward A Langhans, *A Biographical Dictionary of Actors, Actresses, Musicians, Dancers, Managers & Other Stage Personnel in London, 1660-1800*, Carbondale, Illinois, Southern Illinois University Press, 1991
Hillary, W, MD, *An Inquiry into the Contents and Medicinal Virtues of Lincomb Spa Water near Bath*, London, 1742
Ison, Walter, *The Georgian Buildings of Bath*, revised edition, Bath, Kingsmead, 1980

Kerr, John, *Sydney Gardens Vauxhall, Bath: Syllabus, or Descriptive Representation of the Numerous Productions of Nature and Art, Presented in this Extensive Establishment*, Bath, Meyler, 1825
Lancaster, Rev Ronald, *Fireworks: Principle & Practice*, 4th ed., Palm Springs, California, Chemical Publishing Co, 2005
Loudon JC, ed., *The Architectural Magazine, and Journal*, Volume 3, London, Longman, Rees, Orme, Brown & Longman, 1836
Macky, John, *A Journey through England: Letters from a Gentleman here, to his Friend Abroad*, Volume 2, London, J Pemberton, at the Buck and Sun against St. Dunstan's Church in Fleet Street, 1722
Mainwaring, Rowland, *The Annals of Bath from the year 1800*, Bath, Mary Meyler & Son, 1838
Manco, Jean, 'Pulteney Bridge', in *Architectural History*, 38 (1995), pp.129-45
Merlin, John Joseph, *Merlin's Mechanical Exhibition: Catalogue of the Different Pieces of Mechanism Exhibited at his Great Room*, n.d.
More, Martha, *Mendip Annals; or A Narrative of the Charitable Labours of Hannah and Martha More in their Neighbourhood, being the Journal of Martha More*, ed. Arthur Roberts, 2nd ed. London, James Nisbet & Co, 1859
Murray, John, *Practical Observations on the Phenomena of Flame and Safety Lamps*, London, Holdsworth & Ball, 1833
Parry, Eric, *Context: Architecture and the Genius of Place*, Chichester, John Wiley & Sons, 2015
Peach, REM, *Historic Houses in Bath, and their Associations*, London & Bath, Simpkin, Marshall & Co, 1883
Penrose, Rev John, *Letters from Bath: 1766-1767*, ed. Brigitte Mitchell & Hubert Penrose, Gloucester, Alan Sutton, 1983
Pepys, Samuel, *The Diary of Samuel Pepys MA, FRS*, ed. Henry B Wheatley, George Bell, London, 1893
Pococke, Dr Richard, *The Travels through England of Dr Richard Pococke, successively Bishop of Meath and of Ossory, during 1751, 1752 and Later Years*, ed. James Joel Cartwright, Volume 2, London, Camden Society, 1889
Rack, Edmund, *The Journal of Edmund Rack: An Enlightenment Gentleman's Observations on Georgian Bath*, Bath, Bath Royal Literary & Scientific Institution, 2018
Rolls, Roger, *The Hospital of the Nation: The Story of Spa Medicine and the Mineral Water Hospital at Bath*, Bath, Bird Publications, 1988
Simon, Jacob, *Directory of British Picture Framemakers, 1600-1950*, London, National Gallery, 2007 (now an online resource provided by the National Gallery and selectively update twice yearly; www.npg.org.uk/research/conservation/directory-of-british-framemakers)
Smollett, Tobias, *The Expedition of Humphrey Clinker* (1771), Ware, Hertfordshire, Wordsworth Classics, 1995
Snaddon, Brenda, *The Last Promenade: Sydney Gardens, Bath*, Bath, Millstream Books, 2000
Swift, Andrew & Kirsten Elliott, *Awash with Ale: 2000 Years of Imbibing in Bath*, Bath, Akeman Press, 2004

Swift, Andrew & Kirsten Elliott, *Lost Pubs of Bath*, Bath, Akeman Press, 2005
Swift, Andrew & Kirsten Elliott, *The Year of the Pageant*, Bath, Akeman Press, 2009
Swift, Andrew, *All Roads Lead to France: Bath and the Great War*, Bath, Akeman Press, 2005
Swift, Andrew, *The Ringing Grooves of Change: Brunel & the Coming of the Railway to Bath*, Bath, Akeman Press, 2006
Sydenham, S, *Bath Pleasure Gardens of the Eighteenth Century issuing Metal Admission Tickets*, Bath, Bath Herald, 1907
Thicknesse, Philip, *Valetudinarians Bath Guide*, 2nd ed., London, Dodsley, Brown, Pratt & Clinch, 1780
Tunstall, James, *Rambles through Bath and its Neighbourhood*, London & Bath, Simpkin, Marshall & Co, 1847
Ward, Edward, *A Step to the Bath: with a Character of the Place*, London, J How, 1700
Winter, Andrew, 'Bath', in *The Land We Live In*, Volume 3, London, Charles Knight, 1847, pp. 25-56
Wood, John Wood, *An Essay towards a Description of the City of Bath*, Bath, printed for W Frederick, Bookseller, 1749
Wood, John, *A Description of Bath*, 2 volumes, 2nd edition, London, W Bathoe in the Strand & T Lownds in Fleet Street, 1765
Woodforde, James, *The Diary of a Country Parson*, ed. John Beresford, Volume 2, 1782-87, London, Oxford University Press, 1926

Documents

Bath Record Office (www.batharchives.co.uk)
Map showing Bath and five miles round, surveyed by Thomas Thorpe, 1742
Map of the Manor of Bathwick circa 1770
Map of Bath by Taylor and Meyler 1793
Maps of Bath by Harcourt Masters 1795 & 1800
Maps of Bath from a survey conducted by Cotterell & Spackman in 1852-53
Deeds and plans of Grosvenor Gardens
Deeds and plans of Sydney Gardens
Sales catalogues and plans relating to the proposed hotels.
Architectural drawings by Sir Reginald Blomfield of the Holburne Museum alterations
Minutes of the Parks Committee and Sydney Gardens sub-committee
Planning application to make a public entrance from Sydney Gardens onto the canal towpath

Bristol Archives (www.bristolmuseums.org.uk/bristol-archives)
Inventory of goods of William Hull, gardener, tenant of Spring Gardens, Bathwick, made by Jarrit Smith preparatory to carrying out a distraint for arrears of rent, August 7 1742

Letter and draft reply: Earl of Bath to Jarrit Smith concerning a lawsuit brought by William Hull, claiming damages suffered by distraint, April 3 and 7 1753

Draft agreement for lease between 1) Earl of Bath 2) Richard Collins and others of premises formerly let to William Hull, September 4 1742

Paragon School

Various documents donated by George Moger were held at the Paragon School and are now held at Prior Park College. These include an inventory of 1746, a copy of William Hillary's investigation into the waters of the spa, and the accounts from 1767 when the spa was sold to William Street.

Websites

Ancestry: www.ancestry.co.uk

British History Online: www.british-history.ac.uk

British Weather from 1700 to 1849: www.pascalbonenfant.com/18c/geography/weather.html

History of Bath Research Group: historyofbath.org

Legacies of British Slave-ownership: www.ucl.ac.uk/lbs

Measuring Worth: Relative Worth Comparators and Data Sets: www.measuringworth.com

PICTURE CREDITS

Austenonly website 104; Bath Central Library 137, 140, 212; Bath in Time 28, 144, 149, 167 (bottom), 170, 178, 191, 198, 211 (bottom); Bath Record Office 12, 18, 22, 33 (both maps), 34 (top), 35, 38, 40 (both maps), 56, 59 (bottom), 79 (top), 84, 122, 124, 128, 129, 131, 132, 138, 143, 154, 157, 163, 164 (top),166 (top & middle), 167 (top),168, 169 (pictures on left), 176 (map), 214, 222, 240, 245 (top), 247, 248, 258, 264, 267 (bottom), 277, 283, 337, 338, 340; British Library 198; Christopher Wheeler 19 (top), 210; Coasters World website 193; Geoffrey Hiscocks 324 (top); Houghton Library, Harvard University 112 , 173 (Playbills and Posters Concerning Magic, 1800-1936 Harvard Theatre Collection); L'Institut National d'Histoire de l'Art, France 153; Iveagh Bequest 161 (bottom left); Know Your Place website 256; Mary Britton and Thomas Harper, 343; Metropolitan Museum of Art, New York 223 (top; Gilman Collection, Purchase, Mrs Walter Annenberg and the Annenberg Foundation Gift, 2005), 230 (Gilman Collection, Museum Purchase, 2005), 233 (top: Purchase, Robert Alonzo Lehman Bequest, 2005); Mike Williams, Museum of Bath at Work 245 (bottom); Patricia Humphrys 341 (top); Paul De'Ath 139; Prior Park College 45 (bottom), 46, 49, 50, 51; Royal Collection 219; Sinebrychoff Art Museum, Finland 151 (top: Hjalmar Linder Donation); Smithsonian National Air and Space Museum 180 (A20140948000 1802 Sept. 7th. Mr Garnerin and Mr Glaishford Ascended at Sydney Gardens, Bath, and Afterwards of an Hour's Voyage Descended in a Field Here Represented, Near Mells Park, Somerset); Somerset Archives 175, 208; Steve Lord 342; University of Michigan Special Collections Research Center 262; Vauxhall History website 185 (top); Victoria and Albert Museum 37, 48,103 (purchased with Art Fund support), 196, 201, 232; Wellcome Collection 8, 14, 17, 71, 87 (top),111, 119, 203; Wikimedia Commons 2, 34 (bottom), 68, 94, 102,123, 146, 179, 230 (bottom), 234; Yale Center for British Art, Paul Mellon Collection 8, 63, 66, 72, 87 (bottom), 100, 101, 113, 116; Yale Center for British Art, Yale Art Gallery Collection 70.

All other pictures are from the Akeman Press Archive. These include photographs by Kirsten Elliott and Andrew Swift.

INDEX

Adam, Robert 155-57
Adelaide, Queen 220
Adeler, Edwin 271-72
Alcoholic beverages 34, 75, 84, 90, 92, 95-96, 107, 109, 118, 127, 132, 147, 165, 175, 182, 221, 253, 335
Alexandra Park 260
Alkmaar, the Netherlands 318
Allen, Ralph 38, 40, 41-43, 61, 78-79, 337, 346 n2 (chap 3)
Amburgh, Van 219-20, 230
Amelia, Princess 22-23, 29, 315
Andrews, General Augustus 213, 241-44, 252, 354 n48, 354 n51
Angling 29, 118, 121, 127
Anne of Denmark 7
Anne, Queen 17-18, 21
Anorexia nervosa 48-50
Anstey, Christopher 61-62, 66-67, 91
Archery 134, 207, 220, 245-46, 249-50
Argyle Street 98, 107, 156-57, 209
Assembly Rooms, Lower Rooms (both sets) 21-22, 26, 30-33, 69, 182, 319
Assembly Rooms, Upper or New Rooms 65, 69, 182, 280
Astley's Riding School 61, 111-12
Atwood, Thomas Warr 40
Aust, James 246-47, 330
Austen, Jane 174, 303

Bagatelle Gardens 77-83, 87, 91, 325
Baldwin, Thomas 119-20, 127, 132, 136, 156-58, 164-68, 181, 227, 282-84, 287, 299, 351 n11 (chap 2)
Ballooning 100-1, 179-80, 202, 234, 235, 236, 237, 254, 273-74
Balls, 68, 102, 179, 280
Bankruptcy 86, 91, 132, 136, 141, 143, 165, 186, 207, 235, 237, 330, 353 n72
Banks, Failure of 117, 127

Barbadian Steel Band x, 306
Barrett, W & J 142
Barrow Hill, see Twerton Roundhill
Bath Abbey 6, 18-19, 23, 31, 83, 194, 204, 252, 316-18
Bath Canoe Club 209
Bath Floral & Horticultural Society 209, 213, 215, 218-19
Bath Horticultural Society 219, 221-22, 225, 234, 239, 241, 245, 353 n8
Bath Pageant 276-82, 286-87
Bath Proprietary College, see Sydney Gardens: Sydney College
Bath Rowing Club 262
Bath Spa Hotel, see Vellore House
Bathampton 40, 338, 341
Bathing facilities 79-82, 120, 128, 330, 332
Bathwick Mill 33-34, 37-38, 59, 107
Bathwick Park, see Henrietta Park
Bathwick Villa 91-97, 99-114, 141, 326-30
Beacon Hill 137, 158
Beazer Maze 59, 139, 322
Beer, see alcoholic beverages
Ben Greet Players (Woodland Players) 254, 261-62, 273
Bennet, Philip 38-39, 41, 43, 47
Bird impressionists 101, 110, 114, 174
Blomfield, Sir Reginald 282-84, 308-9
Boatstall Lane 61, 269-70
Bowers, Mr and Mrs 79-80, 83
Bowling greens 17, 18, 25, 30, 71, 72, 118, 120-21, 127, 132, 138, 163, 191, 199, 200, 284, 289, 290, 294, 307, 318-19, 320-21, 345 n14
Breakfasts, Public 47, 58, 62-64, 66-67, 68-69, 79, 90, 99, 100, 127, 147, 165, 179, 180-81, 189, 203, 206, 347 n8
Bridle, William 194-97, 201-7, 217-18, 220, 224, 354 n 44, 353 n72

Brown, Lancelot 'Capability' 43
Brunel, Isambard Kingdom 159, 208, 209, 215, 221, 225-27, 255
Buck, Samuel & Nathaniel 26-28, 33-34, 42
Burney, Fanny 9, 93-95
Buxton, Derbyshire 4, 7

Cannons, presented by Beau Nash 32-33, 69, 107, 118, 132, 295
Cantelo family 69
Cavendish Crescent 137, 332
Chandler, Mary 27-28
Charles II 16-17
Chatterton, William 209, 213
Cheapside, *see* Grove Street
Cheltenham 10, 37, 202, 213, 218, 219
Children 178, 191, 192, 205, 247, 248-49, 250, 254, 272-73, 279-80, 291, 293, 295, 301-2, 303-5, 335, 340, 343-44
City walls 12, 19, 26-27
Civil War, English 15-16
Cleveland Bridge 209
Cleveland, Dukes of 211, 233, 237, 255-57, 263, 326-28, 338
Clitherow, Benjamin 108-9, 111
Cody, Samuel 273-74
Collibee, William 31
Concerts, *see* music
Connaught, Duke & Duchess of 254
Cornish, Thomas 31
Countess of Huntingdon's Chapel 92, 350
Cremorne Gardens, *see* Folly
Crotch, William 99
Cruttwell, Mr (Surgeon to the Humane Society) 72-73
Cunliffe, Barry 269
Cupid's Garden, *see* Bagatelle

D'Ernst, John George 220
Dancing 17, 22, 31, 36, 47, 58, 64, 65-68, 79, 130, 152, 235, 262, 278, 290, 292, 300, 303, 304, 305, 340; cotillions 65-68; waltzing 270
Darlington, Earl of, *see* Vane, William Harry
Daubeney, Colonel 206
Davis, E (of Grosvenor) 141, 351
Davis, Edward 221-23, 260, 274
Davis, John 237

Davis, Major Charles Edward 268-70
Defoe, Daniel 21
Delia's Grotto 27-28, 322, 353 n37
Distin Family Quintet 233
Drake, Captain Peter 41, 46, 85
Dudley 3rd Baron North 13

Eaux-Bonnes, France 223
Edmondson, Francis 36, 57
Edward VII 260, 286
Egan, Pierce 189-92, 194, 200, 332
Elephant & Castle Inn 9
Elizabeth I 7
Empire Hotel 269-70, 317
Epsom, Surrey 14-15
Eveleigh, John 109, 115, 117-24, 127-29, 132-35, 141, 163

Farnham, G 188, 192-94, 196, 201
Farwell, Frederic 328
Ferries: Grosvenor 118, 121, 132, 141, 337; Spring Gardens 36, 56-57, 61-63, 113, 318; Walcot 96, 108-9; South Parade 109, 113, 194
Ferry, James 91-95
Fiennes, Celia 17, 18-19, 23, 315, 318
Fireworks 23, 32, 36, 69-71, 84, 90, 97, 100, 102-14, 121, 124, 128, 130, 132, 134, 136, 138, 141-42, 150, 163, 172, 174, 179, 182-89, 193, 196, 203, 214, 220, 228, 234, 236, 237, 250, 251, 253, 261, 265, 277, 278, 281, 289, 303-5, 336, 347 n15
Florists' feasts 39-40, 185
Flowers 27, 28, 39-40, 58, 74-75, 84-88, 120
Forester, Captain Francis 263, 268, 276, 328-29
Fragonard, Jean-Honoré 146-47, 148
France, War with (1793-1815) 73, 117, 127
Frere, George 215
Frog Lane 57, 124, 347

Gainsborough, Thomas 116-17, 161
Gale, John 147-48, 163, 168, 171-74, 179-80, 182-84, 185-86
Garnerin, André-Jacques 179-80, 273
George III 117
George IV 203-4
Giller, Daniel 336

Glendurgan Gardens, Cornwall 192
Gloucester 203
Gordon Hotel Company 268-70, 275-76
Gordon Riots 88
Gravelet, Monsieur & Mademoiselle 202
Gray, Master (singer) 105, 108
Great Pulteney Street 98-99, 112, 115, 138, 145, 148, 149, 155-58, 164-65, 172, 227-28, 232, 236, 249, 255, 268, 277, 280, 282, 294
Great Western Railway 10, 162, 169, 197, 208-9, 215, 216-18, 220-21, 224-28, 230-31, 236, 246, 248, 254-55, 262, 263, 301-2, 334-35, 338, 340
Green, Mowbray 282
Grieve, Thomas 232
Grosvenor Brewery, *see* Folly
Grosvenor Gardens 115, 117-23, 125-29, 131, 132-36, 138, 140-44, 147, 151, 160, 162, 163, 172, 330-32, 336-38
Grosvenor Suspension Bridge 331, 338
Grottoes vii, 27-28, 121, 160, 162-63, 189-90, 198, 200, 227, 229, 239-44, 322, 352 n37, 354 n48
Grove Street 117, 120, 127, 141, 326
Grove Tavern, Orange Court 109-10
Guillet, James 80-82, 348
Guinness clock 305
Gyde, Cam 68, 69, 71, 72, 73, 75, 320, 348

Hall, John 27, 31
Ham House, Surrey 30
Hand & Flower Ground, Lansdown Road 39-40, 324, 335
Handy, Benjamin 111-12
Hare & Hounds Inn, Lansdown 344
Hare, Albert Alfred 252-53
Harper, Tom x, 343
Harris, James 99
Harrison, Mr T (of the Bagatelle) 82-83
Harrison, Thomas 21-23, 25, 27, 30-32
Harrison's Walks 21-23, 25-33, 50, 71, 138, 285, 318-22
Harrogate, Yorkshire 15, 271
Hawley, Lord Francis 31-32
Hayes, Elizabeth 31-32
Hayman, Francis 103, 349 n8
Hayward and Wooster 266, 270
Heal, Sir Ambrose 296-98
Hedgemead Park 259-60

Helena, Princess, Duchess of Albany 254-55
Henrietta Maria, Queen 14
Henrietta Park 157, 259, 260, 355 n2
Herschel, Alexander 108
Herschel, William 108
Hewlett, Richard 134, 136, 143
Hewlett, William 136
Hickes, John 44, 45-46, 50, 54, 75
Hill, Walter 263
Hillary, William Dr 45-46, 48-50, 54, 75
Hobhouse, Henry 206, 208
Holburne Museum 153, 157-58, 255, 276, 282-85, 294-95, 301, 303, 308-10
Holland, Alfred 269-70
Holloway, Thomas 174-75, 178-79
Holy wells 5-7, 13
Hospitals: General (Mineral Water Hospital) 237-38; United/Royal United 218, 231, 251, 291; War Hospital, Combe Park 290
Hulbert, Matthew 338-39
Hulbert, William 337
Hull, William 34-35
Humphreys, Glenn 4, 307
Hunt, Henry 195-96, 217, 220

Ilchester Gaol 195
Ilfracombe, Devon 262, 266-67
Illuminations 79, 84, 90, 93, 97, 100, 105, 106, 108, 138, 139, 172, 174, 188, 189, 207, 224, 235, 247, 250, 251, 262, 276-78, 292, 303-6, 309-10
Inoculation, smallpox 76-77
Institution Gardens 285, 318, 319-21
Invetto, Giovanni Antonio (John Anthony) 97, 106, 111, 113-14, 124, 130, 134, 136, 138, 141-42, 172, 175, 182-83, 350 n38
Ivatts, James 235-36

Jackson, Mr, 'the Black' 112
James I 7
James II 41
Jardin du Luxembourg, Paris 24-25
Jelly, John 130-31, 136
Jelly, Thomas 92-93
Jenkins, Mr (of Sydney Gardens) 231
Joel, Herr David 207
Johnstone Street 114, 138, 322-23, 349 n25

Jones, Davey 265-66, 270
Jones, Richard 61
Jones, Robert 130, 137
Jullien, Louis-Antoine 234, 249

Kennet & Avon Canal 175-81, 190, 200, 215, 225, 228, 236, 248, 262, 302, 303-4, 306-7, 337, 338, 339; Darlington Wharf 176, 180-81; Sydney Wharf 176, 262; passenger boats to Bradford on Avon 180-81
Kemble, Charles, Rector of Bath Abbey 252
Kensington Meadows 142-43, 332
Keppel, Admiral 93
Kerr, John 145, 197-201, 241
King James's Palace 41, 46, 83-91, 113, 186, 326
King's Meads 16, 18-19, 22-23, 315-16
Kingsmead Square 315-16
Kingston, Duke of 31
Kinneir, David 75-77
Knight, Charles 227

Labyrinths 121, 141, 153, 159-60, 162-63, 190, 192, 197, 200-1, 227, 229, 232, 235, 236, 239, 240, 248
Lalanne, Baptiste 201-2
Lancashire, Richard 85
Lane. Josiah 241, 243
Langslow, Monsieur & Madame 254
Lansdown Grove Hotel 268
Lansdown, Robert 90, 186
Larkhall Inn 342-44
Laura Place 98-99, 107, 117, 120, 133, 157, 165
Leamington Spa 202-3
Leopold, Prince, of Belgium 204
Lindsey, Mary 'Dame' 30-32
Linley, Elizabeth 26-27, 79, 190, 200, 227, 352 n37
London Pleasure Gardens: Cremorne 340; Cupid's Garden 82; Green Park 70; Gunnersbury 108; Marylebone 9, 108; Ranelagh 41, 57, 64, 108, 119, 120; Spring Gardens 9, 33; Vauxhall 8, 9, 33, 41, 57, 64, 100, 102-3, 106, 120, 141, 165, 183, 185, 189, 196, 202, 203, 220, 247, 340
London theatres: Astley's Amphitheatre 112; Covent Garden 102, 232; Drury Lane 102, 103, 232; Sadler's Wells 111

Loudon, John Claudius 221-22, 316, 319
Lovelace, Catherine 30, 32
Lunardi, Vicenzo 100-1
Lyncombe Spa X, 38-39, 41-54, 75-78, 83, 85, 86, 325

Macky, John 21, 25, 27
Madron, Cornwall 5-6
Mainwaring, Captain Rowland 180-81, 186-87, 206-7
Maltby, Richard 45-46, 83
Marrett, Joseph 95-97, 100-13, 120
Mary of Modena 41
Masonic Lodge of Perfect Friendship 83, 86, 90
Mastalier, Dr AE 231-32
Masters, Charles Harcourt 132, 165-67, 282, 287, 351, 352; 1795 Map of Bath 337; 1800 Map of Bath 122, 131, 132, 138, 154-55, 163, 194, 240, 243
McAdam, John 197
Mells, Somerset 179-80
Merlin, John Joseph 121, 147, 152, 159-63, 171, 190-91, 200, 227, 229-30
Migasi, Antonio (Il Diavolo Antonio) 196
Milgrove, Benjamin 103-4, 349 n9
Milsom, Charles 44-46, 83
Mitre Green 23, 345 n12
More, Hannah 259
Mortram, Henry 234
Mortram, Vincento de 183-88, 193, 196, 203, 352 n29
Music vii, 9, 24, 31, 36, 47-48, 50, 64-69, 79-80, 87, 90, 97, 99-106, 108, 110-12, 114, 120, 127-30, 140-41, 152, 162, 172, 174, 183, 185, 189, 196, 202-3, 206, 230, 233-36, 239, 244-45, 247-50, 252-53, 260-62, 265, 271-72, 276-81, 281, 284-85, 289, 291-93, 300, 303-4, 306, 321-22, 344, 347 n13, 349 n9, 355 n 54; child prodigies 99, 110, 111; clarionets 67, 69, 83, 87, 152; Glass armonica 68, 347 n 13; harps 69; harpsichords 136, 162; horns 47, 65, 67, 69, 83, 87, 152, 233; Irish pipes 127-30; organs 120; Pandean band 196; pianos 99; trumpets 291; violins 65, 69, 99, 114

Napoleon, Louis (Napoleon III) 229-30, 232, 234

Nash, Richard 'Beau' 10, 13, 21, 23, 30, 32, 69, 295
National Trust 326, 344
Nattes, Jean-Claude 167, 182
Nixon, John 121-22, 178, 191, 349 n6
Norrison, Francis 207-9
North Parade 27, 257, 319-22
North Parade Bridge 156, 319, 322

Orange Court 37, 57, 109-10
Orange Grove 19-20, 22-27, 31, 40, 58, 61, 63, 71, 77, 257, 269, 316-18, 345 n12
Orange, Prince of 23, 317
Osmond, Thomas 340

Padmore, John 42, 346 n2 (chap. 3)
Palmer, General Charles 206
Parade Gardens 23, 27, 319-22, 344
Paragon School x, 325
Parry, Eric 227, 308-9
Peach, REM 229
Peacock, James 239
Pearce, WS 290
Penrose, Rev John 62-64, 75, 86, 273
Pepys, Samuel 16, 18-19
Persian gardens 1-2
Phipps, Charles 250
Pinch, John 139
Pinch, John, the Younger 209-10, 212, 227, 282
Poole, Maria 101-3, 106, 350 n9
Pope, Alexander 43
Porter Butt Pleasure Gardens, London Road 335-36
Powlett Road 328-29
Powlett, Lord William 233, 236-38
Prior Park College 325
Prior Park Landscape Garden 38-44, 326, 344
Pritchard, Meshach 113, 117, 120, 138, 349 n10
Prostitution 9, 237
Pulteney Bridge 62, 72-73, 98-99, 106-7, 112, 155-57, 194, 230, 269, 317, 319, 347 n4
Pulteney, Frances 73, 346 n4
Pulteney, Henrietta Laura 210-11, 256
Pulteney, William Johnstone 73, 105, 116-17, 210, 346 n4, 350 n10, 350 n5 (chap 1)

Pulteney, William, Earl of Bath 33-6, 57, 73
Purdie, William (and Purdie family) 36-37, 57-59, 61-62, 64, 68-69, 71-73, 75, 90, 95-97, 99-111, 113-15, 117
Purlewent, Samuel 36

Rack, Edmund 87-88
Rauzzini, Venanzio 102, 349 n9
Rebecqui, J 172-73
Recreation Ground 157, 257, 322-24
Retreat public house, Primrose Hill 342-43
Richmond, Surrey 30, 104
Ridout, Alfred 320
River Avon 20, 26-29, 33-37, 38-39, 56-57, 61-62, 72-73, 98-99, 113, 118, 121-22, 133, 141, 143, 194, 320, 324, 330, 337-39; drownings and rescues 61, 72-73, 111, 338-39; *see also* ferries
Robins, Thomas 28-29, 37, 47-48
Roebuck, John 206, 208
Rogers, Mr, of the Hand & Flower 39-40
Roman Baths 3-4, 6, 269, 271
Roman Catholic Chapel, Lower Borough Walls 88
Rose, Bill 325
Rossignol, Signor 101, 114, 175
Royal celebrations 22-23, 102-5, 107-11, 114, 124, 138, 172, 174-75, 181, 183, 185, 207
Royal Victoria Park 205, 209, 218-19, 221-23, 245, 247, 259, 274, 276, 280, 282, 285, 287, 300, 307, 355 n2
Rudge, John Arthur Roebuck 251, 355 n68

Sage, Letitia Anne 101
Sally Lunns (Spring Gardens Rolls) 64, 71, 124-25, 152-53, 347 n8
Saqui, Madame 201-2
Sartain, Rita 301
Savile, Henry 33
Schöttler, WFC 278-79, 284
Seymour, Henry 213-15, 218-20, 225
Sham Castle 261, 337
Shell, Thomas 141
Sheridan, Betsy 83
Sheridan, Richard Brinsley 26-27, 79, 83, 189-90, 200, 227, 229, 352 n37
Shew, Thomas 331, 338
Siamese twins (Chang and Eng) 203

INDEX 369

Simpson, Charles 32, 37, 68-69, 71, 347 n12
Simpson's Walks, *see* Harrison's Walks
Slavery: abolition of 210; William Johnstone Pulteney's involvement in 210-11
Smallpox 31, 76-77, 347 n2
Smith, Jarrit 35-36
Smith, Sydney 205
Smollett, Tobias 58-59
Smyth, James Carmichael 162
Soane, Sir John 221-23
South Parade 95, 109, 113, 194, 322
Southby, Chevalier 203
Southport, Lancashire 232
Spa culture 1, 7-9, 13-25
Spa, Belgium 1, 7-8, 15, 37
Speed, John 6, 33
Spring Gardens 33-37, 50, 56-73, 91, 95-111, 113-14, 120, 123-27, 130, 132, 134, 136, 138-39, 141, 153, 172, 263, 273, 295, 318, 322-24, 335, 345 n1 (Prelude), 349 n10
Stanhope, Erroll 272
Stevenson, Bennett 57
Stothert, George 175
Stothert, Percy 266
Street, William 75-77, 85
Subscriptions to Pleasure Gardens 58, 90, 118-19, 122, 127, 130-31, 137, 163, 191-92, 213, 235, 260, 320-21, 355 n2
Sutton, WG 271-72
Swings 121-22, 132, 134, 141, 147-48, 150-53, 159-62, 171, 189-91, 194, 199, 227, 229-30, 239, 246, 249, 254, 280, 290, 294, 332, 340, 349 n4, 351 n6-7 (chap 2)
Swings, Merlin 121, 147, 152, 159-62, 171, 190-91, 227, 229-30, 350 n4, 351 n6-7 (chap 2)
Sydenham, Kent 15
Sydenham Ground, Lower Bristol Road 249
Sydney Gardens vii-viii, ix-x, 10, 115, 120-24, 126-27, 131-32, 134, 136, 138, 143, 145-312, 333, 340, 344, 349 n3, 349 n6 (chap 4), 352 n37, 354 n50, 356 n49; animals and birds 178, 218-20, 235, 251, 261; archery 207, 220, 245-46, 249; as a hydropathic establishment 231-32;

bandstands 165, 168, 170-71, 185, 189, 250, 253, 260, 276, 278, 281, 285-86, 288, 292, 299-300, 302; bowling greens 138, 163, 199-200, 284, 289-90, 292, 294, 296, 307; building of houses on 165, 168-69, 181, 212-15, 239-40, 244, 258-59, 263, 265, 275-77; cascades 149, 150, 183, 189, 191, 197; castle 149-50, 159, 163, 186-87, 198-200, 226-27, 295; coffins, discovery of 200, 250; complaints from residents 233-39, 252, 260, 265, 284, 294-96, 303-4; concerts 172, 174, 183, 233-34, 236, 239, 245, 247, 253, 260-61, 265, 277-80, 292, 300; Cosmorama 197, 199; Crystal Palace (proposed) 239; dinner boxes 150, 165, 167, 170-71, 189, 211; electric lighting 254, 266, 274, 277, 288, 355 n77; entrances to 158, 168, 172, 182, 188, 247-49, 285, 288, 294, 305, 309; fêtes 180, 245, 247-54, 260-63, 265-66, 270-72, 274, 280, 290-91, 293-94; fireworks 150, 163, 172, 174, 179, 182-89, 193, 196, 203, 214, 220, 228, 234, 236, 237, 250, 251, 253, 261, 265, 277, 278, 281, 289, 303-5; Floral Fete & Band Committee 252-53, 260-61, 263, 265-66, 270-71, 284-85; galas 172, 174-75, 179-80, 185-87, 189, 191-92, 194, 196-97, 201-3, 207, 213, 217, 220, 235, 237, 251; gardener's Lodge 222-23, 289, 311; gas lighting 205, 224, 232, 251, 254; Gothic Hall 232, 235, 237, 239, 245; grotto 160, 162-63, 189-90, 198, 200, 227, 229, 239-44, 354 n48; Hanoverian Band 245, 247, 249-52; Heritage Lottery Fund grant x, 10, 307, 311; hermit's cottage 192, 198, 201; illuminations 172, 174, 189, 207, 224, 247, 250-51, 277, 303-6, 309-10; in World War One 288-91; in World War Two 299-302; labyrinth 153, 159-60, 162-63, 190-92, 197, 200-1, 227, 229, 232, 235-36, 239-40, 248; Merlin swing 147, 152, 159-62, 171, 190-91, 227, 229-30; Middle Bar 163, 209, 221, 226-27, 309; military manoeuvres 172, 206-7, 244; named after 1st Viscount Sydney 350 n3;

obelisk 165, 168; pavilion/loggia 149-50, 158-59, 177, 189, 199, 213-14, 285, 290, 295-99, 311-12; Peace Day celebrations 291-93; Pierrots 271-72, 274, 280, 291; public conveniences 163, 191-92, 213; Pulteney Hotel, see Sydney Hotel; pump room 202-3; purchase by corporation 255, 266, 275, 282; purchase by Mineral Water Hospital (proposed) 237-38; rebuilding of hotel (proposed) 252-53, 256-59, 263-70; reservoirs 199, 350 n5 (chap 1); ride 163-64, 179, 182, 191, 197, 199, 212-15, 230, 239-40, 259, 263, 275-77, 295; Russian Mountains 193-94; Rustic Pavilion 222-24, 246, 260, 274; scientific demonstrations 202, 204, 224, 251; swings 147-48, 150-53, 159-62, 171, 189-91, 194, 199, 227, 229-30, 239, 246, 249, 254, 280, 290, 294; Sydney College 244-48, 250-2, 255, 257, 263, 265, 268, 275-76, 294; Sydney House (at top of gardens) 213-15, 230, 297, 299; Sydney Hotel/House/Tavern 153, 163-68, 170-72, 174-75, 178-79, 181-82, 186, 189, 191, 197, 201-3, 205-9, 213, 215, 225, 228-29, 231-32, 234-37, 244, 353 n88; Sydney Tap 181-82, 207, 221, 236; Temple of Minerva 285-88, 290, 311; tennis courts 263, 266, 285, 294, 296, 312; watchmen's boxes 188; water features 149-50, 159, 163, 191, 200, 202, 224, 226

Taber, John 47
Tanner, Robert 90-91, 113
Taylor, AJ 288
Teas, Public 64-65, 85
Tennyson, Alfred Lord 229, 354 n17
Terrace Walk 27, 32
Thayer, Humphrey 31
Thicknesse, Philip 40, 347 n8
Thorpe, Thomas 35-36, 38-39, 41, 337
Thrale, Mrs 93, 99
Tightrope (and slackrope) walking 192, 196, 201-3
Tiley, Edward 230
Toilets 64, 128, 163, 191-92, 213, 320
Tokens for admittance to gardens 122, 131-32, 168-69, 349 n7
Towers, William Colborne 320-21
Townsend, William & John 134, 136, 138-39
Townshend, Thomas, 1st Viscount Sydney 349 n3
Tramway, Ralph Allen's 38-39, 42, 78, 346 n2 (chap 3)
Trusler, Rev Dr John 326-27
Tuileries Garden, Paris 25
Tunbridge Wells 13-14, 16-18, 345 n1 (chap 1)
Tunstall, James 327
Twerton Roundhill (Barrow Hill) 158, 199, 232

Unitarian Chapel, Frog Lane 57
Upper Borough Walls 107, 336

Vane, William Harry 211
Vaughan, John 239-40
Vellore House 213, 239-44, 252, 354 n51
Versailles, Le Petit Trianon 123
Victoria, Queen 205, 219, 261-62
Villa Fields 246-7, 326-30
Villa Fields Tea, Pleasure & Aquatic Gardens 246-7, 330
Villa Gardens, see Bathwick Villa
Vivier's Glaciere Gardens 137-38, 332

Walcot Botanic Gardens 130-32, 136-37, 332-33
Wansbrough, HC 265-66, 270
Ward, Edward (Ned) 19-20
Wardour Castle, Wiltshire 241, 243
Warminster Road 209
Waterhouse, Alfred 268
Waterloo Gardens 194, 332
Waters, Charles 83-87, 89-91
Watson, Barnard 229, 231-35
Watteau, Jean-Antoine 151
Weather conditions, adverse 18-19, 61-62, 70, 100, 104-5, 108, 110, 113, 128, 143, 172, 174-75, 202, 204, 218, 220, 239, 252, 260, 262, 291-93, 318, 353 n2
Wellingborough, Northamptonshire 14
Westbury Court Gardens, Gloucestershire 60
Weston-super-Mare, Somerset 265, 268, 272, 355 n54
White Hart, Stall Street 83, 86
White Hart, Widcombe 73

Whittington, John S 265, 267-68
Wicksteed, James 77-78, 346 n7 (chap 3)
Wicksteed, John 40-41, 43, 77-80, 83
Wicksteed's Machine, 39-41, 43, 77 *see also* Bagatelle
Widcombe Manor 39-43, 47
Widcombe Terrace 89
Wilkinson, Dr Charles 111, 202, 204, 231, 354 n22
William IV 204, 207, 215
Wills, Alfred 292-93
Wine, *see* alcoholic beverages
Winter, Andrew 227
Wood, John 21-25, 27-32, 34-35, 42, 44-46, 158, 320, 345 n12, 346 n7 (chap 3)
Woodhouse, Samuel 86
Woodland Players, *see* Ben Greet Players
Wooten, Doug 343